"*Surviving the Future* is a testament
only possible, our people are makin
queering how we get there through (
Now is the perfect time to interrogate how we are with each other and
the land we inhabit. This collection gives us ample room to do just
that in a moment of mass uprisings led by everyday people demanding
safety without policing, prisons, and other forms of punishment."
—Charlene A. Carruthers, author of *Unapologetic: A Black,
Queer, and Feminist Mandate for Radical Movements*

"*Surviving the Future* is an essential text for this moment.
This anthology is the toolbox we need right now, filled with
contributions that show the conditions and the stakes of
the crises we're facing through the lens of queer abolitionist
resistance. Reading this book raised urgent questions for me that
I had not even thought to ask yet. *Surviving the Future* is a much-
needed resource for our movements, as we simultaneously face
worsening crises and grow queer abolitionist resistance."
—Dean Spade, author of *Mutual Aid: Building Solidarity During
This Crisis (and the Next)* and *Normal Life: Administrative
Violence, Critical Trans Politics and the Limits of Law*

"*Surviving the Future* is not an anthology that simply includes queer
and trans minorities in a mix of existing abolitionist thought. Rather,
it is a transformative collection of queer/trans methods for living
an abolitionist life. Anyone who dreams of dismantling the prison-
industrial complex, policing, borders, and the surveillance state should
read this book. Frankly, everybody who doesn't share that dream
should read it too, and maybe they'll start dreaming differently."
—Susan Stryker, author of *Transgender History: The Roots of Today's Revolution*

Surviving the Future

Abolitionist Queer Strategies

edited by Scott Branson,
Raven Hudson, and Bry Reed

Surviving the Future: Abolitionist Queer Strategies
© 2023 Scott Branson, Raven Hudson, and Bry Reed
This edition © 2023 PM Press

ISBN: 978-1-62963-971-0 (paperback)
ISBN: 978-1-62963-986-4 (ebook)

Library of Congress Control Number: 2022931959

Cover design by Drohan DiSanto
Interior design by briandesign

10 9 8 7 6 5 4 3 2 1

PM Press
PO Box 23912
Oakland, CA 94623
www.pmpress.org

Printed in the USA.

Contents

Foreword

Mimi Thi Nguyen

In 1987, I was in new braces and a new middle school, and a California Highway Patrol officer was arrested for the murder of a young white woman named Cara Evelyn Knott. Her car was found abandoned on a dead-end road at the incomplete I-15 Mercy Road exit into Rancho Peñasquitos from San Diego County, and her body was discovered at the bottom of a nearby ravine. The officer had been harassing other women driving alone while on duty in his marked patrol car, pulling them over and stroking their hair, their shoulders, in the swallowing darkness of this unlit off-ramp. Knott had threatened to report him, so he bludgeoned her with his flashlight and strangled her to death before throwing her body over the edge of a nearby bridge.

Mercy Road was about a mile or two from my parents' house, in a suburb that was still being built, one cookie-cutter stucco-and-tile residence at a time. (Ours was built on the parking lot for the model homes of our development; for years we would find chunks of asphalt in the soil.) That was the year I split my time between the long-haired skaters and metalheads and the Asian girls with the oversized tops and teased bangs, fanning out like sparkling sugar-spun clouds. In the waning days of Satanic panic (when subculture was seized upon as a breeding ground for lawlessness), the skaters and the metalheads were harassed by security guards for "destruction of public property" or for loitering in the convenience store parking lot. Meanwhile, a new moral panic about Southeast Asian gangs that was sweeping Southern California—fears of Vietnamese home invasions, Filipino petty crimes—underwrote a racial-sartorial profiling that caught even middle schoolers in its crosshairs; you could not wear black and be Asian without attracting suspicion from authority figures.

To fourteen-year-old me, who grew up on stories of a war from which we fled to the empire that inflicted much of its violence, Knott's death at the hands of an officer seemed all too possible. I remember the murmurings, the disbelief from some and the shrugs from others, and the nascent consciousness that the police do not protect you. What Mercy Road taught me was: *they can murder you too.*

In the years that followed, I traded metal braces for combat boots, and I also came to know that others were being murdered with much more impunity and much less scrutiny. I heard about the high school boys who would shout from the crests of ravines crisscrossing our suburb, *La migra!* just to fuck with the Mexican migrants camped out in the scrub in between construction or landscaping gigs, and about the white supremacist militias who "volunteered" to police the border between San Diego and Tijuana. I saw the feminist public art project called "NHI—No Humans Involved," which addressed the sexual assault and murder of forty-five women in San Diego from 1985 to 1992 and the chilling shorthand that police used to describe such violence. On two billboards, a black-and-white photograph of Donna Gentile, her hair softly feathered, and the pale-yellow letters "NHI" were placed side by side; Gentile was a sex worker found strangled to death, gravel and dirt stuffed into her mouth, a month after she testified against two police officers. When a reporter compared the swift investigation of Knott's death with this series of unsolved murders, a sheriff responded, "It's hard to evoke as much empathy for a prostitute as there is for a pretty little college co-ed."[1]

I remember shuddering at the videotaped assault of Black motorist Rodney King on the shoulder of highway I-210, which played on every television station, and reading that then LAPD Chief Daryl F. Gates claimed that Black persons being choked with a police baton could endure more than "normal people." One year later, just weeks before my high school graduation, four LAPD officers were acquitted for King's beating; instead of being proof that King did not resist arrest, the video instead became evidence, according to the defense, that his raised arms were potentially lethal weapons. I was a young punk who had just learned about the covert wars of the Reagan administration in Central America, propping up dictators who were waging Indigenous genocide with cadres trained at the US Army School of Americas, and who understood the first Gulf War as an extractivist imperial war ("No blood for oil!"). I didn't yet have the critical theory to make sense of all these pieces (I would read Sylvia Wynter and

Judith Butler years later), but I was already familiar with the language of *fuck this*.

I am reminded of some of these early lessons when I reflect upon the wreckage around us. It can be hard to know how to grasp all these ruins of moral panics, forever wars, global pandemics, austerity measures, and racial terrors.

Still, the first time I read this passage from *You Can't Shoot Us All*, a firsthand account of the riots in Oakland following the murder of Oscar Grant at the hands of transit police, I saw in it a way to survive the future:

> When we realized that, in the eyes of the powerful, our lives are just piles of bones waiting to be shattered, arteries and veins on the verge of tearing open, hearts and lungs that stop beating and expanding at the moment they pull the trigger, the only thing left to do was to come together and make them tremble before us. . . .
>
> I wanted to break windows, to set fires, to strike fear into every cop on the streets that night. I wanted to show the powerful that they, too, would learn the meaning of violence, just as we have been forced to learn it time and time again. They needed . . . to feel that we were still alive.

I saw the future again in 2020 when, in the midst of a pandemic that disproportionately kills Black and brown people, the Third Precinct police station in Minneapolis was burned to the ground by protesters, after the police murder of George Floyd on a late spring day. As bystanders pled with him and filmed him, an officer knelt on a Black man's neck for over nine minutes as he lay on the ground, asphyxiating Floyd as he cried, "I can't breathe." The tavern at which Black trans woman CeCe McDonald was assaulted years before by a white supremacist, and then arrested by Third Precinct officers and later imprisoned for not dying quietly, also collapsed in flames the same week.[2]

That same spring, in Louisville, Kentucky, Breonna Taylor was murdered by plainclothes officers executing a no-knock warrant late at night. Alleging that the warrant was part of a broader effort to evict residents frustrating the city's redevelopment initiative, her family's lawyers accused the city of targeting an associate of Taylor's former boyfriend so it could repossess the house he rented; a few months after her death, the city and a land bank purchased the house for one dollar.[3] Although more than twenty properties on the two-block stretch were also purchased following foreclosures, Louisville officials in the economic development department claimed there was no conspiracy, but they did note, "The community has told us they want to get criminal activity off this block, to get the properties torn down and returned to productive use."[4] Consecutive nights of protest followed in Louisville, and Breonna Taylor's name continues to be a rallying cry. Two months later, after Jacob Blake was shot in the back seven times as he walked away from Kenosha, Wisconsin, police, a Department of Corrections building was burned to the ground; another building was spray-painted with: "You have stolen more than we could ever loot."

"Protect and serve" is racial capitalism; growth is dispossession; law is violence. Conversely, then, we can also say that what is understood as "waste" to be discarded and demolished is actually *life*. Rebellion against this lethal order is spreading (as is the brutal counterrevolutionary response of state apparatuses), and in response to the hand-wringing appeal, "But why are you destroying your own communities?" others responded, "We are not burning our communities; we are burning our plantations."

Anti-eviction activists sealed shut the doors to courthouses with spray foam insulation to keep dwellers safe for another day, another week, another month. Housing advocates seized foreclosed homes from the dead pledges of financial lenders for living beings. Repurposed refrigerators parked on public sidewalks and private lots were stocked with donated provisions. We sent out what dollars we have to mutual aid funds and individual payment app accounts.[5] The destruction of law, and especially the law of property—as that which transforms Black life and death into "no humans involved" and demands subservience to forms of debt that diversify endlessly—becomes necessary to build other social bonds. A week after it was burned, signs were affixed to the security fence around the burned-out and emptied Third Precinct reading, "Designate this site as a historic monument." The anonymous social media account Seize the Museums captioned a photograph of these signs and the destruction behind them: "Let the people decide to leave it in rubble, or build a park for children to play in, or a museum to honor Black rebellion, the possibilities are endless." The inside is turned out; we are born in flames.

The authors collected here know what the horizon must be—including *abolish police, stop landlords, tell our stories, fuck gender, build mutual aid, end state violence*, and truly nourish Other being. They tell us, as riots also do, that it is necessary to call for creating more life while destroying capital and empire, permanently. Or, as the protest graffiti on a subway wall promises: "Another end of the world is possible."

Notes

1   "NHI—No Human Involved" was a collaborative project by Deborah Small, Elisabeth Sisco, Scott Kessler, Carla Kirkwood, and Louis Hock. Elizabeth Sisco wrote about it for the collection *Critical Condition: Women on the Edge of Violence*, ed. Amy Scholder (San Francisco: City Lights Books, 1993), accessed May 25, 2022, https://public.csusm.edu/dsmall/public_art/nhi_text.html.

2   Aren Aizura, "A Mask and a Target Cart: Minneapolis Riots," *New Inquiry*, May 30, 2020, accessed May 25, 2022, https://thenewinquiry.com/a-mask-and-a-target-cart-minneapolis-riots.

3   Brendon Beck, "The Role of Police in Gentrification," *Appeal*, August 4, 2020, accessed May 25, 2022, https://theappeal.org/the-role-of-police-igentrification-breonna-taylor.

4   Bailey Loosemore, "'A False Narrative': Louisville Leaders Scoff at Gentrification Claims in Breonna Taylor Suit," *Louisville Courier Journal*, July 6, 2020, accessed May 25, 2022, https://tinyurl.com/2p8s5t5a.

5   I borrow the term "dead pledges" from Annie McClanahan, *Dead Pledges: Debt, Crisis, and Twenty-First Century Culture* (Palo Alto, CA: Stanford University Press, 2017).

Introduction
Betraying Institutions

Scott Branson

The pieces of this book meet at the intersection of many seemingly endless cycles, some that have been repeating for years, some that promise to continue into a never-ending future: a global pandemic, mishandled to deadly results and irrevocably changing our lives; the boom and bust of capitalist markets, alternatively showing their fragility and their resilience; the biggest militant street movement the US has seen, echoing the various global uprisings of the 2010s, followed by the election spectacle that utterly demoralized the grassroots as usual (the beautiful moment of burning the police precinct in Minneapolis got lost in the old story of pointless liberal protests and legible demands); the continual normalization and rise of fascist street violence and infiltration into local power structures; the more and more incontrovertible evidence of the nearness of environmental collapse.

I had hoped at the onset of the 2020 COVID-19 pandemic that the contradictions of a world that demands we pay to live yet forces us out of work would lead more people to take matters into their own hands. When the collective refusal finally happened, it was a magnified echo of Ferguson, in response to the state violence delivered to George Floyd, one among several police killings of Black people in that week alone. The George Floyd uprising brought the terms of abolition to a wider public, just as it became a focal point of Black queer/trans militant organizing. If it introduced new radicals to street movements, it also gave them firsthand experience of the violent hand of the state, as, in city after city, people in the street were hailed with rubber bullets, tear gas, and other forms of police assault. For some queer and trans people, this experience only solidified a commitment to abolition—of police, of prisons, of capital, of the settler state and all its institutions.

However, in the aftermath of the uprisings, we saw once again that radical militancy is always vulnerable to recuperation by the systems in place, and abolition is a slippery term. Just as "decolonize" has become an abused metaphor that no longer threatens the colonial power structures,[1] we have witnessed calls for abolition either turn into a watered-down version of "Defund the Police" or simply be emptied of any material meaning. So how do militant queers attach ourselves to an ongoing abolition movement that can be traced back to the self-liberation of Black African people who were enslaved and the armed resistance of Indigenous people to the theft of land and genocide? What does abolition mean and how does it apply to queer and trans life in a paradoxical moment of increased assimilation and increased violence?[2]

In a foundational text for thinking abolition through a queer/trans lens, included in the groundbreaking edited volume *Captive Genders*, Morgan Bassichis, Alexander Lee, and Dean Spade make a call for an "Abolitionist Trans and Queer Movement" as a way to choose a radical legacy for trans and queer militants. To call ourselves queer abolitionists means we name our ancestors in struggle and embody the counter-history of insurgency against the state. Bassichis, Lee, and Spade set our current moment in the aftermath of counterrevolution by the state, which decimated the liberation movements of the 1960s and 1970s, alongside the neoliberal turn that decimated the minimal safety net afforded to people living within the parameters of the state. One of the effects of this double campaign of counterinsurgency was to silo queer issues into white bourgeois–led demands for inclusion in the dominant structures, to gain some benefits for the few. In this process, the ongoing, even deepening, plight of queer/trans people, especially racialized queer/trans people, those who work in informal economies, those who are unhoused, and those people with HIV/AIDS who could not access medicine or treatment, was erased. This history is also the history of the explosion of the prison-industrial complex, which has become such an ingrained fixture of our hellish landscape, serving the purpose of further invisibilizing people who are pushed to the margins and continually subject to state or vigilante violence. In this moment, the call for a trans and queer abolitionist movement aims to demolish the racialized hierarchy of white gay rights and connect with ongoing and historical work of abolition to "weaken oppressive institutions, not strengthen them" and to build a world based on care, desire, and joy.[3]

In fact, on both a theoretical and material level, we have to recognize the violence of the police and the prison-industrial complex as two areas where the ongoing process of gendering and racialization that began with colonialism, capitalist extraction, and the development of the state are concentrated. A queer/trans abolitionist strategy, thus, names the institutions that continue to create our positions as marginalized identities and is ever committed to their destruction, all while building a world here and now for our survival, even for our thriving. In the spirit of the Combahee River Collective, we have to organize from the point of the "interlocking forms of oppression"—race, gender, class, ability, citizenship status, and more—in order to envision collective liberation. As they said in the 1970s, liberation won't come without the abolition of capitalism—and we can add to that the litany of state-built institutions and state-sponsored identities.[4] On the one hand abolition means destruction, in particular of the future the system posits as a reproduction of its business as usual, while, on the other hand, abolition is a building of another world of survival in mutual aid, love, and care—work that queer/trans people have been doing all along.

Surviving the future is a tall order when we are surrounded with regimes of violence. The future itself is a form of violence. This book is written within the settler context of the United States and Canada, where the very fact of the state is a perpetuation of violence: in its continual occupation of lands, its profiting off the extraction of labor and resources of racialized, enslaved labor, and the daily disciplining of bodies along the identity lines of race, ethnicity, gender, and sexuality. We know well the now-old tune of Lee Edelman's "no future," an institutionalized version of a deeper queer nihilism that insists on now as an ever-vanishing queer moment to disrupt the regimes of futurity that recreate past forms of oppression. We get caught up in the play of survival, for example, in an election year, when liberals moralize about voting Democrat as blackmail for preserving the minimal protections the state offers queer and trans people (in a clearly racialized, colonial way). Perhaps even more salient for queers today than the trap of electoralism is the social justice–oriented idea that consuming the right media is in itself akin to an act of rebellion or some kind of ethical proclamation. Focusing our struggle on representation is just another lure away from our movements. Certain queers, certain trans people, have been included in institutions and, thus, no longer pose a threat to their continued domination. The coded ways that queers in institutions try to weave their rebellion into their work subterraneously is no longer enough; it's time we take sides. Explicitly. Some of us with more access and more safety nets might risk less with these acts (or perhaps risk more, like jobs), but it often falls to those who are the most precarious to be the bravest in irrevocably calling for abolition.

The fact is that folks have always been working on surviving the violence of the future. With the pandemic, environmental collapse, and insurgent antiauthoritarian movements, state forces have used the opportunity to intensify both their explicit violence and their blatant disregard for most lives, under the guise of safety. Abolition became defund became increase the police budgets. In answer, queer and trans militants have (as usual) helped lead efforts at mutual aid, tenant organizing and eviction defense, and service worker organizing. Black queer and trans people helped spearhead a nationwide rebellion after the murder of George Floyd that brought more people into the streets than any other US movement and faced nightly onslaughts by the police, as well as violent white supremacists. Despite relief from Trump, the grim picture of the future has been reestablished by another Democrat centrist who will perpetuate the continual wasting away of the earth, the hoarding of resources, and the dwindling of the quality of our lives, and queers are still fighting for survival against all odds. Fighting must be a way of life, an outgrowth of our reckoning with the continual process of transformation. Queers, better than anyone, know how to do it with joy, with the pleasure of perversion, and with the deviancy of the criminal.

"Queer-friendly" institutions are not our allies. They are avenues for assimilation and the defanging of our radical queer liberation movements. They put in place the divides that keep some people perennially out of the picture, while rewarding a lucky few with means for survival, however temporary. We may do some good within them, but we must always keep in mind the limits of that good, as they exist within the gates of professionalization, legacies of exclusion, and the hierarchies of knowledge and privilege. Incidentally, this book came into existence with the support of people within institutions who used their access to promote radical content—not only in this instance but consistently—content that often went against the interests of the institutions that funded them.

From a queer anarchist point of view, I am wary of institutions, because they are semipermanent structures in which power inheres. Instead, I favor bottom-up, temporary forms of infrastructure, semiformal networks of delivery, preparation, and action that can be spread within and among communities. The queer nihilist in me pushes for the dissolution of such infrastructure projects that no longer work, that start to coalesce into concentrated power, that have served their purpose and can move on, or that often end up sheltering forms of abuse and unaccountability. In our movements, we don't need to aim for forever, or even tomorrow. There's enough work right for us to do now, and we need to start here, the place and the moment where we are.

The kind of infrastructure I'm referring to can be created within and beyond institutions; as the pandemic settled in, I saw this with students who used their access to school resources to set up mutual aid networks for community members in need. When the uprisings kicked off across cities after George Floyd's murder, this organizing created infrastructure that connected medics, provided jail support, and formed other affinity groups to help each other as they confronted the murderous state in the streets night after night. In this way, queer radicals in the institutions can help sow the seeds for this kind of temporary extra-institutional infrastructure, as well as bringing outside organizing to bear on the institution itself, including pushing for commitments toward abolition and transformative justice in the institutions, however unlikely it might be for the powers to comply. Still, speaking the truth matters. The mutual aid network can precede the movement to stop campus police, for example, and can also provide the backup needed when a campus cop targets a queer student, say, in a mental health crisis. We've seen campus labor organizing meet the violent hand of university police, transforming the organizing to target "Cops Off Campus." These groups can then lead to divestment movements, settler colonial reckoning, removal of monuments to slavery, and ways of shifting the landscape of a school toward acknowledgment of institutional complicity with the violence that queer people face, specifically Black and Indigenous queer people, and eventually to the abolition of the institution itself, vacating the stolen land and leaving room for queer/trans Black and Indigenous people to envision other ways to fulfill our community needs.

This introduction is meant to provide context for this collection's inspiration and compilation, to acknowledge the wonderful support we gained along the way from people inside and outside of institutions, but also to provide an instructive story about the stakes of organizing radical queer content within academic institutions and the persistent perils of coming out, both as queer/trans and as anarchist. In the end, my hope for radical queers is not new but remains no less imperative. We must betray the institutions that try to house us, to domesticate us. Yes, we may gain entry and take the paycheck, but we must then use the access we have gained to spread the resources available and to fight the institutions themselves—not simply from the inside through reform and change but through direct action. This direct action must take form against the policies that embed the institutions within the state, against their occupation of land that furthers settler colonialism, and against the ways they hold our futures for ransom in preconceived and yet unattainable career paths, which only result in the withering away of our time and energy.

In that light, we have chosen to title this compilation of current thought from queer radicals, activists, scholars, academics, and students *Surviving the Future*. Bassichis, Lee, and Spade use the very *impossibility* of queerness and transness as the motivation of an abolitionist movement: our lives are deemed impossible, we shouldn't exist, and our goals of abolition and liberation are similarly impossible.[5] This "beautiful impossibility" they gear us toward also comes with the daily experience we have of this world not being made for us. On the negative side, the writers of *Baedan* "overthrow" Edelman's notorious "no future" thesis of queerness, radicalizing it as a form of "social war": "our queer project must also pose itself as the denial of the future of civilization."[6] Capitalism depends on the future, in terms of labor source, profit, and social reproduction—civilization as we know it. The future we must survive is, therefore, *their* idea of the future, merely an empty repetition of the painful present, now under the guise of progress along with a glorious revision of the violent past. Here, *Baedan* adds the argument by Jacques Camatte against domestication:

> To say "no future" means to say that we have no future except for one drifting at sea, blown at all times by the winds of the unfolding crisis of the capitalist mode of production. Precarious employment, lifetimes of debt, the impossibility of retirement, the need to constantly remake oneself through countless techniques-of-the-self in order to bring oneself to market as a pretty new commodity, rent, bills, credit: the facts of our own daily reproduction force us to continually sell, not just our bodily capacity, but our futures as well. Every time we offer up our body in a medical study, or turn a trick, or run a scam, we are wagering our futures against the daunting task of surviving another month in hell.[7]

Abolition is a means for surviving the future. As Black, queer abolitionist and poet Alexis Pauline Gumbs has envisioned, abolition isn't a future event, a goal we aim for, but "something that grows." Her beautiful impossibility includes an abolition that "sprouts out of the wet places in our eyes, the broken places in our skin, the waiting places in our palms, the tremble holding in my mouth when I turn to you."[8] We are constantly surviving countless futures, countless presents, countless pasts. Not only because many queer people are survivors of trauma, abuse, and violence, but also because our oppositional communities are continuously developing that temporary infrastructure, the momentary collectives, to deal with the shit that comes up.

The following collection of essays was initially inspired by two conferences that I helped organize when I was associated with the University of North Carolina, Asheville (UNCA), and then Davidson College in North Carolina. As the project grew, my coeditors, Raven Hudson and Bry Reed, and I have tried to make it also serve as a reflection on queer liberation movements during the COVID-19 pandemic and the uprisings. In first joining the conference organizing committee, I was becoming part of a long-running biannual queer studies conference that has been influential in the region and, as many students have remarked to me, has greatly impacted queer undergraduate lives. The committee still consists of people who organized the first conferences, and so it contains a special repertoire of history and continuity, with more experienced faculty and staff passing the torch to newer faculty, staff, and students in a welcoming way. I heard from attendees across a few generations that they date important encounters and revelations to their attendance or participation in various vintages of the UNCA queer conference. It was always conceived by its initiators as a meeting place for academics and organizers and for fostering connection between the on- and off-campus queer communities.

Yet my experience organizing this conference—despite the general enthusiasm of the committee and their solid support for both the theme and me as an organizer—is that it was the event that finally pushed me out of formal institutional lodging as an academic. In that light, I want to set up this collection from the contradictory position that Eli Meyerhoff writes of in *Beyond Education*, echoing Fred Moten and Stefano Harney's undercommons: "How to organize 'in but not of' the dominant institutions while also struggling 'against and beyond' them."[9] However, I want to add the important caution that Nick Mitchell advises in an essay on professionalization, politicization, and (the lack of) solidarity of queer academics: "Probably never are we more of [the university] than when we think we are outside of it."[10] My experience organizing this conference as an explicitly radical—and, in all but name, anarchist-inspired—disruption within the university simultaneously provided a prime opportunity for symbolic sacrifice, co-optation, and liberal self-congratulation, while also opening real space and resources for radical queer/trans people to meet and share ideas.

Given the conference's inception within the institution yet honoring its aim to bridge that gap to community—and reflecting that we are publishing with a radical press, not an academic press—we have sought to provide an inclusive compendium of thoughts and strategies written by queer people in the midst of the struggle. Queer theory holds a particular status in the university; along with gender studies, Black studies, Indigenous studies, and other so-called identity-based departments or fields, it seems to speak to a particular political conviction. Regardless, these fields of study and departments remain an important place of radicalization for undergraduates, or, at the very least, a threshold for students to push further in their own analysis of the world surrounding them. But beyond the seeming radicality of queerness, its symbols of left-leaning attitudes, or what often get called "progressive positions," it is still a clearly domesticated, colonized form of study that is housed and funded by elite institutions. There is a gulf between the labor done in the university and the work done in the streets (or communities)—and this is true even if the same person performs both kinds of labor. Part of this is due to material circumstances and the tracks of professionalization. To jump through the hoops and win the prize of secure employment within the university system means acceding to its formal recognition of value and its hierarchies of knowledge and power. Most often, it means identifying with that power, or, at the very least, the institution's continuation. I've seen committed radicals get beaten down and broken by the tenure system. It's hard to emerge unscathed, and it is unusual for the rare professor who reaches that level of comfort to remain a radical. The people within the institutions who helped support this book are important exceptions. Nonetheless, when we examine the scope of what must be abolished, we include the university.

On the other hand, there is a growing number of precarious professors and graduate student workers who don't have the same material conditions or resource access as tenured or tenure-track academics, and who, therefore, feel less allegiance to the institution that doesn't support them but gives them occasional employment. These people tend, despite the risk, to put themselves on the line by taking a more explicit stance in their approach to education, whether that means employing radical forms of pedagogy, giving students access to different, revolutionary ways of thinking, or even just redistributing office supplies. As it becomes less and less likely for college graduates to find any kind of secure professional status with their degree (and they are more and more saddled with unpayable debt), these revolutionary ideas are even more pertinent and prevalent. It must also be noted that the work of political education is quite often done by queer/trans, Black, Indigenous, Latinx, and Asian faculty—those people who already need to fight for a voice and position within the university, and who, by taking sides, face the most dangerous backlash from privileged (cisgender, heterosexual) white students, faculty, and administration, when their very lives are threateningly questioned.

I came to Asheville in 2016 with the conviction that I would no longer hide myself in the interests of holding down an academic position, even though it was my lecturer position at UNCA that brought me there. Asheville is known as a queer-friendly, liberal, white-dominant enclave in the conservative Christian environment of Western North Carolina. Asheville is a relatively small city, though its population continually grows, yet its police have an arsenal of military-grade weapons on hand. Aside from the police, the Tourist Board is a primary beneficiary of city and county money, and most political decisions are made to benefit the owners. In the years since I arrived, it has become increasingly difficult to afford to live here—it is one of the top ten most gentrified cities in the US. Yet it still has a reputation for its supposed tolerance.

UNCA is the UNC system's "liberal arts" college, providing a relatively small campus experience in a more rural/small urban setting. I had fled an abusive relationship and, before that, a long attempt at a closeted life in academia, both with my militant convictions and my queerness. I had long been fed up trying to accommodate myself to the demands of the profession, to twisting myself into the appropriate forms of presentation, both of myself and of my interests, that supposedly fit the tenure-track job. It's an impossible demand, since, as my advisor told me, even getting an interview for a tenure-track job is like winning the lottery. Well, I had a one-year renewable lecture position, so I resolved to use my institutional access to spread resources, as well as to live as far out as I could, come what may. I was in a new place, surrounded by a vibrant queer/trans anarchist community that saw me for who I was. Immediately, the long-time organizers of the queer conference opened the call for new faculty to join in the organizing of the queer conference, so I signed up as a vocal participant.

The moment of my arrival in Asheville was also pivotal in the liberal city's long-running assault against its residents, with a particular focus on the Black community and houseless people. The day after I arrived, July 2, 2016, the Asheville Police Department (APD) shot and killed a Black man, Jai "Jerry" Williams, in the parking lot of the Deaverview Apartments, a public housing complex. Though Asheville has a reputation for diversity in the region, this mostly means a liberal assortment of white hippies, punks, anarchists, and queers. Asheville is a city that is almost completely segregated and has a long history of municipal and county assaults on its Black and Latinx communities. But, at the time, the police department had a (white) lesbian chief, so, of course, that's progress.

The APD killed Jerry during a summer in which a series of police murders were highly publicized, caught on phones or even police body cams, leading to various uprisings across the country. The case in Asheville culminated in an occupation of the police department, with Jerry's family demanding justice. The media painted him as violent and criminal—as Jackie Wang discusses in "Against Innocence," he wasn't the right kind of victim to birth a liberal-inclusive movement.[11] Asheville District Attorney Todd Williams didn't charge Tyler Radford; the officer who killed Jerry Williams seemed to fade from view, all while the city keeps devoting more funds to the police (to make tourists feel safe), continues its violence against its Black residents, and makes symbolic gestures toward reparations and acknowledgment of its legacy of slavery and settler colonialism—it sits on Cherokee land. This story, of course, is not unique, but it gives a sense of the backdrop against which the queer conference took place, with the campus often in complete ignorance of the racialized political conflict that occurred every day around it.[12]

Given the events transpiring around us, I helped steer the conference toward a radical theme and tried to highlight the work of southern Black queer organizing. The 2018 conference that initially inspired this book was titled "Prisons, Borders, and Pipelines: Toward a Queer/Trans Abolitionist Movement." We planned it such that the typical academic boundaries were crossed by radical content and participants, and we were able to feature outspoken critiques of the state and its relationship to academic institutions.

One of our dynamic keynote speakers was glo merriweather, who was, at the time, facing state charges. Only a few months after the Asheville Police Department murdered Jerry Williams, the Charlotte-Mecklenburg Police Department killed Keith Lamont Scott, leading to a citywide uprising, during which the police killed Justin Carr and framed Black organizers, including glo, for his death and for inciting a riot. (Currently, Rayquan Borum is in prison, framed for the police killing of Justin Carr.) We were able to give financial support to a Black, radical, trans movement worker who was then fighting the killer police and corrupt courts. glo delivered a beautiful talk linking radical trans lineage to current movements for police and prison abolition.

The conference also featured a keynote discussing the insidious political underpinnings of the call for "resiliency," by Mimi Thi Nguyen, the inspiring queer punk academic who is one of those rare people with institutional leverage who speaks the truth, takes sides, and sticks her neck out for others. Mimi provides the foreword to this book.

The last day of the conference was organized around a panel with Durham Jewish Voice for Peace members Sandra Y.L. Korn and Beth Bruch, who contribute a piece here reflecting the work they've done in their community, along with Palestinian activist Samir Hazboun and Dean Spade, who presented the film *Pinkwashing Exposed: Seattle Fights Back!*[13]

Developing this conference at a supposedly liberal southern university wasn't without its controversies. That same year, I had invited members from anarchist collective CrimethInc. to speak as the culminating event of a week I helped organize at the initiative of radical undergraduates (a "Radical Rush," on the model of UNC Chapel Hill's "Disorientation"). I had to assure the head of the humanities program that if he supported this talk, it wouldn't be too political. He had serious regrets that the school had hosted Pussy Riot to talk about the similarities between Trump and Putin, calling it one of the biggest embarrassments of his academic career, since he feared that a student—a young cis straight white man, I assumed—wouldn't be able to make up his own mind about the world if he was subjected to this perspective.

Interestingly, one of the former core members of the queer conference organizing committee became one of the conference's antagonists and eventually made the call that led to the termination of my academic career.

She had been on the queer conference committee in the initial stages—I suppose we had butted heads when she wanted to spend a good chunk of our limited budget on flying an esteemed trans academic from Australia to give the keynote, even though the committee had come to a consensus to devote our funds to supporting Black trans organizers from Appalachia, though I had no idea there were bad feelings. As the organizing progressed, we had slated a keynote who was currently a target of state repression, and our call for papers made a public declaration of our radical ideas, leaving her purportedly afraid of right-wing backlash on the campus. Though this is a real fear—Asheville has seen white nationalist action, and UNCA has been the target of racist threats—her ultimate aim was questionable. She forced a meeting with the provost of UNCA. According to her explanation, the purpose of the meeting was to warn him that our conference would potentially make the campus a target. She felt it was imperative to notify campus police and the city, despite the arguments we brought up against an abolitionist conference staffed with law enforcement. In effect, as I discovered in further conversation with her and the provost, she was really asking for permission from the school administration to hold the conference, ceding whatever idea of autonomy we had as organizers. The provost didn't care, promised some funding, and ushered us out of his office.

An unforeseen institutional shakeup came when the university chancellor took a more prestigious northern university job, the provost became interim chancellor, and our queer conference snitch became the interim provost. A week before the conference, I was notified that the funding for my position was cut (tellingly, she only cut one position with a person occupying it, relying on the financial support for survival). She swooped in at the provost reception during the conference to tell a keynote, Mimi, how important she thought this abolitionist work was, turned her back to me, and left, never attending another moment of the conference. As she told me later, when it came to my job, her hands were tied—a simple question of funding. I lost my position at the end of the semester, with no time to look for other academic work. But, through the conference, I was saved significantly by Davidson College professor Melissa González. Melissa had attended the conference and had a vision of Davidson becoming a partner in the conference. Davidson College is situated outside Charlotte, and professors and students in the Gender and Sexuality Studies (GSS) Department have programmed radical content and provided support for the Black queer/trans movement fighting the state and police.

Melissa helped me continue to be part of the UNCA queer conference, now with the cosponsorship of Davidson College. Working with the Charlotte Uprising group, including glo, Ash Williams, Jamie Marsicano, Myka Johnson, and youth from the Southeast Asian Coalition (SEAC) Village, for the Davidson College community, I also got the chance to help organize a symposium called "Breaking Cages, Building Community, Queering Justice: A Symposium on Abolition and Queer/Trans Liberation." This event consisted of two days of workshops and talks centering abolition and transformative justice, with the goal of building inclusive queer community, especially for youth. I had truly never seen a university or college—let alone a wealthy elite school—devote resources and time like this to explicitly radical content. This access to resources was thoughtfully planned and executed by the comrades in the GSS Department. With Davidson's support, we continued to steer the UNC Asheville conference toward radical content, the wonderful committee now headed by Jordan and Shawn. We developed a follow-up conference titled "Fitting In, Sticking Out: Queer (In)Visibilities and the Perils of Inclusion." This theme was inspired by the collection of essays *Trap Door: Trans Cultural Production and the Politics of Visibility*. The conference was slated for 2020, though the COVID-19 pandemic delayed it, and we eventually held a virtual conference in April 2021. Our keynotes included the poet Kay Ulanday Barrett and Wriply Marie Bennett, one of the Black Pride 4 from Columbus, who contributes a beautiful piece and artwork here.

In the meantime, I had been invited to speak on a panel titled "Abolitionist Solutions to Social Problems" at the 2018 Society for the Study of Social Problems "Abolition vs. Reform" conference in Philadelphia. Steven from PM Press was tabling at the conference, and we struck up a conversation, leading to the idea to make a book from the two conferences. Eventually, again with Melissa's generous help, we were able to get financial support from a Mellon Justice, Equality, Community Grant that Davidson College received, which helped fund everything from the abolition symposium to a one-off course I taught at Davidson on queering transformative justice and eventually provided a subvention for the book and a grant for two student editors of color, Raven Hudson and Bry Reed, who became significant visionaries of the ultimate book. It is important to note that Raven and Bry, as Davidson students, were lucky to be able to find mentorship and support for radical learning and projects in an elite predominately white institution. Of course, this kind of support in alliance with faculty tends to come from the smaller number of Black and brown tenured and contingent faculty.

As the essays in this volume attest, the idea of queerness right now exists in a strategically contradictory place. On the one side, the signs of queerness—and their radical sheen—are trendy. The wages of inclusion are enticing, especially when any wage at all is less and less likely. Institutions—from universities through nonprofits to businesses—that want to seem progressive will tout their LGBT allyship, and they might take advantage of young queers to help prove it. On the other side, a radical lineage of queerness continues and, arguably, has further reach through social media, not only providing young queers with formerly impossible access to community and models of queer (deviant) living but also disseminating the radical analysis of abolition, anticapitalism, and collective liberation. These sides—the institutional and the communal—can intersect, especially as queer traitors enter institutions under the guise of tokenism to help spread resources, in an echo of the mutual aid (and forms of reparations) that we see spearheaded by queer/trans anarchists and others in communities across the US and the world. We've known, going back to Cathy J. Cohen's seminal call for a radical queer commitment, "Punks, Bulldaggers, and Welfare Queens," that queerness alone doesn't promise good politics.[14] This is why abolition has to be a daily practice, a continual question of where we stand in our relationship to each other and the world, with the ultimate horizon being liberation. The essays in this book, inspired from the conferences, give a wide range of strategies to question our inclusion in the institutions that always betray us, asking us to enter them at our peril. It demands that we, in turn, betray these institutions, betray racial and class hierarchies, white supremacy, anti-Blackness, and transmisogynoir, and even, eventually, queerness itself, since it is not immune to the processes of co-optation.

In the end, our slate of contributors extended beyond conference participants, and the final collection presents an exciting mix of artists, scholars, and movement workers, along with a mix of newer and more well-known voices. As circumstances continued to shift during 2020, we worked very hard to produce a book that responded to the state of queer life and organizing under COVID-19 and during the George Floyd uprisings. The book takes an explicitly radical stance, inspired especially by the initial abolitionist framework. We launched a fundraiser in May to be able to pay some of our writers, specifically in the hope of giving financial support to

QTBIPOC thinkers. We raised $2,400, therefore, allowing us to offer $300 to eight of our contributors. Though a book like this is often a labor of love, it is important, wherever possible, to give whatever financial resources we can to the often undervalued and mostly unpaid work of thinking, writing, organizing, and fighting. Though the work included in this volume spans a variety of topics pertinent to militant queer abolition movements, there is a shared emphasis in each to working toward liberation, to breaking down the systems that oppress us, and to imagining liberated places where there is no longer (their) future to survive.

The book opens with E Ornelas's important contribution to connecting the legacies of the settler state with the slave state in the formation of the modern carceral state's attack on Black and Indigenous people, specifically Black and Indigenous individuals who identify as queer, transgender, gender nonconforming, and/or Two Spirit. This piece sets the historical stage as well as the political stakes for the book as a whole. Diving into this crossover from another angle, Che Gossett contributes an important piece on the Indigeneity of Blackness, following the analysis of the land and the water. Both zuri arman and Zaria El-Fil build on recent work in Black studies on Blackness, gender, the human, representation, and essentiality in the COVID-19 landscape.

On the specifics of COVID-19 and queerness, we have a range of pieces, from Kitty Stryker's overview of the overlooked ways that marginalized queers are affected by this pandemic to Adrian Shanker's detailing of the need for queer-specific and nonjudgmental health care in every context. Following this, Yasmin Nair theorizes that the campaign for gay marriage pushed actual accessible health care off the table with disastrous results seen in the severity of the pandemic in the US.

In the middle, Mattilda Bernstein Sycamore provides an interlude with a beautiful twinning of her experience of the pandemic with the experience of the uprising in Seattle. This summer matched loneliness with the need for solidarity and a thrilling hope of abolition coming.

Our next section details the many facets of abolition: Darian Razdar explores how urban planning has both used and refused queerness, while proposing an abolitionist planning that rethinks the city. Amalia Golomb-Leavitt, Ryan Becker, and Rebecca Valeriano-Flores make an important call for an expansive understanding of our abolition work to include those who are convicted for sex offenses, framing transformative abolition work in a larger context of antiviolence work and rejecting the violent punitive measures of the state. Raxtus Bracken provides a theory and case study of how white queers serve the settler colonial and white supremacist needs of the university at the expense of Black students. Kai Rajala analyzes the failures and hopes of solidarity among radical queer settlers in Canada and Indigenous resistance movements, with a final call for queer settlers to join in Indigenous refusal of the state.

We move on to a series of reports from the midst of movement work. Toshio Meronek and Stasha Lampert give an overview of Gay Shame's vitriolic campaigns against white LGBT urban development in San Francisco that leaves out poor and working-class queers, particularly BIPOC. Beth Bruch and Sandra Y.L. Korn offer an argument for solidarity among targeted groups, detailing the Durham chapter of Jewish Voice for Peace's most recent campaigns against police training in Israel. Yold Yolande Delius theorizes the exclusion of queers left out of Black organizing toward a queer Blackness that would spell real liberation.

Turning to the archives of queerness, aems dinunzio makes a strong argument for a militant memory praxis that disrupts archives from a Black trans anarchist perspective. We also have two more historical documents: Jonesy and Jamie Knight's excerpt from their film *The Figa*, which consists of an interview with queer anthropologist Gayle Rubin on San Francisco's S&M scene, alongside artistic reenactments, and Scott Chalupa's combination of theory and poetry from the height of gay decimation by HIV/AIDS.

Finally, we end with the formation of queerness. Examining how health care and schooling institutions destroy queer bodies, Cassius Kelly and emet ezell propose ways to undiscipline our bodies from these violent regimes. The last pair of pieces approach representation in art, with Jamie Theophilos's call for new radical strategies in media making that resist co-optation but expand possibilities and Wriply Marie Bennett's beautiful written and illustrated piece, which details her own Black trans experience.

Notes

1   Eve Tuck and K. Wayne Yang, "Decolonization Is Not a Metaphor," *Decolonization: Indigeneity, Education and Society* 1, no. 1 (January 2012): 1–40, accessed June 8, 2022, https://tinyurl.com/5n6nnx9k.

2   On the connections between inclusion and violence, see Eric A. Stanley, *Atmospheres of Violence: Structuring Antagonism and the Trans/Queer Ungovernable* (Durham, NC: Duke University Press, 2021).

3   Morgan Bassichis, Alexander Lee, and Dean Spade, "Building an Abolitionist Queer and Trans Movement with Everything We've Got," in *Captive Genders*, ed. Eric A. Stanley and Nat Smith (Oakland: AK Press, 2011), 34.

4   "The Combahee River Collective Statement," in *How We Get Free: Black Feminism and the Combahee River Collective*, ed. Keeanga-Yamahtta Taylor (Chicago: Haymarket Books, 2017).

5   Bassichis, Lee, and Spade, "Building an Abolitionist Queer and Trans Movement," 24.

6   *Baedan: A Journal of Queer Nihilism* no. 1 (Seattle: Contagion Press, 2012), 39.

7   Ibid., 57.

8   Alexis Pauline Gumbs, "Freedom Seeds: Growing Abolition in Durham, North Carolina," in *Abolition Now! Ten Years of Strategy and Struggle against the Prison Industrial Complex*, ed. Critical Resistance CR10 Publications Collective (Oakland: AK Press, 2008), 145.

9   Eli Meyerhoff, *Beyond Education: Radical Studying for Another World* (Minneapolis: University of Minnesota Press, 2019), 191.

10   Nick Mitchell, "Summertime Selves (On Professionalization)," *New Inquiry*, October 4, 2019, accessed June 8, 2022, https://thenewinquiry.com/summertime-selves-on-professionalization.

11   Jackie Wang, "Against Innocence: Race, Gender, and the Politics of Safety," *LIES* 1 (2012): 1–27, accessed May 26, 2022, https://tinyurl.com/3as7uf6u.

12   As in many supposedly liberal cities across the country, in May 2020, Asheville hosted a face-off of Black youth–led organizers with the riot cops, who unloaded tear gas and rubber bullets on the rebels, and, then, at the appropriate time, the cops took a knee for the cameras. The uprising in Asheville was ultimately squashed, as many across the country were, by claims of white anarchist agitators and demands to listen to "Black leadership," which ended up being a few liberal voices claiming the Black Lives Matter moniker and silencing younger Black militants.

13   Dean Spade, dir., *Pinkwashing Exposed: Seattle Fights Back*, Vimeo, 2015, accessed June 1, 2022, https://vimeo.com/126391030.

14   Cathy J. Cohen, "Punks, Bulldaggers, and Welfare Queens: The Radical Potential of Queer Politics?" *GLQ* 3, no. 4 (May 1997): 437–65, accessed June 8, 2022, https://tinyurl.com/2p9bmp8b.

Land and Water
Blackness and Indigeneity

Telling "Our Stories"

Black and Indigenous Abolitionists (De)Narrativizing the Carceral State

E Ornelas

In *Why Indigenous Literatures Matter*, Daniel Heath Justice (Cherokee) considers stories to be of utmost importance for Indigenous peoples. Justice delineates between "stories that wound" and "stories that heal,"[1] the former being the dominant settler colonial narratives told *about* Native and First Nations peoples on Turtle Island (i.e., North America).[2] These stories, ranging from incomplete to downright toxic, are harmful.[3] Quite likely, any person—Indigenous or not—growing up on this continent could, if called upon, regurgitate these *stories that wound*: false images of brave "explorers" penetrating untouched virgin land; Thanksgiving (or, more accurately, Thanks-*taking*) meals involving happy, patriarchal, nuclear families of pilgrims and Natives; young, properly heterosexual Indigenous ciswomen who fall in love with benevolent white cismen; the "progress" of westward expansion bringing Christian sexual norms; "primitive savages" who antagonize settlers with deviant gender identities and expressions; "noble savages" who are able to adapt and assimilate to Euro-American ideals...

I argue that *stories that wound* are an integral part of the carceral state. These stories supply the justifications for how the carceral state purports to mete out justice and redress harm, and excuse the violence inherent to it.[4] My approach makes the case that Black feminist, queer, and trans theorizations of the slave state, as well as of Indigenous feminist, Indigiqueer, and Two Spirit critiques of the settler state are indispensable for more thorough and enriched queer and trans abolitionist conceptions of the carceral state. The development of the slave state and the settler state are not discrete meaning-making practices but are concomitant, parallel phenomena that culminate in the carceral state. Both are central to the creation of the US state as an Othering and punishing apparatus. In *As Black as Resistance*, Zoé Samudzi and William C. Anderson cite the forced kidnapping, trade, and servitude of Africans, alongside Indigenous genocide, as "intrinsic to American settlement."[5] To demonstrate these "intrinsic" foundations, I provide an overview of the white supremacist settler colonialism that informs the carceral state today. Specifically, I discuss the Othering narratives of certain bodies and lives—in particular, those of Black and Indigenous individuals who identify as queer, transgender, gender nonconforming, and/or Two Spirit—which marks them as needing to be controlled through a myriad of punitive practices.

In this essay I present the *how* of carcerality and the carceral state, rather than *which* specific institutions, ideologies, and discourses have taken shape. To give texture to this investigation into *how*, I ask these guiding questions: How do Othering narrative regimes inform the carceral state? How do these very narratives create the conditions of possibility for carcerality? How do they justify and bolster certain practices? How has this endured for centuries, in particular harming Black and Indigenous peoples deemed "deviant" and "less than" for their gender identities and sexual orientations? These questions are best answered through what Seneca Nation scholar Mishuana Goeman calls (re)mapping and unsettling settler narratives.[6] Intervening into or "unsettling" the *stories that wound* requires a practice of digging into and exposing their roots and simultaneously emphasizing and affirming the importance of Indigenous peoples and people of color. Goeman's practice of (re)mapping and unsettling is helpful in articulating the conceptual resonances between dominant narratives of the slave/settler/carceral state throughout the last five hundred years.

In recent years, rates of incarceration among American Indian and Alaskan Natives have been rising faster than in any other racial or ethnic group.[7] "Because we are a colonized people," Luana Ross (Salish and Kootenai) relates, "the experiences of imprisonment are, unfortunately, exceedingly familiar. Native Americans disappear into Euro-American institutions of confinement at alarming rates."[8] It is also widely reported that "African Americans are incarcerated at grossly disproportionate rates throughout the United States."[9] According to data from the Centers for Disease Control, the groups most likely to be killed due to injuries inflicted by law enforcement are Native Americans, followed by African Americans.[10] I do not cite statistical evidence to make a claim of identical intentions or impacts, but I also don't find these numbers to be a coincidence.[11] Indeed, these numbers "reveal discretion in defining and apprehending criminals."[12] In other words, official crime statistics tell stories about the deliberate "defining" of bodies and lives as "criminal" and in need of "apprehending" through a myriad of state punishing practices. Hence, I argue that the carceral state is an instantiation—a white supremacist settler colonial fiction made real—of the Othering narratives that have pervaded the last five hundred years of this continent's history.

The dominant narratives throughout this five-hundred-year time frame (re)present an Other—*several* Others, in fact. As Justice avers, these narratives are not "our own" but are, instead, full of deceit, lies, and deficiency "imposed on us *from outside*."[13] The protracted unfolding and dissemination of these *stories that wound* has served the slave/ settler/carceral state and has accumulated in such a way that we now lie, as Christina Sharpe might say, *in the wake* of a half-millennia-long narrative genealogy, or "a past that is not past." Sharpe describes the tracing of these reverberations, as well as the interruptions of them, as *wake work*, a "method along the lines of a sitting with, a gathering, and a tracking of phenomena that disproportionately and devastatingly affect Black peoples any and everywhere we are" as well as "tracking the ways we resist, rupture, and disrupt that immanence and imminence aesthetically and materially."[14] My task accounts for a "past" narrative "that is not past," that is very much a reverberating disturbance on the surface of an Othered existence. The historical narratives of Othering, or *stories that wound*, culminate in *a past that is not past*, in parallel patterns of present-day policing, prison, and punishment practices aimed at Black and Indigenous queer, trans, gender nonconforming, and Two Spirit people.

The Slave/Settler/Carceral State

In 1441, the first Portuguese ships carrying West African peoples sold into slavery arrived in Europe. Half a century later, Spanish ships landed on the shores of a "new" world and confronted its Indigenous peoples. Alongside these events in the fifteenth century, a new taxonomy of the (hu)man emerged, a Eurocentric conception that, according to Sylvia Wynter's "Unsettling the Coloniality of Being/Power/Truth/Freedom," relied on subjugation through constructed human difference and the naturalization of this subjugated difference.[15] While this taxonomy marked Black and Indigenous bodies—individual, communal, and geographic—differently, the effects it engendered frame(d) the Other as extractable, disposable, and violable, and advance(d) a variety of murderously, psychologically, and sexually violent tactics and seizures to ensure the progress of the modern Western project of domination and expansion.

At first, this approach to a history of Euro-American racialization and Indigeneity appears grounded in Western-centric worldviews and time-telling, setting the clock back only as far as the fifteenth century when recounting complex and expansive narratives. Yet marking this period— not as a singular event but as a mushrooming of practices, codifications, and justifications that would come to resonate for centuries—is crucial to understanding a genealogy of punishment and resistance as it relates to gender and sexuality on Turtle Island. Following this genealogy, the twin processes of the creation of a slave *and* settler state are revealed to culminate in the creation of the US carceral state, or what I refer to as the slave/settler/carceral state. I contend that these twin processes cannot be grappled with separately, especially when considering the contemporary carceral state's Othering narratives about Black and Indigenous queer, trans, gender nonconforming, and Two Spirit people.

The slave/settler/carceral state's *stories that wound* are often presented as discrete, yet Tiffany Lethabo King's *The Black Shoals* works against typical conceptions of Blackness and Indigeneity "as emerging independently of one another," as well as clarifying "their co-constitution or oneness."[16] King chafes against the continual juxtaposition of Blackness and Indigeneity, specifically the likening of Indigeneity to land and landedness and of Blackness to water but *not* land, with landlessness but *not* landedness. This juxtaposition is commonly exemplified by narratives of US state–based Othering that go something like this:

> Government racism has not been uniformly applied to all groups of color, but has been manifested through different mechanisms for different ethnic groups over the centuries. *Native Americans were displaced from their land by force and then faced constantly changing conceptions of their status dreamed up in Washington, D.C. African Americans were enslaved and then kept at the bottom of the economy by legal segregation and violence.*... One after the other, these groups were racialized, that is, made into a legal entity subordinate to white people.[17]

While the heterogeneous application of oppressive policies and practices that Lui et al. describe in *The Color of Wealth* is accurate, this continual representation separates land theft and chattel slavery from one another, as if these were not inextricably linked and dependent on each other for the US to establish itself. In other words, focusing on Indigenous *displacement from their own land* and Black *enslavement on others' land* mischaracterizes these as discrete forms of meaning-making that separately serve white supremacist settler colonial control. King intervenes thusly: "The practice of enslaving Black people and making them fungible and accumulable symbols of spatial expansion happens *alongside* and *in relation to* Indigenous genocide."[18] Here, I draw from *The Black Shoals* not to equivalize experiences but, instead, to interrupt narratives constructed about them.

Acknowledging the colonial extraction of Blackness is a disruption to the "rootless" figure of the enslaved arrivant. Samudzi and Anderson offer an alternative depiction of Blackness, more compatible with King's: "Through enslavement in the Americas and histories of Indigeneity and migration on the African continent, Black identity is in many ways inextricably linked to land."[19] Yet due to "the forced extraction of Africans during the transatlantic slave trade, blackness has come to symbolize a kind of rootlessness."[20] Linda Tuhiwai Smith (Ngāti Awa and Ngāti Porou) briefly touches on how colonialism worked as a driving force for both the enslavement of indigenous Africans and the land theft and genocide of Indigenous peoples on Turtle Island. She explains, "Millions of indigenous peoples were ripped from their lands over several generations and shipped into slavery" to "lands already taken from another group of indigenous peoples."[21] The slave/settler/carceral state requires land—and, thus, the elimination of those already existing on said land—and it *also* requires the stealing of those existing on their own lands to perform forced labor elsewhere.[22] Both of these existences are simultaneously linked and delinked from land, both are wracked by resource extraction, both are defined as distinct from one another (yes, even in liberal discourse, as exemplified above), and both are narrated through harmful stories not of their own making.[23]

To be clear, I am not suggesting that Black people on Turtle Island are indigenous to this place. This is also not to confuse Chickasaw theorist Jodi Byrd's question of how "arrivants and other peoples forced to move through empire use Indigeneity as a transit to redress, grieve, and fill the fractures and ruptures created through diaspora and exclusion,"[24] because I genuinely believe it is possible to redress the harms of Othering narratives without claiming equivalencies or appealing to state recognition. However, I do take seriously King, Samudzi, and Anderson, as well as Smith, in imploring for more complex narratives of the constructions of Blackness and Indigeneity than the ones we are given: Blackness as not simply *landless* and Indigeneity as not solely *landed*.[25] As I see it, telling *stories that wound*, stories that separate, stories that allowed (and continue to allow) for bodies "to have been taken and to have been made to leave" is a cornerstone of the slave/settler/carceral state and its effects on both Black *and* Indigenous peoples from the Middle Passage and post-Columbian contact onward.[26] In what follows, I distinguish (some of) the multiple intersecting experiences of being gendered, sexualized, racialized, and/or colonized that resemble a particular kind of Otherness under the slave/settler/carceral state and its attendant narratives.

Punishing the Other(s)

Early penitentiaries claimed to be based in ideas of the penitence and rehabilitation of the mind and soul. Providing background on prisons as "institutions of modernity" that were a "central feature in the development of secular states," Ruth Wilson Gilmore notes that prisons made it possible to "depersonalize social control" in order to make such control more bureaucratically manageable, as well as to meet the historical reformist demands for less corporal punishment.[27] Concomitant with the rise of the rhetoric of "freedom" and "liberty," prisons were meant to be a consequence (e.g., a loss of freedom) due to one's actions,[28] promising societal "stability" through justifications, such as "retribution, deterrence, rehabilitation, or incapacitation."[29] At that time, "irrational" racialized, colonized Others were not believed to have access to such promise of change through penality. For example, "Black men and women were ideologically barred from the realm of morality and ... were not even acknowledged as ever having been epistemological subjects and moral agents."[30] Prisons, police, and courts have, therefore, never been "neutral" arbiters of "justice" but, rather, highly biased systems that stem from and continue to enact punishment on Othered Blackness. Joy James reminds us that inequities along racial, class, and gender lines exist at every level of the criminal punishment system, from prosecution and sentencing to abuses within policing and imprisonment, etc.—practices that don't materialize from the ether but from narratives of difference and disposability.[31] According to Angela Davis, the "promise" of the prison had little or nothing to do with redemption and has instead shown how white settler interests have a stake in controlling Black bodies as "raw materials"—whether as chattel slaves, chain gang members, or prisoners—"for as long as possible."[32] Founding the US slave state on murderous anti-Blackness demanded the practice of punishment as a form of *controlling whether and how Black people may even exist*. White supremacist narratives of "deviance" and "irrationality" justified this punishment and carcerality.

Black feminists, queer, trans, and gender nonconforming people offer specific gendered and sexualized critiques of this slave/settler/carceral state that constructs narratives of certain bodies and existences as able to be robbed of autonomy. Scholarship around the countless Black folks who identify as queer, trans, and gender nonconforming throughout US history whose assaults have not only been undertheorized but completely overlooked points to the Othering that occurs not simply at the axis of race but of gender and sexual orientation as well.[33] Saidiya Hartman contextualizes this historically in the colonial and antebellum eras, when the confluence of racialized and gendered Othering became enshrined in law: "The failure to comply with or achieve gender norms would define black life; and this 'ungendering' inevitably marked black women (and men) as less than human."[34] And this would further mark Blackness as a "condition of unredressed injury."[35] In other words, the racialized, gendered "condition" of Blackness is not represented within the genre of (hu)man enough to be considered harmed by sexual violence, enslavement, and other forms of white supremacist terror. This echoes queer of color critiques from scholars like C. Riley Snorton and Roderick Ferguson.[36] Snorton recounts that often, regardless of being cis or trans, "black genders are figured outside the traditional symbolics of 'male' and 'female.'"[37] It is not just nonnormative Black gender identities and presentations that are "figured outside," punished, and threatened with death. Cathy J. Cohen's seminal article "Punks, Bulldaggers, and Welfare Queens" reminds us that the sexual and kinship practices of Black folks, poor folks, and others in marginalized social positions "have been [and continue to be] prohibited, stigmatized, and generally repressed," even if *seemingly* straight.[38] While Black women who identify as cisgender and/or straight certainly still benefit in some ways from the cisheteropatriarchy of dominant US society, Samudzi and Anderson emphasize that both Black cis and *especially* trans women and girls are vulnerable, targeted, murdered, and yet continually invisibilized, "because women's safety is a non-priority of the state and because patriarchal gender structures are ultimately grounded in transmisogyny."[39] In sum, the *stories that wound* Blackness hinge on the condemnation of an Other that is both a racialized *and* gendered body. Therefore, narratives of Blackness must account for the creation of this Othered body that is seen as both unable to be violated or to be redressed due to (trans)misogynoir and white supremacist sexual norms.[40]

Deemed simultaneously further from whiteness *and* femininity and, therefore, further from innocence, Black trans and gender nonconforming folks are viewed through a lens that Andrea Ritchie highlights as "criminalizing narratives"[41] or that Patricia Hill Collins might call "controlling images."[42] Ritchie insists the "false gender binary" in the US "tolerates no deviation in appearance, behavior, or expression from characteristics associated with the gender assigned at birth," and that any such deviation leads "to a suspicion and presumptions of instability, criminality, fraud and violence in police interactions with transgender and gender-nonconforming people, particularly of color."[43] Criminalizing narratives paint a picture of these gendered Black lives as Others, threatening, and in need of control, which, therefore, justifies the use of slave/settler/carceral state violence against them. Yet at the same time, mainstream LGB (and sometimes T) activism has colluded with slave/settler/carceral state interests and focused on legal reform efforts, such as passing hate crime laws. Dean Spade maintains that being a crime victim grants the legal protection that is often desperately sought by vulnerable populations.[44] But state protection entails competing for safety and security as a subject who conforms to norms of good citizenship and simultaneously distancing oneself from what Amy Brandzel describes as less desirable, abject (non)citizen positions[45]—requirements that Black queer, trans, and gender nonconforming people are *always* denied under the settler/slave/carceral state.[46] Ultimately, any legislation bolsters punitive, retributive justice systems and "serves as an alibi to state violence" within white supremacist, settler colonial, cisheteropatriarchal "structures that cannot be redeemed."[47]

Just as carcerality is foundational to the US slave state, it is equally true that founding the US settler state on genocidal coloniality demanded *controlling if and how Indigenous people might even exist*. This is too often framed as a story of how the enclosure and punishment of individual, communal, and geographic bodies produces safety. Concerns over security are only a motivation insofar as the state manages Othered populations deemed dangerous, pathological, disposable, criminal, guilty, and deserving of punishment for the sake of the white, cisheteropatriarchal settler population. Similarly to Davis, Ross contends that the bodily subject of the original penitentiary was a white one, and the punishment of colonized Indigenous peoples (as well as other people of color) has always been detached from any goal of instilling morality or penitence. We can see this in the ways gendered settler norms and restrictions of the outside world are reproduced inside jails and prisons. Not only are these spaces antithetical to any traditional healing practices—in reality, they are actively antagonistic to those aims—they also subject Native individuals who identify as queer, trans, gender nonconforming, and/or Two Spirit to the cisheteropatriarchal whims of non-Native police, corrections officers, wardens, doctors, counselors, etc.[48]

The methods settler colonialism has used to instill cisheteropatri-archal norms operate at multiple registers, through Indigenous peoples' forced assimilation into institutions like prisons and residential schools. For Native Americans, Ronald Takaki notes that punishing and isolating mechanisms—such as the asylum, the boarding school, the penitentiary, and the reservation—all serve "the principle of separation and seclusion" that "would do more than merely maintain Indians: It would train and reform them."[49]

I would go further and argue that separating people from their community and culture is not merely *reform*; it is death. Following the pronouncement that the US must "kill the Indian . . . and save the man,"[50] Indigenous assimilation is, in fact, an iteration of genocidal control. This resonates with A. Dirk Moses's discussion of defining colonization as cultural genocide, a more expansive view that encompasses cultural—not just physical—destruction.[51] The US settler state has certainly employed both culturally and physically eliminatory practices and justified them through narratives of Otherness, savagery, and "deficiency."[52]

The white supremacist settler colonial narrative of Native Otherness and inferiority in contrast to a Euro-American rational modernity sought to destroy Indigenous bodies and minds and strip them of humanity from first contact. Specifically, through law, "Native people . . . became 'criminals.' *Criminal* meant to be anything other than Euro-American."[53] Similarly—as a deviant, punishable, Othered definition of Indigeneity— settler colonialism also "framed Native people as queer populations marked for death" due to how settlers "interpreted diverse practices of gender and sexuality as signs of a general primitivity among Native peoples."[54] Deborah Miranda (of the Ohlone-Costanoan Esselen Nation) demonstrates that part of the murderous momentum of settler colonialism has been the deliberate "gendercide" of these Native identities and practices deemed "queer" in terms of gender and/or sexuality.[55] Other Indigenous feminists also confirm that the settler state actually *requires* the violence and death of the gendered and sexual Other, because, as Audra Simpson (Kahnawake Mohawk) indicates in the article "The State Is a Man," an agentic, autonomous, and self-determining Other poses a threat to the settler state's sense of sovereignty.[56] Sarah Deer (Muscogee Creek) provides a comprehensive overview of US settler colonialism's sexually violent history, in which there is an inseparable connection between the sovereignty of Native bodies and the sovereignty of tribal nations. "It is impossible," Deer tells us, "to have a truly self-determining nation when its members have been denied self-determination over their own bodies."[57] The loss of self-determination on an individual level creates the conditions for a loss of political self-determination, and vice versa.[58] Furthermore, in place of "the more open gender possibilities" and sexual possibilities that settlers have demonized in Indigenous communities is the implementation of "a binary gender system based on a hierarchy of male supremacy over women that erased nonbinary Indigenous gender roles, such as those we now call transgender and Two Spirit."[59] By erasing gender and sexual diversity, bodily autonomy, and, ultimately, tribal sovereignty, narratives of "backward" people are formative to the violent, even deadly, punishment of Indigenous peoples under the slave/settler/carceral state.

Forging Paths Beyond

All of this is to say that stories matter; stories have an impact. If the dominant ones told about Black, Indigenous, and people of color (BIPOC) communities have wounded and continue to wound—specifically by justifying the deadly punishment doled out by the carceral state—then any attempt to tear down and exist outside and in spite of these conditions must confront these stories. Overall, I see the stories told *about* Black and Indigenous peoples to be central to the carceral practices that need to be combatted. Conversely, the stories told *by* Black and Indigenous feminists, queer, trans, gender nonconforming, and Two Spirit people help to challenge policing, prisons, and punishment. I am in no way saying that to be Black is the same as to be Indigenous, or vice versa. What I am arguing is that to be either (or both) means that narratives that are not our own are foisted upon us. These narratives have formed parallel justifications and valences of Othering as it pertains *specifically* to the carceral state. (For instance, Black and Indigenous peoples are both overrepresented in incarcerated populations.) If these *stories that wound* precipitate parallel effects, then it behooves those of us invested in prison abolition to investigate and counter them and to create our own.

However, the narratives of the slave/settler/carceral state belie the continued existence, resistance, and survivance of Black and Indigenous lives that *exceed* the forces that seek to control, punish, and kill with impunity. We certainly need to tell our stories of lives that have not been entirely determined by and, indeed, have forged sociality in spite of the restrictions of the slave/settler/carceral state.[60] These are what Daniel Heath Justice might call *stories that heal* or alternative visions that speculate beyond the many harmful narrativizations I've laid out above. At the same time, a dream of abolition from BIPOC communities must also counter the *stories that wound* by (de)narrativizing the Othering lies that the slave/settler/carceral state requires to define itself in relation to. Following the abolitionist and decolonial practice of Black and Indigenous feminist, queer, trans, gender nonconforming, and Two Spirit theorizations of the slave/settler/carceral state, I have attempted to *(re)map* and *unsettle* white supremacist, settler colonial, cisheteropatriarchal narratives by exposing them as the constructed fictions that they are. It is only by exposing and *unsettling* these narratives as centuries-long *stories that wound*, which prop up attempts to dictate lived realities, that we can then see we are living in *a past that is not past*. We are living with the historical resonances in the present day, and we must do the work of (de)narrativizing them to resist retelling them.

For Black and Indigenous individuals who identify as queer, trans, gender nonconforming, and/or Two Spirit, the connections between historical precedent and contemporary punishment are salient. As Davis conveys, Black, Indigenous, and people of color community members "are sent to prison, not so much because of the crimes they may have indeed committed, but largely because their communities have been criminalized."[61] This criminalization has a history and a language. Narratives of gendered, sexualized, racialized, colonial Othering, or *stories that wound*, have been central to US carceral state formation. In the preceding pages I have focused on the institutions, ideologies, and discourses that have turned Black and Indigenous people into living fictions, Othered figures not of "our own" making. As I've determined, these Others are not entirely discrete or simplistically defined as *landed* or *landless*. Nor is the narrative told about these Others singular and monolithic. Although these stories deem *all* Blackness and Indigeneity as various shades of always already "deviant," "debased," and "dangerous," those who are additionally Othered due to nonnormative gender identities and sexual orientations are at further risk of being subjected to present-day patterns of policing, prison, and punishment practices. For the contemporary carceral state to function it is necessary for it to take cues from narratives foundational to the slave state and the settler state, narratives that make clear who is to be punished, controlled, and killed under the purview of law. These are narratives that must be actively opposed. Black and Indigenous peoples working toward the abolition of the slave/settler/carceral state challenge what we have all been told are the limits of possibility and actively forge paths beyond.

Notes

1   Daniel Heath Justice, *Why Indigenous Literatures Matter* (Waterloo, ON: Wilfrid Laurier University Press, 2018), 1.

2   Here, I rely on the distinction of *settler colonialism* "from the more traditional ideas of colonialism (wherein invaders claim resources but return home) by emphasizing the settler population's creation of a new social order that depends in part on the ongoing oppression and displacement of Indigenous peoples"; ibid., 9.

3   Ibid., 2.

4   The white supremacist, settler colonial US state advances the police, the judicial system, and mass incarceration's imposition of retribution, torture, and even death as means of "redress" for harm. It is this imposition that exemplifies the *carceral state*, a governing constellation that "anticarceral feminists" have analyzed as not only encompassing the criminal punishment system but also "the interrelationship of state abandonment and state violence in communities of color, the entanglements of carceral and psychiatric power, and the racial constitution of gender and sexual norms and their brutal modes of enforcement in [and outside of] locked institutions"; Emily Thuma, *All Our Trials: Prisons, Policing, and the Feminist Fight to End Violence* (Champaign: University of Illinois Press, 2019), 3. It is this lens through which I view the US as a carceral state.

5   Zoé Samudzi and William C. Anderson, *As Black as Resistance: Finding the Conditions for Liberation* (Oakland: AK Press, 2018), 4.

6   Mishuana Goeman, *Mark My Words: Native Women Mapping Our Nations* (Minneapolis: University of Minnesota Press, 2013), 3.

7   According to the US Department of Justice, between "1999 to 2014, the number of AIAN jail inmates increased by an average of 4.3 percent per year, compared to an increase of 1.4 percent per year for all other races combined." In federal corrections,

the United States Sentencing Commission states that, as of 2013, the "number of Native American offenders has increased by 27.2 percent over the last five years."

8   Luana Ross, *Inventing the Savage: The Social Construction of Native American Criminality* (Austin: University of Texas Press, 1998), 1.

9   Michelle Alexander, *The New Jim Crow: Mass Incarceration in the Age of Colorblindness* (New York: New Press, 2012), 99.

10   Mike Males, "Who Are Police Killing?" Center on Juvenile and Criminal Justice, August 24, 2014, accessed December 6, 2019, http://www.cjcj.org/news/8113.

11   I am also cognizant of many Black scholars' critiques of the use of statistics, mathematics, and numerical figures in the valuation of Black life; see Katherine McKittrick, "Mathematics Black Life" *Black Scholar* 44, no. 2 (June 2014): 17, accessed June 8. 2022, https://antiableistcomposition.files.wordpress.com/2020/06/mathematics-black-life.pdf; Khalil Gibran Muhammad, *The Condemnation of Blackness: Race, Crime, and the Making of Modern Urban America* (Cambridge, MA: Harvard University Press, 2019), 13–14.

12   Luana Ross, *Inventing the Savage: The Social Construction of Native American Criminality* (Austin: University of Texas Press, 1998), 33.

13   Justice, *Why Indigenous Literatures Matter*, 2; emphasis added.

14   Christina Sharpe, *In the Wake: On Blackness and Being* (Durham, NC: Duke University Press, 2016), 13.

15   Sylvia Wynter, "Unsettling the Coloniality of Being/Power/Truth/Freedom: Toward the Human, After Man, Its Overrepresentation—An Argument," *CR: The New Centennial Review* 3, no. 3, (Fall 2003): 257–337, accessed May 27, 2022, https://tinyurl.com/bdh9ddkz.

16   Tiffany Lethabo King, *The Black Shoals: Offshore Formations of Black and Native Studies* (Durham, NC: Duke University Press Books, 2019), 28.

17   Meizhu Lui, Bárbara Robles, Betsy Leondar-Wright, Rose Brewer, and Rebecca Adamson, *The Color of Wealth: The Story Behind the US Racial Wealth Divide* (New York: New Press, 2006), 19; emphasis added.

18   King, *Black Shoals*, 11; emphasis added.

19   Samudzi and Anderson, *As Black as Resistance*, 21.

20   Ibid., 23.

21   Linda Tuhiwai Smith, *Decolonizing Methodologies: Research and Indigenous Peoples* (London: Zed Books, 2012), 69–70.

22   Patrick Wolfe, "Settler Colonialism and the Elimination of the Native," *Journal of Genocide Research* 8, no. 4, (December 2006): 387, accessed June 8, 2022, https://www.scinapse.io/papers/2018276495#fullText.

23   Obviously, there are complexities and problematics in comparing and conflating Black and Indigenous struggles with one another. This is not to say that these are discrete communities, which would ignore the lived existence of Black Indigenous people. Regarding language around social and racial justice concerns, Eve Tuck (Unangan) and K. Wayne Yang chasten against allowing other liberatory aims to obscure Indigenous efforts for sovereignty. Decolonization "is not a generic term for struggle against oppressive conditions and outcomes. . . . By contrast, decolonization specifically requires the repatriation of Indigenous land and life"; Eve Tuck and K. Wayne Yang, "Decolonization Is Not a Metaphor," *Decolonization: Indigeneity, Education and Society* 1, no. 1 (January 2012): 21, accessed June 8, 2022, https://tinyurl.com/5n6nnx9k. Similarly, Mark Rifkin's *Fictions of Land and Flesh* outlines how

comparisons between Black and Indigenous struggles risk omitting important differences, such as issues over sovereignty, settlement, and strategy. Rifkin understands that situating concerns over a slave state and a settler state under a singular analytical structure "aims to think together the uneven distributions of power, resources, and life chances for a range of oppressed racialized populations while suggesting that these groups share a set of objectives in the dismantling and transformation of that larger matrix of ideologies, institutions, and coercions" but ultimately believes that this approaches totalization; Mark Rifkin, *Fictions of Land and Flesh: Blackness, Indigeneity, Speculation* (Durham, NC: Duke University Press, 2019), 15. Instead, Rifkin proposes understanding the different "conditions of emergence" that shape contemporary Black and Indigenous movements, which should be seen "less as incommensurable than as simply *nonidentical*, as having distinct kinds of orientation shaped by the effects of histories of enslavement and settler colonial occupation"; ibid., 4; emphasis added.

24   Jodi A. Byrd, *The Transit of Empire: Indigenous Critiques of Colonialism* (Minneapolis: University of Minnesota Press, 2011), 39.

25   Vicente Diaz (Chamorro) considers more expansive views of Indigenous place and simultaneously de-emphasizes the privileging of continents and land, a narrow view that illuminates "how we as Native peoples sometimes unwittingly perpetuate colonial definitions of land (and self) through ways that we invoke primordial connectedness to landedness, particularly in political programs of reclaiming stolen land bases"; Vicente Diaz, "No Island Is an Island," in *Native Studies Keywords*, ed. Stephanie Nohelani Teves, Andrea Smith, and Michelle Raheja (Tucson; University of Arizona Press, 2015), 91. Diaz is not discounting land-based claims but is, instead, demanding conceptions of continents and islands that include non-land as valuable and valued within Indigenous and decolonial movements.

26   Fred Moten, *Black and Blur* (Durham, NC: Duke University Press, 2017), 199.

27   Corporal punishment "nevertheless endures in the death penalty and many torturous conditions of confinement"—indeed, I would argue torture is *the* condition of confinement; Ruth Wilson Gilmore, *Golden Gulag: Prisons, Surplus, Crisis, and Opposition in Globalizing California* (Berkeley: University of California Press, 2007), 11.

28   However, *un*freedoms were always guaranteed by other legal and extralegal means for disenfranchised individuals and communities throughout US history; ibid., 12).

29   Ibid., 13.

30   Angela Davis, "From the Convict Lease System to the Super-Max Prison," in *States of Confinement: Policing, Detention and Prisons*, ed. Joy James (New York: St. Martin's Press, 2000), 66.

31   Joy James, introduction to James, *States of Confinement*, x–xvi.

32   Davis, "From the Convict Lease System to the Super-Max Prison," 69.

33   Although it is beyond the scope of this chapter, the highly gendered and sexualized nature of narratives about and violence against Black masculinity throughout US history should also be noted.

34   Saidiya Hartman, *Wayward Lives, Beautiful Experiments: Intimate Histories of Social Upheaval* (New York: W.W. Norton, 2019), 186.

35   Saidiya Hartman, *Scenes of Subjection: Terror, Slavery, and Self-Making in Nineteenth-Century America* (Oxford: Oxford University Press, 1997), 101.

36   Roderick Ferguson, *Aberrations in Black: Toward a Queer of Color Critique* (Minneapolis: University of Minnesota Press, 2004), 3.

37   C. Riley Snorton, "Gender," in *Keywords for African American Studies*, ed. Erica R. Edwards, Roderick A. Ferguson, and Jeffrey O.G. Ogbar (New York: New York University Press, 2018), 92.

38   Cathy J. Cohen, "Punks, Bulldaggers, and Welfare Queens: The Radical Potential of Queer Politics?" *GLQ* 3, no. 4 (May 1997): 437–65, esp. 453, accessed May 31, 2022, https://tinyurl.com/2p9bmp8b.

39   Samudzi and Anderson, *As Black as Resistance*, 68.

40   Moya Bailey, "They Aren't Talking About Me . . . ," Crunk Feminist Collective, March 14, 2010, accessed May 26, 2022, http://www.crunkfeministcollective.com/2010/03/14/they-arent-talking-about-me.

41   Andrea J. Ritchie, *Invisible No More: Police Violence against Black Women and Women of Color* (Boston: Beacon Press, 2017), 236.

42   Patricia Hill Collins, *Black Feminist Thought: Knowledge, Consciousness, and the Politics of Empowerment* (London: Routledge, 2014), 69.

43   Ritchie, *Invisible No More*, 127.

44   Dean Spade, "Their Laws Will Never Make Us Safer," in *Against Equality: Queer Revolution, Not Mere Inclusion*, ed. Ryan Conrad (Oakland: AK Press, 2014), 170.

45   Amy Brandzel, *Against Citizenship: The Violence of the Normative* (Champaign: University of Illinois Press, 2016), 14–15.

46   Samudzi and Anderson, *As Black as Resistance*, 69.

47   Amy Brandzel, *Against Citizenship* 38–42; Dean Spade, "Their Laws Will Never Make Us Safer," 172.

48   Kalaniopua Young, "From a Native *Trans* Daughter: Carceral Refusal, Settler Colonialism, Re-Routing the Roots of an Indigenous Abolitionist Imaginary," in *Captive Genders: Trans Embodiment and the Prison Industrial Complex*, ed. Eric A. Stanley and Nat Smith (Oakland: AK Press, 2011), 87.

49   Cited in Ross, *Inventing the Savage*, 21.

50   Richard H. Pratt's famous words endorsing settler colonial practices were actually uttered in the same breath with the championing of similar practices for "civilizing" enslaved Africans.

51   Despite detractors who claim it is not to the letter "genocide," because genocide requires total destruction and intentionality; A. Dirk Moses, "Genocide and Settler Society in Australian History," in *Genocide and Settler Society: Frontier Violence and Stolen Indigenous Children in Australian History*, ed. A. Dirk Moses (New York: Berghahn Books, 2004), 17–18.

52   Justice, *Why Indigenous Literatures Matter*, 19.

53   Ross, *Inventing the Savage*, 14.

54   Scott Lauria Morgensen, "Settler Homonationalism: Theorizing Settler Colonialism within Queer Modernities," *GLQ* 16, nos. 1–2 (April 2010): 106, accessed June 8, 2022, http://985queer.queergeektheory.org/wp-content/uploads/2013/04/morgensen-settler-homonationalism.pdf.

55   Deborah A. Miranda, "Extermination of the Joyas: Gendercide in Spanish California." *GLQ* 16, nos. 1–2 (April 2010): 258.

56   Audra Simpson, "The State Is a Man: Theresa Spence, Loretta Saunders and the Gender of Settler Sovereignty," *Theory & Event* 19, no. 4, (October 2016): 1–30.

57   Sarah Deer, *The Beginning and End of Rape: Confronting Sexual Violence in Native America* (Minneapolis: University of Minnesota Press, 2015), xvi.

58   For example, the ability for tribal nations to respond, especially in traditionally affirming ways, to gendered and sexualized violence has dwindled over the years, leaving many Native individuals who identify as women, girls, transgender, gender nonconforming, and/or Two Spirit vulnerable. *Oliphant v. Suquamish Indian Tribe* (1978) divested tribal courts of jurisdiction over non-Natives, meaning such courts cannot criminally prosecute non-Native defendants. This is part of a larger pattern of Native nations' diminished and constrained self-determination—over outcomes for Indigenous bodies and for those that cause harm to Indigenous bodies—which US federal powers like the Bureau of Indian Affairs embody.

59   Ardele Haefele-Thomas, *Introduction to Transgender Studies* (New York: Harrington Park Press, 2019), 241; Sarah Hunt, "Representing Colonial Violence: Trafficking, Sex Work, and the Violence of Law," *Atlantis* 37, no. 2 (2015–2016): 27, accessed June 8, 2022, https://1library.net/document/yewm627y-representing-colonial-violence-trafficking-sex-work-violence-law.html.

60   In *Fugitive Poses*, Gerald Vizenor provides the following definition: "Native survivance is 'more than survival, more than endurance or mere response... survivance is an active repudiation of dominance, tragedy, and victimry'"; cited in Grace L. Dillon, "Imagining Indigenous Futurisms," in *Walking the Clouds: An Anthology of Indigenous Science Fiction*, ed. Grace L. Dillon (Tucson: University of Arizona Press, 2012), 6.

61   Angela Davis, *Are Prisons Obsolete?* (New York: Seven Stories Press, 2003), 57.

Sovereignty Imperiled

Blackness and "Unsovereign" Indigeneity

Che Gossett

"Why is black movement indigenous movement?... Black people
are indigenous people, doubly displaced—from the land and from
the socius, in the land and in the socius. This displacement placed
black people no place, but no place is not nowhere."
—Fred Moten and Stefano Harney

"Abolition is beyond (the restoration of) sovereignty. Beyond
the restoration of a lost commons through radical redistribution
(everything for everyone), there is the unimaginable loss of that all
too imaginable loss itself (nothing for no one). If the indigenous
relation to land precedes and exceeds any regime of property, then
the slave's inhabitation of the earth precedes and exceeds any prior
relation to land—landlessness. And selflessness is the correlate. No
ground for identity, no ground to stand (on)."
—Jared Sexton

Jamaican novelist and critical theorist Sylvia Wynter's unpublished manuscript "Black Metamorphosis," held at the Schomburg Center for Research
in Black Culture, bears the subtitle "New Natives in a New World." The
manuscript, written in the 1970s and towering at over 800 pages, prompts
me to consider Blackness as the metamorphosis of Indigeneity. I'm interested in how Blackness radicalizes the conceptualization of Indigeneity,
as it is rerouted not through the sovereign treaty but, rather, through the
void of the slave ship's abyss and the forced deportation and inhuman
trafficking of the Middle Passage (to invoke and extend Édouard Glissant's
terminology). Blackness has been figured as Indigeneity placed under

erasure, barred from recognition due to what Nahum Chandler describes as its "originary displacement."[1]

The sundering of Blackness from Indigeneity has been repeated at the level of the episteme, academic discourse, and even disciplinarity. Sylvia Wynter's contributions to the rethinking of Indigeneity are at once indispensable and yet also widely underthought. The Caribbean is one place where Blackness and Indigeneity are entangled with and in the plantation. Wynter's "archipelagic thinking," in contrast to and undermining "continental thinking," reveals how the Caribbean fractures and fragments not only Western philosophy's conceit of the subject but the conceptualization of Indigeneity as the underside to Western *nomos*, or law, and sovereignty.[2] In this brief essay—essay in the sense of an experimental proposition—I think through how Blackness undoes sovereignty and the political coordinates of Indigeneity that are given and maintained through anti-Blackness. Not only does Blackness demand a dismantling of anti-Black structuration of any formation of Indigeneity that would deprive Blackness of Indigenous ontology, but Blackness also prompts a reconfiguration of the ontology of Indigeneity itself. I take up the contributions of Wynter, as well as Édouard Glissant, Hortense Spillers, Fred Moten, and Nahum Chandler, and bring them to bear on Blackness and Indigenous ontology.

Black and Native studies are the result of the disciplinary as ontological fissure: the consolidation of each as mutually exclusive objects of study, disciplinary formations, and methodologies within the larger academic edifice of the humanities means that they are figured as separate and siloed. The bracketing of Black from Native studies is emblematic of the discursive violence of anti-Blackness that figures the slave as "nowhere"—as Moten and Harney state in the epigraph—without cultural coordinates.[3] The scholarship of Achille Mbembe and Mahmood Mamdani have been central to bringing African Indigeneity into the fold of postcolonial theory. Likewise, Tiya Miles and Tiffany Lethabo King have intervened in Native studies in the US settler academic context to consider the entanglement of Blackness and Indigeneity. Yet, to borrow Nahum Chandler's grammar once more, Black Indigeneity is "unsovereign" and fugitive, outlaw to the authenticity politics of Indigenous sovereignty (a cardinal example being the Cherokee Freedmen's anti-Black exiling from the Cherokee Nation).

Anti-Blackness means that the Blackness of Indigeneity is placed under erasure—barred, foreclosed, and canceled. Black Indigeneity. Here, what was first Heidegger's and later Derrida's syntax of *sous rature* is applicable. As Gayatri Spivak writes of the critical gesture in her preface to *Of Grammatology*: "Since the word is inaccurate, it is crossed out. Since it is necessary, it remains legible."[4] The violence of the slave ship was not only its carceral function as a nautical prison. It is also worth noting that racialized capture itself in the Western world traces not to policing and prisons but, rather, earlier, to the slave dungeon and the slave fort that preceded and prefigured their existence. Before the ship was the hold of the dungeon. Then the hold of the ship.

The slave ship in its hellish apparatus figures for Glissant as a void, and yet the void is not the nothingness of the negative vortex but, rather, an ontology of capture that is deconstructive (generative as opposed to destructive) in its violence. "Yet, the belly of this boat dissolves you, precipitates you into a nonworld from which you cry out. This boat is a womb, a womb abyss."[5]

The sea is vertigo-inducing. *Vertigo* traces back to the Latin for the dizzying sensation of whirling, the loss of anchoring coordinates, and the dispossession that accompanies the slow or rapid decomposition and evaporation of the sense of stable orientation. It is this sense of vertigo that Glissant describes in "The Open Boat," the first chapter of *Poetics of Relation*. The vertigo that accompanies the "dizzying sky plastered to the waves" is a meta/physical undoing and disorientation. Similar to Hortense Spillers in her version of the hold of the ship as a reformulation of the Freudian oceanic and to Edward Kamau Brathwaite's poetics of the hold as limbo—which, in the theological sense, marks the atopic space and suspended temporality of purgatory—the hold for Glissant is a "nonworld."

What is a nonworld? The grammar of capture, here of the hold, even as it is an entirely different politics and poetics, in this case of the Black radical poetic and literary tradition, still fails to adequately account for and communicate that which it aims to describe. In the midst of torture, the voice, words, and the power of linguistic narration—which is seen as one of the central tenets of the human, demarcating the human from the category of the animal that has sounds but not *logos* and reasoned speech—fail to register. The voice fails as a register, and, instead, language fractures and decomposes into haunting screams, moans, and cries. The slave ship is an ontological enterprise, an anti- and ana-anthropological machine for the negation of persona and lifeworld, a space of oblivion wherein being is bracketed, shackled, thrown overboard, devoured, and murdered. The planet is an archive of slavery.

For Glissant, the ocean is part of the political ecology of anti-Blackness and racial slavery:

> Whenever a fleet of ships gave chase to slave ships, it was easier just to lighten the boat by throwing cargo overboard, weighing it down with balls and chains. These underwater signposts mark the course between the Gold Coast and the Leeward Islands. . . . In actual fact the abyss is a tautology: the entire ocean, the entire sea gently collapsing in the end into the pleasures of sand, make one vast beginning, but a beginning whose time is marked by these balls and chains gone green.[6]

Here, the sea is in fact in vertigo, flipped upside down. There's an inversion from the terrestrial to the oceanic topology; the optics move from earthly to subterranean. The signposts are underwater, a submerged route that lies beneath the "human" world and haunts it. The human world is the earthly world, which is why the oceanic world is often experienced as so foreign. The human is etymologically of the earth as well, one of the biological tenets and registers of man as an anthropological being is evolutionarily bipedalism (an attribute rooted in the distinction of human from animal, which in its ableism bifurcates between the trope of the naturalized human body and its animal and disabled/crip other). The human is shadowed by its Latinate root, *humus*, for *ground* or *earth/soil*. The ocean is the afterlife of slavery and racial capitalism.

The slave ship is a deportation machine, and the transatlantic slave trade was the greatest forced migration in modern world history. Who was deported?

> African aristocrats were not only complicit in the trade but protected from it. Now, what do we call the people this royalty helped track and capture and trade from their hinterlands, margins, and among their "subjects"? Those people were indigenous, displaced in the most brutal way by European sociopathic greed with the aid of African kings and queens and aristocrats. In other words, from the beginning, indigeneity and class are given in the Africans who suffered Middle Passage.[7]

The African aristocrats, however, were neither protected from nor could they anticipate colonialism's dispossession of their aristocratic station and the recursive violence of ideological anti-Blackness and racial capitalism that would fold back onto the continent in their near future and in our historical present.

Glissant differentiates the experience and ontological condition of the exile from that of the enslaved: "Exile can be borne, even when it comes as a bolt from the blue. The second dark of night fell as tortures and the deterioration of person, the result of so many incredible Gehennas."[8] The Gehenna is a state of liminality and limbo, between hell and the world, a grave and a condemned site in biblical and rabbinical eschatology. This "deterioration of the person" is one of the signatures of racial slavery, the slave ship, and its technologies of torture and the hold, which are designed to both extinguish the coordinates of personhood of the enslaved and to affirm the sovereignty of the category of the person as the exclusive property of whiteness.

The negative horizon of racial slavery was the violent reduction of the figure of person to "flesh," that which, as Spillers argues, was available to anyone (any white/person). What exactly is flesh? To parse out the political vernacular, flesh shares an anatomical imaginary with cadaver (the etymology tracing to fallenness) but denotes sensation, perhaps overwhelming sensation. Flesh is the sphere of the living; the cadaver is the sphere of the dead. The skin is subtended by flesh, yet flesh is what is exposed when the skin is cut, riven, or, to use Spillers's description, "ripped apart."[9] Flesh is sentient but not conscious. Flesh can be eroticized. Saidiya Hartman's work traces the anti-Black libidinal violence of sensuality of the flesh, where white pleasure is made possible through the death and torture of the enslaved. "More than lynched," as W.E.B. Du Bois writes in *Black Reconstruction*, attempting to describe the horrific nature of anti-Black libidinal violence that was in excess of lynching itself.[10] It was the event of encountering the paraphernalia of lynching—discovering that Sam Hose's body parts were for sale at a local business when he was on his way to deliver a letter for publication in the *Atlanta Journal Constitution* protesting the lynching—that drove Du Bois to radicalize and antidiscipline sociology.

To return to the opening epigraphs, the quotes from Fred Moten and Stefano Harney and Jared Sexton point toward how Blackness troubles and is askew from the coordinates of Indigeneity that are proscribed and prescribed through the logic of political representationalism. What does Indigeneity mean and become without the "claim" to sovereignty—neither the sovereignty of the modern capitalist nation-state nor the hierarchical proto-sovereignty of the ethnic group, which is absorbed into the slave/

master, capitalist, and colonial relations?[11] How to think the genocide of the slave trade as Indigenous genocide? How to think "landless" Indigeneity? These questions are an invitation, as well as a way to also show how the struggle against anti-Blackness cuts in a transversal and diagonal movement across political axes, forcing us to consider that the perennial pursuit of the abolition of anti-Blackness radicalizes struggles for postcolonial and Indigenous independence, such that these are thought with and through Blackness, instead of unthought without Blackness.

Notes

1   Nahum Dimitri Chandler, "Originary Displacement," *boundary 2* 27, no. 3 (Fall 2000): 249–86.
2   John E. Drabinski, *Glissant and the Middle Passage: Philosophy, Beginning, Abyss* (Minneapolis: University of Minnesota Press, 2019), xv.
3   Yollotl Gómez Alvarado, Juan Pablo Anaya, Luciano Concheiro, Cristina Rivera Garza, and Aline Hernández, "Conversación Los Abajocomunes: Stefano Harney and Fred Moten in conversation on the occasion of the Spanish translation of *The Undercommons*," *New Inquiry*, September 5, 2018, accessed May 26, 2022, https://thenewinquiry.com/conversacion-los-abajocomunes.
4   Jacques Derrida, *Of Grammatology*, trans. Gayatri Chakravorty Spivak (Baltimore, MD: Johns Hopkins University Press, 2016), xxxii.
5   Édouard Glissant, *Poetics of Relation*, trans. Betsy Wing (Ann Arbor, MI: University of Michigan Press, 2010), 6.
6   Glissant, *Poetics of Relation*, 5.
7   Gómez Alvarado et al., "Conversación Los Abajocomunes."
8   Glissant, *Poetics of Relation*, 5.
9   Hortense J. Spillers, "Mama's Baby, Papa's Maybe: An American Grammar Book," in *Black, White, and in Color: Essays on American Literature and Culture* (Chicago: University of Chicago Press, 2003), 206.
10 W.E.B. Du Bois, *Black Reconstruction in America* (New York: Free Press, 1998), 728.
11 Gómez Alvarado, et al., "Conversación Los Abajocomunes"; Jared Sexton, "The *Vel* of Slavery: Tracking the Figure of the Unsovereign," *Critical Sociology* 42, nos. 4–5 (July 2016): 593.

Claiming Alterity

Black, Gender, and Queer Resistance to Classification

Zaria El-Fil

> "That man over there says that women need to be helped into carriages, and lifted over ditches, and to have the best place everywhere. Nobody ever helps me into carriages, or over mud-puddles, or gives me any best place! And ain't I a woman?"
> —Sojourner Truth

Sitting among many white abolitionists at the 1851 Women's Rights Convention, Sojourner Truth spoke out extemporaneously and delivered the famous speech posthumously entitled, "Ain't I a Woman?"[1] According to the Anti-Slavery Bugle, Truth began by asking if she might say a few words, and then asserted, "I am a woman's rights."[2] While there is much debate surrounding the exact details of her speech, all versions of the speech display Truth's persuasive oratory style as she questions where she stands in terms of "man" and "woman." In the Anti-Slavery Bugle, Truth is cited as saying, "I can carry as much as any man, and can eat as much too, if I can get it," before pleading with the male audience to give women their rights. It is very clear that such a speech was considered extreme at the time, both because of the political plea for equality and the fact that Truth herself was formerly enslaved. While the historicity of the speech is largely debated, much of the language regarding the precarity of womanhood and manhood as they are mapped onto Black flesh offers an important opening to rethink the perceived universality of national body politics. Whether Truth asked, "Ain't I a woman?" or declared, "I am a woman's rights," an answer in the affirmative offers no assurances. The suffering that Truth bore as an enslaved woman exceeded the assumptive logic of gender, making the hegemonic code for "woman" insufficient to account for her

Blackness. Consequently, in this essay, I will ask as Saidiya Hartman has asked, "Can we employ the term 'woman' and yet remain vigilant that all women do not have the same gender?"[3]

Western gender works as an organizing principle that names a particular subject-object relation. Similar to other *things*, gender is constructed by countless grammars of capital, power, and consciousness.[4] Once Blackness is added to the frame, the grammars of capital and power that secure gender as a form of normalized, hegemonic body-reasoning are unearthed. If Blackness fundamentally disrupts gender in a way that makes "women" and "men" errors of classification, then it is possible that this site of error and disruption can be the very entry through which a queer resistance to classification can occur. In other words, to be omitted from traditional gender and only included at the moment of your erasure is to occupy an insurgent site from which a reverse discourse can be articulated. What new questions on Blackness and *being* can be asked when consulting this liminal space of ontological exclusion? How can Blackness be articulated within a queer realm of being? I argue that these questions extend across time—leading our inquiry from enslavement and Truth's provocative speech onward into the present "afterlives of slavery."[5] Written in the midst of an interminable catastrophe, this project started as my own venture to seek a nonbinaristic relationship to my own understanding of my gender and grew into a larger discussion with other Black people seeking to delink from gender as defined by Western hegemony. The ideas here are porous and insist on transformation beyond their present spatiotemporal frame. Which is to say, this article is unfinished—patiently awaiting thoughtful engagement to push it beyond its manageable limits. I will continue to wrestle with Blackness and gender now, as an undergraduate student, and forever. While the present intervention is not intended to be exhaustive or to completely decipher the opaque, it opens a space to ask questions about the dialectic between our bodies and the grammar of meaning they have been placed into.

In "Imitation and Gender Insubordination," Judith Butler makes the critical point that the bifurcation of gender derives less from physiology and more from socially derived codes of being and their performances. Due to the fluidity of these codes, they need to be performed, elaborated, and insisted upon constantly to warrant any validity. Therefore, queerness is a socially defined identity slippage that exists opaquely as a disavowal of the clearly legislated norms under the heterosexual matrix. Butler recognizes this slippage as a spatiality where new inquiries can be articulated in the service of displacing hegemonic heterosexual norms. In this essay, I propose that Blackness and queerness overlap in their blurring of ontology by way of decentering and disrupting normative structures. My meditation on "queer" and "queering" is not necessarily synonymous with "LGBTQIA+" as an identity; rather, it is a zone of instability, a "doing for and toward the future."[6] It is a refusal of the present with an aim toward futurity.

While folks identifying within the LGBTQIA+ spectrum possess a powerful critique due to their material experiences and daily refusals, I also call for a movement toward queer as praxis. Just as Black radical thinkers have called for a Black consciousness, I argue that the full embodiment of a revolutionary consciousness is not complete unless it is rooted in (and informed by) both individuals who identify themselves as queer as well as a queer social consciousness. In this essay, I am careful not to remove queer identity from its experiential foundations and would instead like to think about "queer" as a space. As the Mary Nardini Gang asserts:

> Queer is a territory of tension, defined against the dominant narrative of white hetero monogamous patriarchy, but also by an affinity with all who are marginalized, otherized and oppressed. Queer is the abnormal, the strange, the dangerous. Queer involves our sexuality and our gender, but so much more. It is our desire and fantasies and more still. Queer is the cohesion of everything in conflict with the heterosexual capitalist world. Queer is a total rejection of the regime of the Normal.[7]

In other words, queerness *is* a rebellion refusing enclosure. This is consistent with multiple readings of Blackness as an inherently destabilizing force. Thinking from a position of Blackness presents us with a critique of the world that is so totalizing it can only be described as "the end of the world."[8] Or, more precisely, the end of the world as it is now. In this way, queerness and Blackness put forth a myriad of ways of being and resisting that ultimately disavow the present order in favor of new worlds.

My reading practices are deeply influenced by thinkers like Sylvia Wynter, Hortense Spillers, Zakiyyah Iman Jackson, and C. Riley Snorton. I build from Wynter's critical intervention, which redefines human life and sociality as both biology and culture, bios and mythos, skin and mask. Moving beyond biocentric and ethnocentric determinism, my analysis is attentive to sociogenesis and the role of narrative in creating and assigning codes/categories of being. To elaborate on this point, I consult Hortense Spillers's renowned essay "Mama's Baby, Papa's Maybe: An American Grammar Book," which details the (mis)mapping of genders onto Black flesh. In this essay, Spillers lays down the critical framework for understanding the centrality of Black female flesh to the emergence of transatlantic slavery as the underpinning of modern historical governance. According to Spillers, flesh is the conceptual and temporal precursor to the body that is not postulated as a matter of pure biology but, rather, is the result of a collection of narratives transcribed and seared into the body by "the calculated work of iron, whips, chains, knives, the canine patrol, the bullet."[9] The narratives (American grammar) produce a rupture between the Black female body and the rhetorical core that secures womanhood as coherent—expressed through motherhood and sexuality. Attempting to repair rupture through the gender binary reifies gender stratifications that have historically relegated Black people to the outside of "American grammar."

Zakiyyah Iman Jackson further explores Black genderedness through her concept of "ontologized plasticity," which defines the marginalizing chaos associated with Blackness's arbitrary remapping of gender "nonteleologically and nonbinaristically, with fleeting adherence to normativized heteropatriarchal codes."[10] In conjunction, these scholars' work opens a space for reconceptualizing what *being* means through the rupture of white normative gender constructs. Keeping these ideas in mind, I hope to pose questions to try to understand how Blackness operates, both inside and outside of modernity, and throws the general theory of the human and gender into crisis. Furthermore, I envision this work as an acceptance of the opacity and inversion of Black genderedness through a queer political operation. In this way, queer isn't another identity to be placed into neat social categories but, rather, an opposition to the manageable limits of identity. It is the "total rejection of the regime of the Normal."[11]

Race against the Binary

"The colonial world is a world cut in two."
—Frantz Fanon

In the 1961 text *The Wretched of the Earth*, Frantz Fanon employs dualistic imagery to uncover the nature of the colonial encounter. According to Fanon, the colonial world is a world divided into compartments—two compartments inhabited by two different species. In the Manichaean sense, the good is pitted against the bad, the white against the Black, the rich against the poor. The dividing line in this dichotomy is made coherent through symbolic and material political violence.[12] One important societal bifurcation that occurs through the colonial encounter is the distinction between Man and Other. In *Black Skin, White Masks*, Fanon makes the provocative statement, "At the risk of arousing the resentment of my colored brothers, I will say that the black is not a man."[13] Fanon's point here has roots in the Hegelian assumption that *proper* recognition is the mutual recognition between two conscious agents. Mutual recognition allows for a cognitive awareness of the self and its relation to the Other (and the world).[14] This "coming into self-awareness" is skewed for Black people by the way the white colonial gaze functions to obscure and define the Other's bodily schema. When describing how his body created a dialectic with the world, Fanon notes, "my body was given back to me sprawled out, distorted, recolored, clad in mourning."[15] In other words, the colonial encounter transforms the colonial subject into a body emptied of being into which new interpretations can be planted. In this section, I follow Oyèrónké Oyěwùmí and Hortense Spillers in their historical assessment of the complex naming system imposed by colonial domination, which misidentified and miscategorized Black genderedness. It should be noted that some Black feminists critique the category of "Black woman" but assert that the nascent colonial understanding of the term does not necessarily twin our contemporary understanding of category. I am not suggesting that the violences of slavery and colonization are unchanging and all-consuming, but, rather, that the legacies of such carry "living effects, seething and lingering, of what seems over and done with."[16] Put differently, Black genderedness is not static or ahistorical, it is constructed and, therefore, intimately connected to the past.

In *The Invention of Women*, Oyèrónké Oyěwùmí traces the connection between colonization and the emergence of gender as an organizing principle in Yorùbá social life. As a Nigerian feminist and critic of the equation of sex with gender (a phenomenon she terms "biologism"), Oyěwùmí asserts that Western gender is derived from biocentric assumptions that are both culturally and historically bound. Oyěwùmí pushes against the Western preoccupation with the visual and hence physical aspects of human reality. The mistranslation of *obinrin* and *okunrin* into *female/woman* and *male/man* is a direct reflection of Western dominance in interpreting and organizing the world. In the West, men and women are binarily linked, hierarchical, and social categories. Biocentric definitions of humanness and gender assume that these categories are universal and maintain that men are the norm against which women are defined. The Western preoccupation with biology seeks to solidify portions of power from a biological basis and instate a biological supremacy to affirm privilege and dominance. The body is said to produce a logic of its own and, once gazed upon, can tell a person's beliefs, social position, and morals or lack thereof.

The biologic of the Western episteme presents the body as "always *in* and *on* view."[17] As such, the colonial gaze rests upon the body to determine difference, one difference that Oyěwùmí cites as being historically constant is the gendered gaze. In Oyěwùmí's words: "The social categories 'man' and 'woman' are social constructs deriving from the Western assumption that 'physical bodies' are social bodies." Western gender organizing principles were applied transculturally through colonial domination and passed as *natural* fact. However, Yorùbá language does not rely on gender as a mode of relation, as illustrated in the lack of gender-specific and body-specific first-person pronouns, kinship terms (i.e., son, daughter, brother, sister, etc.), as well as personal names. With European colonial rule in Africa came the importation of body-centered gender logic as a social organizing principle. Oyěwùmí asserts that the British system of indirect rule disregarded the existence of women as chief authority and consequently displaced them from all political affairs that they previously participated in. In Oyěwùmí's words: "The very process by which females were categorized and reduced to 'women' made them ineligible for leadership roles. The basis for this exclusion was their biology, a process that was a new development in Yoruba society."[18] This colonial development has persisted and has placed individuals gendered as women at an acute disadvantage. Oyěwùmí asserts that in the colonial situation "there was a hierarchy of four, not two, categories. Beginning at the top, these were: men (European), women (European), native (African men), and Other (African women)."[19] In Oyěwùmí's calculus, African women become the Other—a zero degree of social conceptualization.

Moving forward toward transatlantic slavery, Hortense Spillers attends to the idea of "body reasoning": gendered narratives and grammars are pinned to Black women in relation to enslaved people. According to Spillers, before the body, there is the flesh. Flesh is not postulated as a matter of pure biology but, rather, as the result of a collection of narratives transcribed and seared into the body. Locating the Middle Passage, Spillers posits that enslavement and colonization marked a theft of the body, wherein "the female body and the male body [became] a territory of cultural and political maneuver, not at all gender-related, gender-specific."[20] The captive body is woven into anecdotes and assumptive logics that secure it as being *for* the captor. This means the captive body is reduced to flesh, vulnerable to the projections of the captor, and translates into what Hortense Spillers describes as pornotroping:

> This profound intimacy of interlocking detail is disrupted, however, by externally imposed meanings and uses: (1) the captive body as the source of an irresistible, destructive sensuality; (2) at the same time—in stunning contradiction—it is reduced to a thing, to being for the captor; (3) in this distance from a subject position, the captured sexualities provide a physical and biological expression of "otherness"; (4) as a category of "otherness," the captive body translates into a potential for pornotroping and embodies sheer physical powerlessness that slides into a more general "powerlessness."[21]

Hortense Spillers's term "pornotroping" linguistically stages both the sexualization and the brutalization of enslaved people and names the process of becoming flesh. Simultaneously, pornotroping marks the ungendering of Black *bodies* turned *flesh*, erased of past gender-social identities. The inclusion of flesh throws biologized gender into peril, because it asserts that the historical, philosophical, and material experiences of Black women deviate significantly from the social scripts holding the concept "woman" together. Spillers's use of pornotroping and flesh are touchstones for configuring how we can account for the "female flesh 'ungendered'" birthed by the Middle Passage.[22] Moreover, Spillers's discussion of flesh opens a site to think about how sex and gender are fixated, expressed, and arranged within logics that sustained racial slavery and colonization. Reading Spillers alongside Oyěwùmí in the context of gender and colonial domination uncovers the lack of a universal instantiation of gender. Black feminist theorists, including Patricia Hill Collins, Angela Davis, and Darlene Clark Hine, have also taken up the question of gender universality and concluded that Black subjects' genders and sexualities are formulated differently from those found in the mainstream of the world of Man. This is further illustrated in the way the Western episteme has constructed Black people as "sub, supra, and human simultaneously and in a manner that puts being in peril, because the operations of simultaneously being everything and nothing for an order—human, animal, machine, for instance—constructs Black(ened) humanity as the privation and exorbitance of form."[23]

Given the colonial origin of Black genderedness, it is scarcely possible to construct a Black "woman" or "man" identity that is reliant on a perceived universality of these gender experiences in a patriarchal world order. As posited by Sylvia Wynter, such universal codification of gender circumvents and ignores the "negro question," such that gender functions simply as a genre of Man.[24] The peril of inclusion into liberal humanism is that it reifies normativized heteropatriarchal codes and enforces the subjecthood/objecthood separation that has historically served to oppress the captive body. Instead of repairing the grammatical mismatch with increased pleas to be included in Western womanhood and white feminisms (which she calls a "monstrosity"),[25] Spillers asserts:

> This problematizing of gender places [Black women], in my view, out of the traditional symbolics of female gender, and it is our task to make a place for this different social subject. In doing so, we are less interested in joining the ranks of gendered femaleness than gaining the insurgent ground as female social subject. Actually claiming the monstrosity (of a female with the potential to "name"), which her culture imposes in blindness.[26]

Claiming the monstrosity of one's alterity throws traditional feminism into crisis and sabotages "[feminism's] own prescribed role in the empirical articulation of its representations in effect by coming out of the closet, moving out of our assigned categories."[27] The monstrosity is an insurgent space from which new questions about being can be articulated. Starting from an understanding of flesh and the monstrosity thereof can lead to new understandings of fugitivity and freedom. Instead of acceptance into normative structures, the insurgent ground of a queer politic enables a space for riot, revolt, refusal, and insisting *otherwise*. Therefore, a politic centered on Blackness's articulation within a queer consciousness throws gender as Western genre into crisis and leads to a different freedom praxis. The goal of liberation changes from "becoming human"—via adherence to normative gender structures—to abolishing those very structures that secure white supremacist cisheteropatriarchy.

Toward a Black Queer Revolution

> "We have no place that we can claim without contention
> We are constructing a whole new edifice of boxes to put people in . . .
>
> And the most significant thing that any person can do
> But especially Black women and men
> Is to think about who gave them their definitions
> And rewrite those definitions for themselves."
> —Moses Sumney, "boxes"

As we move into the present, the epistemic weight of biocentric coding remains a prevalent issue. Black culture presents a social heterogeneity that refuses the boundaries of gender propriety and sexual normativity.[28] In the 1960s, the Moynihan Report aimed to pathologize the Black family and naturalize the family as the ordering episteme of social life from an unmistakably white Western perspective. In doing so, Moynihan castigated Black matriarchal households as deviant and vilified Black single women's sexual autonomy, fortifying an "ethos of personal responsibility and disavowed structural inequality."[29] Instead of holding onto liberal humanist conceptions of filial organization, Black feminists have pushed to identify other ways of living in relation outside of the categories that currently name humanness—what the individuals featured in Moses Sumney's "boxes" describe as writing "those definitions for themselves."[30] I argue that this rewriting includes making the leap from the epistemic violence of Western gender and the nuclear family toward other ways of living. The pessimism toward the promise of social position secured through colonial gender categories forces us to seek out an *elsewhere*. There is a realm of possibility and futurity when one is delimited to outside the anthropology of the human. As Tiffany Lethabo King asserts, when one is not afforded gender and subjecthood, one occupies a unique position of having nothing to prove.[31] Yet nearly two centuries after Sojourner Truth's infamous speech, many movements are still rooted in liberal humanism via Western binary gender. Tying the previous sections together, this section aims to leap from the binds of Western gender toward an acceptance of queer subject positioning.

During July 5–10, 2020, there was a mass social media trend wherein Black individuals typed "I Am Black Man" or "I Am Black Woman," followed by affirmative adjectives and powerful messages of positivity. The original trend included the following copied-and-pasted instructions:

I am a Black man.... I build.... I don't tear down other Black men!
... I have felt the pain of being torn down and I have decided I will be
deliberate about building others! If I didn't tag you, please don't be
offended. I tried to pick people I thought would do this challenge!!
All too often, we men find it easier to criticize each other instead of
building each other up. With all the negativity going around let's
do something positive!! Upload one picture of yourself... only you.
Then tag as many brothers to do the same. Let's build each other up,
instead of tearing ourselves down.[32]

It should be noted that the trend started out as only Black men, but
Black women slowly started to take part in the challenge. The goal was to
uplift Black people in the wake of the murder of George Floyd, Ahmaud
Arbery, Breonna Taylor, and the mass uprisings thereafter. An article
discussing the trend described it as functioning to combat harmful stereotypes of Black men in particular, with no acknowledgment of the women
utilizing the trend. While it was a wonderful mode of confidence, when
coupled with the worldwide movement for Black lives, the trend seemed:
(1) to adhere to the politics of representation that conflates the disavowal
of stereotypes through positive representation as providing reprieve from
ontologizing violence, and (2) to make a determined attempt for human
recognition via adherence to Western binary genders. Recuperation of
humanity through appropriating institutions like Western gender that
rendered Black people outside of its symbolic economy is a never-ending project. There are colonial histories and discursive frameworks that
secure Black genderedness as incompatible with white Western gender.
However, a true acceptance of Black ontological opacity is an important site
for thinking and worlding from outside of our present governing system of
meaning. This vision of a reimagined future will need to arise from Black
LGBTQIA+ individuals who break with normativity in their historical
positioning and embodiment and show us how to imagine otherwise. It
also will come from an acceptance of the Black queer political positioning
that acknowledges the way that social scripts securing Western traditional
gender fail to encapsulate Black cultural life historically. Now, more than
ever, I think it is important to analyze one's commitments to traditional
symbolics of Western gender. In the fight for a reimagined future, one
must lean into these categorical antagonisms instead of seeking to join
the ranks of the white hegemonic social subject.

Notes

1   Sojourner Truth, *The Narrative of Sojourner Truth, Dictated by Sojourner Truth*, ed. Olive Gilbert (Boston: Self-published, 1850), accessed June 9, 2022, http://www.libraryweb.org/~digitized/books/Narrative_of_Sojourner_Truth.pdf.

2   *Anti-Slavery Bugle* (New-Lisbon, Ohio), June 21, 1851, accessed May 26, 2022, https://chroniclingamerica.loc.gov/lccn/sn83035487/1851-06-21/ed-1/seq-4; for the sake of this article, I consult this version of the speech, because it was the first to be published.

3   Saidiya V. Hartman, *Scenes of Subjection: Terror, Slavery, and Self-Making in Nineteenth-Century America* (New York: Oxford University Press, 1997), 99–100.

4   C. Riley Snorton, *Black on Both Sides: A Racial History of Trans Identity* (Minneapolis: University of Minnesota Press, 2017). On page 6, Snorton discusses "Thing Theory," which describes the process by which an object becomes a thing as one that relies on a particular subject-object relation. This relation is one that is laden with power and defines "things" by differentiation that lacks absoluteness. I argue that gender is a thing in so far as it outlines a relation reliant on differentiation— what a man *is* relies heavily on what a woman *is not* (and vice versa). The grammars insist on a particular relation that is performed and articulated.

5   Saidiya V. Hartman, *Lose Your Mother: A Journey Along the Atlantic Slave Route* (New York: Farrar, Straus and Giroux, 2007), 6.

6   José Esteban Muñoz, *Cruising Utopia: The Then and There of Queer Futurity* (New York: New York University Press, 2009).

7   *Toward the Queerest Insurrection*, printed clandestinely by the Mary Nardini Gang, 2008.

8   Aimé Césaire, *Notebook of a Return to the Native Land*, trans. and ed. Clayton Eshleman and Annette Smith (Middletown, CT: Wesleyan University Press, 2001). This apocalyptic invocation has been taken up by Frantz Fanon as well.

9   Hortense J. Spillers, "Mama's Baby, Papa's Maybe: An American Grammar Book," *Diacritics* 17, no. 2 (Summer 1987): 65–81, accessed June 9, 2022, https://people.ucsc.edu/~nmitchel/hortense_spillers_-_mamas_baby_papas_maybe.pdf.

10 Zakiyyah Iman Jackson, *Becoming Human: Matter and Meaning in an AntiBlack World* (New York: New York University Press, 2020).

11 Mary Nardini Gang, *Toward the Queerest Insurrection* (Seattle: ZAPP Zine Project, 2008).

12 Fanon describes the dividing line as being shown by "barracks and police stations." I read this as specifically speaking to the state-sanctioned nature of such a division. Political actors, such as police officers and soldiers, are deployed to solidify the violent dichotomy of the colonial world.

13 Frantz Fanon, *Black Skin, White Masks*, trans. Richard Philcox (New York: Grove Press, 2008).

14 Georg Wilhelm Friedrich Hegel, *The Phenomenology of Spirit*, trans. and ed. Terry Pinkard (Cambridge: Cambridge University Press, 2018).

15 Fanon, *Black Skin, White Masks*, 259

16 Avery F. Gordon and Janice Radway, *Ghostly Matters: Haunting and the Sociological Imagination* (Minneapolis: University of Minnesota Press, 1997), 195.

17 Oyèrónké Oyěwùmí, *Invention of Women: Making an African Sense of Western Gender Discourses* (Minneapolis: University of Minnesota Press, 1997), 2.

18 Ibid., 124.

19 Ibid.

20 Hortense J. Spillers, *Black, White, and in Color: Essays on American Literature and Culture* (Chicago: University of Chicago Press, 2003), 67.

21 Ibid., 20.

22 Ibid., 27.

23 Jackson, *Becoming Human*.

24 Sylvia Wynter, "Unsettling the Coloniality of Being/Power/Truth/Freedom: Toward the Human, After Man, Its Overrepresentation—An Argument," *CR: The New Centennial Review* 3, no. 3 (Fall 2003): 313, accessed May 27, 2022, https://tinyurl.com/bdh9ddkz.

25 Spillers, *Black, White, and in Color*.

26 Ibid., 24.

27 Sylvia Wynter, "Beyond Liberal and Marxist Leninist Feminisms," *The CLR James Journal* 24, nos. 1–2 (July 2018): 16.

28 Roderick A. Ferguson, *Aberrations in Black: Toward a Queer of Color Critique* (Minneapolis: University of Minnesota Press), 2004.

29 Tiffany Lethabo King, "Black 'Feminisms' and Pessimism: Abolishing Moynihan's Negro Family," *Theory & Event* 21, no. 1 (January 2018): 68.

30 Moses Sumney, "boxes," on *græ* (Bloomington, IN: Jagjaguwar, 2020); this interlude features Taiye Selasi, Michael Chabon, Ezra Miller, and Ayesha K. Faines, with each person's voice overlaid by the others, creating a mosaic of thoughts and feelings.

31 King, "Black 'Feminisms' and Pessimism," 80.

32 Abi Travis, "Here's Why You're Seeing the 'I Am a Black Man' Challenge on Your Feed Today," Distractify, June 5, 2020, accessed June 9, 2022, https://www.distractify.com/p/i-am-a-black-man-challenge.

Feeling Unsentimental

Black Essentiality and Queer Black Questioning of the Human

zuri arman

"And I warped you in the interest of design
It's just because I love you"[1]
—Mavi, "Self Love"

"Is abolition a synonym for love?"[2]
—Saidiya Hartman, "The End of White Supremacy, An American Romance"

"The impasse is reconciled by the mutual acceptance of risk and vulnerability that comes with interdependence and symbiosis."[3]
—Zakiyyah Iman Jackson, *Becoming Human*

"Said, we got to go down, down to the wire
I'll go through the fire with you"[4]
—D'Angelo, "The Line"

God's not dead (but maybe He should be)

a gust of wind lifted the veil
from my eyes,
a commandment
questioning the wholly holiness of 'holy' matrimony
that weds flesh to flesh
as if they've ever been strangers.

white lace:

obscuring the radiance
of a black face,
its ability to hold me
as we descend into chaos.
whispers made me doubt
i could love it.

white lace:
putting my faith in preacher
Man to guide me
down the aisle.
He takes from my pockets,
breaks my spine
in two, and
calls that an election
(among other things,
like freedom)

if not the wind,
then who would've told me
that I could love you?

that we could have
it all as the

horizon collapses

and the sun sets
as the backdrop to ruins.

Introduction

The COVID-19 pandemic has revealed the specificities of anti-Black violence in the wake of climate change–related and ecological disaster. The revelation/reclamation of our "interconnectedness" is often touted as a solution to the perils of climate change, a predicament that is most commonly framed as panhuman: if "we" can come together and realize the stakes of the situation through an existential awakening of sorts, both the planet and "our" lives will be saved. Beginning in 2020, the social protocols surrounding COVID-19 promoted by governments and governmental agencies around the globe claimed that each person could do their part for the public good primarily by staying inside to prevent the spread of the virus. This reliance on a coming-together-in-species narrative, however, prematurely "disavow[s] and erase[s] racial antagonisms."[5] The solution is not as simple as everyone working from *inside* their homes or being incorporated *into* humanity, because some people—and their labor—are the constitutive *outside*. Black labor, even while devalued, is still required for society to run its business as usual. Therefore, as Axelle Karera explains: "It is no longer sufficient to abide to liberal romantic dictums according to which any configuration of a 'we'—'we' the people, 'we' the post-Human, 'we the hyper-objects,' 'we' earthy beings—can secure the good life so long as we can escape the constraints of the state, of racial capitalism, and now of our ecological demise."[6]

I propose that an interrogation of "we" reveals differing relations to COVID-19 and its effects and, more broadly, to climate change–related disaster, particularly along what W.E.B. Du Bois terms the "color line."[7] This "we" encompasses all of humanity, but it is stratified in accordance with a specific expression or "genre" of the human, as described by Sylvia Wynter. This Eurocentrically defined human—referred to as *man*—is a white, cisgender, heterosexual, economically affluent male in its most perfect form and overrepresents itself by portraying its own "interests, reality, and well-being" to be the same as those of every other life form on earth.[8] Man not only relegates Black people to the "nadir" or bottom rung of society, it further uses the Black worker as a dispensable yet necessary tool for its capital-seeking endeavors in the face of climate change, a relation revealed by—and predating—the current nomenclature "essential worker." I posit that the "essentiality" of Black "nonessential" workers, who I will refer to as the "Black human," such as the Black middle class and affluent, lies in the symbolic coherence they bring to the human through their abject status as Blackened people who are, nonetheless, still humanized. Therefore, regardless of occupation, Black people (also referred to abstractly as "the Black" to denote the living object-status) exist in a state of *essentiality* that turns the definition of the word and the connotative meanings we ascribe to it on its head.

In its continued attempts to "master" nature, man forces primarily Black essential workers into deadly positions. When the Black worker is coerced into accepting this new title of "essential" they are also conditionally accepted into the economic "we" and work to meet its ends. To be clear, "essential" brings the Black into conversation with humanity and even humanizes them to an extent, but with a muffled voice and no aims of their own. Therefore, "if being recognized as human offers no reprieve from ontologizing dominance and violence," then we must consider what can be gained by refusing humanhood, specifically man's overrepresentation as the human.[9] Furthermore, I propose that this refusal shifts the struggle being waged away from one of incorporation into society's established practices toward an engagement in the "politics of existence." Importantly, this entails attempting to enact what Karera calls an "ethic of non-relation" relative to man because the intensification of ethical relations creates fertile ground for the proliferation of anti-Black violence. The struggle for the Black is to create the conditions to coexist with the self and others in ways antithetical to man. In what follows, I will interrogate what I term "Black essentiality" before turning my attention to the role of queer Blackness in this socio-politico-ecological moment.

COVID-19 and Black Essentiality

Millions of workers across the United States from various fields such as food and agriculture, transportation, and health care have seen their positions labeled "essential," forging a new relation with civil society that now relies upon their labor during environmental and economic crisis. This renaming, however, has very different impacts on communities that are dependent on race. Workers in the (predominately white) health care field have undoubtedly faced increased danger from this highly contagious virus, but they are aided by their many years of training, workplace conditions conducive to limiting its spread, and access to medical care. Conversely, Black and brown laborers in other fields, including those that support the functioning of health care facilities, are not given the proper training or precautionary protective equipment to maintain their safety.[10]

Colloquially, *essentiality* is associated with the reception of care and regard. This assumption has been true for the case of doctors and nurses who, in the early stages of the COVID-19 pandemic, were heralded as heroes and afforded the opportunity to speak about the dangers of their work environment on a national scale. As the novelty of the pandemic faded, the health and safety of health care workers has been increasingly overlooked. Their bravery, though, is still acknowledged even if the praise does not lead to material change. Conversely, *Black* essentiality *continues* a relation in which the Black worker "cannot take but by which he or she [or they] can be taken."[11] By virtue of their "essentiality" the Black worker can be used and abused as a means to an end. That end is the resumption of ordinary business operations in the interest of man's pursuit of capital accumulation—even as this pursuit degrades the environment through its extractive logics, which, ironically, contribute to the emergence of previously unseen viruses similar to the current moment.[12] Civil society structurally degraded the Black worker before the pandemic as well; workplace conditions were still treacherous, the pay was still lacking, and the soul was still crushed. Therefore, civil society has no desire to speak of the Black essential worker's precarious workplace conditions, because precarity *is* the condition of Black essentiality under man's tyrannical reign.

For the Black, "essential" operates on a different register. The Black doesn't simply provide labor. As Sylvia Wynter notes in an unpublished essay titled "'We Know Where We Are From': The Politics of Black Culture from Myal to Marley," while orthodox Marxism defines the worker as "economically powerless," the *Black* worker is both economically and *symbolically* powerless within a global symbolic order that defines Black as abject, disposable, and, thus, worthy of deathliness. Their forced precarity also provides coherence to the non-Black subjects who contra-define themselves as a "workers" against the Black;[13] they are exploited and alienated, but *at least they aren't Black*. This is the essentiality of the *Black* worker. They are necessary as a marginal(ized) limit case for non-Black workers and, *additionally*, for Black people who have been humanized (i.e., have been whitened). The Black human retains their essential object status relative to white counterparts but are projected to have "evolved" past their less-affluent Black counterparts, concealing that they too are the symbolic limit case for the human and, thus, always deemed lesser relative to others.[14] Through man's gaze, "human recognition is extended, but only to serve further objectification."[15] The Black can be humanized, but only as an object in human form that is more or less proximate to (but never fully) the proper human. Society uses the Black worker, in particular, for symbolic *and* economic activity. The "essential" label simply demarcates this current historical moment which is a perpetuation of an anti-Black past. Christina Sharpe refers to this as a "singularity—a phenomenon likely to occur around a particular time, date, or set of circumstances," such as those we find ourselves in now.[16]

This pre- and post-COVID-19 continuity begins to explain the position of the Black worker (and, therefore, the Black, in general), whose labor requires proximity to death for the sake of the "we." Indeed, this present ecological moment—sparked by COVID-19—and the consequent renaming of workers perpetuates relations that have always placed the Black in a position of precarity and in routine proximity to deathliness. This constant closeness to mortal threat has now been labeled "essential" labor. In moments when Black labor is not labeled "essential," our carceral and anti-Black society still subjects the Black worker (and to varying extents, the Black human) to quotidian violence, such as police brutality or the lack of access to clean water and air; the same relation leads to each of these outcomes. In fact, as Jared Sexton and Steve Martinot note, "racism is a mundane affair," present at every level of society, its ordinariness camouflaged by the spectacle of police violence.[17] Regardless of naming, Blackness emerges in an overdetermined relation of violence predicated on fatality and disposability that materializes with fluctuating levels of visuality and viscerality. The Black worker, as a precarious figure perpetually confronting death, reveals the limitations of incorporating the Black into the "we" of society. The Black worker's dilemma reveals the dangers of continuing to accept the ongoing humanization of Black people into our currently ordered ways of being.

Attempts to bring the Black "inside" society, while simultaneously requiring them to be corporeally outside—such as the "essentializing" of the Black worker—rely on the same ethical relation that requires the death of the Black (worker) as a condition of humanhood. Labeling the Black "essential" masks the fact that the Black is already *essentially* outside society by bringing them within it through a violent, ongoing, and repetitive initiation. Before COVID-19, however, Black experiences of nonessentiality and routine abjection from a dominant political system also yielded anti-Black violence. Black workers are then faced with the choice of fulfilling their essential duty to society and continuing to succumb disproportionately to the virus or quitting their job through a politically legible and perfectly acceptable act of resistance only to be faced with the material consequences of unemployment. The choice is a coercive nonchoice between two fatalities: a position of being damned if you do and damned if you don't.[18]

Black Essentiality in a Global Context

Moreover, Black bodies outside the United States are also positioned to perform a distinct labor. On a global scale, Black people continue to be "thingified."[19] While speaking on French national television, a doctor asked,

"If I can be provocative, shouldn't we be doing this study in Africa, where there are no masks, no treatments, no resuscitation?"[20] The doctor's first instinct, which undoubtedly mirrors larger sentiments of anti-Blackness, is the "total objectification" of Black African people by using the continent as a "living laboratory."[21] The Black is reduced to flesh to be toyed and tampered with, again for man's gain, as it attempts to procure a vaccine for its own safety, which can also double as a product to be sold. Again, it must be remembered that society could simply pause its capital-accumulating activity to ensure safety for everyone but chooses not to. This living laboratory is reminiscent of the Tuskegee experiments in Alabama and the experimentation on the bodies of enslaved peoples—female slaves, in particular—for the sake of the "we," demonstrating that the relation resulting in the objectifying instrumentalization of the Black is global in nature *and* atemporal; it is a cycle that continues anywhere Blackness is to be found. Following this genealogy of Black death, it almost seems common sense for the non-Black to refuse to treat Black Africans for COVID-19 or to supply them with the necessary protective equipment, because Black death is inevitable, lucrative, and symbolically necessary for the world's functioning under the guidance of man.

In the West, the only relation that is currently imaginable for a Black population with greater society seems to be, again, one that relies on Black proximity to death. If we look at this relation through the lens of *Black essentiality*, then perhaps we can say the "essentiality" of Black Africans lies in their exposure to COVID-19, similar to Black essential workers in the United States; for the Black African to be inside society—in order to receive any type of international medical attention and be conditionally accepted as human—they must first be diseased. Help, then, only arrives for the sake of the rest of the world's health. Incorporation into present society would require Black people to be recognizable, legible, and respectable in the hopes of "overcoming" their Blackness to be recognized as "white," a corporeal impossibility.[22] Therefore, attempts to comport the Black body into more "upright" (and uptight) figurations of always already debased flesh should be rejected as a solution to anti-Black violence.

The Impossibility of Incorporation

"As long as the United States government keeps the masses of Black and other Third World people as cannon fodder, and uses force to maintain its domination over us, and i am alive, i will resist, knowing that my fate as a resister irregardless [*sic*] of the state's consequences is better than the fates of those who accept oppression and pass it on to coming generations."[23]

—Kuwasi Balagoon, *A Soldier's Story*

Amid this pandemic, what is the role of the queer Black person? What is their function at this intersection of ecologically related disaster and quotidian anti-Black violence? Because their queerness positions them as even further opposed to man in its most ideal form, I posit that the queer black people, including the queer Black worker, are actually key actors, particularly when "performing" queerness, which is to say acting "Black."[24] I propose that we first understand queerness, which is to say queer Blackness, as a "relational ethic and site of alternative political and representational possibility" that materializes as an act of self-destruction.[25] To actively "queer" is to incessantly question the foundational and normative understandings structuring our political and social realities that *seemingly* aid us in some way; the Black is the embodiment of the dangerous question, while the queer Black *asks* the dangerous question already inscribed in their flesh. Here, I am inspired by Safiyah Bukhari who writes:

> We must not be afraid of allowing the old self, rife with the negativisms of this society, to die so that a new, more revolutionary and progressive self can be born. Then and only then do we stand a chance of destroying this oppressive society. It is with this thought in mind that we use the weapon of criticism and self-criticism to correct the way we deal with each other. . . . We must exorcise those characteristics of ourselves and traits of the oppressor nation in order to carry out that most important revolution—the internal revolution. This is the revolution that creates a new being capable of taking us to freedom and liberation. As we are creating this new being, we must simultaneously be struggling to defeat racism, capitalism, and imperialism.[26]

The act of self-destruction moves past the self, as the queer Black attempts to bring the world into a state of "nigger chaos" through various modes of confrontation.[27] Through radical embodied criticism, the queer Black drags the world to its personal hell. This goes beyond seeking "justice," since the justice we might seek may actually render us something akin to "emancipated but subordinated"; the definition of justice that stabilizes current political discourse relies on the existence of anti-Black violence.[28] I argue that queer Blackness requires what Zakiyyah Iman Jackson describes as "reframing black subjection not as a matter of imperfect policy nor as evidence for a spurious commitment to black rights ... but rather as necessitating a questioning of the universal liberal humanist project."[29] Therefore, to be Black and queer is to continue to chisel away at the foundations of a society that places the Black in a position of precarity and to *internalize* the understanding that no performance of gender, sexuality, labor, etc. will lead to society's structural accommodation of Blackness into man's humanity—other than through violence and as abject. But there are other praxes of existing for the queer Black person (those illegible to man's realm of politics) that begin to set the stage for a conflictual ceremony, the destruction of this queerphobic (because foundationally anti-Black) world.

In "Unsettling the Coloniality of Being/Power/Truth/Freedom," Sylvia Wynter explores the origins of Western humanism and its onto-epistemological (questions of our being and our ways of knowing our reality) implications to reveal that our current definition, or "descriptive statement," of the human is such that to be human is to be the "masterer of Natural Scarcity," one who is able to achieve economic freedom, as opposed to the jobless, the homeless, or the poor.[30] Therefore, succumbing to natural scarcity, being impoverished, or being left vulnerable to deadly disease, as in the case of the Black worker today, serve as "proof" of one's natural Otherness. Wynter outlines our current situation: the Black, being the Other, is rendered vulnerable to death by the human to allow its own flourishing.

An uncritical solution, however futile, may be to somehow overcome this scarcity by putting one's head down and laboring through the situation to "prove" one is human, or to mirror the white, cisgender, heterosexual male human through the impossible suppression of queerness and Blackness within oneself and one's community. Both are an attempt at "self-mastery," as described by Saidiya Hartman: attempting to discipline the Black into a proper (Eurocentrically defined) being, primarily expressed through the physical or symbolic "laboring body," the only praxis of being that is afforded to the Black by man.[31] For the Black (worker), self-mastery might look like working in conditions of precarity for low wages without complaint and maintaining a safe distance from queerness to avoid blowback. But anti-Black violence is not enacted because the Black exists in a particular way to be corrected or because the Black may be queer but, instead, simply because the Black is Black.[32] This is why violence follows the Black worker, whether economically incorporated as "essential" or remaining unincorporated. The only safeguard from man's anti-Black violence is to not be the Other and, thus, to not be Black—an impossibility.

Importantly, Wynter highlights that within a hierarchical structure of humanity, the Black has always been "on a rung of the ladder lower than that of all humans" and always will be as long as humanism's (dis)possession continues.[33] The Black's position is predestined, because the human's current descriptive statement is the result of the continued secularization of an originally religious ordering schema based on "degrees of spiritual perfection." That is, the ordering of humans and "the Other" in Western thought was originally rooted in the calculated proximity to a Christian God, wherein one was a part of the clergy or one was "sinful by nature"; there was the Christian, and there was the Other.[34] As secularization continued, Europe understood the human as a hybridly religio-secular being with a rational self and political subjecthood (man 1); the proper practice of political subjecthood affirmed one's reason while the Other lacked both.

Following Charles Darwin's contributions to science, this same onto-epistemological infrastructure mutated into a homologous social structure that defined the human as "homo economicus," a purely biological (rather than religious) being able to overcome the aforementioned natural scarcity (man 2). It maintained the same structural "space of Otherness," however, and imposed this on the Black.[35] The Black fills a structural position in the ordering of humanity, justified through biological determinism (a secularization and "scientification" of the "supernatural") that represents itself as a priori. In other words, within the logics of Western humanism, the Black worker succumbs to scarcity and sickness, because that is what is "natural," and even *desired* and *rewarded*. It is a sign that the social order is still intact.

I want to emphasize the religious infrastructure that orders thought, which suggests anti-Blackness is a matter of "faith" or deals with the "sacred." Therefore, I would like to suggest we begin thinking about how to collectively "kill Gods" while retaining a semblance of a "religious attitude."[36] I characterize this as questioning a priori assumptions that we consider "common sense," remaining skeptical of even our surest thoughts, and rejecting structures that prevent what I call "flesh speaking to flesh" by alienating (Black) people both from one another and from their needs for survival.[37] These "Gods," or sacred epistemic artifacts and properties, mediate and dilute contact with others and desires of the self. For example, in the context of the United States, electoral politics overrepresents itself as the only form of politics and, therefore, structures the political imagination. Every political suggestion must encircle or be adjacent to electoral politics to be seen as legitimate. What does it mean to limit one's political imagination to two opposing parties that are each equally incapable of and unwilling to address topics like anti-Black police violence, climate change, or environmental injustice? The effects of these social ills escape the political. These are matters of survival that require our re-self-conceptualization against, through, and beyond homo economicus, and even beyond "human." We must think outside of the acceptable terms of liberal humanist politics. At the same time, while in the company of one another, we must be willing to lose ourselves to that which is unseen (and perhaps even unheard) yet perceived like the lowest growl of a steady bass line, a distant hum that beckons. Nikki Giovanni's "For Saundra" begins to demonstrate a conscious awareness of one's position in an anti-Black world that requires "killing Gods" and breaking through the glass ceiling constructed by humanity.

Potentiality without Certainty

> "Revolution within a modern industrial capitalist society can only mean the overthrow of all existing property relations and the destruction of all institutions that directly or indirectly support existing property relations."[38]
> —George Jackson, *Blood in My Eye*

Wynter makes apparent why the Black worker—and Black people in general—are damned from all angles. Within the current structuring of being, knowing, and politicking, Black people comprise the bottom tier of society. Without any attempts to disrupt this current line of thinking and way of being, this ethical relation will continue for the foreseeable future until our certain demise.

Radical queer Blackening suggests that our struggle in the present moment is over the politics of existence or the "praxes of existing," a question about who defines what it is to exist. The battle being waged is over more than political recognition or rights; it concerns *who* is human and, therefore, who is granted these rights. We must also be astute about *what makes one human* and move beyond it.

Nikki Giovanni may provide a helpful point of reference for queer Black people engaged in struggle over the politics of existence. In "For Saundra," published in 1968, Giovanni describes a time she was writing a poem:

> i wanted to write
> a poem
> that rhymes
> but revolution doesn't lend
> itself to be-bopping
>
> then my neighbor
> who thinks I hate
> asked—do you ever write
> tree poems—I like trees
> so I thought
> i'll write a beautiful green tree poem[39]

Instead of writing her original poem, she is challenged by a neighbor to describe the natural life around her. She notes, however, that this neighbor thinks Giovanni hates, which sets the stage for a conflict between the neighbor and Giovanni that mirrors the conflict between man and the Black, with the former Othering the latter. Given the time in which Giovanni was writing, the "hate" disregarded by her neighbor is likely a false characterization of her militant way of being that typified many at the time. The neighbor reduces Giovanni's reaction to centuries of racial violence simply to "hate" in order to make this Black expression of affect understandable to herself. This attempt at making her legible humanizes Giovanni, but only as a "hateful" Black human, particularly a hateful Black woman. This grossly mischaracterizes Giovanni's emotion, which cannot be properly described by the constrictive language and grammars afforded by (the) man. Nonetheless, after acknowledging what is, at best, a misunderstanding, she accepts the invitation to write a poem and, thus, to write her way into the environmental humanities—and into humanity, in general, to engage in aesthetic confrontation. Giovanni surveys her environment for signs of life and beauty. She realizes, however, that from her Manhattan apartment there is no such reality to describe. There are no trees, and the sky is not worth noting:

> peeked from my window
> to check the image

noticed that the school yard was covered
with asphalt
no green—no trees grow
in manhattan

then, well, I thought the sky
i'll do a big blue sky poem
but all the clouds have winged
low since no-Dick was elected[40]

Because race (even more so than class) determines the environmental health of one's community, it should come as no surprise that these are the conditions Giovanni faces.[41] As previously stated, Blackness is always proximate to death. Environmental injustice is *essential* for this capitalist society to economically function; many of the pollution-emitting facilities located in Black communities are commercial, meaning that not only is the Black *body* essential for the economy, but so is the Black *home*—the very home that the Black human "remotely" works from, meaning humanization is not an escape.[42] If communities attempt to "green" their space, they create conditions ripe for developers to gentrify and displace the community.[43] It is not just a matter of Black people creating or demanding healthy environments for themselves. The Black, regardless of income, is essential for man's attempted mastery of nature in all places and forms.[44] But Black people, themselves, are not allowed to assert any claim to nature, particularly healthy ones, because they inescapably represent death in the eyes of man.[45] Importantly, these deadly conditions lead to increased morbidity that serves to naturalize and support the categorization of Black people as diseased. To riff off Fanon, Blacks are diseased because they are Black, and they are Black because they are diseased (or dead).

Giovanni understands the antagonistic relationship between Blackness and aliveness within the current order of society, demonstrated by her reflection that perhaps now is no time to write a nature poem:

so I thought again
and it occurred to me
maybe I shouldn't write
at all

but clean my gun
and check my kerosene supply

perhaps these are not poetic
times
at all

Writing a traditional nature poem would inevitably lead to Giovanni's humanization and the naturalization of her environment as her proper place of being. She would remain stuck as her words calcify on the page. Instead, I suggest she refuses the relation of Black essentiality. She refuses any relation, because her gaze is on her own material needs. She is as disinterested in spiting the human's canon of environmental literature as she is in seeking incorporation into it. She troubles the idea of the nature poem with her refusal of traditional form. In her praxis as a writer, she bleeds her angst onto the page in an attempt to *exist* otherwise to the human and to *write* otherwise to the forms in which the human writes of nature. She stages an aesthetic confrontation, "a presentation that refuses representation," because an attempt to represent would amount to nothing more than a lie.[46] Because of her relation to nature and the necessity of her proximity to death, she cannot afford to act in ways that mirror the human, including writing a simple "tree poem." While the human can rely on the liberal politics to which it properly belongs for its political engagement, the Black is concerned with something wholly different. They are concerned with ridding themselves of the complete domination of both their body and home. They are concerned with survival. This is a matter of life and death: a situation that cannot be resolved within the dominant logics of civil society.

What would it mean for Giovanni to simply write a poem about a serene and pastoral natural that does not exist *for her* and to be violently and passively incorporated into a canon of environmental literature that disacknowledges and disavows Black death? Similarly, what does it mean to appeal to a political system that relies on a definition of justice, environmental or otherwise, that makes Black death essential for humanity to function? Instead of grabbing materials for incorporation like a ballot, Giovanni has other plans. There are no trees where there is Blackness; where there are no trees, there must be no peace. She grabs her gun and gasoline—tools more contextually fitting for revolutionary struggle when solutions do not seem to present themselves naturally—to confront the powers that have purposefully and perpetually rendered her environment lifeless and continue to strangle the life from her body and our collective body. The words leave the page, and where they end they begin to demand the action required to struggle over the politics of existence. This shift in consciousness is important, because new praxes of existence must be enacted for the Black to begin destroying whatever is necessary to create conditions that allow for Blackened people to exist within an environment not fraught with death. Giovanni demonstrates an "expression of potentiality" with no certainty of success, but with vigorous action, nonetheless.[47]

In the same way that Giovanni's subject did not have the conditions or the infrastructure to write a poem about that which did not exist, there is no viable opportunity for Black liberation in general, or for queer Black liberation in particular, within the Western liberal humanism of man. As Giovanni powerfully declares, "Perhaps these are not poetic times at all." Perhaps these are no longer—and never have been—times to *talk* within the realm of politics, because commotion happens in silence. Instead, perhaps we need to disrupt politics without fixating on and centering the disruption. Centering disruption masks itself as refusing to engage with politics, but I argue it leads to the seeking of a different recognition—recognition as a "worthy adversary"—without actually enacting an adversarial *praxis*. This is dangerous, because it limits one's politics to attempts to *appear* capable of causing harm to dominant structures without meaningfully destroying any of them; it is another trap of representational politics, a desire to be seen.

Describing and imagining Black liberation requires something other than the human, particularly during this continuing environmental crisis, which is itself a continuation of man's persistent and processual claim to life, both Black *and* green. So just as Giovanni's subject puts down her pen, Black people must put down the hopes that a full life can be lived today under such soul-crushing conditions of anti-Blackness. Just as her gun provides the means for creation, Black people—and anyone who wishes to learn the steps to the "dance of social death"—too, must equip themselves *however necessary*, both intellectually and materially, to construct an otherwise—because it won't appear organically.[48]

I do not wish to be prescriptive or offer a solution. Instead, I will describe the potential terrain for struggle. On this terrain, practices may mean increasing our investment in mutual aid networks to decrease our

reliance on the nation-state for relief—beginning the process of delegiti-
mizing the state and revealing it as an unnecessary mediator that limits
people's ability to imagine a new existence and to work alongside one
another to construct new ways of existing. It may also look like divesting
from climate-change inducing industrial agriculture and, instead, growing
one's own food in community with others. We must end the teleological
thinking that legitimizes man and reinforces its hold on our imagination,
resulting in the construction of life within this current genre of the human
without questioning any underlying assumptions about *why* we do what
we do.[49] It is not that we need to refine our way of living; we need to dramatically destroy it before creating it anew. Furthermore, the "elevated" Black
human, who—by virtue of Blackness—is always essential for society must
reject narratives that position them as more evolved than those of a lesser
socioeconomic status and refuse selective incorporation at every possible
turn. Amílcar Cabral refers to this as "class suicide," and it *does not feel good*;
it feels as if one is dying a necessary death. Finally, practices of freedom
undoubtedly require strategic conflict and direct action because of man's
reliance upon anti-Black violence for the symbolic coherence of reality. As
argued previously, anti-Black violence is not contingent. It has no cause,
so it has no end. Yet it must be ended, and this is no small task.

A Benediction

Cultivating the "otherwise" to humanity is akin to sowing a garden off the
edge of a dangling cliff: dangerous, seemingly (and perhaps) impossible,
and an ongoing process. Still, I hope to build upon the work of others in
describing and discrediting that which will *not* result in liberation in the
hope of pushing us toward the horizon of an existence not haunted by the
specter of anti-Blackness and ecological ruin (which is to say anti-Blackness twice over). I hope you will join me as I join you in assembling a
"we" capable of bringing about the end of the world—beginning with the
Black radicals currently incarcerated for sketching choreographies aimed
at introducing social inventions previously unimaginable and unfathoma-
ble. *Together*, we can inherit their steps and *move* toward the materializing
manifestation of the unrepresentable.

> Love is contraband in Hell
> cause love is an acid
> that eats away bars.

But you, me, and tomorrow
hold hands and make vows
that struggle will multiply.

The hacksaw has two blades.

The shotgun has two barrels.

We are pregnant with freedom.

We are a conspiracy.[50]

Ashe.

Notes

1   Mavi, "Self Love," on *Let the Sun Talk* (Rosmalen, NL: de Rap Winkel Records, 2020).

2   Saidiya Hartman, "The End of White Supremacy, An American Romance," *BOMB*, June 5, 2020, accessed May 27, 2022, https://bombmagazine.org/articles/the-end-of-white-supremacy-an-american-romance.

3   Zakiyyah Iman Jackson, *Becoming Human: Manner and Meaning in an Antiblack World* (New York: New York University Press, 2020).

4   D'Angelo, "The Line," on *Voodoo* (Los Angeles: Virgin Records, 2000).

5   Axelle Karera, "Blackness and the Pitfalls of Anthropocene Ethics," *Critical Philosophy of Race* 7, no. 1 (January 2019): 32–56, esp. 33.

6   Ibid., 50.

7   W.E.B. Du Bois, *The Souls of Black Folk* (New York: Barnes & Noble Classics, 2003 [1903]), 3.

8   Sylvia Wynter, "Unsettling the Coloniality of Being/Power/Truth/Freedom: Toward the Human, after Man, Its Overrepresentation—an Argument," *CR: The New Centennial Review* 3, no. 3 (Fall 2003): 257–337, 262, accessed May 27, 2022, https://tinyurl.com/bdh9ddkz.

9   Zakiyyah Iman Jackson, *Becoming Human: Matter and Meaning in an AntiBlack World* (New York: New York University Press, 2020).

10 Emily Stewart, "Essential Workers Still Lack Basic Safety Protections on the Job," Vox, May 7, 2020, accessed May 27, 2022, https://tinyurl.com/37ynnn5w.

11 Fred Moten, "Blackness and Nothingness (Mysticism in the Flesh)," *South Atlantic Quarterly* 112, no. 4 (October 2013): 737–80, 749, accessed May 27, 2022, https://americanhorrorstoriessite.files.wordpress.com/2017/08/fred-moten-blackness-and-nothingness.pdf.

12 E. Gould, "Clinical Microbiology and Infection," *Clinical Microbiology and Infection* 15, no. 6 (June 2009): 503–98.

13 Jackson, *Becoming Human*, 49. The human subject and Black object are always in relation to one another, even as each takes on the identity of "worker," meaning

that the limit case for the human subject-worker is the Black (essential) object-worker. The human worker maintains their identity through not being the Black worker. Here I'm thinking of the history of unions banning Black workers from joining them while being supportive of "worker's" rights.

14   Sylvia Wynter, "No Humans Involved: An Open Letter to My Colleagues," *Forum N.H.I.: Knowledge for the 21st Century* 1, no. 1 (Fall 1994): 42–73, esp. 53, accessed May 27, 2022, https://files.libcom.org/files/Wynter5.pdf.

15   Jackson, *Becoming Human*, 50.

16   Christina Sharpe, *In the Wake: On Blackness and Being* (Durham, NC: Duke University Press, 2016), 106.

17   Steve Martinot, "The Avant-Garde of White Supremacy," in *Afro-Pessimism: An Introduction*, ed. Jarrod Sexton (Minneapolis: Racked & Dispatched, 2017) 49–66, esp. 55, 56.

18   Saidiya V. Hartman, *Scenes of Subjection: Terror, Slavery, and Self-Making in Nineteenth-Century America* (New York: Oxford University Press, 1997). Here I am thinking of Hartman's description of the "burdened individuality" of former slaves, in which they were "freed from slavery" yet "free of resources." Similarly, the Black worker can "choose" to stop working in dangerous conditions but in doing so would also face certain poverty.

19   Aimé Césaire, *Discourse on Colonialism* (New York: Monthly Review Press, 2000), 42.

20   "Coronavirus: France Racism Row over Doctors' Africa Testing Comments," BBC News, April 3, 2020, accessed May 27, 2022, https://www.bbc.com/news/world-europe-52151722.

21   Hortense J. Spillers, "Mama's Baby, Papa's Maybe: An American Grammar Book," *Diacritics* 17, no. 2 (Summer 1987): 65–81, esp. 68, accessed May 27, 2022, https://www.sas.upenn.edu/~cavitch/pdf-library/Spillers_Mamas_Baby.pdf.

22   Frantz Fanon, *Black Skin, White Masks* (New York: Grove Press, 2008 [1952]), xi–xviii, esp. xiv.

23   Kuwasi Balagoon, *A Soldier's Story: Writings by a New Afrikan Anarchist*, 3rd ed. (Oakland: PM Press, 2019).

24   If Blackness is constructed in contradistinction to the human, then Blackness, in its purest form, is directly oppositional to the human. Then perhaps we can say that Blackness is a precondition to queerness in relation to the human, in the sense that it will always present a theoretical problem for the human in this position as a "liminal group." Perhaps, then, even queer Blackness is redundant, because the Black is always queer in relation to the human, regardless of attempts to mirror the praxes of the human to achieve human status. Perhaps "quareness" is what queerness seeks to be but can never quite accomplish; for more, see Mae Henderson and E. Patrick Johnson, "'Quare' Studies, or (Almost) Everything I Know about Queer Studies I Learned from My Grandmother," in *Black Queer Studies: A Critical Anthology* (Durham, NC: Duke University Press, 2007).

25   Aliyyah I Abdur-Rahman, "The Black Ecstatic," *GLQ: A Journal of Lesbian and Gay Studies* 24, nos. 2–3 (June 2018): 352.

26   Safiya Bukhari, *The War Before: The True Life Story of Becoming a Black Panther, Keeping the Faith in Prison and Fighting for Those Left Behind* (New York: Feminist Press at the City University of New York, 2010), 60–61.

27   Sylvia Wynter, "The Ceremony Must Be Found: After Humanism," *Boundary 2* 12, no. 3/13, no. 1 (Spring/Autumn 1984): 19–70, accessed May 27, 2022, https://

trueleappress.files.wordpress.com/2020/04/wynter-the-ceremony-muyst-be-found-after-humanism.pdf.

28   Hartman, *Scenes of Subjection*, 117; Christina Sharpe, *In the Wake: On Blackness and Being* (Durham, NC: Duke University Press, 2016), 7. Indeed, the "justice" served for violence against Black people requires the initial violence. "Justice" is not interested in *ending* the violence but in narrating it.

29   Jackson, *Becoming Human*, 28.

30   Wynter, "Unsettling the Coloniality of Being/Power/Truth/Freedom," 321.

31   Hartman, *Scenes of Subjection*, 134.

32   Wynter, "Unsettling the Coloniality of Being/Power/Truth/Freedom," 296. Here I am referring to Wynter's description of the religio-secular formation of race in which "Indians" were classified as "'irrational' because 'savage,'" while enslaved Africans were classified as "subrational" Negroes. I want to highlight the lack of conditionality within the "grounds of legitimacy" for African enslavement signaled by the omission of "because." Whereas the Indian is defined as irrational and, *thus*, a savage, as a means of justifying the expropriation of Indigenous lands, the Negro is simply subrational, seemingly a priori. Therefore, while the Indian can theoretically escape land expropriation by striving for rationality to negate the savagery, the Negro has no such escape. This means the Negro is subjected to violence not contingent upon rationality but, instead, on the basis of simply being a Negro. There is no praxis of being human that relieves this tension. This is a result of the color Black coming to symbolize "sin" and "demons" within Christian thinking and, as a result, the Negro occupying a position of dysselected "degen-era[cy]" always outside of the Christian (302). If we take Wynter's assertion that each iteration of the human retains the same ordering structure seriously, then we must consider the possibility that this lack of conditionality for violence is still present. This means that Black people are certain to continue facing violence by virtue of being Black, regardless of other performances of gender, sexuality, and labor.

33   Ibid., 301.

34   Ibid., 276.

35   Ibid., 314.

36   Joshua Dubler and Vincent W. Lloyd, *Break Every Yoke: Religion, Justice, and the Abolition of Prisons* (New York: Oxford University Press, 2020), 17.

37   "But I would make a distinction in this case between 'body' and 'flesh' and impose that distinction as the central one between captive and liberated subject-po-sitions. In that sense, before the 'body' there is the 'flesh,' that zero degree of social conceptualization that does not escape concealment under the brush of discourse, or the reflexes of iconography. Even though the European hegemonies stole bodies—some of them female—out of West African communities in concert with the African 'middleman,' we regard this human and social irreparability as high crimes against the flesh, as the person of African females and African males registered the wounding. If we think of the 'flesh' as a primary narrative, then we mean its seared, divided, ripped-apartness, riveted to the ship's hole, fallen, or 'escaped' overboard." Spillers makes a crucial distinction between the body and the flesh. While the human has a body, the Black is reduced to flesh. Following her logic, I believe liberal representational politics are for those with bodies and those who aspire to have a body. I do not believe we should aspire for such if we

aim for the radical upending of the world as such. For more, see Spillers, "Mama's Baby, Papa's Maybe."

38 George Jackson, *Blood in My Eye* (Baltimore, MD: Black Classics Press, 1996 [1972]).

39 Nikki Giovanni, "For Saundra" (1968), in *Black Nature: Four Centuries of African American Nature Poetry* (Athens: University of Georgia Press, 2009), 151.

40 For a critical discussion of masculinist attitudes in the Black Arts Movement, see Phillip Brian Harper, *Are We Not Men? Masculine Anxiety and the Problem of African-American Identity* (New York: Oxford University Press, 2010).

41 *Toxic Wastes and Race in The United States: A National Report on the Racial and Socio-Economic Characteristics of Communities with Hazardous Waste Sites*, (New York: United Church of Christ Commission for Racial Justice, 1987), xi–xvi, accessed May 27, 2022, https://www.nrc.gov/docs/ML1310/ML13109A339.pdf.

42 Liam Downey and Brian Hawkins, "Race, Income, and Environmental Inequality in the United States," *Sociological Perspectives* 51, no. 4 (December 2008): 759–81, accessed May 27, 2022, https://www.ncbi.nlm.nih.gov/pmc/articles/PMC2705126.

43 Melissa Checker, "Wiped Out by the 'Greenwave': Environmental Gentrification and the Paradoxical Politics of Urban Sustainability," *City and Society* 23, no. 2 (December 2011).

44 Downey and Hawkins, "Race, Income, and Environmental Inequality."

45 Katherine McKittrick, *Sylvia Wynter: On Being Human as Praxis* (Durham, NC: Duke University Press, 2015), 47.

46 Denise Ferreira da Silva, "Reading Art as Confrontation," e-flux no. 65 (May 2015), accessed May 27, 2022, https://www.e-flux.com/journal/65/336390/reading-art-as-confrontation.

47 Jackson, *Becoming Human*, 36.

48 Frank B. Wilderson III, "The Prison Slave as Hegemony's (Silent) Scandal," *Social Justice* 30, no. 2 (2003): 18–27, accessed May 27, 2022, https://ufmrg.files.wordpress.com/2017/12/frank-b-wilderson-iii-the-prison-slave-as-hegeomnys-silent-scandal.pdf.

49 Sylvia Wynter, "The Ceremony Must Be Found," 19–70, esp. 23.

50 Assata Shakur, *Assata: An Autobiography* (London: Zed Books, 1987), 130.

COVID-19 and Queerness

Seeing Queerness in the Time of COVID-19

Kitty Stryker

I'm going to start this with an admission. I was originally planning to submit something to this anthology about the queer community, sex positivity, and fatphobia as they all relate to visibility/invisibility. Then the virus now known as COVID-19 hit, sweeping through my community in a flash. The United States government's inaction felt eerily familiar to many who had lived through the AIDS epidemic. As someone who is a bit of an infectious disease nerd, and as a queer person who is witnessing too many people die before their time, I couldn't find it in me to write about anything else.

I want to say that the spectrum between visibility and invisibility is a complex one. Queer people are often shapeshifters, needing to code-switch from one environment to another for safety. I'm not trying to say in this essay what way is best, as it's each person's choice where they want and need security and where they want and need freedom. I do want to illustrate how our society keeps us constantly uncertain of our footing, and how we can stay grounded despite (and to spite) them.

What Good Is Visibility if It Just Makes Them Hurt You?

The impact of a pandemic on marginalized communities is multifold, particularly when the people in those communities share other marginalized identities, such as sexuality, transness, ethnic minority status, disability, insecure housing, or poverty. For example, initial reports on who is getting hit hardest by this virus say that Black folks make up 33 percent of the hospitalizations, while making up only 13 percent of the population.[1] Additionally, people of color are more likely to have jobs considered "essential work,"[2] and many of those companies—meat processing facilities, online warehouses, food delivery services—have poor working conditions and union-busting histories. Immigrant laborers are still at risk of arrest by Immigration and Customs Enforcement agents,[3] but their absence is destroying our food supply chain.[4] Black people especially, and people of color in general, are often given lower wages when employed, struggle harder to get promoted, and are often relegated to underpaid, working-class labor thanks to racist hiring practices. Add being less likely to have access to health insurance and being more likely to live in shared housing to that,[5] and infectious disease has ideal conditions in which to spread.

These risk factors associated with COVID-19 are especially true among the queer population. One in five LGBTQ people live in poverty,[6] a number that increases when you look at the intersection of poverty with people of color, transgender people, and rural communities. LGBTQ people are more likely to be smokers,[7] another possible risk factor for COVID-19.[8]

Meanwhile, President Donald Trump and Vice President Mike Pence have used this pandemic as an opportunity to move forward on rolling back health care discrimination protections for LGBTQ people.[9] Initially proposed in 2019, the rule would reverse the Obama-era decision to include queer and trans people under the umbrella of sex discrimination under Section 1557 of the Affordable Care Act. Allowing hospitals to deny care to people they perceive to be trans or queer during a pandemic, when medical supplies are hard to come by, is an effective death sentence.

What are queer populations to do when their clinics are threatened with drastic cuts? Lyon-Martin Health Services, a San Francisco health clinic focusing on transgender people and cisgender women, was forced to shut its doors amid COVID-19, thanks to budget cuts passed down from parent company HealthRIGHT360.[10] Many of Lyon-Martin's clientele were uninsured or underinsured, and most felt invisible, unsafe, or unheard by the practitioners at general clinics. Clinicians at Lyon-Martin were offering COVID-19 tests to transgender people living in shelters, a necessary service that is now gone. Some blame HealthRIGHT360 for not prioritizing Lyon-Martin, others blame the city of San Francisco for not offering financial assistance.

Blame, however, won't keep the doors of needed services open. Health care is a necessity, not just for our physical bodies but also for our minds and hearts. The mental health of queer and trans people is also at risk, and with clinics that are focused on their needs shutting down, there are fewer places for them to seek help.[11] Stress has drastically increased for many, especially when you consider mass unemployment and worries about housing loss. Judging from articles and social media, loneliness is a major concern when we can't meet up in person. Many folks I know are talking about feeling "touch starved," particularly my LGBTQ friends, as we moved into Pride month. It stung (and was sometimes unsafe) to be stuck at home, our celebrations canceled, during mass political unrest, when queer defiance is usually at its sweetest. Being isolated from each other caused many in the queer community to feel deflated. Because the queer community regularly reports higher instances of mental health issues, particularly anxiety and depression, it follows that sheltering in place while friends and family die has been especially difficult. For many, the inability to spend time with chosen family in person during this instability was a real blow. For those struggling with suicidal feelings, it could become a fatal one.

Not helping with mental health issues, particularly for queer and trans youth, is many universities closing their on-campus housing in an attempt to stop the spread of the virus.[12] The consequence of this, of course, is that many LGBTQ youths are then faced with a difficult decision—go back in the closet and go home with a potentially abusive family or live on the street, which is incredibly risky, even without a pandemic. Queer and trans youth disproportionately experience homelessness, with 40 percent of the unaccompanied homeless youth population in the US identifying as LGBTQ.[13] Considering that homeless populations are often at higher risk of infection from any illness, COVID-19 is a devastating nightmare.[14]

Queer and trans college students sent home to quarantine may have to choose between the risks of homelessness to the risks of being at home. Survival may be dependent on being unseen, whether by hostile family members at home or by the police on the streets. What is called "passing privilege," or the ability to pass as heterosexual, white, and/or cisgender, makes a complex identity invisible but may also allow it to pass under a bigot's radar. This success is a mixed blessing, especially when many states allow the trans panic defense: using claimed unawareness of someone's transness to justify violence against them. It's unsafe to be blatant, and it's unsafe to be too private, with many having to make split-second decisions every day as they interact with others about which risk to take.

Staying at home may be dangerous for adults as well. Domestic abuse calls have seen a sharp increase during sheltering in place, in part due to the isolation, and in part due to the financial stress.[15] Domestic abuse shelters are also being forced to cancel planned fundraisers due to the shutdown, costing them a percentage of their annual budget during a time when it is needed the most. Bisexual women report incredibly high instances of intimate partner abuse, with 61 percent saying they had experienced it according to the CDC's 2010 study *The National Intimate Partner and Sexual Violence Survey*.[16] A study by UCLA's Williams Institute on Sexual Orientation and Gender Identity Law carried out in 2015 reported that 31 to 50 percent of trans people have experienced dating violence[17]—in half of the cases in 2018 where trans people were murdered, they were murdered by an intimate partner, according to advocates.[18] Trans people also struggle to find shelters where their gender identity is accepted. Black trans women in particular are the most likely to be murdered in the United States, and they often bear the brunt of both state and personal violence.

Visibility, as one of my friends says every Trans Day of Visibility, can be a curse.

Being Invisible Also Sucks

Invisibility is also a curse. COVID-19's impact on the queer and trans community may be masked by a lack of LGBTQ health data being collected during this crisis.[19] As of this writing, Washington, DC, was the only jurisdiction reporting collection of this information, and even they admitted the data was incomplete. Without adequate statistics gathering practices, it will be impossible to truly measure how COVID-19 swept through queer and trans populations.

Access to hormones and gender-affirming surgeries has also been negatively impacted by this pandemic. Many lifesaving trans surgeries were pushed back to prioritize COVID-19 patients, an unfortunate but inevitable result of widespread infectious illness.[20] As of May 2020, some are tentatively rescheduling, but the trickle-down effects will lead to many whose appointments were canceled waiting for months or years for another chance. Not all trans people can inject their hormones at home, leaving them without treatment during a time of uncertainty and instability. Mass unemployment has made paying for hormone treatments too expensive for others to manage, leaving them to rely on mutual aid networks to connect with other trans people who are willing to share.[21]

To make matters worse, doctors in some areas are attempting hormone replacement treatments on cisgender men to see if it impacts their likelihood of getting the novel coronavirus.[22] Considering that in some places cisgender men are twice as likely to catch COVID-19, there is some suspicion that it may be affected by testosterone, so estrogen is now being trialed to stop the spread. Granted, it's also true that studies have suggested men are 50 percent less likely to wash their hands, and 31 percent are less likely to use soap even if they do, but I suppose hormone replacement treatment is an easier sell.[23]

The affordability of health care is further complicated as COVID-19 effectively shuts down multiple industries, as those industries try to mitigate the spread and flatten the curve. Food services, hospitals, retail, and education (both K–12 and higher education) have all suffered as schools, restaurants, hotels, bars, and stores have become ghost towns. Forty percent of the LGBTQ community work in one of these impacted industries, double the rate of their cisgender, heterosexual counterparts.[24] As of May 2020, thirty million people have filed for unemployment insurance in the US. Many workers have been furloughed as they wait for business to resume. Some, like bar workers and event staff, may be waiting months (or years) longer.[25]

Many cities also canceled in-person Pride events in anticipation of festival shutdowns lasting until at least the fall, much to the dismay of queer businesses. Gay Pride is often celebrated in June to commemorate the Stonewall riots in New York City, when LGBTQ people fought the police for their right to gather at the Stonewall Inn in one of the most famous gay protests. It was mourned fiercely, especially as Pride is an important public recognition of the impact of the HIV epidemic on LGBTQ people, something that feels especially pertinent now as another virus threatens people around the world.

As July came and went, and shelter-in-place orders stretched further, any in-person gathering like Pride became less and less likely. Many small businesses that cater to the queer community worried that they wouldn't be able to afford to continue to operate due to the financial losses.[26] The Castro, one of the oldest gay neighborhoods in the United States, submitted a letter pleading with the mayor to postpone Pride until the fall in the hopes things will be different then, as it's an important financial and historical event for the area, and many local businesses in the neighborhood are owned by LGBTQ people.[27] Interestingly, while in recent years corporate floats have outnumbered community floats in the annual parades, my research didn't show many corporations reallocating that money to small queer businesses to help them through this current financial crunch.

Even as I write this, I realize that I am listing endless problems, exclaiming, "but wait, there's more!" I have to be honest, COVID-19 is exposing all the cracks and margins we knew were there and laying bare these systematic failures. It's rough out there. I'm bitter and angry.

The tightrope walk between visibility and invisibility feels even more perilous now as I struggle to navigate surviving during COVID-19. My visibility as a queer person is courted during Pride Month or as a diversity hire, but if I want a stimulus check from the government or a small business loan, I don't want to be too visible, lest I be considered prurient and, thus, ineligible.[28] With LGBTQ content often censored for being explicit just for talking about our lives, the concern about accessibility of content is a valid one.[29] Never mind that many LGBTQ people work in the adult industry, whether it be stripping, selling sex toys, or working in porn—all legal and considered businesses when it comes to paying taxes but not seen as legitimate enough for stimulus relief.[30] Sex workers in areas of the industry made illegal, such as street-based sex workers, brothel workers, and some professional dominatrices, are still expected to pay taxes on their income but without access to unemployment insurance.

It's Not All Bad—Glimmers of Hope

COVID-19 has increased overall political and social awareness of the working class and their needs, from demands for universal basic income to single-payer health care, particularly in the United States. The capitalist, every-man-for-himself values that have dominated our politics have fallen far short during a pandemic. While small groups of conservatives are gathering in defiance of the shelter-in-place orders, demanding that businesses to be allowed to open before a vaccine has been discovered,[31] most people understand the need to stay home for the sake of the community at large.[32] Mass unemployment has exposed how precarious our economy is, to an extent that even the Republicans can't ignore.[33] Stimulus payments made available in April 2020, while inadequate and riddled with logistical issues, have demonstrated a need for some form of basic income to prevent societal collapse.

The issues around health care have also become apparent during this. The underfunding of public health agencies has created a massive issue in containing COVID-19.[34] Widespread shortages of hospital beds and ventilators, as well as personal protective equipment (PPE), have received a great deal of local and national media coverage. (I myself donated forty

N95 masks, set aside for the next fire season, to an ER doctor.) A recent Gallup poll found that 14 percent of Americans who likely have COVID-19 would avoid seeking medical care because of a fear of the cost—an alarming statistic during a highly infectious, airborne pandemic.[35] Universal basic income and single-payer health care, often ideas relegated to the far left of our political discourse, are now finding support among liberals during an election year. Both initiatives, if passed, would have significant impact for the LGBTQ community, who are statistically more likely to live in poverty, to be unemployed,[36] and to lack access to affordable health care.[37] It will be interesting to see if this enthusiasm for these causes continues as we start to rebuild in the wake of this plague.

Another interesting area of improvement during this crisis is blood donation protocols. After the AIDS epidemic, men who have sex with men were banned from blood donations for their lifetimes, as we didn't have the technology to effectively screen blood. This ban was upheld in 2015, though the lifetime ban was reduced to a year-long ban, thus requiring men who have sex with men to be celibate for a year before they could donate.[38] COVID-19 and the resulting blood shortage caused the FDA, even under a markedly anti-LGBTQ Republican president, to reduce the ban to three months.[39] Still, a straight man, regardless of safer sex practices and number of partners, has no restrictions, whereas a monogamous gay man is still unable to donate blood or plasma. As blood drives beg for participants, particularly those recovered from COVID-19, the FDA is now reportedly considering lifting the ban entirely, finally catching up to the science indicating our blood tests are now sufficient to make bans based on sexual orientation unnecessary.[40]

Society is also beginning to catch up to what queer and trans people have known all along: mutual aid networks are often more reliable than government agencies. GoFundMe, a popular crowdfunding platform, has a whole section dedicated to gender-affirming surgeries, since, for many people, crowdfunding has been the only way to afford medical care not covered by insurance.[41] It's not just financial support either. Mutual aid networks, often fronted by leftist activists, have mobilized in breathtaking numbers to support marginalized communities through this pandemic, from grocery delivery to free therapy sessions.[42] These networks have always quietly existed, and COVID-19 is giving mutual aid the chance to demonstrate a reliability and resilience that our infrastructure so clearly lacks. I deeply hope that this trend will continue past a vaccine, because it's one of the best ways for us to be an actual community—showing mutual care, mutual responsibility, and mutual accountability.

Of course, queer and trans folks know how to utilize the internet in all sorts of creative ways to connect, care for each other, hook up, and hold space. Some are discovering new erotic frontiers by camming with each other or attending virtual sex parties.[43] Others are partying with each other via club nights hosted on Zoom or Twitch.[44] Pride and Folsom Street Fair are exploring ways to provide entertainment and community through online means.[45] One of my friends hosts a twenty-minute ABBA dance party every day. We are learning that we don't need to rely on bars or dance parties or even a Pride celebration to gather and experience community, and people who have historically felt left out and left behind—sober people, people with disabilities, people in areas without much of a LGBTQ community—are finding themselves able to engage in these spaces now. Hopefully, those considerations won't vanish again as we return to seeing each other in person.

We adapt. We evolve. We mourn our dead, and we fight for the living.

Notes

1   Reis Thebault, Andrew Ba Tran, and Vanessa Williams, "The Coronavirus Is Infecting and Killing Black Americans at an Alarmingly High Rate," *Washington Post*, April 7, 2020, accessed June 9, 2022, https://tinyurl.com/4cpwka9e.

2   Kadia Goba, "New York City's Coronavirus Essential Workers Are Overwhelmingly People of Color," Buzzfeed News, April 22, 2020, accessed June 9, 2022, https://www.buzzfeednews.com/article/kadiagoba/coronavirus-new-york-brooklyn-essential-workers-black-poc.

3   Ted Hesson, "Explainer: How the US is Handling Immigration Enforcement during the Coronavirus Crisis," Reuters, April 24, 2020, accessed May 27, 2022, https://tinyurl.com/2n3aa299.

4   Chase Purdy, "The Stability of the Global Food System Relies on Immigrants," Quartz, April 26, 2020, accessed May 27, 2022, https://qz.com/1844194/covid-19-exposes-how-the-global-food-system-relies-on-immigrants.

5   Linda Carroll, "LGBT Adults in US Less Likely to Have Jobs, Health Insurance," Reuters, July 26, 2018, accessed May 27, 2022, https://tinyurl.com/ctsrws4m; "LGBT People Are More Likely than Non-LGBT People to Face Housing Instability," Williams Institute, UCLA School of Law, April 2, 2020, accessed May 27, 2022, https://williamsinstitute.law.ucla.edu/press/lgbt-housing-press-release.

6   Meera Jagannathan, "1 in 5 LGBTQ Americans Lives in Poverty—and Some Groups are Particularly Worse Off," MarketWatch, October 23, 2019, https://tinyurl.com/48nfst74.

7   "Tobacco Use in the LGBT Community: A Public Health Issue," US Food and Drug Administration, updated June 2, 2021, accessed May 27, 2022, https://www.

fda.gov/tobacco-products/health-information/tobacco-use-lgbt-community-public-health-issue.

8 Mary Van Beusekom, "Studies: Smoking, Age, Other Factors Raise Risk of COVID-19 Death," CIDRAP, April 9, 2020, accessed May 27, 2022, https://tinyurl.com/bp6uta77.

9 Selena Simmons-Duffin, "'Whiplash' of LGBTQ Protections and Rights, from Obama to Trump," NPR, March 2, 2020, accessed May 27, 2022, https://tinyurl.com/2tcumjye.

10 Michael Barros, "California LGBTQ+ Health Clinic Faces Drastic Cuts," KCBX News, April 13, 2020, accessed June 9, 2022, https://www.kcbx.org/post/california-lgbtq-health-clinic-faces-drastic-cuts#stream/0.

11 Amy Green, Samuel Dorison, and Myeshia Price-Feeney, "Implications of COVID-19 for LGBTQ Youth Mental Health and Suicide Prevention," Trevor Project, April 3, 2020, accessed June 9, 2022, https://tinyurl.com/2h9mmm9b.

12 Li Cohen, "Coronavirus Closed Down Colleges—Now Some LGBTQ Students Fear an Abusive 'War Zone' at Home," CBS News, April 16, 2020, accessed June 9, 2022, https://www.cbsnews.com/news/coronavirus-lgbt-college-students-homelessness-abuse-campuses-closed.

13 "New Report on Youth Homeless Affirms That LGBTQ Youth Disproportionately Experience Homelessness," Human Rights Campaign, November 15, 2017, accessed May 27, 2022, https://www.hrc.org/blog/new-report-on-youth-homeless-affirms-that-lgbtq-youth-disproportionately-ex.

14 Emma Grey Ellis, "For Homeless People, Covid-19 Is Horror on Top of Horror," *Wired*, April 2, 2020, accessed May 27, 2022, https://www.wired.com/story/coronavirus-covid-19-homeless.

15 Tyler Kingkade, "Police See Rise in Domestic Violence Calls amid Coronavirus Lockdown," NBC News, April 5, 2020, accessed May 27, 2022, https://tinyurl.com/3k2vnvbu.

16 Mike L. Walters, Jieru Chen, and Matthew J. Breiding, *The National Intimate Partner and Sexual Violence Survey: 2010 Findings on Victimization by Sexual Orientation* (Atlanta, GA: National Center for Injury Prevention and Control, Centers for Disease Control and Prevention, 2013), accessed May 27, 2022, https://www.cdc.gov/violenceprevention/pdf/nisvs_sofindings.pdf.

17 Taylor N.T. Brown and Jody L. Herman, "Intimate Partner Violence and Sexual Abuse among LGBT People: A Review of Existing Research," UNCA School of Law Williams Institute, November 2015, accessed May 27, 2022, https://williamsinstitute.law.ucla.edu/publications/ipv-sex-abuse-lgbt-people.

18 "Violence against the Transgender Community in 2018," Human Rights Campaign, accessed May 27, 2022, https://www.hrc.org/resources/violence-against-the-transgender-community-in-2018.

19 Chris, Johnson, "States Won't Collect LGBTQ Data on COVID-19—and Advocates Aren't Happy," Washington Blade, April 1, 2020, accessed May 27, 2022, https://tinyurl.com/58jue6zp.

20 "An Update on Gender Affirming Care During the COVID-19 Pandemic," Human Rights Campaign, April 6, 2020, accessed May 27, 2022, https://www.hrc.org/blog/an-update-on-gender-affirming-care-during-the-covid-19-pandemic.

21   Amelia Abraham, "How Coronavirus Is Affecting Trans People's Access to Hormones," Dazed, April 1, 2020, accessed May 27, 2022, https://tinyurl.com/2xm938c3.

22   Vic Parsons, "Plot Twist: Doctors Try Giving Men the Female Sex Hormone Oestrogen to Save Them from Coronavirus," Pink News, April 28, 2020, accessed May 27, 2022, https://tinyurl.com/582fep9x.

23   Katie Hunt, "Men Wash Their Hands Much Less Often than Women and That Matters More Than Ever," CNN, April 1, 2020, accessed May 27, 2022, https://www.cnn.com/2020/04/01/health/handwashing-gender-gap-wellness/index.html.

24   David Rae, "LGBTQ Finances Are at Risk amidst COVID-19 Pandemic," Forbes, April 20, 2020, accessed May 27, 2022, https://tinyurl.com/373zwu3y.

25   Melissa Gomez, "This Is California's Reopening Plan for Stores, Offices, Schools, Sports, Concerts, Theaters," Los Angeles Times, April 28, 2020, accessed May 27, 2022, https://tinyurl.com/2p8w67mz.

26   Manola Secaira, "Seattle's Queer Businesses Struggle as Pride Goes Virtual," Crosscut, April 28, 2020, accessed May 27, 2022, https://crosscut.com/2020/04/seattles-queer-businesses-struggle-pride-goes-virtual.

27   Steven Bracco, "Pride Cancellation Intensifies COVID-19's Impact on Castro Bars, Restaurants," hoodline, April 23, 2020, accessed May 27, 2022, https://hoodline.com/2020/04/pride-cancellation-intensifies-covid-19-s-impact-on-castro-bars-restaurants.

28   Otillia Steadman, "If You Strip, Make Porn, or Sell Sex Toys, You Might Not Get Any Coronavirus Aid Money. That's Where the First Amendment Comes In," Buzzfeed, April 11, 2020, accessed May 27, 2022, https://www.buzzfeednews.com/article/otilliasteadman/coronavirus-sex-industry-strip-clubs.

29   Aja Romano, "A Group of YouTubers Is Trying to Prove the Site Systematically Demonetizes Queer Content," Vox, October 10, 2019, accessed May 27, 2022, https://tinyurl.com/8zdx5tb2.

30   Stephanie Farnsworth, "Why LGBT and Sex Worker Rights Go Hand-In-Hand," Huffington Post, April 14, 2016, accessed May 27, 2022, https://tinyurl.com/e2mxp2y7.

31   Lisa Graves, "Who's Behind the 'Reopen' Protests?" New York Times, April 22, 2020, accessed June 9, 2022, https://www.nytimes.com/2020/04/22/opinion/coronavirus-protests-astroturf.html.

32   "Poll: 8 in 10 Americans Favor Strict Shelter-in-Place Orders to Limit Coronavirus' Spread, and Most Say They Could Continue to Obey Such Orders for Another Month or Longer," KFF, April 23, 2020, accessed June 9, 2022, https://tinyurl.com/4cwccy3u.

33   Erin Mansfield and Kevin Crowe, "Unemployment Funds Were in Trouble Before Coronavirus. Now Claims Are Sky High," USA Today, March 20, 2020, accessed June 9, 2022, https://tinyurl.com/yckncs64.

34   Steven Ross Johnson, "Report: Public Health Funding Falls Despite Increasing Threats," Modern Health Care, April 24, 2019, accessed June 9, 2022, https://www.modernhealthcare.com/government/report-public-health-funding-falls-despite-increasing-threats.

35   Dan Witters, "In US, 14% with Likely COVID-19 to Avoid Care Due to Cost," Gallup, April 28, 2020, accessed June 22, 2022, https://news.gallup.com/poll/309224/avoid-care-likely-covid-due-cost.aspx.

36   "Economic Opportunity," LGBT Funders, accessed June 9, 2022, https://lgbtfunders.org/resources/issues/economic-opportunity.

37   Jennifer Kates, Usha Ranji, Adara Beamesderfer , Alina Salganicoff, and Lindsey Dawson, "Health and Access to Care and Coverage for Lesbian, Gay, Bisexual, and Transgender (LGBT) Individuals in the US," KFF, May 3, 2018, accessed June 9, 2022, https://tinyurl.com/yck6utr8.

38   Bobby Allyn, "FDA Loosens Restrictions On Gay Blood Donors amid 'Urgent Need' Caused by Coronavirus," NPR, April 2, 2020, accessed May 30, 2022, https://tinyurl.com/3c53k7my.

39   Tony Morrison, "FDA 'Commencing a Study' That Could Lead to the Removal of a Once-Lifetime Ban on Gay Men Donating Blood as COVID-19 Survivor Says He Was Turned Away from Blood Center for Being Gay," ABC News, April 24, 2020, https://abcnews.go.com/US/fda-reveals-generating-scientific-evidence-lead-removal-lifetime/story?id=70251561.

40   Tim Fitzsimons, "FDA Eases Restrictions on Gay Blood Donors amid 'Urgent Need,'" NBC News, April 2, 2020, accessed May 30, 2022, https://www.nbcnews.com/feature/nbc-out/fda-reduces-restrictions-gay-blood-donors-amid-urgent-need-n1175141.

41   "Be Yourself: Gender Confirmation Surgery Fundraising," GoFundMe, accessed May 30, 2022, https://www.gofundme.com/c/gender-confirmation-surgery-fundraising.

42   Nico Lang, "Behind the Fundraisers Saving Queer and Trans Lives during COVID-19," them, April 27, 2020, accessed May 30, 2022, https://www.them.us/story/coronavirus-lgbtq-mutual-aid-fundraisers-charity-financial-help.

43   Naveen Kumar, "How Queer People Are Getting Off While Staying In," them, March 20, 2020, accessed May 30, 2022, https://www.them.us/story/lgbtq-gay-sex-hook-ups-coronavirus-grindr-scruff-lex; Brit Dawson, "Inside the Virtual Sex Parties and Orgies Heating up Lockdown," Dazed, April 30, 2020, accessed May 30, 2022, https://tinyurl.com/mupc484n.

44   Katelyn Burns, "What Will Pride Mean This Year?" Vox, April 29, 2020, accessed May 30, 2022, https://www.vox.com/2020/4/29/21227999/online-pride-coronavirus-pandemic.

45   Ibid.; Precious J. Green, "2020 Folsom Street Fair Moves Online," KALW, April 28, 2020, accessed May 30, 2022, https://www.kalw.org/post/2020-folsom-street-fair-moves-online#stream/0.

When "Fitting In" Is Bad for Our Health

Adrian Shanker

We've all heard a doctor say: "I welcome all patients; I treat everyone the same." When a doctor says that in my presence, I cringe. It's a cute sentiment though, and it's nice to know they aren't one of the *truly bigoted* doctors who would put a sign on their door saying they don't serve my kind, but when it comes to my health care I want more than that. We should all want more.

For more than seven years I led an LGBTQ+ community center in Allentown, Pennsylvania. Shortly after the center opened in 2016, a community member came in for HIV testing. After his test, he found me in my office and had money in his hand. He wanted to donate his co-pay. I let him know that our services were free, and there was no need to pay, but he cut me off. He said, "I didn't come here because I couldn't afford an HIV test; I came here because when I went to my doctor's office, I felt sex-shamed and judged. My doctor asked why I was having sex with so many people. I left, and I came here for my HIV test instead." He wanted to donate what he would have paid at his doctor's office so that nonjudgmental HIV testing would be available for others as well.

I'll never know who the doctor of this community member was, but I'm pretty sure that there wasn't a sign on the front door of the doctor's office saying, "No gay clients allowed." This doctor likely presumed that the care they were providing was open to anyone, offered equally, and without discrimination. Clearly, however, this doctor lacked an understanding of the lived experiences of queer people and the health care we need. Unfortunately, this doctor is just one of many health care professionals queer people interact with. Stories like this one are a common experience for LGBTQ+ people when it comes to accessing care. Stories like this one are what cause LGBTQ+ people to delay or avoid care altogether.

That's why fitting in is bad for our health. Our queer bodies are not the same as everyone else's. Our lives are not the same. Our health care needs are not the same. It is impossible to provide culturally responsive, nonjudgmental care by treating us the same as everyone else when our lives are so different.

As a population, LGBTQ+ people experience health disparities by almost every indicator. We consume tobacco at more than double the rate of the majority population, and we engage in higher risk factors for HIV and other sexually transmitted or chronic diseases. We even use tanning salons at higher numbers than our straight, cisgender peers. All coping mechanisms to survive a world that wasn't created for us. Then we avoid seeking care, from annual physicals to preventative cancer screenings, because of the storied history of health care bias and discrimination in our community, as well as the negative past experiences with health care in our own lives. This is complicated by the way that LGBTQ+ people experience barriers to care throughout our lives, from birth to death. As a result of these increased risk factors, barriers to care, and outright discrimination, our health outcomes as a population are worsened.

The hard-fought victories to bring about greater acceptance of LGBTQ+ people have allowed the narrative of assimilationism to stick. Throughout recent history, there have been those who have argued, sometimes quite fiercely, that we should all try to fit in with society. For example, in his 1996 book *Virtually Normal*, Andrew Sullivan argues that with same-sex marriage and open military service gay people would be virtually normal if we were to assimilate into the broader society. The publisher's description of the book states, "[Sullivan] calls for a politics of homosexuality that would guarantee the rights of gays and lesbians without imposing tolerance."[1] In a critical review of *Virtually Normal*, Lillian Faderman excoriated Sullivan's argument, writing "in still another baffling leap, [Sullivan] takes all liberationists to task for imposing the word and concept of *queer* on all homosexuals."[2] In the book, Sullivan literally calls his same-sex attraction his "apparent aberration."[3]

The politics of queer assimilation are a politics of convenience. They only work for those who either don't desire to live authentically or who prefer the power of alignment with mainstream society. For those reasons, efforts to advance queer assimilation leave most of us behind.

The presumption that one can fit in is grounded in privilege and excludes the parts of the queer community that are not able to or have no desire to conform. Fitting in means mirroring conventional standards created by and for cisgender, heterosexual people.

Where the fight for basic acceptance falls short is where we stand out. Sometimes we want to stand out. Sometimes we need to stand out. We need to be, in a word: queer.

Being queer means we are living our lives authentically. For many of us, our queer identity is not limited to our sexual identity or our gender identity. It's how we vote. It's how we build community. It's how we live. For many of us, our queer identity is inseparable from our being, not just one minor aspect of our lives that can be brushed aside for safety or convenience or our medical visits.

For some of us, our queerness means we have whatever number of sexual partners we want, but it also means we must go to great lengths to find accurate and accessible sex education that speaks frankly to the liberated sexuality we engage in. For others, our queerness means that vanilla is not an ingredient in our sexual appetite, and we may have questions for health care professionals about kink that our doctors are wholly unprepared for—or, worse, uncomfortable with answering.

For some of us, our queerness means multiple romantic partners, which means we may not find ourselves *fitting in* on medical intake forms as they are often written. For others, our queerness means that we consider our circle of closest friends to be our chosen families, and we may have rotating chosen family members accompanying us to medical visits.

For some of us, our queerness means our gender identities or our gender performances fall outside of the binary genders that health insurance companies and government identity documents often restrict us to, making it harder to seek medical care, or even to fill prescriptions at pharmacies. For others, our queerness means that we resist the shame and stigma surrounding HIV that the broader society still holds on to.

For most of us, our queerness is also political. It's one of the lenses through which we view the world, and a lens through which we view the health care system. It's why so many of us feel that the broken health care system leaves our queer bodies behind.

If the sex we have is queer sex, the love we experience is queer love, and the lives we live are queer lives, then the health care we need must be queer health care—or, at the very least, we need to actively *queer* health care so that it reflects our authentic lives.

We need our primary care doctors to ask us appropriate questions about our sex lives so they can inform us about protective factors (like internal condoms, pre-exposure prophylaxis, commonly called "PrEP," and birth control), relevant vaccines (e.g., for hepatitis A or HPV), and screenings (e.g., anal or cervical Pap tests). We need to know that our care professionals have more information about our health care needs than we can find with our own internet searches. We need intake forms that allow us to bring our whole selves to the clinic. We need waiting rooms to feel affirming. We need insurance companies to cover the health care services and prescriptions we need. We need schools to teach queer-inclusive sex education. We need a health care system that works for us.

What does that even look like?

A fourteen-year-old youth program participant at Whitman-Walker Health Clinic in Washington, DC, once said that "wellness is about surviving in a world that wasn't made for you." What would it look like if we actually queered the health care system so it reflects our lives and our health care needs? What would it look like if rather than trying to fit into a broken system, we insisted on a system that actually worked for us?

I'm pretty sure it would look like an elimination of the health disparities that shorten queer lives. It would look like health equity, defined by the US government as "the attainment of the highest quality of health for all people." Perhaps if we are to achieve health equity, we need to stop trying to fit in. We need to stop attempting to be treated the same as everyone else. We need to demand that our health care providers see us—and treat us—as authentically queer people.

Notes

1   Andrew Sullivan, *Virtually Normal: An Argument about Homosexuality* (New York: Alfred A. Knopf, 1996).
2   Lillian Faderman, "To the Manner Born," *Advocate*, September 19, 1995.
3   Sullivan, *Virtually Normal*.

The End of Gay History, or This Is Not the World We Asked For

Yasmin Nair

"A specter is haunting the world, the specter of AIDS."
—with apologies to Karl Marx

"And you may ask yourself, 'How do I work this?'
And you may ask yourself, 'Where is that large automobile?'
And you may tell yourself, 'This is not my beautiful house'
And you may tell yourself, 'This is not my beautiful wife'"
—Talking Heads, "Once in a Lifetime"

Happiest Season—Hulu's in-house, queer, Christmas-themed rom-com—may be the most boring Christmas movie ever made, quite an achievement given that we now have over a century's worth of such content piling up in the annals of film history. It comes with a queer twist: Abby Holland (Kristen Stewart) and Harper Caldwell (Mackenzie Davis) are two lesbians in what a friend John (Dan Levy) describes as a "perfect" relationship. It's all quite predictable: if you leave the room, as I did, to get a snack while the movie continues on your screen and then come back in, say, ten minutes, you will have lost none of the plot and whatever transpires will remain entirely predictable.

Since it's a 2020 production, even this queer, pro-marriage film felt the need to reflect that the cultural conversation around gay marriage has shifted to the point where there is a more widespread critique of the institution. John, played easily by Levy, is the witty, smart homo with a witty, smart takedown of the conventional romance and marriage Abby is about to enter. Clearly, someone at the writer's table said, "*It's 2020—we've got to get some criticism of marriage in here.*" As he walks Abby back from the jewelry store where she has picked up the engagement ring she plans to use to propose to Harper, he's compelled to ask, "Abby, you and Harper have a perfect relationship. Why do you want to ruin that by engaging in one of the most archaic institutions in the history of the human race?"

"Because I want to marry her," she responds; to which he replies, "Okay, you *say* that, but what you're actually doing is tricking the woman you claim to love by trapping her in a box of heteronormativity and trying to make her your property. She is not a rice cooker or a cake plate. She's a human being." Abby protests that marriage is "about building a life with her," and then reveals her plan to ask Harper's father for her hand, to which John can only sniff: "I'm sorry: Ask her dad for his blessing? Way to stick it to the patriarchy. Really well done." All the key words are there—*heteronormativity, property, patriarchy*—and John's sentiments will ring true to anyone, queer or straight, who is weary and wary of marriage.

Had this movie been made in, say, 2010, when the issue was only just gaining ascendancy, and when I, as a freelance journalist for the *Windy City Times*, Chicago's gay paper, covered innumerable rallies and protests for gay marriage, there wouldn't have been a whiff of such politics in the film. Instead, the plot would have centered entirely on the tension between a loving gay couple and a cruel world that would tear them apart, with much the same progression as *Happiest Season*: family tensions and secrets, some mayhem, some drama, and a happy ending.

That such a segment, inserted somewhat clumsily into the narrative of this film and packing in a *lot* of political issues (which, even if expressed with a degree of sophistication and verve, are not necessarily connected to each other) should exist might persuade some that the work of radical queers is now over. Of course, as we might expect, the critique doesn't extend much into the actual film; it's an evanescent bit that flashes up and is then quickly swallowed up by a, well, deeply heteronormative film that really doesn't contest the idea that a woman is a piece of property to be handed down by a man to her spouse. (There is, admittedly, a stunningly beautiful bit about coming out, also articulated by John, but that beauty is a rare moment in this otherwise hackneyed tale.)

More important, though, is not the fact that even this fragile critique does not run through the entirety of the film, but that this *is* the only critique of gay marriage that really exists in popular media today—and it's not a particularly good one.

The problem with gay marriage is not that it's a patriarchal, heteronormative institution. The problem with gay marriage is that it's a movement that led to other conservative gay movements like inclusion in the military and hate crimes legislation that, in collusion with gay marriage, allowed the last shreds of resistance to neoliberalism to be torn apart. Gay marriage led to the gentrification of AIDS, making the "gay disease" something that wealthy gay white men in particular could be protected from.[1] Gay marriage led to the end of the last consistent movement for the institution of universal health care, a fight that continues to meet resistance even as millions suffer and die. Gay marriage, in short, led to the increase of suffering we see in the COVID-19 era.

Let me state that as bluntly as possible: if gay marriage had never been won, if it had never even been a fight to begin with, and if the gay community at the time had continued after the "end" of AIDS (an end that only exists for a particular segment of the gay community) to take on other and more relevant issues, including the end of the prison-industrial complex and the military expansion of the United States, we would not be where we are today. A the time of this writing, the country has seen over a million deaths, and the number of infections hovers at around ninety million; given the United States' rudimentary health care system and its long-standing impulse to deny reality, these are both more than likely undercounts (and by the time this goes to print, both numbers will undoubtedly be much higher). COVID-19 has demonstrated that the United States is not only the world's leader in deaths and infections, but that the supposedly richest country in the world has a health care system so broken that all we can do is stand back in shock and watch as the numbers escalate every day.

All of this could have been prevented if we had health care freely available to all, without the requirement of marriage or employment. It's not so much that the virus kills people, but that robust health care and other social systems could help keep them alive and get them back on their feet. In Canada, residents were assured of months of a monetary stipend to keep them afloat, buttressed by an already strong health care system that, even when strained, did not completely fail the population (even as it hurtles further toward ruinous privatization). Here, the poorest were told to continue serving as fast-food workers, delivery persons, and frontline workers without even the hope of tests. In return, the rest of us were able to work from home and isolate and bang pots and pans and clap safely from behind our windows.

Today, vaccines exist, but, at the time of this writing, little is known about their long-term efficacy and effects. More importantly, the structural problems of distribution in the United States, now exposed as substandard, and the massive amounts of poverty—not just inequality but actual, gaping, festering poverty—will mean that COVID-19 will continue to blight millions, while remaining something of no concern to the elites.

How, you might ask, could gay marriage possibly be responsible for all this? What might be the connection between AIDS and COVID-19? How does gentrification play a role in both?

Gentrification is both a physical and a conceptual matter. When we talk about neighborhoods being gentrified, we usually mean that entire populations—poorer, more marginalized, usually people of color—are physically swept out of areas that were formerly considered "ghettos" and are now being cleaned up as desirable places in which to own or rent property. Cities in particular, owing to their density, are constantly in flux as developers expand in search of more expensive properties to buy and sell. Gentrification means that a neighborhood will magically get resources long denied: in the corner of Hyde Park where I lived for a few years before moving to another location, the sewer outside my window regularly stank even in the winter months. As soon as a powerful developer, Mac Properties, began building a massive rental high-rise in the former parking lot opposite my building, the sewers were thoroughly cleaned out, the street was newly paved, the pavements were redone, the old streetlights were replaced, and perennial floral arrangements were hung on the corners. All of this coincided with the arrival of a Whole Foods down the street, as well as a Marshalls and a Michaels (now gone), which meant that Hyde Parkers, historically underserved like many other neighborhoods in Chicago's largely African American South Side, would no longer have to leave the neighborhood to buy essentials like socks and groceries (our main grocery store, Treasure Island, had been closed for a few years). At the same time, predictably, rents everywhere shot up. About a decade ago, you could find massive multi-bedroom apartments for less than $1,000, a steal for students living together. Now, there are far more amenities readily available, but a studio can cost $2,000 (an actual price in the aforementioned new Mac property).

This has meant that longtime Hyde Parkers, denizens of a neighborhood that's unusual in Chicago because generations of families have lived here, are being phased out if they lack the resources to buy or rent in the neighborhood, outward to other parts of the South Side, which are often food deserts, lacking basics like grocery stores. This is the story everywhere in the city, including Pilsen, a longtime Mexican American neighborhood increasingly taken over by hipsters, and in other cities like San Francisco and New York, which are mostly unaffordable.

Gentrification is also a conceptual shift: it reifies the dominant ideology that some—a few—deserve privileges that others don't, including clean streets and access to fresh produce, when these are, in fact, simply basics that should be accessible to all—but that's the definition of gentrification: it not only grants access to some but also actively works to further disenfranchise those considered expendable or less deserving.

In a similar way, gay marriage, ensconced in the rhetoric of love and acceptance, helped gentrify AIDS. As the fight for AIDS research and pharmaceuticals became successful, the movement mostly benefited well-off white gay men. Access to medications and treatment was made available to those who needed it, but it's people with workplace health care or private funds who mostly benefit from the fact that AIDS is not, strictly speaking and in the US, a lethal but a manageable disease. For those lacking insurance, receiving treatment and medications is harder and is compounded by inefficient transportation systems. A vaccine for COVID-19, which requires two doses two weeks apart, can be impossible for many if health care workers can't track patients.

This never had to be the state of affairs. Up until the early 1990s, ACT UP and other queer activist groups fought strenuously for the state to recognize that there was an epidemic, one that, at least in the US at the time, mostly affected gay men. But as AIDS stopped being a medical crisis for white gay men, it became less of a concern for the mainstream gay community, which, in the early 1990s, was beginning to think about and center gay marriage as an issue. The Human Rights Campaign Fund, birthed in the mid-1980s, eventually became the Human Rights Campaign (HRC) and extensively revamped itself in the early 1990s as a political lobbying group concerned with "the social welfare of the gay and lesbian community." It also began endorsing politicians, most notoriously at the time Senator Alphonse D'Amato, an arch Republican, thus, proving that HRC would never care about a truly liberatory ideology but only about furthering what it saw as its "social welfare" mission, one that centered a conservative agenda around marriage and other socially conservative values.

HRC and similar groups began to be heavily funded in the context of a political and social order that was now interested in the kind of well-off gays and lesbians who could potentially make or break political candidates. AIDS dropped off the radar, as did the myriad related issues like housing and poverty, issues that were increasingly urgent as more and more people began coming out and subsequently losing jobs and families due to a combination of societal stigma and discrimination. Within the United States, we saw the gentrification of AIDS, in the sense that poorer men of color were pushed out of the range of easily affordable health care and public health measures that could prevent infection in the first place and, if infected, provide the right kind of care and access to more than medications, such as therapy, counselling, and housing: more than 40 percent of HIV infections in the United States are among African Americans. African American men account for more than 70 percent of the infections. One in sixteen African American men and one in thirty-two African American women will be diagnosed in their lifetimes, and African Americans with HIV/AIDS are dying at ten times the rates of whites (numbers are available from the American Psychological Association).[2]

The lack of economic opportunities and access to steady, reliable health care, along with factors such as a lack of stable housing, or even groceries in severely underserved neighborhoods like the South Side of Chicago, means that African Americans are not only susceptible to infection but lack the means to sustain effective treatment regimens once infected. In a city like Chicago, the majority of health care available to gay men is still concentrated in the toxically racist white North Side—traveling there from the South Side can take hours each way. As Steven Thrasher points out, HIV treatment is difficult to maintain when it's compounded by homelessness.[3]

For LGBTQ people who are not wealthy, life can be not only difficult but dangerous, given that homophobia and transphobia continue to be linked to extreme forms of violence and exclusion, including displacement from housing and job opportunities, and Black and brown LGBTQ people face multiple forms of economic and political oppression. COVID-19 makes their lives particularly fraught and dangerous: it's easy to see that even with available vaccines, the virus will be gentrified, much as AIDS has been. Given that the United States has no definitive mass vaccination program and, as a result, no real way to ensure herd immunity (real herd immunity, not the sort that simply decimates millions without a vaccine), it's more than likely that COVID-19 will remain a health concern for many without health care and without the stability that ensures they can, for instance, get the second shot in a two-step process. A vaccine is even potentially problematic for those without health care, if it causes side effects. Already, there is little to aid survivors suffering from the "long-tail" effects: the debilitating long-term, possibly life-long, lingering health issues that affect so many and that are still not fully understood by the scientific community.

What if, instead of health care being tied to marriage and employment, we lived in a country where it was available easily, freely, and automatically to all? What if we had chosen to abjure the central message of the gay marriage movement and, instead, demanded a system where the quality of one's life was not determined by one's ability to enter and stay in a rickety, dying institution but by the sheer fact of existing? Instead, for nearly two decades, wealthy and powerful gays and lesbians, who could have used their considerable power to other ends, chose to take the momentum *away* from universal health care, something that AIDS activists had vigorously demanded. The mainstream gay community could, with its growing power, have been instrumental in demanding such an agenda but, instead, literally chose the opposite: its chief rationale for demanding marriage was that uninsured gays and lesbians needed marriage to get spousal health care, never mind that a divorce would mean the end of such for some individuals.

How did we get here?

Ten years ago, in October 2010, Against Equality (AE), the radical queer editorial group I cofounded with Ryan Conrad, published the first of three books on the mainstream gay agenda, *Against Equality: Queer Critiques of Gay Marriage*. We followed this, over the span of a couple of years, with *Against Equality: Prisons Will Not Protect You* and *Against Equality: Don't Ask to Fight Their Wars*. The books (now all collected as an anthology *Against Equality: Queer Revolution, Not Mere Inclusion*) were collections of essays archived on our website, the brainchild of Ryan, who decided, in the first months of the gay marriage hysteria, that the world needed an alternative history of queer and gay resistance to the movement.[4] As the years went on, we also spoke about hate crimes legislation and how it extended the prison-industrial complex and critiqued the call for gay inclusion in the military, which uncritically bolstered the strength of the United States empire.

When AE first set about publishing our critiques of the institution, we found ourselves barred from universities by gay student groups who insisted we were homophobes. Ryan and I received death threats, telling us we would be dismembered and thrown into dumpsters. (I faced the additional threat of being sent back to whichever place people imagined I came from, and it was never clear if the dismemberment came before or after I had been expelled.)

Much has changed since then. Gay marriage is now legal, hate crimes legislation has come to pass, and Don't Ask, Don't Tell (DADT) has been erased, only to be replaced by a new call to exclude trans soldiers. These issues form the Holy Trinity of the gay movement. Gay Christmas movies with brief critiques of gay marriage now exist. No doubt, with a liberal Biden-Harris administration—one that has already made clear that it has an agenda of strengthening American military might across the world—the exclusion of trans soldiers will soon end.

To some of us, the present state of affairs is deeply frustrating. Radical queers who have militated against the Holy Trinity might be tempted to see all that has transpired as a mark of failure on our part. Ten years later: What is the legacy of the left/radical queer critique now that gay marriage is legal? What do we do with our ongoing critique, given that not all parts of it have actually been absorbed into the mainstream gay agenda, and given that we have not been completely co-opted by it?

The point of AE's critiques was never that we actually hoped they would decisively decimate and end the movements. We persisted in our work to create a discursive space of resistance, where the problems with these crusades might exist in a way that could be retrieved—whenever necessary, even years into a future when gay history's ostensible future had been gained. Our central critique of marriage has never been that it's too assimilationist, but that it's an economically and politically disastrous way to structure people's lives and collective worth. Ours was always a materialist critique of the gay agenda, starting with our point that gay marriage pushed forward a neoliberal agenda that privatized benefits like health care that should never be linked to individual relationships or employment.

That materialist critique remains, but it's much less likely to be adopted even by those who consider themselves queer lefties. Rather, the more popular critique of gay marriage is the sort we hear articulated in *Happiest Season*: about patriarchy, sexism, and gender. That's an important critique, sure, but it keeps marriage as a problem of interpersonal relationships; abjure marriage for yourself, and you effectively end its evil effects, goes the logic. But the problem with marriage, in fact, is that it's an instrument of the state, directing people's lives toward a personal dependency on others so that the state might accrue more benefits through the consolidation of capital.

The success of gay marriage emboldened mainstream gays and lesbians, hungering for power and what they saw as "equality," to push for other retrograde measures like inclusion in the military and hate crimes legislation. Even the straight left, too cowed by fears of being called homophobic, dispensed with its antiwar politics to support these causes. *Democracy Now*, which has always been critical of American imperialism, centered Dan Choi, the gay veteran at the heart of the anti-DADT movement, as a frequent guest, and its founder and key journalist Amy Goodman also wrote an op-ed praising Choi's work.

Gay marriage made its way into public consciousness as a finely crafted piece of emotional blackmail. At a time when liberals, leftists, and progressives were straining to prove their pro-gay cred, the marriage movement essentially argued that anyone who did not support gay marriage was against "us." If you think I'm exaggerating, take the following as an example: at a public debate on gay marriage that I had with Andy Thayer, a Chicago gay activist, Keeanga-Yamahtta Taylor, who was a member of the International Socialists Organization (ISO) at the time and a fervent public defender of the cause, stood up in front of the room and proclaimed, "You're either with us or against us" when it came to gay marriage, going on to say that to be against gay marriage was to be against gay *people*. Oddly, Taylor didn't seem to see the irony of using words associated with George Bush as he argued for endless war. This was an ostensibly queer left activist using the words of an American imperialist to rhetorically manipulate her listeners into agreeing with a conservative gay agenda. By then, all factions of the left, straight and gay, demonstrated such muddied politics, leaving radical queers like those in and affiliated with AE as the pariahs and outcasts.

In 2005, Cheryl Jacques left her post as executive director of the Human Rights Campaign after a year (the post would be filled by Joe Solmonese). In an interview with *Windy City Times*'s Marie-Jo Proulx, a friend and coworker of mine, Jacques casually and inadvertently revealed much of the callousness of the gay marriage movement and how the issue became a catalyst for a series of legislative shifts that furthered a neoliberal agenda (in this case, the privatization of benefits and resources that should be the responsibility of the state). The segment in question is worth quoting in full:

> **MJP:** The increasing push for equal marriage rights has left a lot of single LGBT people feeling somewhat left out. They are asking, "What about our rights?"
>
> **C.J.:** I don't draw a distinction between single people and coupled people. It's equality for all. . . . What has happened is gay marriage has become the vocabulary for equality. . . . People talk about equality, and they quickly jump to gay marriage because it would be fairly symbolic and representative of almost achieving full equality. Because with marriage rights come thousands of benefits and tax protections and so forth. So I can understand why single people might say, "That won't benefit me." But it will and here is how: whether they ever choose to get married or not, whether they have a partner or not, it's symbolic of society moving forward and understanding that it's right to treat people equally under the law. If we achieve marriage equality, as I fully believe we will, we will achieve workplace equality, our right to serve in the military, we will get hate-crimes laws passed, get fair and full funding of HIV/AIDS research. The rest will flow. . . . It's all interconnected. We are all in this together.
>
> **MJP:** But won't gay partners feel like they must get married to gain benefits?
>
> **C.J.:** I think gay couples will feel the same as straight couples. If you get married, there's a host of responsibilities and rights and protections that come with that, and if you don't, those don't.

Jacques, whose logic and politics are perfectly representative of the gay marriage movement then (and now), said she didn't draw a distinction between single people and couples. This might prove bemusing to single people in the US who continue to bear the brunt of unfair laws in every arena, from employment to taxation, and who, as the sociologist Bella DePaulo points out, are effectively subsidizing coupled people (your two-for-one meal or cruise ticket is being paid for by the singles near you, for instance, to use one tiny example).

Perhaps even more important is the way that Jacques links gay marriage to, well, everything else: "symbolic of society moving forward and understanding that it's right to treat people equally under the law."

She goes on to argue that achieving "marriage equality" would inevitably bring forth everything else mainstream gays should desire in terms of policy matters. Here, Jacques is explicitly making a connection between gay marriage, hate crimes legislation, and inclusion in the military, as AE does, but where we pointed to the problems with such an interconnection, she was bursting with optimism about it. The workplace equality she speaks of is, in fact, not available to millions of people, regardless of their sexual orientation. Except for Montana, all states are "right to work," which (despite what the phrase appears to mean) simply means that employees can be fired at will. As for the right to serve in the military: while the overt exclusion of gays and lesbians in the military is certainly egregious, generations of antiwar LGBTQ people have worked to dismantle the military, not fought to enter it. Activists like Jacques argue that the military allows queers and other poor people to gain a measure of economic mobility, because it gives them a steady job and health care: But why should queers have to sign away their lives and limbs for what should be the basics of life? Finally, Jacques bluntly stated that, in essence, unmarried people unwilling to take on the "host of responsibilities and rights and protections" don't deserve benefits anyway.

Which brings us back to the question of health care for all and to Jacques's point about HIV/AIDS research funding.

HIV/AIDS activists, the queer radical ones left from that struggle and not the ones who would go on to become major gay marriage activists, might wonder why their efforts, which never had anything to do with marriage, are not only slighted in this interview but completely erased, as if they never existed without the marriage movement. In fact, at its height, AIDS activism centered around the idea of universal health care—which is to say, health care that would not be determined by spousal or family relationships. When ACT UP Philly staged a twentieth anniversary march in 2007, it launched a call to support a "Medicare for All" bill, but by then the gay marriage crowd was powerful and paid no attention, seeing no need for such a thing, given that it was arguing that gay marriage should be what structures people's access to insurance.

By the early 2000s, the war was on; you had to pick a side, and anyone remotely critical of gay marriage, even if from the left, needed to be silenced and expunged. It also helped, of course, that even conservatives loved gay marriage, proving AE's point that this was an issue beloved of fiscal and social conservatives. In 2011, David Cameron endorsed gay marriage with the words: "I say this: Yes, it's about equality, but it's also about something else: commitment. Conservatives believe in the ties that bind us; that society is stronger when we make vows to each other and support each other. So I don't support gay marriage in spite of being a conservative. I support gay marriage because I am a Conservative."[5] While Cameron and other conservatives echoed their support for gay marriage in terms of social stability and the benefits to society, what they really meant, as exemplified by Cameron's political career and beliefs, was that gay marriage was a good thing for the state, because it would consolidate families into taxable units.

With supporters of gay marriage coming from such seemingly disparate people (ISO leftists, gay liberals, and political conservatives), how could it not succeed in garnering massive amounts of support, especially when its benefits were couched in terms of the greater good? In a neoliberal world, few would raise the objection that AE kept emphasizing: gay marriage was both a socially and economically conservative move that would only bring disaster for millions down the road.

I am writing this in what will undoubtedly be the worst and most dangerous year of our lives—or, at least, we can hope so. Anything worse than this, a year dominated by a virus that transmits far more easily than HIV, a virus that can be breathed on you, can only be an episode of *The Walking Dead*. Even as we mask and distance from each other, we are reminded that what's killing us is not the virus alone but also a lack of health care and the complete breakdown of all social and political systems.

It never had to be this way. As Nancy Polikoff indicates so fully in her book *Beyond (Straight and Gay) Marriage*, there are a myriad of ways to construct a society where marriage does not guarantee life itself.[6] None of that was heeded.

As I write this, groups like HRC and Lambda Legal have been regularly sounding the alarm over the last four years of a Trump presidency that gay marriage will be rescinded and, then, oh, horrors, where will we all be? But in the year of a plaguey virus, the likelihood that some or many people will have their marriages torn asunder seems, well, not that serious considering that millions are dying or infected.

It's easy to blame Trump for the deaths and suffering, and, certainly, his callousness and desire to profit off the crisis is greatly responsible for where we are now. But, in the end, Americans died in such large numbers—and many more will continue to suffer long-term effects over their entire lives—because we never had even a commitment to health care for all, other than initiatives like the Affordable Care Act, which, even if resurrected by Biden, will still penalize people for not buying in (making it yet another punitive system for the poorer among us).

What if we had not suffered that depletion of political energy with the fight over HIV/AIDS? What if the mainstream gay movement, now so large and ubiquitous that it's referred to as Gay Inc., had not swooped in and distorted that struggle? What if it had not turned the very fact that people were dying from a lack of health care into a reason to then deny health care to millions of others by demanding that it should be yoked to marriage? What if it had not, thus, reified the idea that it was perfectly okay to live in a world where employers, not the state, should be the guarantors of health care?

AIDS continues to be a crisis across the world: there are currently thirty-eight million people living with HIV, and its effects in poorer countries are devastating. In the US, HIV has become a racialized disease that also marks poverty and lack of access to resources. The mainstream gay community pays attention to AIDS when it's a convenient fundraising trope (mostly around December 1, World AIDS Day). For Black men in particular, here and in Canada, HIV has become a tool of surveillance and punishment. Michael Johnson, whose case went unreported until Steven Thrasher picked up the story in Buzzfeed, faced twenty-five years in prison under laws that continue to target and criminalize Black gay men in particular for supposedly willfully infecting others. This is the gentrification of AIDS: white gay men get to do what they want behind closed doors, while Black men's sexual lives are placed under public scrutiny. In prison, where Johnson spent five years, access to medications can be volatile at best. HIV/AIDS, with its unequal and disproportionate effects based on race and class, is now further exacerbated by COVID-19, which has left prisoners everywhere deeply, hopelessly vulnerable.

That moment, when the idea of universal health care just slipped between the cracks and then disappeared from our radar until now, has been severely undertheorized. Today, as this country deteriorates into a death spiral, we are seeing things get worse and worse. Medical costs are the leading cause of bankruptcies in this country. It needs repeating: at the time of this writing, the United States, ostensibly the world's richest country, leads in COVID-19 deaths and infections. Medical care has never been so lacking, and the bodies and infections are piling up.

It never had to be this way.

This was never the future we needed or wanted; this was never the world we asked for.

With many thanks to Gil Spears for the untangling.

Notes

1   I do realize that combining "AIDS" and "gentrification" will bring to many people's minds Sarah Schulman's *The Gentrification of the Mind: Witness to a Lost Imagination* (Berkeley: University of California Press, 2012). I've not read the book, but I have no doubt that there is a confluence between her work and mine.

2   "Ethnicity and Health in America Series: HIV among African-Americans," American Psychological Association, 2012, accessed May 30, 2022, https://www.apa.org/pi/oema/resources/ethnicity-health/hiv-african-americans.

3   Stephen Thrasher, "World AIDS Day Is a Grim Reminder That We Have Many Pandemics Going On," *Scientific American*, December 1, 2020, accessed May 30, 2022, https://tinyurl.com/2p83dmj7.

4   Ryan Conrad, ed., *Against Equality: Queer Revolution, Not Mere Inclusion* (Oakland: AK Press, 2014).

5   See, e.g., Nick Duffy, "Five Years Ago Today: David Cameron Urges Tories to Back Gay Marriage," Pink News, October 5, 2016, accessed June 9, 2022, https://www.pinknews.co.uk/2016/10/05/five-years-ago-today-david-cameron-urges-tories-to-back-gay-marriage.

6   Nancy D. Polikoff, *Beyond (Straight and Gay) Marriage: Valuing All Families under the Law* (Boston: Beacon Press, 2008).

Interlude

Dispatch from the Uprising

Things That Make Me Feel Less Lonely

Mattilda Bernstein Sycamore

I dream that I'm walking into a public square during some kind of street festival, and there are a bunch of styley punkish weirdos who are excited to see me. Maybe this is what I'm always looking for, a sudden home in someone else's eyes, and now we are here together. The sky is orange and red, and everyone is flailing their arms, so I join them. Someone leans his back against mine, and we start dancing like that, our bodies moving slowly around, arms up in the air, and we're leaning against one another, movement rolling over movement so we can fly. The feeling of his neck against mine, looking up at the sky for a moment and, everything in my body says, "Yes." Even though I know I'll smell like someone else's smoke and booze and sweat, I'm ready to make out, as lips roll over neck. Except then I remember the coronavirus, and I pull myself awake in fear before our lips meet. I try to get back to that space where my whole body comes alive in anticipation, but all I can sense is exhaustion.

For those of us growing up knowing that touch meant violence, that it could never be safe, that we would never be safe, I wonder about the long-term ramifications of this time when so many of us are avoiding touch, for our safety and the safety of others. I've spent so long trying to find the physical intimacy that I crave in my life. The physical intimacy that feels like safety. The safety I never experienced as a child. Leaving touch behind, especially in a time of fear, feels like going back to a traumatized place.

Embodiment, for me, is a bridge between trauma and possibility. It's harder to feel this without feeling it with other people.

I just don't want touch to become impossible again.

Hold me. Wait, don't hold me. Do you see what I mean? I had no idea that I could hate this country even more than I already did.

Then I'm screaming on my balcony at 8:00 p.m., the way we do, and I hear some guy yell, "That's not how you do it!" I can't see him, so I don't know if he's talking to me, but I yell "Tell me how to do it, BABY..."

He screams.

I scream.

He screams.

I scream.

He screams.

Who says you can't have sex without touch?

For those of us going without touching any other human being for this long, do we have a sense of what happens after? I mean how to make it better, this touch, when it returns.

More intimate. More solid. More fluid. More constant. More evolved. More comfortable. More dependable. More present. More consistent. More expressive. More honest. More whole. More sensual. More supportive. More emotional. More grounded. More open.

That feeling in my body that I don't have to hold everything in. That I don't have to hold everything on my own. That I can let go. That I can let the world in. This is what I've wanted for a long time.

Wait, the police station in Minneapolis is burning, and we are watching. Then, we are in the streets too.

Of course, the cops can only react to protests against their brutality with more brutality, over and over and over again. You'd think they would learn something, but all they learn is more brutality. It's my birthday, and all I want is an end to this country. All I want is an end to the genocidal reign of the white imagination. I want an end to the cops and the military and the idea that the cops or the military could ever be a force for good. I want the immediate redistribution of their resources to everything that will help us heal and grow and nurture and dream.

I don't want an end to good cops, or bad cops; I want an end to policing in all its forms. I want an end to mass death disguised as profit. I want an end to swing states, and states, and nations, and nation-states. I want an end to voting for the lesser of two evils. The lesser of two white supremacists. The lesser of two rapists. I want an end to voting, if this is all it means. I want an end to alternatives that reenact the same brutality, over and over and over again. I want an end to false hope.

Whenever I wake up thinking I might feel okay, just today, this might be the day, finally, maybe today, then I crash into a puddle of doom so fast.

I don't want to live in that puddle of doom. So I hope that I wake up crying, because when I wake up crying, then I know I can feel. Everything. That's how I woke up today.

It's my birthday. Should we light a candle? Don't blow it out.

Things that make me feel less lonely tonight: rabbits chasing each other across the street, diagonal tree trunks, the light between the clouds, the way the pattern of the leaves against the sky looks like lace.

Why are they using tear gas? Why? Why is this allowed? Anywhere. George Floyd was murdered by the cops in Minneapolis while gasping, "I CAN'T BREATHE." So now police departments across the country are using tear gas and pepper spray on protesters so no one can breathe.

What would it look like if these liberal mayors just sent the cops home? Permanently. How could they possibly think that the damage would be greater than the damage their cops enact every day? Why can't they imagine something else? Why can't they allow us to create it?

It is so inspiring to see people on their porches with water, masks, and first aid to offer protesters. "We're in this together," I think. This is rarely something I feel in Seattle.

Yes, the 8:00 p.m. balcony screaming in my neighborhood is starting to merge with chants of "Black Lives Matter," even if that's only me and a few people around the corner. And "Abolish the Police," even if that's just me, but I'll assume the crescendo of sound afterward is in our favor. I'm getting pretty good at blowing extremely loudly on my whistle to the tune of "Black Lives Mat-terrrrrrrrrr, Abolish the Police." Also, I found a cute barrette to wear while screaming and blowing my whistle on my balcony, so my hair doesn't get in my face while I'm swaying side to side, and you can't really argue with a cute barrette, right?

I'm starting to wonder if this burning in my eyes and intense sinus congestion isn't a sudden spike in allergy symptoms but is the lingering effects of tear gas in my neighborhood every night. Luckily, I haven't been gassed while at the protests, but I have been there before and after.

And now I'm realizing that my lips are burning too, which isn't an allergy symptom I've ever experienced.

When your neighborhood suddenly turns into a destination for protest, a battleground, a party, a surveillance spectacle, a war zone—all in the midst of a pandemic that is always visually present through the variety of masks and avoidance and care, everything at once. "How are you?" people say, and I have no idea. I mean, I'm devastatingly exhausted, as always, but also inspired, enraged, horrified, broken open, shut down, enervated, suffocating, screaming, appreciating all the flowers, trying to hope, trying to breathe.

It seems like the Seattle police attack protesters every day night around 8:00 p.m., when people across the city are making a joyful noise in support of essential workers. Maybe cops think that beating up protesters is supporting essential workers by sending more people to the emergency room.

"COP FREE ZONE" spray painted directly on the police station. This is how to dream. I'm taking pictures of all the graffiti, and this guy comes up to me to tell me where to get a good deal on my sunglasses. Then he says: "We have locksmiths. If we wanted to get inside, we'd be inside, right?" If that's not an undercover cop, I don't know what is.

Update: one other person is now screaming "Black Lives Matter, Abolish the Police" with me as the opening to the daily 8:00 p.m. neighborhood noise extravaganza—here we go.

But did I tell you about the guy who was waiting across the street the other night when I went out on my balcony? He said, "Are you the one with the whistle—I get so much joy hearing you from my place that I decided to come down to meet you." That was a beautiful moment. I said maybe we should go on a walk and chat sometime, but I couldn't tell what he thought of that idea.

I'm thinking about what it is that has made my headaches so bad over the last several months, so that every day I'm basically fighting off a migraine, and then I realize, "Oh, that's the same amount of time I've gone without touching another human being." How sad that what heals me the most has become the riskiest. When can I go back to risking what will help?

Before this pandemic started, I had finally found a way toward the intimate touch I need in everyday experience, through ecstatic dance and contact improv, and I was searching for more, more of these forms of intimacy, to extend the possibilities, and then just like that I lost it all. And then the other forms of touch, Feldenkrais and craniosacral massage, which I usually rely on to keep me somewhat in balance, gone. It's just me and my body. I still have what I've learned and that is helping me through, but I would also like more help.

A hug is just a hug, something soft to rely on, but what does a hug become when there are no hugs? Where is the softness? To be self-reliant was something I learned as a child, but that was from trauma. Anything not to go back to that place of shutting off just to survive. And yet, how? How exactly? To move forward. Loneliness can be a gateway, but only if there's something on the other side.

And yet just speaking all of this does help. I can feel the air in my body now; there's a softness there. How to stay open to everything?

Things that make me feel less lonely tonight: graffiti, trees, the moon, hydrangeas, the breeze, the coolness of my fingers.

Things that make me feel less lonely tonight: one tiny cloud floating past the half moon, the way the trees are reaching up, how the sky is still so blue after the sun goes down.

This person actually has an "All Lives Matter" sign displayed on their rear windshield. How is there still glass there? Also, they have a rainbow teddy bear on the dashboard, proving, yet again, that sometimes the gays can be the worst.

Too tired to be this sad. Too sad to be this tired.

Too exhausted to be this exhausted.

I wake up, and the helicopters are flying over again. Every time I hear the helicopters, I think about the cops shooting tear gas at everyone night after night. Tear gas, rubber bullets, stun grenades, pepper spray. And the residue of the poison stays in the air for days and days.

After violently forcing protesters out of the Capitol Hill Organized Protest, the city of Seattle is saving the protest signs that covered the police precinct and cataloging them. This was a well-planned operation involving the mayor's office, the police, the Seattle Department of Transportation, the Parks Department, the FBI, and who knows how many others. The cops pulled people out of their tents in the middle of the night, arrested at least thirty-five people, confiscated everyone's belongings, and threw everything into dumpsters, and, then, within minutes, city employees were already painting over the graffiti covering the police precinct.

I wonder which robber baron institution will showcase these protest signs in an upcoming exhibit, which hypocritical nonprofits will step forward to claim ownership of the relics of protest, while furthering the destruction of Black lives, and which hideous corrupt politicians will show up to smile for the cameras and take credit for supporting activism.

Every restriction on police force includes the provision that the cops can use force if they feel they are in danger. They always claim to be in danger, so that they can continue to be the danger.

And now the city has painted over the gorgeous George Floyd graffiti in the park, gigantic puffy letters stretching across the old pump station for the reservoir, reflected in the water; it was such an inspiring sight for me every day. But the city of Seattle destroyed this beauty. This statement. This remembrance. This resistance. They've replaced it with beige.

No one can enter the park. They've mowed the lawn, and the cops have driven their cars inside to protect the beige. How many city employees participated in this erasure, and how many cops are being paid overtime to keep protest out?

The city of Seattle wants us to know that they are saving confiscated protest signs in vaults; they call this preserving the art. But the actual art is in the streets, spray painted on buildings that are now being whitewashed to return the neighborhood to its gentrified banality.

Art is just art, and yet. When it is such a beautiful tribute to someone's life. To George Floyd's life. And then the city paints it over, just like that. You can't help thinking about all the violence this represents.

Things that make me feel less lonely tonight: the cat that came down a flight of stairs to join me on the sidewalk, the flashing yellow lights of the new walk signal, a friendly person who said hello on the corner, the smile her boyfriend gave me, the coolness of my lips.

This guy is telling his friends about the union organizing he does, and then they're getting ready to say goodbye, and he says: "I haven't hugged anyone since March, so it'll be weird." He puts his mask on, and they hug goodbye, and I'm crying. I haven't hugged anyone since March either.

I used to hug people all the time. How weird it sounds to say something like that. How the sadness hits you all the sudden; suddenly you're lost. You're feeling the loss. How sad that a hug is no longer just a hug. How sad that a hug is no longer.

So much hope, and so much hopelessness, they are so close together. Have they ever been this close?

I decide to visit the toppled Confederate monument in Lake View Cemetery again; it's a pick-me-up every time. But then this guy stops his car and looks out at me with some strange confused look: "Why," he's asking, "why?"

"Because it was a Confederate monument," I say.

"But why would they do this to it?" he asks.

"Because it was a monument to slavery," I say.

"But why would they do this?" he says.

"It was the Democrats who owned slaves," he says, and this is when I realize he tricked me into this conversation, that he drove by just to see the toppled Confederate monument and argue with someone about it. If he was a white guy, I would have suspected a racist agenda right away, but he does not appear to be a white guy.

His wife, who does appear to be white, says, "Do you know who was buried there?"

"No one was buried there," I say. "It was a monument to the Confederacy."

"At least it wasn't a grave," she says.

"Why would it matter?" I say. "It's just a piece of stone."

"It's terrible," she says, "just terrible."

And then the guy says, "Why would they do this?"

And that's when I say, "I can't talk to you. This is ridiculous," and I walk away, and they continue driving. An interracial couple of Confederate sympathizers—oh, this country.

I'm still crying about Summer Taylor, murdered on a Seattle freeway during a Black Lives Matter protest when a driver entered through an exit ramp to avoid a police blockade, gunned his engine, and sped into the protesters. I didn't know Summer, but I used to see them on the street and think who is this styley genderqueer person, and we would acknowledge one another in a way that rarely happens in Seattle. Is it okay to say that I miss them, even if I didn't know them?

I'm still crying about Charleena Lyles, murdered by the cops in her home after she called for help. I didn't know her, but I brought roses to her memorial, and her relatives asked if I knew her. There was something so welcoming in that question; it made me feel like I did know her. Maybe I could have known her, except she was already dead.

And then yesterday, two years after the cops murdered Charleena Lyles, the head of the Seattle police union said her death was "suicide by cop." On a Black news program famous for covering current protests. How is this allowed?

I do not want to give the cops the right to do anything but leave the police force. For good. They should not be allowed to do anything until then. Why would we want to hear from them? They don't deserve to speak to us.

Charleena liked to dance; that's what her relatives told me. They thought we partied together, something like that. I wish I could dance with Charleena.

Summer Taylor was dancing on the closed highway at a Black Lives Matter protest when a driver entered the highway in the wrong direction to murder them. I wish we could dance together, all of us dancing on the highway until the murders stop. Don't you?

I can't think about Summer Taylor without thinking about Breonna Taylor. Because they shared that last name. Breonna Taylor wanted to save people's lives; that's what she wanted. She helped start a movement, but that was after the cops killed her. They didn't even give her a chance.

I just keep thinking: How many more people need to die? How many more will the cops kill? The cops, and the people who think like the cops. How many more? This is not a question that should ever be answered. I mean, there should be a different answer.

We don't need more trauma in order to know what trauma is; that much I can tell you.

Let the grief bloom. Do you know what I mean? So we won't only have more grief.

The surveillance helicopter is circling the area, so there must be a protest nearby, but where? I'm trying to find it.

One day I'd like to live in a country that I don't hate as much as I hate this one, and, strangely, I'd like that to be this country.

Things that make me feel less lonely tonight: rabbits hopping in the unmowed park grass, the orange light on the top floor of a house on the hill and the silhouette of a person leaning against the windowsill, the cool air, the way the street lights illuminate the leaves.

Things that make me feel less lonely tonight: the curve of the moon, rubbing my chest to remind myself what's inside, the ACAB chant on repeat in my head, "A, C, A, B, all cops are bastards."

Things that make me feel less lonely tonight: the half moon, the shape of this tree that looks like it's dancing, a stained-glass rose in someone's bay window, the sound of a fountain that competes with the highway noise, if I listen carefully enough.

Hooray for the ivy, escaping through the fence, we all need some good news.

If writing isn't memory, I don't know what is. Writing as a way through trauma. "Can you show me the way?" I'm writing. Writing as a way into trauma. Writing as a way out.

There is no hope without honesty, and in this sense hopelessness may be the most honest form of hope.

Are people in your neighborhood still making noise at 8:00 p.m.? It's quieting down over here, and I'm worried, because this is my most reliable moment of the day, and what would I do without it?

Things that make me feel less lonely tonight: moving my hands in the shape of the flatter side of the moon, looking up at the top parts of the trees to see how the leaves meet the sky, the light of the fake candles in someone's wide-open windows.

Things that make me feel less lonely tonight: how a wall can be cracked and still stable, a lovely sofa sitting outside in someone's entryway, realizing that strange bird sound is actually my right shoe, how a street can be so quiet in the middle of a city.

Things that make me feel less lonely tonight: leaning against the trunk of a holly tree on the sidewalk, running my hands along the surprising roughness of the bark, how the air can be warm and cool at the same time.

Things that make me feel less lonely tonight: how a tree can reach out in so many directions, how the bright light behind this fence means you can see through it, how the sound of the highway can somehow feel comforting when it's not too close.

Someone yelled "love you" to me today from the building across the street after our 8:00 p.m. neighborhood noisemaking—this is what sustains me. Love as a public force, not a private impulse. Why is this so rare? Love as an engagement with the everyday, not only the extraordinary.

Things that make me feel less lonely tonight: the smell of rosemary on my fingers after I pick it from a sidewalk planter, the way a cat has eight legs when it runs across the street, everything growing on top of this old cement garage.

Things that make me feel less lonely tonight: the sound of the breeze, the trees that grow across the street like there's no street, the feeling of dry moss on a tree trunk, the way the best meditation is the one you don't expect.

Watching a video of white vigilantes blocking the street to prevent protesters from reaching the suburban home of Seattle's Black police chief is one way to summarize the American dream. Yes, I hate this world, but I hate this country even more.

Let the record show that for a little while I actually had people in my neighborhood screaming "Abolish the Police" with me every day at 8:00 p.m., and while I'm now alone in that daily balcony chant, I will keep screaming.

Things that make me feel less lonely tonight: finding a neighborhood cat in the park and sitting together, touching the ferns growing out of a retaining wall and sensing their strength, noticing that someone changed their lighting from fluorescents to something softer.

Things that make me feel less lonely tonight: walking by the apartment building where I had sex with someone in the laundry room when I was visiting in 2000, thinking about sunflowers as people but without the damage, how a square can become a diamond can become a square inside this window frame.

One of my favorite graffiti messages from recent days says, "Kill the cop inside yourself." I wish everyone would take this advice.

This drunk fag is yelling "not all cocksuckers are leftists," and, while he may not know it, this is a very succinct summation of one key problem in my life.

Things that make me feel less lonely tonight: singing "nothing nothing nothing" in my head until I notice the yellow orange of the headlights on this old bus, the red pink orange of the horizon, and the way window panes can turn almost the same color as the sky.

Yes, I'm the one who crossed the street to watch these people make out in their window, but now I can't find them.

Things that make me feel less lonely tonight: the way the lights on this rooftop umbrella make it look like a spaceship, everyone who has their doors open to let the cool air in, the way music from far away can still sound like music.

The thing about loneliness is that it's always there, and yet sometimes, suddenly, it isn't.

"BURN IT DOWN," spray painted on the courthouse steps—I knew there was a reason I walked downtown. Honey, if I lose my shit entirely, you will be here to witness, right? Yes, I went on a walk to calm my brain, but then I'm thinking about how the police state includes the parks department, fire department, public works, transportation, and every other agency complicit in police brutality, over and over and over again. How will this ever end?

Suddenly, struck by the devastating sadness that is everything, I'm trying not to fall on the ground and just lie there. But would it feel good; okay, let me try it. It does feel good, actually, the dry grass and the stars, the way my body can relax into the ground, my breath going back, maybe I should do this more often.

Things that make me feel less lonely tonight: leaning against the ivy and how it takes over, noticing how red a stop sign can be, looking up at the sculpture created by the tree branches.

To hear an unanticipated protest and rush toward it is one of the greatest joys in the world—to dance in the street in rebellion, no matter what, no matter what, no matter what. Five months ago, if someone had told me that my neighborhood in Seattle would become a central place for Black Lives Matter protests, I would have laughed my ass off. And yet here we are. The persistence, in the face of relentless police brutality and the vicious hypocrisy of liberal authoritarianism, this persistence no matter what. Over and over again, every day, in every way. Here we are.

I'm leaning against the railing on the stairway leading into this tiny park at night, and a woman living in the park comes up to ask me if I'm okay, do I need any water, and this gesture of kindness makes me feel so present and so sad at once. How this city destroys the people who will offer you water, pushes them aside.

Then she goes over to give water to the giant tree in the traffic island, before saying a prayer for it, and then goes back to dismantling shopping carts to place them upside-down on the stairway. I'm saying this is someone we need, even if this country tells us to discard her.

We don't need this country, but this country needs us.

Abolish Cities, Prisons, Universities, and the State

The Question of Planning

Transformation, Abolition, and Queer Space

Darian Razdar

> "The vanguard demands that the revolution go on forever and so
> demands that the celebration only be planned, never enacted."
> —Larry Mitchell, *The Faggots and Their Friends between Revolutions*

Since 1979, Buddies in Bad Times Theatre, a queer performing arts company, has called Toronto home. Buddies built a name for itself by producing performances that were "unapologetically political, fiercely pro-sexual, and fundamentally anti-establishment."[1] In 1991, the nomadic troupe found its home in a garage on George Street in Toronto's not-yet-gentrified Downtown East neighborhood. There, Buddies blossomed into an erotic and experimental world of its own, where queers gathered to perform, play, party, witness, and organize. The George Street squat birthed iconic productions—such as Sky Gilbert's *Suzie Goo: Private Secretary* (1991), Daniel MacIvor's *2–2 Tango* (1991), and the BDSM *Dungeon Parties*—and held queer space during the height of the AIDS epidemic.

In 1993, Toronto officials launched a competition to find new occupants for the Alexander Street Theatre: a postindustrial, two-venue building in the Gay Village. The competition offered the lucky winner a rent-free lease with the City of Toronto, drawing the attention of Buddies' directors Sky Gilbert and Johnny Golding. After the city's initial selection fell through, certain municipal officials advocated for Buddies as the successful runner-up. Accepting the offer and negotiating a forty-year lease, Buddies opened its black box and cabaret stages on Alexander Street in 1994. Today, Buddies is the "largest and longest running queer theatre company in the world."[2]

For some, the move was worth the risk; it offered the possibility of a long-lasting and well-resourced queer theater. For many, however, the move from George Street represented the end of Buddies' militant era. With nearly three decades of hindsight, it is clear today that this change renewed Buddies' commitment to queer performance, although in a more institutionalized manner. Buddies now operates as a highly planned nonprofit theater. Buddies' Alexander Street building has become a popular venue for independent LGBTQ events and parties. Its place on the Village's nightlife circuit gives Buddies a hard-to-shake reputation for attracting white gay cismen, though Toronto's diverse queer and trans communities still use the space to party, perform, and organize. Most recently, Buddies faced allegations of anti-Blackness, tokenization, and violence toward Two Spirit, Black, Indigenous, and People of Color (2SQTBIPOC) artists, as a result of which the organization has launched an ambitious restructuring process.

Buddies' trajectory raises questions for queer space in relation to planning—specifically, because the organization had no plan. I refer to *planning* as the common verb for *to arrange in advance*, as well as the professional field of urban planning tasked with arranging cities. Planning is both, for example, how organizers strategize around common goals, as well as how capitalists regulate, oversee, and police others. The contradictions within the word *planning* are exactly why it must be questioned. For queers, especially 2SQTBIPOC, for whom planning implies access to unassured futures, the question of planning is one of life or death.

In a 2019 interview with Buddies' acting artistic director Evalyn Parry, I learned that club nights were integral to offset costs associated with the 1994 move "because of the last-minute way that Buddies came here, without much of a business plan. It wasn't the plan to be here at all."[3] While Buddies did not plan its move, it acquired the high-capacity, rent-free building because of the city's decision to support artists. To offer a queer theater company a marquee venue was extraordinary in the early 1990s, and this decision reflected an urban planning attitude tolerant of deviance—albeit the marginally acceptable deviance of a majority white queer theater. At the same time, Toronto's planning regime displaced and dispossessed queers of all stripes of their right to housing, public space, social spaces, and healthy lives. For example, due to the Kings Redevelopment Plan, Buddies' 1994 move occurred in a context of sweeping redevelopment and displacement in Toronto's Downtown East, which the theater called home.[4] By accepting the city's offer, Buddies conceded autonomy in exchange for longevity, while Toronto's planning regime continues to destroy queer spaces.

This essay explores the questions of planning through three Toronto queer spaces: Buddies in Bad Times Theatre, Unit 2, and Videofag. How do queers make and hold space? How do we create a radical politics of queer space, learning from transformative justice (TJ) and brick-and-mortar queer spaces? Is planning enough for queer spaces to survive and endure?[5]

Transformation and abolition, as mutually inclusive approaches to change, inform grassroots responses to the above questions. In the following sections, I analyze (mis)uses of the term "transformative" in the planning field, explore queerness in relation to planning, and learn from the experience of queer space makers. Drawing lessons from Buddies, Unit 2, and Videofag, I hope to explore the tensions between abolition and planning—guiding us toward an actionable, visionary politics of queer space.

Transformative Planning

Transformative justice (TJ) emerged as "a political framework and approach for responding to violence, harm, and abuse."[6] TJ repairs harm by changing how we respond to violence via "collective action toward addressing larger issues of injustice and oppression," and "without relying on alienation, punishment, or [the] State."[7] Whether change is induced or spontaneous, TJ creates conditions ripe for liberation.

Transformative planning integrates TJ into the planning profession to stem the systemic violence of "the dark side of planning."[8] Transformative planning seeks to change violent planning regimes and is gaining traction among left-aligned planners.[9] Planning scholar Leonie Sandercock presaged the transformative turn in "Toward a Planning Imagination for the 21st Century."[10] Sandercock's "four keys qualities" of a renewed planning imagination—political, audacious, creative, and therapeutic—all resonate with the justice-aligned lineages collected in the 2019 anthology *Transformative Planning*.[11] Transformative planning, however—as I explore through LGBTQ planning and social economy below—often struggles to embrace TJ. Transformative planners, like planners in other traditions, often uphold institutions that perpetuate state, racial, and capitalist violence. For queers and planners in search of more radical approaches, TJ is a useful measure to evaluate planning discourse and reflect on our own efforts to transform space.

A subfield of transformative planning, LGBTQ planning discerns how "planning reproduces structures of heterosexual domination" in the built environment.[12] This movement asserts that planning institutions exclude

LGBTQ communities from the scope of public interest, thereby facilitating "the development and control of [certain] spaces" and certain people.[13] The overwhelming response by planners has been to *include* LGBTQ people and places in current planning regimes, assuming that queer inclusion as a "community of interest" allows governments to account for the services and resources on which we rely.[14] The inclusionary focus of many LGBTQ planning interventions calls upon policing and top-down authority, acquiesces to for-profit development and boosterism, and reproduces settler property rights.[15] While capable of redistributing some resources to marginalized communities, these interventions do not propose a thorough change.

Social economy, another transformative planning subfield, responds to spatial violence by recognizing and mobilizing alternative planning practices around three pillars: economic democracy, redistributive justice, and relational autonomy.[16] Social economists study with working classes to reveal the violence of capitalist institutions and struggle for a variety of alternatives—or counterinstitutions—like co-ops, trusts, and unions. In return, feminist social economy argues that counterinstitutions do not account for social reproduction, which is the everyday replication of social relations. Feminist social economy unveils how counterinstitutions become sites of violence and struggle, despite their transformative aspirations.[17] Feminist social economies offer potentially transformative alternatives to the institutions and relations of capitalist subjugation.

Efforts to embrace transformative planning evidence incremental progress in the planning discipline. However, transformative planning, particularly LGBTQ planning and mainstream (i.e., heteropatriarchal) social economy, often falls short of TJ's aims. When planners transform spaces without meaningfully changing the dominant systems in which they exist, these spaces continue cycles of violence that especially harm queer communities. The following sections learn from these shortcomings to inform a radical politics of queer space.

Abolition and Planning

Let us remember that transformative justice requires abolition. Transformative justice organizer Mia Mingus writes that "TJ is an abolitionist framework that understands systems such as prisons, police and I.C.E. as sites where enormous amounts of violence take place.... TJ works to build alternatives to our current systems."[18]

Transformation framed as inclusion is not enough to address the roots of such violence. To be sure, inclusion and recognition in liberal institutions benefit some marginalized individuals and groups. Buddies in Bad Times Theatre, for example, only won access to the Alexander Street Theatre because of a logistical error and backroom advocacy. Most of us still live in precarity, however, and working within dominant systems has not benefited the majority of queer people. Including marginalized voices, bodies, or places in planning regimes might reduce but cannot undo the harm these regimes perpetrate.

There is an instructive dynamic between *abolition* and *planning*. Are we planning abolition or abolishing planning? *Planning abolition* places agency in planners to end violent institutions. *Abolishing planning*, on the other hand, gives power to abolitionists to end planning regimes specifically. Both commit to the task of abolition, the opposite of assimilation. Yet if the subject doing abolition work is contained within a professionalized class of planning experts, as in the former, planning must betray its allies in police, prisons, and private capital.[19] *Planning abolition* entails planning's eventual, though uncertain, end. *Abolishing planning*, conversely, presents planning—and its allied institutions—as the primary object of abolition and in favor of alternatives. This semantic dynamic reveals the tension between abolition and planning. The following paragraphs explore this tension to respond to the question of planning for queer spaces.

Kian Goh, queer organizer and urbanist, asks, "How might we conceive of a radical planning for radical queer activism?"—*radical* meaning *at the root* and signifying efforts to abolish violent regimes.[20] Goh asserts that "it is crucial ... [for planners to] confront and attempt to dismantle power structures" that displace and dispossess queers and many others.[21] Goh's call to planning action is a radical LGBTQ planner's strategic use of inclusion and recognition, while acknowledging that such strategies do not transform or abolish anything on their own.

At its best, LGBTQ planning holds the aforementioned tension by *planning abolition*. However, LGBTQ planning's prevailing politics of inclusion cedes change-making work to professional planners who "plan *for* LGBTQ community."[22] The "planning for" stance confers authority to so-called experts, leaving the rest of us with little power to make our own spaces.

Social economy holds the tension between abolition and planning in varied terms. In an effort to upend the "dark side of planning,"[23] social economy employs strategic moves "from below."[24] Heteropatriarchal social economies, as seen in some unions and nonprofits, *plan abolition* through institutional transformation. The site for such struggles is institutions and counterinstitutions. However, Buddies in Bad Times Theatre, as a queer counterinstitution in itself, attests to possible alliances between labor and queer struggles in *planning abolition*.

Feminist social economy, however, aligns with *abolishing planning* to avoid the pitfalls around counterinstitutions. Feminist social economists discern that many violences still run rampant in counterinstitutional settings, because liberal capitalism traps them in competition with mainstream capitalist institutions.[25] From here, feminist social economists turn to everyday noninstitutional spaces—such as homes, restaurants, streets, and relations—as sites of exploitation, struggle, and potential liberation. Feminist social economists, such as Silvia Federici and J.K. Gibson-Graham, push *against* patriarchal planning regimes and *for* grassroots planning practices. They tie liberation to transformed social relations rather than (counter)institutions. Feminist social economists present a rare example of the *abolishing planning* approach from within transformative planning, theorizing a useful response for queers to the question of planning.

Toronto Queer: Case Studies

The tensions between abolition and planning, as explored above through LGBTQ planning and social economy, have everything to do with actual queer spaces. Queer spaces demand that we both plan and celebrate revolutions.[26] With Unit 2 as our point of departure, I revisit Buddies in Bad Times Theatre, look back at Videofag, and finally return to Unit 2, in an effort to understand how queers respond to the question of planning in Toronto. In this effort, I uplift the lessons of redistributive justice, anti-institutionality, and radical vulnerability that queer organizers in Toronto use to claim space.

Unit 2 is a do-it-together arts space for QTBIPOC and friends in Toronto's West End and was founded in 2008 by Rosina Kazi and Nicholas Murray. The live-work space brings transformative justice's abolitionist politics to life. Through my relationship with Unit 2's community of organizers, I learned how the space leverages community assets to share art, food, shelter, skills, connection, and other necessities among left-aligned communities. Unit 2 thinks of its organizing as a type of (counter)planning, while recognizing that planning is only part of the work. The beauty of queer space at Unit 2 happens when the planning ends: in performance, dance, shared meals, discussions, and all sorts of play. Intermittent refusals to plan are especially noteworthy when liberal funding systems try coercing autonomous formations like Unit 2 into nonprofit structures.

Unit 2 unlocks the binary between abolition and planning to make space for queer survival in the here and now. The space is a useful starting point to grapple with the question of planning, in queer terms, because its organizers explicitly frame their work in terms of abolition and transformation.

Buddies in Bad Times Theatre, as previously mentioned, has a colorful history of organizing militant queer performance in Toronto. Buddies offers lessons on redistributive justice—the idea that radically sharing resources disrupts cycles of oppression—given its mandate to serve local queer artist communities. Over its forty-year history, Buddies has provided innumerable queer artists with space, resources, funding, and inspiration.

In socioeconomic terms, Buddies is a counterinstitution wherein business proceeds and grant funding redistribute resources among an interdisciplinary ecosystem of queer artists. Theater revenues go to a staff of queer and trans people and back to the community in the form of new productions and educational programs. In our interview, Buddies' artistic director Evalyn Parry mentioned that community education programs attract "queer communities of all dimensions" with free drop-in programs and artist workshops.[27] By redistributing resource access, Buddies seeks to fulfill its nonprofit mandate for queer communities, which has profound ripple effects in the broader queer cultural ecosystem. Still, the question of who is prioritized in the redistribution of Buddies' sought-after resources has yet to be resolved, as repeated allegations of anti-Blackness, tokenization, and resource inequities emerge.

The potential pitfalls of redistribution become clear in the pervasive inequities between white queers and 2SQTBIPOC in Toronto, a city that prides itself on multicultural tolerance. Redistribution alone only goes as far as inclusion and recognition. Redistributive *justice* goes further by prioritizing resources for those most in need. By reinvigorating its redistributive justice practice and returning to its militant roots, Buddies could replan its theater with 2SQTBIPOC at its core. To radically redistribute access in a diverse city of queers like Toronto, this queer counterinstitution must challenge and refuse the oppressive systems in which it operates.

Moving onto another crucial space in Toronto's recent queer history, Videofag was an independent arts space run out of Will Ellis and Jordan Tannahill's Kensington Market apartment from 2012 to 2016. As if in response to Buddies' counterinstitutional dilemma, Videofag offers the lesson of anti-institutionality as an asset for queer space-making. Ellis and Tannahill founded a space where queer artists shared and witnessed new work in its most raw and spirited forms.[28] Videofag's small storefront regularly hosted film screenings, plays, performance art, and live music that pushed against not only *what* was programmed but *how*. In an interview with Ellis and Tannahill, I learned that the two programmed the space by drawing on an ever-expanding network of queer artists and their friends, whose work was either too experimental, too explicit, or too rudimentary for institutional settings. Rather than measuring success in terms of revenue or audience numbers, Ellis and Tannahill value the relationships and artwork made at Videofag beyond the idea of success itself.

Videofag, while short-lived, is well-remembered for liberating queer space outside institutional walls. Videofag addressed "the real need for space for different parts of the queer community to screen, share, meet, and to make work" without institutional barriers like formal proposals, budgets, or timelines.[29] Despite a lack of material infrastructure, an anti-institutional approach enabled Videofag to support artists who did anything "a little off the walls or experimental, who didn't feel like they could be programmed or curated or screened at an established arts space."[30] Videofag responded to the tension between abolition and planning by subverting the drive to make new counterinstitutions, thus, transforming the conditions of queer possibility in Toronto forever.

Similar to Videofag, as a live-work anti-institution, Unit 2 offers a third lesson for queer space: radical vulnerability as a practice of building solidarity and sustaining community. Over its twelve years—full of celebration and comradery—Unit 2 has also held space for communities to grieve. In this space, I have repeatedly witnessed the power of grief and hardship to ignite struggles for justice and mutual aid. This power, in response to 2020's many crises, inspired care team organizing, crisis intervention without cops, and grassroots fundraising efforts for Unit 2 community members in need.

Learning with Billy-Ray Belcourt and Jack Halberstam, Unit 2 fits into a queer lineage of "bad affect" and "failure."[31] Meaning, the erotics of pain, vulnerability, and failure hold answers to the question of planning and point to a radical politics of queer space.³² Holding radical queer space means holding space for vulnerability and the political work of feeling, trying, and failing. In its acceptance of vulnerability, Unit 2 offers a glimpse into a world where abolition is already at work.

Unit 2, Buddies in Bad Times Theatre, and Videofag point to redistributive justice, anti-institutionality, and radical vulnerability as ways queers make and hold space in Toronto. The lessons they offer speak to a politics of queer space that holds the abolitionist potential of TJ, while showing how planning can be used and refused for the benefit of queer communities.

The Question of Planning

How do queers make and hold space? How do we create a radical politics of queer space, learning from transformative justice and brick-and-mortar queer spaces? Is planning enough for queer spaces to survive and endure?³³

This essay traces the contours of transformation and abolition in relation to LGBTQ planning, social economy, and queer spaces in Toronto. I am not ending here with any particular answers but with ever-changing responses to the above questions.

Any endeavor toward transformative justice or transformative planning must integrate abolition. As learned from LGBTQ planning and Buddies in Bad Times Theatre, transforming spaces must coincide with the abolition of oppressive systems. Transformative planning *for* queers, within existing regimes and institutions, may benefit certain individuals. Entire communities will continue to suffer until inclusion and recognition become the floor, not the ceiling, of queer space-making. Thinking with brick-and-mortar queer spaces as feminist social economies themselves, we learn that planning is only transformative when it is abolitionist.

Still, planning is neither omnipotent nor ubiquitous, and it does not have the final word in queer spaces. Queer organizers strategically use and refuse planning to make and sustain queer space. Queer planning is not used to fix or predetermine outcomes but to open future possibilities that are best left unplanned. For Buddies, Unit 2, and Videofag, planning is one tool among many; they regularly hold space via performance, play, dance, cooking, eating, and other unplanned ways of doing. There is much to celebrate in the un-, non-, and antiplanned of queer space. In these spaces, uses and refusals of planning constitute a diversity of queer spatial tactics.

The question of planning for queer spaces, in Toronto and beyond, is not simply *how to plan* but, rather, *how to get free*. Queer organizers on

Toronto's grassroots and around the world respond daily to this very question. As queers committed to making better worlds and our collective liberation, we must be careful to identify all forms of violence and be unyielding in our efforts to abolish and transform.

Notes

1   "Our History," Buddies in Bad Times Theatre, accessed May 30, 2022, https://buddiesinbadtimes.com/about/history.

2   "About," Buddies in Bad Times Theatre, accessed May 30, 2022, https://buddiesinbadtimes.com/about.

3   Evalyn Parry (artistic director, Buddies in Bad Times Theatre) in discussion with the author, December 2019; emphasis added.

4   The King-Parliament Secondary Plan (the Kings Plan), adopted by Toronto City Council in 1996, sought to plan for mixed-use redevelopment and densification in Toronto's Downtown East neighborhood, where Buddies had formerly existed on George Street. This neighborhood was identified as underutilized and unsafe, even though a variety of people used it for informal and nonprofit services in the area.

5   Gerold Vizenor, "Aesthetics of Survivance: Literary Theory and Practice," in *Survivance: Narratives of Native Presence*, ed. Gerold Vizenor (Lincoln: University of Nebraska Press, 2008), 1–23. Vizenor developed the term "survivance" explicitly in terms of Indigenous North American expressions of sovereignty that fuse "survival" and "endurance." The term has subsequently been taken up by a range of other cultural studies to explain the more profound aspects of surviving.

6   Mia Mingus, "Transformative Justice: A Brief Description," Transform Harm, accessed May 30, 2022, https://transformharm.org/transformative-justice-a-brief-description.

7   Sara Kershnar, Staci Haines, Gillian Harkins, Alan Greig, Cindy Wiesner, Mich Levy, Palak Shah, Mimi Kim, and Jesse Carr, *Toward Transformative Justice* (San Francisco: Generation FIVE, 2007), 5, accessed May30, 2022, https://www.transformativejustice.eu/wp-content/uploads/2010/11/G5_Toward_Transformative_Justice.pdf.

8   Oren Yiftachel, "Planning and Social Control: Exploring the Dark Side," *Journal of Planning Literature* 12, no. 4 (May 1998): 395–406, accessed May 30, 2022, https://tinyurl.com/37e83xmz.

9   Marie Kennedy, "Roots and Reflections on Transformative Planning," in *Transformative Planning: Radical Alternatives to Neoliberal Urbanism*, ed. Tom Angotti (Montreal: Black Rose Books, 2019).

10   Leonie Sandercock, "Toward a Planning Imagination for the 21st Century," *Journal of the American Planning Association* 70, no. 2 (June 2004): 133–41.

11   Angotti, *Transformative Planning*.

12   Michael Frisch, "Planning as a Heterosexist Project," *Journal of Planning Education and Research* 21, no. 3 (March 2002): 256.

13   Michael Frisch, "Finding Transformative Planning Practice in the Spaces of Intersectionality," in *Planning and LGBTQ Communities: The Need for Inclusive Queer Spaces*, ed. Petra L. Doan (London: Routledge, 2015), 129–46.

14 Petra L. Doan, "Why Plan for the LGBTQ Community?" in Doan, *Planning and LGBTQ Communities*, 1–15.

15 Petra L. Doan, "Beyond Queer Space: Planning for Diverse and Dispersed LGBTQ Populations," in Doan, *Planning and LGBTQ Communities*, 256. In the conclusion to her edited volume, Doan advocates for representatives from the "LGBTQ community" to serve as liaisons to municipal planning departments much like "many cities have done for the Police Department," without remarking the violence police represent for poor, working-class, BIPOC, and many other groups. Doan also advocates for planners to learn from "edgy" neighborhoods for their inclusion of sexual and gender diversity, while these neighborhoods usually only accept those who are white and able to buy into commodity culture.

16 Katharine Rankin, "Polanyian Pedagogies in Planning and Economic Geography," *Environment and Planning A* 45, no. 7 (July 2013): 1651, accessed May 30, 2022, https://journals.sagepub.com/doi/pdf/10.1068/a45582.

17 Nicole Cox and Silvia Federici, *Counter-Planning from the Kitchen*, (Bristol, UK: Falling Wall Press, 1975), accessed May 30, 2022, https://caringlabor.files.wordpress.com/2010/10/counter-planning_from_the_kitchen.pdf.

18 Mia Mingus, "Transformative Justice: A Brief Description," Transform Harm, accessed May 30, 2022, https://transformharm.org/transformative-justice-a-brief-description.

19 Deshonay Dozier, "A Response to Abolitionist Planning: There Is No Room for Planners in the Movement for Abolition," PN: Planners Network, August 9, 2018, accessed May 30, 2022, https://www.plannersnetwork.org/2018/08/response-to-abolitionist-planning.

20 Kian Goh, "Place/Out: Planning for Radical Queer Activism," in Doan, *Planning and LGBTQ Communities*, 222.

21 Ibid., 230.

22 Doan, "Why Plan for the LGBTQ Community?" 1; emphasis added.

23 Yiftachel, "Planning and Social Control."

24 Silvia Federici and Campbell Jones, "Counter-Planning in the Crisis of Social Reproduction," *South Atlantic Quarterly* 119, no. 1 (January 2020): 161.

25 Peter Staudenmaier and Jay Driskell, "From a Critique of Corporate Power to a Critique of Capitalism," in *Bringing Democracy Home* (Plainfield, VT: Institute for Social Ecology, 2000): 25.

26 Mitchell and Asta, *The Faggots and Their Friends Between Revolutions*, 22.

27 Evalyn Parry in discussion with the author.

28 For more information on the work produced at Videofag, see William Christopher Ellis, Greg MacArthur, Aisha Sasha John, and Jordan Tannahill, *The Videofag Book* (Toronto: Bookthug, 2017).

29 Jordan Tannahill (arts organizer, Videofag) in discussion with the author, October 2019.

30 Ibid.

31 For "bad affect," see Billy-Ray Belcourt, *This Wound Is a World: Poems* (Calgary: Frontenac House Poetry, 2017); for "failure," see Jack Halberstam, *The Queer Art of Failure* (Durham, NC: Duke University Press, 2011); for "constitutive non-sovereignty of the sexual," see Billy-Ray Belcourt, "Indigenous Studies Beside Itself," *Somatechnics* 7, no. 4 (September 2017): 182–84, cited in Tiffany Lethabo King, "Our

Cherokee Uncles: Black and Native Erotics," in *The Black Shoals: Offshore Formations of Black and Native Studies* (Durham, NC: Duke University Press, 2019), 146–47.

32   Audre Lorde, "Uses of the Erotic," in *Sister Outsider* (Berkeley: Crossing Press, 1984), 56, accessed June 10, 2022, https://tinyurl.com/yckkxxfp.

33   Vizenor, "Aesthetics of Survivance: Literary Theory and Practice."

Unconditional Abolition

Ending State Violence against People with Sex Offenses

Amalia Golomb-Leavitt, Ryan Becker, and Rebecca Valeriano-Flores

In recent years (and most especially in the June 2020 uprising against white supremacy), we have witnessed a much-needed shift in public discourse: the concept of prison abolition is increasing in visibility and popularity. More people every day are recognizing both the drastic harm and deplorable wastefulness of the US prison-industrial complex, which includes not only prisons but also police, schools, hospitals, courtrooms, and all other public institutions implicated in alienating and criminalizing people and locking them up.

However, when we call for abolition it is imperative to include every one of us that is criminalized, incarcerated, and killed by the various iterations of the prison-industrial complex. Abolitionists frequently focus on case examples and rhetoric that underscore the need to release those accused of misdemeanors or drug charges: sympathetic narratives of "victimless crimes." The movement frequently skirts over acts with very visible victims, particularly those involving people incarcerated for causing sexual violence.

This essay aims to demonstrate that prison abolition means abolishing punishment systems for *everyone*, including those of us in prison convicted of sex offenses. True abolition must be unconditional. It is grounded in the human right to live outside of a cage—in the conviction that no one deserves to be locked up, no matter what type of harm we have caused. Prison abolition, queer liberation, and the fight against rape culture are all rooted in the need to end violence. If we maintain that we support these movements, and, thus, that ending violence is our goal, then we must fight to end the severe state violence enacted against all people in prisons, as well as sexual violence, homophobia, transphobia, and all other forms of harm.

For these reasons, we advocate that queer liberation must specifically address issues surrounding people convicted of sex offenses, the people so often left behind in abolitionist rhetoric. LGBTQ+ people are disproportionately subject to the violence of the prison system and are disproportionately detained for sex offenses.[1] To omit people convicted of sex offenses in our advocacy for abolition is to endorse prisons for *some* people, a move that we argue is directly opposed to the abolitionist framework of ending all violence. In short, such exclusion makes advocates of abolition complicit in state violence.

The importance of ending sexual violence is irrefutable. We recognize the desire to end harm and ensure safety feels especially dire for those of us who are most vulnerable to sexual violence. But this sense of urgency is often used to excuse the omission of people convicted of sex offenses from calls for abolition. To this end, we highlight the wisdom of activist Mimi Kim, cofounder of Incite! Women, Transgender and Gender Nonconforming People of Color Against Violence. Kim explains in detail how valid concerns about safety often lead to an excessive and misguided focus on immediate physical safety. There is a widespread presumption that immediate physical safety is an unarguable priority for preventing violence, despite the many different ways that exist to address violence. Such fetishization of safety, as Kim demarcates, leads to an overreliance on the carceral system to remedy those worries.[2] This trend is especially true in addressing sexual violence; worries about physical safety in combination with an overreliance on the criminal legal system to solve interpersonal harm lead many to believe that the carceral system is the only way to prevent sexual violence.

It is this trend that so often shapes abolitionist work, advocacy, and community organizing that leaves out, ignores, or makes invisible people convicted of sex offenses, despite evidence that the carceral system itself perpetuates sexual violence in prisons. This essay explores the ways that prisons do not reduce sexual violence, but, rather, distract us from developing other ways to address sexual violence. The failure to advocate equitably for holistic abolition thus not only fails in effectively reducing state violence for all, rather than some; in fact, it also fails to address sexual violence itself in any meaningful way. We fail survivors of both state and sexual violence when we abandon an abolition that includes all of us.

Our campaigns, our words, and our abolition efforts must reflect an unconditional commitment to end all forms of violence for all people. We cannot choose to support some survivors, while allowing the dehumanization of others. It is our commitment to supporting survivors that fuels our need to abolish prisons for everyone. Thus, this chapter is dedicated to those of us so often invisibilized— people convicted of sex offenses— and to the realities of how the prison-industrial complex harms people convicted of sex offenses specifically. We are incarcerated, formerly incarcerated, and free-world activists living in Illinois, and, thus, we focus on Illinois's particular context of sexual violence and criminalization. We detail sex offender registries, residency restrictions, and the imposition of "three years to life" as ways the prison-industrial complex attempts, often successfully, to ruin the lives of people convicted of sex offenses. We provide context for how the image of the "sexual criminal" has been intentionally sociopolitically constructed over time along racist, homophobic, and gendered lines. Finally, we conclude with ways we as abolitionists can hold each other accountable to unconditional abolition work.

The Harms of the Carceral System
Sex Offender Registries

The carceral systems designed to reduce sexual violence are not only ineffective at that goal, but they also cause further harm to marginalized communities. Sex offender registries exemplify the specific and ongoing failure of the carceral system. Registries became widespread in the mid-1990s after the implementation of the Jacob Wetterling Act and Megan's Law, federal laws that require states to institute a registry and to release registry information to the public. By the mid-2000s, all states had registries accessible through the internet. Empirical research suggests that sex offender registries have not reduced the number of sex offenses in the US, nor have they reduced recidivism—they may have actually led to an increase of recidivism, because residency restrictions can prevent people convicted of sex offenses from accessing treatment, stability, and support networks.[3] Otherwise, people convicted of sex offenses are generally less likely than people convicted of other offenses to be rearrested or go back to prison, despite the Bureau of Justice Statistics' misleading statements.[4]

In Illinois, people convicted of sex offenses who qualify as "sexual predators" are required to register in person and pay a $100 fee annually for their entire lifetime. Illinois is one of the strictest states in terms of registration requirements. A person on the registry must report to the police department every time they have a change of address, phone

number, job, school, or email address. If they don't update this information within three days, the police issue a warrant for their arrest, and
they could face five additional years in prison. The system is difficult to
navigate and is set up for people to fail. Furthermore, people convicted
of sex offenses are under surveillance not only by the prison-industrial
complex but by their neighbors and communities. Personal information
about all of those forced to register can be found by anyone with access
to the internet. This puts people convicted of sex offenses in danger of
harassment and violence and entails stigmatization for themselves and
their families.[5]

These issues become even more difficult for individuals experiencing
homelessness. According to the Chicago 400 Campaign, a group organized
to support the four hundred Chicagoans who are experiencing homelessness as a result of being on the sex offender registry, the registry makes
it incredibly difficult to find stable work and housing. If the individual is
experiencing homelessness, Illinois requires that the individual registers
weekly and provides the exact location of where they slept every night to
ensure they follow residency restrictions. A stark racial and economic
disparity is clear in the demographics of this group: nearly 80 percent of
Chicagoans on the registry who are experiencing homelessness are Black
men from impoverished areas of Chicago. Although many of the Chicago
four hundred have jobs, they often miss work or lose employment opportunities because of these weekly registration requirements. These formerly
convicted and incarcerated people must stay in contact with the police for
years, and, for most of them, for the rest of their lives.[6]

Residency Restrictions

People convicted of sex offenses leaving prison after completing their
sentences are required to abide by unique and draconian sets of residency
restrictions, making it difficult to find viable housing or host sites for their
parole. For example, at least twenty-nine states in the US have restriction
laws that prohibit people convicted of sex offenses from living near schools,
parks, and daycare centers.[7] Studies suggest that residency restrictions
have little effect on preventing sex offenses against children and that very
few sex crimes against children even occur at schools, parks, and daycare
centers near residences of people convicted of sex offenses.[8] Illinois is
one of these states, according to Illinois Voices, an organization focused
on legislation and litigation concerned with public registries. Illinois

residency restrictions prohibit people convicted of sex offenses against children from living within five hundred feet of schools, playgrounds, daycares, and other facilities that provide programs for minors. However, this restriction is often imposed on all people convicted of sex offenses, irrespective of whether their convictions were related to minors.

Other restrictions include prohibition from residing in an apartment complex if another people convicted of sex offenses already lives there and the requirement to wear an electronic monitoring (EM) device that can be tracked within ten feet at all times by a parole officer.[9] People convicted of sex offenses are routinely subjected to random searches of their computers and other devices, are not allowed to use social networking sites, and have only restricted access to devices with internet capability. They must obtain approval for employment or training, maintain a daily written log, take an annual polygraph test, and get approval to drive alone in a vehicle. People convicted of sex offenses do not qualify for halfway housing.

We have listed here only a few of the dehumanizing restrictions upon reentry on parole.[10] In summary, restrictions and increased surveillance provide steep barriers to reentering society after incarceration and often prevent people convicted of sex offenses from reentering society at all.

Three Years to Life

If people convicted of sex offenses are not able to find a site from prison that meets Illinois residency requirements, they remain incarcerated even after serving their initial sentence. For a person to be released on parole, the individual must register a host site, the place the individual plans to live after release. It is increasingly difficult to find host sites that satisfy the multiple arbitrary residency restrictions. The host site must meet requirements set by Illinois law; however, the Illinois Department of Corrections interprets the law in excessively strict and arbitrary ways. Because of the way the department interprets Illinois law, people convicted of sex offenses are kept in prison far beyond their release dates due to their inability to meet the department's arbitrary standards.

As of September 2020, there are roughly 1,200 people held in Illinois prisons past their release dates.[11] Residency requirements that are often impossible to meet result in people convicted of sex offenses remaining incarcerated indefinitely; parole is set anywhere between three years to a life sentence at the court's discretion: hence the phrasing "three years to life."[12]

J.D. Lindenmeier's story is an example of how difficult residency restrictions make release for people convicted of sex offenses. Lindenmeier was a plaintiff in a class action lawsuit filed against the state of Illinois for civil rights violations. He told WBEZ that he couldn't afford his own apartment and that residency restrictions kept him from living with his family: his father lived too close to a park, his mother had a computer and smartphone with internet capability, his sister had children, and his dad's girlfriend's home was too close to a daycare center. Lindenmeier spent a total of eight years in prison after serving his sentence, because he could not find a place to live that met the parole conditions.[13] Lindenmeier and several other plaintiffs filed the class action lawsuit in early 2019.

In March 2019, Judge Virginia Kendall ruled that the host site requirements violate fundamental rights and constitute cruel and unusual punishment. Kwame Raoul, the attorney general of Illinois, filed a compliance plan in February of 2020 that made changes to some of the explicit residency restrictions and established guidelines for their proper implementation. These prior inhumane restrictions included the interpretations that people convicted of sex offenses were prohibited from living in homes with internet access and banned from living near schools, playgrounds, day-care facilities, or parks. The Illinois Department of Corrections additionally interpreted residency restrictions to prohibit more than one person convicted of sex offenses from living in the same apartment complex or trailer park.

Following Raoul's 2020 compliance plan, the Illinois Department of Corrections eliminated the ban on internet access for all people convicted of sex offenses and changed residency restrictions related to proximity to public locations so that they only apply to people convicted of sex offenses against minors. The Illinois Department of Corrections will no longer interpret the law as banning more than one person convicted of sex offenses from residing in the same apartment complex or trailer park. The compliance plan also introduces a new grievance process and announces plans to develop transitional centers and housing.[14]

Civil Commitment

Despite these changes, the possibility remains that people convicted of sex offenses will end up detained for the rest of their lives, because the compliance plan includes a partnership with the Illinois Department of Human Services (IDHS) to identify individuals for placement in facilities termed "civil commitment." Civil commitment through IDHS is the practice of incarcerating people deemed to be "sexually dangerous persons" beyond their prison sentence in detention facilities and has taken place in its current form since the 1990s.[15] Civil commitment legislation targets people convicted of sex offenses who are living with mental illness or "mental abnormality." The laws require evidence of a connection between mental illness and either prior sex offenses or risk of future sex offenses.[16] Though civil commitment facilities pose as treatment centers rather than detention centers, residents are involuntarily and indefinitely held until deemed "rehabilitated." Very few people convicted of sex offenses are released, and many die while detained. Like "three years to life," civil commitment outside of the Illinois Department of Corrections keeps individuals detained beyond their court-ordered sentences.

The measures used to determine civil commitment sentencing are inhumane, ineffective, and discriminatory. Tests assessing people convicted of sex offenses for risk of reoffending include the Static-99R and the penile plethysmograph. The Static-99R is a ten-question, points-based checklist that deems people convicted of sex offenses to be at a higher risk for reoffending if they are a man convicted of a sex offense against male-identifying people or if they have not lived with a lover for a minimum of two years. As many queer people are not able to live with their partners due to widespread institutional homophobia, both of these questions lead to discrimination and bias against LGBTQ+ people in the carceral system and to a disproportionate number of LGBTQ+ people being placed in civil commitment. The plethysmograph test, meanwhile, measures blood flow to an individual's penis when they are shown explicit and often disturbing images.[17] In addition to inhumane testing, people convicted of sex offenses must also endure personal interviews as part of their risk assessment. People convicted of sex offenses are asked intrusive questions in these interviews about their sexuality and masturbation, family history, and social media accounts.

In sum, the sex offender registry, the practice of "three years to life," and civil commitment rely on arbitrary and humiliating tests and are based on inconclusive empirical evidence on recidivism's relationship to mental illness, proximity, and commonality with other offenders. As a result, people convicted of sex offenses face lifetime imprisonment, surveillance, and violence beyond the trauma of incarceration. The American Psychiatric Association came out against civil commitment laws in 1998, calling them a "serious assault on the integrity of psychiatry."

Looking Deeper into Sexual Violence, Queerness, and Criminality
There is history and intention behind the way we perceive sexual violence. This history is integral to understanding why people convicted of sex offenses routinely get left behind in queer organizing and abolitionist movements, even when the people incarcerated for sexual violence are disproportionately LGBTQ+.[18] Namely, we equate sexual violence with harmful stereotypes reinforced ubiquitously: adult sexual violence brings to mind a Black man as "perpetrator" with a white woman as "victim"; sexual violence against children triggers imagery of a gay man as "perpetrator" and a young boy as "victim."

The tropes of the Black male rapist and the innocent white woman have existed in the United States since emancipation. After emancipation, as Black men gained political and social power, the US witnessed an increase in accusations against Black men for the rape of white women. Violence and lynching accompanied these accusations.[19] This harmful trope fueled the violence in the famous case of Emmett Till. In 1955, two white men tortured and killed the fourteen-year-old Till after an alleged altercation with Carolyn Bryant Donham. Till's murderers were acquitted by a jury of all white men. Donham, who originally claimed that Till had touched her and talked to her inappropriately, admitted in 2017 that her claim was a lie.[20] The notion that heterosexual sexual violence is most often perpetrated by Black men against white women is part of the very racism that underpins the justification of prisons as a whole.

The victimization of the white woman is in line with racism that paints whiteness as innocent and sexism that paints white womanhood as frail and helpless.[21] This stereotype not only criminalizes Black men but also erases violence against women of color and violence in queer relationships.[22] These tropes are replicated even in our language of perpetrator/victim, which itself paints a black-and-white, all-or-nothing picture of sexual violence that perpetuates stereotypes surrounding sexual violence.

In other words, the carceral system constructs distinct stereotypes of typical perpetrators and typical victims—stereotypes that we reproduce in our media, our court systems, and, importantly, our own beliefs, judgments, conversations, and everyday behaviors. The carceral system is both shaped by and reflected in the language we use, when advocating for abolition and otherwise. Racist, sexist, and homophobic beliefs influence the way we see perpetrators and victims and, thus, they affect the ways we advocate for survivors of sexual violence.

Just as the stereotype of the Black male perpetrator and the white female victim is associated with heterosexual sexual violence, the stereotype of the gay male perpetrator and the male child victim is often associated with homosexual or queer sexual violence. Pedophilia and child sexual abuse are socially conflated with gay and queer men. This myth was the justification behind such actions as Anita Bryant's campaign to repeal antigay discrimination ordinances in Florida in the 1970s, the Vatican's stance that gay men cannot be ordained following child sex abuse allegations in the 2000s, and the Boy Scouts of America's policy to exclude gay men from taking leadership positions (a policy that finally changed in 2015). Antigay religious groups such as the Family Research Council also maintain this myth, despite overwhelming evidence that shows gay men are no more likely to molest children than heterosexual men.[23]

Equating pedophilia with gay men is another way the carceral system criminalizes a marginalized group. There is a long history of the criminalization of "deviant" sexualities; it was illegal to have same-sex sexual intimacy in many states in the US until the criminalization of such intimacy was declared unconstitutional in 2003.[24] Although the bodies and behaviors that society deems acceptable change over time, some humans have been consistently subject to criminalization and victimization by the carceral system. We see people who are Black and/or queer more consistently associated with criminality than white, cis, and/or heterosexual people, and, therefore, people who are Black and/or queer are always at higher risk of experiencing violence from the state and its carceral system.

A vicious and fatal cycle emerges: because Black and gay men are conflated with sexual violence, they end up disproportionately imprisoned; their excessive incarceration guides the public eye to consume such conflations. As such, these racist, misogynistic, queerphobic beliefs are not only imposed on us institutionally by the carceral system but are reproduced when we insist that more prosecution and incarceration are the answers to sexual violence. When our abolition excludes people with sex offenses, we endorse the narrative that the carceral system perpetuates. When we refuse to see people with sex offenses as those in dire need of our advocacy, we are complicit in the violences of the carceral system.

Conclusion

There are perhaps two entwined bottom lines here. First, prisons do not end the problem of sexual violence; rather, they contribute to and perpetuate it. Second, an equally important aim of ours is to honor the lives and specific struggles of people who are incarcerated but who often get left behind in abolitionist narratives. As we have shown, those of us incarcerated for sex offenses face several additional challenges associated with being incarcerated and having a criminal record.

Ultimately, abolition is not just about ending prisons; it is about building the world we want: a world that calls for nuanced and thoughtful solidarity. It is about interrogating the endless and intricate ways we *all* perpetuate carceral logic and valorize a concept of innocence that no one can actually embody. It is about accepting that we all harm and are harmed in different ways. It is about innovating new structures and methods for dealing with harm that are specific to the kind of harm caused, aimed at transforming that harm, and centered around humane consequences, learning, changing, and healing. What does this mean for us, as incarcerated, formerly incarcerated, and free-world abolitionists? How can we further liberate our abolitionist politic?

We provide, here, a few suggestions as starting points. We can note and shift language in our advocacy that perpetuates "us versus them" binaries of perpetrator and victim, guilt and innocence, deserving and less deserving, human and less human. We can bring these dissonances up in our organizations and call our fellow activists, scholars, artists, and comrades into conversations about such discrepancies. We can read the brilliance of Beth Richie, Andrea Ritchie, Mia Mingus, Michelle Alexander, INCITE!, Bay Area Transformative Justice Collective, generationFIVE, Mariame Kaba, Shira Hassan, and other author-organizers of color expanding the intersectional complexities of criminalization. We can learn from and fund organizations, such as Survived and Punished and Love + Protect, which are doing incredible work to end both state and sexual violence against people of color.

We can read, learn, think about, and prepare with our organizations for how to call out rape culture and deal with sexual violence in our own communities in ways that avoid prisons and police, such as transformative justice and community accountability processes. We can learn how other organizations and communities have been dealing with sexual violence and connect with them to share resources and support. We can connect with abolitionist organizations and become pen pals with people locked up for sexual offenses. We can continue to build community with people who are currently and formerly incarcerated and learn endlessly from each other, our stories, and our strengths.

This nuanced solidarity is an unconditional solidarity. It values and validates all of our struggles and all of our histories, and it advocates for a world that allows all of our healing. It acknowledges that we are bound up in each other's liberation and, as Aboriginal Australian organizers once declared, no survivor will heal from the violence they have experienced by disposing of anyone else.[25] We must leave behind the habit of parsing out who does and does not deserve compassion, because no survivor will heal unless all survivors are provided opportunities to heal.

This time of widespread uprising against white supremacy and increased awareness of the violence of policing and incarceration is an enormous window of opportunity to begin all of this work. As we write, we call on ourselves and our readers to make sure the new upsurge of abolitionists understand both the history and the future of what and whom abolition must include.

Notes

1   More specifically, LGBTQ+ people are disproportionately detained in civil commitment centers, as we discuss later in this chapter; see Toshio Meronek and Erica R. Meiners, "The Prison-Like Public Hospital System Disproportionately Packed with Gay Men," *Advocate*, May 31, 2018, accessed May 31, 2022, https://tinyurl.com/4t7p8nrk; Hilary Burdge, Adela C. Licona, and Zami T. Hyemingway, *LGBTQ Youth of Color: Discipline Disparities, School Push-Out, and the School-to-Prison Pipeline* (Tucson: Gay-Straight Alliance Network and Crossroads Collaborative at the University of Arizona, 2014); Jerome Hunt and Aisha Moodie-Mills, *The Unfair Criminalization of Gay and Transgender Youth: An Overview of the Experiences of LGBT Youth in the Juvenile Justice System* (Washington, DC: Center for American Progress, 2012), accessed June 10, 2022, https://www.scribd.com/document/98668589/The-Unfair-Criminalization-of-Gay-and-Transgender-Youth.

2   M.E. Kim, "Challenging the Pursuit of Criminalisation in an Era of Mass Incarceration: The Limitations of Social Work Responses to Domestic Violence in the USA," *British Journal of Social Work* 43, no. 7 (October 2012): 1281–82, accessed May 31, 2022, https://tinyurl.com/yc7ekv4z.

3   Charles Patrick Ewing, *Justice Perverted: Sex Offense Law, Psychology, and Public Policy* (Oxford: Oxford University Press, 2011), 109; for a wide review on literature that looks at recidivism, see chap. 2, 69–116.

4   Wendy Sawyer, "BJS Fuels Myths about Sex Offense Recidivism, Contradicting Its Own New Data," Prison Policy Initiative, June 6, 2019, accessed May 31, 2022, https://www.prisonpolicy.org/blog/2019/06/06/sexoffenses.

5   Erika Davis Frenzel, Kendra N. Bowen, Jason D. Spraitz, James H. Bowers, and Shannon Phaneuf, "Understanding Collateral Consequences of Registry Laws: An Examination of the Perceptions of Sex Offender Registrants," *Justice Policy Journal* 11, no. 2 (Fall 2014): 4, 16, accessed June 10, 2022, http://www.cjcj.org/uploads/cjcj/documents/frenzel_et_al_collateral_consequences_final_formatted.pdf.

6   "Chicago 400 Campaign," Chicago 400, accessed June 10, 2022, http://chicago400.
net/campaign.

7   Ewing, *Justice Perverted*, 83.

8   Joanne Savage and Casey Windsor, "Sex Offender Residence Restrictions and
Sex Crimes against Children: A Comprehensive Review," *Aggression and Violent
Behavior* 43 (November–December 2018): 23–24, accessed May 31, 2022, https://
daneshyari.com/article/preview/8946514.pdf.

9   Unified Code of Corrections, Section 3–3–7, subsection 7.7: Illinois Compiled
Statues, Illinois General Assembly, accessed May 31, 2022, https://www.ilga.gov/
legislation/ilcs/fulltext.asp?DocName=073000050K3-3-7.

10   "Illinois Voices Summary of Laws," Illinois Voices, accessed May 31, 2022, http://
www.ilvoices.org/il-law-summary.html.

11   "People Past Their Release Dates," Chicago 400, accessed May 31, 2022, http://
chicago400.net/how-about-now.

12   Molly Willms, "Sex Offenders Say Illinois Parole System Is Broken," Courthouse
News Service, December 22, 2016, accessed May 31, 2022, https://www.
courthousenews.com/sex-offenders-say-illinois-parole-system-is-broken.

13   Max Green, "Federal Judge Finds Illinois Rules on Sex Offenders Unconstitutional,"
WBEZ, April 1, 2019, accessed May 31, 2022, https://tinyurl.com/mtv3zna9.

14   "Illinois Voices Legal Efforts," Illinois Voices, accessed May 31, 2022, http://www.
ilvoices.org/legal.html.

15   Civil commitment in Illinois can also be found within IDOC as part of the prison
system, however in this article we focus on civil commitment through IDHS to
show how an individual can stay in prison beyond their sentence.

16   "Civil Commitment of Sexually Dangerous Persons," Congressional Research
Service, July 2, 2007, accessed May 31, 2022, https://crsreports.congress.gov/
product/pdf/RL/RL34068/6.

17   Meronek and Meiners, "The Prison-Like Public Hospital System."

18   See Hunt and Moodie-Mills, *Unfair Criminalization of Gay and Transgender Youth*;
Burdge, Licona, and Hyemingway, *LGBTQ Youth of Color*; Movement Advancement
Project and Center for American Progress, *Unjust: How the Broken Criminal Justice
System Fails People of Color*, (Washington, DC: Center for American Progress, 2016),
accessed June 10, 2022, https://www.lgbtmap.org/file/lgbt-criminal-justice-poc.
pdf.

19   Martha Hodes, "The Sexualization of Reconstruction Politics: White Women and
Black Men in the South After the Civil War," *Journal of the History of Sexuality* 3,
no. 3 (January 1993): 402–17, accessed May 31, 2022, http://susannalee.org/courses/
print/Hodes_1993-print.pdf.

20   Richard Pérez-Peña, "Woman Linked to 1955 Emmett Till Murder Tells Historian
Her Claims Were False," *New York Times*, January 27, 2017, accessed May 31, 2022,
https://www.nytimes.com/2017/01/27/us/emmett-till-lynching-carolyn-bryant-
donham.html.

21   George Yancy, interviewed by Merleyn Bell, "Race Relations and the Philosophy
of Whiteness Are Important Subjects for Doctor George Yancy," KGOU, February
20, 2017, accessed May 31, 2022, https://tinyurl.com/57fns438.

22   For more on the erasure of violence against women of color, see Kimberlé W.
Crenshaw, "Mapping the Margins: Intersectionality, Identity Politics, and Violence
against Women of Color," *Stanford Law Review* 43, no. 6 (July 1991): 1241–99, accessed

May 31, 2022, https://blogs.law.columbia.edu/critique1313/files/2020/02/1229039.pdf.

23   Zack Ford, "The Family Research Council's Strange Statement on Josh Duggar's Child Molestation Confession," Think Progress, May 22, 2015, accessed May 31, 2022, https://tinyurl.com/36tdk68b; Gregory M. Herek, "Facts About Homosexuality and Child Molestation," Prof. Herek's Blog, accessed May 31, 2022, https://psychology.ucdavis.edu/rainbow/html/facts_molestation.html.

24   Lawrence v. Texas, Oyez, accessed May 31, 2022, https://www.oyez.org/cases/2002/02-102.

25   The concept of being "bound up in each other's liberation" originates with Aboriginal activists organizing in Queensland in the 1970s.

Adding Insult to Injury

A Case Study of the Institutional Weaponization of White Queerness

Raxtus Bracken

Inhabiting the Ivory Tower

Colleges and universities in the United States are, like the country itself, grounded in principles and practices of inequity and exclusion. The establishment of European-style educational centers in the United States as early as the seventeenth century was part and parcel of the larger Christian colonial project. It simultaneously relied upon and was a primary driver of the violent disruption of Native communities, their forced assimilation, and the ongoing occupation of their land. Additionally, many schools depended on and promoted the use of enslaved labor because they benefited directly from the Atlantic slave trade well into the nineteenth century.[1] These legacies of imperialism and white supremacy have always been tied to the policing of gender, as well as the fascination with and fear of (real or imagined) queer identities, and consequently shape contemporary campus culture throughout the country.[2]

The narratives of diversity and inclusion that have developed within higher education over the last several decades can be understood as a national reaction to these histories.[3] Following racial and gender integration, institutions have understood the concept of diversity as a way of managing—rather than addressing—conflict and difference, avoiding implications of responsibility, and curbing structural change.[4] I argue that institutions situate queerness within these discourses depending on its ability to be assimilated into and leveraged by institutional powers.[5] Essentially, if a particular demand, movement, or phenomenon that is marked as queer can be incorporated into existing policies and structures, it is accepted; if not, it is not only rejected but often actively suppressed. Furthermore, I propose that the primary factor in determining queerness's potential degree of assimilation is its proximity to and embodiment of whiteness.

The threat of queer assimilation is hardly new. The deradicalization of queer movements in the 1960s and 1970s overlapped heavily with racial politics, and white cisgender queers were prominent among those who rebranded the movement for liberation into a campaign of conformity to make the queer community increasingly palatable to mainstream (read: cisgender, heterosexual, and white) audiences.[6] This continues to be mirrored in the (perpetually racialized) nationalization and corporatization of queerness, as well as in the continued willingness of colleges, corporations, and the like to both buy into and co-opt queer rhetoric at the expense of its queer stakeholders.[7]

Sara Ahmed notes that because institutions dedicate so much time and so many resources to denying their white supremacist roots, they imagine accusations of racism "as an injury to whiteness" and see them as the kinds of disruption that diversity work is supposed to protect *against*.[8] Building on Ahmed's arguments, which pertain specifically to institutional and social barriers predominantly faced by people of color, I argue that institutional promises of inclusion for queer students often center white queers and function to the detriment of students of color, whether queer or not.[9] At a predominantly white institution like Davidson College, queerness (like anything that is not explicitly racialized otherwise) is implicitly marked as white; as such, predominantly white institutions may be increasingly willing to capitalize on the relative palatability of predominantly white and/or whitewashed queer experiences, and, in doing so, extend the legacies of white supremacy inherent to such institutions. By constructing white queerness as a more palatable, less disruptive form of diversity than nonwhite marginalized identities, colleges and those in power within them can simultaneously suppress potential dissidence from predominantly white queer populations and deny students of color, particularly Black and Indigenous students, the resources they need to survive ongoing institutional violence. A key danger here is that white queers will (knowingly or unknowingly) fail to acknowledge this administrative strategy, or they will opt for institutional incorporation rather than building coalitions to challenge the structural inequities that undergird their schools.

Of course, the use of the future tense is rhetorical, as this pattern is already underway in many (if not all) colleges and universities. I present some of my experiences and those of my queer peers at Davidson College as a case study to illustrate how institutions seek to subsume and weaponize white queerness against queer students of various racial and ethnic backgrounds who confront these systems of power and their impact on our communities. I discuss some of the primary ways this appropriation manifests at the college and why all of us should be wary of such a pattern and its seductive normative qualities, of which I myself (as a white queer transgender student) have felt the powerful draw. To do so, I draw from the work of Ahmed, who takes an explicitly queer critical lens to structural power, to remind myself and my readers of the dangers of inclusion. While these observations can be useful for many reasons, the trends discussed here should be understood as a warning for fellow white queers in colleges, universities, and comparable organizing spaces in the United States.

Due to my trans identity, I experience gender-based policing and anti-trans rhetoric constantly. Campus spaces heighten my dysphoria, which at times reaches debilitating levels, and friends, family, and strangers critique my self-presentation on an almost daily basis. I understand many of the concerns of queer and trans students, and I experience many of our common obstacles directly and regularly; my goal is not to attack white queers who are subject to these and other difficulties but to reveal the danger of our schools' desire to assimilate us. Similarly, I hope to amplify Ahmed's existing institutional critique by focusing on colleges' misappropriation of queerness and how it serves an institution's surface-level attempts at reconciliation that are, time and time again, offered in place of meaningful transformation.

The Perils of Whiteness: Historical Patterns and Their Impact
In her piece "A Phenomenology of Whiteness," Ahmed investigates how white bodies curate and occupy space in a way that subsumes nonwhite bodies and their experiences.[10]

Just as the construction of whiteness is an "ongoing and unfinished history," the journey of confronting one's own role in white supremacy is lifelong; it is not a project, or even a process, but a way of living in the world, and the institutions we inhabit often shape our (un)willingness to live this way.[11] Davidson College, established on traditional territory of the Catawba Nation and founded in 1837 in collaboration with the Concord Presbytery, reflects the proslavery attitudes of the original church and the colonial ethic of the school's founding family.[12] The planning, construction, and long-term financial support for the school relied heavily on enslaved labor both on and off campus, and the nineteenth and twentieth centuries saw numerous examples of racial violence.[13]

This piece provides the briefest possible introduction to the college's deplorable history and should push us to recover and recall the existence of parallel histories that exist in our own communities, where Indigenous and Black peoples have been mistreated for centuries.[14] The denial of such histories is critical to a school's ability to provide a "happy" community; as Ahmed argues, happiness can be constructed as a promise that pushes us to embrace certain social goods, sites, and bodies, many of which (particularly in the West) are centered around whiteness.[15] Diversity can be made "happy" only when it is predicated upon the incorporation of those seen as "others," usually by bringing them closer (culturally and discursively) to whiteness, thus, revealing that the happiness of certain community members demands the continued invisibilizing or assimilation of others.[16]

Therefore, for institutions, the work of recognizing these histories is an existential threat—it challenges the foundation of a school's power and disrupts the whitewashed, happy histories it presents to insiders and outsiders alike. Because of this threat, the institution may seek to disrupt the potential for radical intercommunity work, and queerness (whether actually predominantly white or simply assumed to be) provides just such a locus of possible intervention. In other words, universities would rather do just enough to keep the majority of white queers *mostly* happy than address the concerns of racism and white supremacy that pertain to all students of color, regardless of their gender or sexuality. Although many of its peer institutions have begun to take some tangible (though often disappointingly cursory) action toward acknowledging their violent pasts, Davidson College remains strongly rooted in historical denial.[17] So how can queer members of the school (particularly white ones) recognize the institution's use of queer stories and bodies as a tactic to delay or even replace a confrontation with such history? How do white queers learn to confront our own complicity in this institutional incorporation? The following trends offer an entry into addressing these questions.

Belonging or Bust: Common Trends of Incorporation
Surveillance Disguised as Support

Colleges and universities today make it clear through websites, pamphlets, monthly publications, and more that they are committed to the idea of supporting students; they proudly offer counseling services, de-stressing events before final exam season, and even the occasional chance to offer feedback. But what is the reality of student care on campus? What does this alleged support look like, and who does it extend to? At Davidson College, queer students have been invited to respond to multiple needs assessments yet have very little to show for it. We are invited to participate in constant data collection of names, emails, and demographics and to observe increasing staff presence at certain community events. While some might argue that these initiatives indicate a growing attention to student needs, the underlying motive may be more sinister.

About a year ago, I attended a dinner for self-identified trans students organized by the Center for Diversity and Inclusion. Despite it being framed as a student event, staff members from the center were present to introduce the dinner and talk with students until the food arrived. Although the stated reason for their presence was to initiate the (fairly self-explanatory) dinner and engage in community outreach, many students felt that they were being watched and that their attendance at the allegedly confidential event was being tracked and possibly even recorded. Besides eliciting some forced thank yous and strained small talk, this student-staff dynamic implied a level of surveillance that students were not prepared for; several students voiced their discomfort with the situation after the staff left.

The trend of monitoring student spaces can be particularly uncomfortable and dangerous for queer students, many of whom are already wary of publicly identifying themselves as queer or being outed to college staff. Concerns around the surveillance of queer spaces may also be heightened on digital platforms, which is particularly relevant in the current context of COVID-19. As queer organizing and events shift to platforms like Zoom, Instagram, and YouTube, there are fewer protections for students who do not wish to be identified or labeled as queer. These issues reflect concerns about surveillance unfolding at the national level, such as the contention over changing gender markers on identification cards and whether or not this option demonstrates a move toward greater rights and protections for trans people or a federally approved tool for tracking and regulation.[18] Nevertheless, several white staff members and multiple white cisqueer students referenced the event described above as proof of Davidson's progressive culture, often reminding their peers that it was "the first event of its kind." In cases like these, it is wise to be wary; free food, fun gadgets, and superficial acknowledgment may appear great in the moment, but what is the price we may unwittingly pay for them? What ammunition do they provide to the institution?

Rhetoric over Resources

As previously discussed, the rhetoric of diversity is pervasive on college and university campuses, and Davidson College is no exception. The website boasts a plethora of student resources and like many liberal arts schools has a specific section for queer students entitled "LGBTQIA Resources," which focuses primarily on support provided by the Center for Diversity and Inclusion. Although conspicuously absent on this webpage, the Center for Student Health and Well-Being frequently markets itself as the most formalized resource for queer students; perhaps unsurprisingly, it is also a primary example of how the rhetoric of support becomes a stand-in for actual resources. While the language of inclusion is common at the health center, certain staff resist queer students' complaints regarding inaccurate health information they have received there, while simultaneously downplaying student demands for more extensive counseling and medical support over the last few years. The staff's responses to student critiques of the existing resources (or lack thereof) reveal the fragility of the school's rhetoric. When student organizers met with staff representatives in fall 2017 to discuss support issues face-to-face, the response was feeble and underwhelming. In spring 2020, student feedback delivered in the form of manifestos and flyers shocked some white staff members, who considered the approach overly aggressive.

In 2019, I attended an upscale college event and was seated next to a well-known white cis staff member who works at the health center. During the meal, they bragged about a new training opportunity for staff and how it would enhance the center's ability to provide tangible resources for trans students. Having experienced their lack of support firsthand and knowing that this provider had misinformed trans students about medical procedures in the past, I calmly added that the changes they were discussing were the result of student demands finally being heard. Before I could finish, they interrupted me and waved their hand dismissively before saying, "Yes, yes, *they* did fine." The staff member proceeded to explain why it was really their own and their colleague's work that had pioneered this change at the college. Their clear annoyance at the suggestion of student-driven change and their evident disinterest in my opinion (all while claiming to be a reliable resource for queer and even specifically trans students) reminded me not only that this rhetoric of inclusion is deep-seated, but that, at the end of the day, it often takes priority over the actual voices and needs of queer people. This provider is held up as a pillar of the community and an essential resource, mostly by white ciswomen; meanwhile, they and their white colleagues have largely failed to address or indeed even involve themselves in the ongoing struggle for adequate queer health resources and continue to contribute to the erasure of queer people of color and their needs across all areas of campus life.

Promotion without Prioritization

The Center for Diversity and Inclusion, the health center, and some of the administrative bodies circulate most information about college events through emails, flyers, and social media. The constant presence of this information in digital and physical public spaces implies that the resources they advertise will also be available and accessible for students, but that is rarely the case. The publicization of various resources and opportunities focuses almost exclusively on bringing more people into "LGBTQIA-designated" spaces and rarely highlights what is useful *about* those spaces. Even the student resource page discussed previously notes that the "A" in the acronym "LGBTQIA" stands for "asexual and/or ally," thus, placing allies not only alongside but essentially *within* the queer community. The constant focus on queer spaces as sites of education and allyship rather than critical support has everything to do with curating outside percep-tions of queerness and little to do with focusing on and meeting the needs of queer people themselves.

The first iteration of the now-annual campus drag show in March of 2019, for instance, showed the institution's willingness to tokenize queer culture but left many queer students—particularly queer students of color and trans students of many races—feeling uneasy.[19] Part of the controversy stemmed from an Instagram post shared by the college social media team the day after the event on March 31, 2019, which happened to be International Trans Day of Visibility. The original post stated "today's . . . a great time to remember (and say it louder for people in the back) that trans rights are human rights" and included a photograph of a white performer from behind, waving a trans pride flag, with their face hidden. There was no credit for the performer or organizers of the event until students requested the caption be edited, and numerous students (mostly students of color) criticized the performativity of the post in the comments.

davidsoncollege Today's International Transgender Day of Visibility, which is a great time to remember (and say it louder for people in the back) that trans rights are human rights. (Big thank you to @davidsonqanda and @dcunionboard for hosting this event, John Crawford for the 📷 and for @channingtaint and all the other performers for joining us.)

Image 1: Post shared by the official Davidson College Instagram page, showing performer Channing Taint on stage during the drag show. (Photo credit John Crawford.)

These students referenced the school's consistent mistreatment of trans students and called for the administration to adopt proposed changes to increase support (which student organizers had previously shared). They were met with standardized replies (which one student called "copy-and-paste" responses), offering the same resources that students were critiquing, and direct threats from other commenters that took the college hours to remove. Meanwhile, white students and staff (queer and otherwise) continued to celebrate the event as an indication of Davidson's inclusivity for weeks afterward.

Another site of publicity that garners internal and external praise is the provision of gender-neutral bathrooms. Access to appropriate facilities is a serious problem for trans students; the 2018 National School Climate Survey revealed that schools forced 60 percent of trans students to use bathrooms that aligned with the sex on their legal ID.[20] Davidson College, eager to signal their interest in accommodations, unveiled their plan to provide increasingly popular gender-neutral bathrooms in 2019.[21]

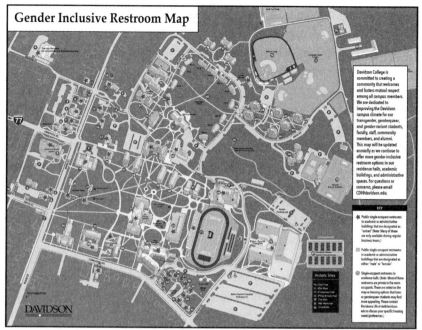

Image 2: Davidson College's map of gender-inclusive restrooms and their (in)accessibility on campus. (Image provided by the Center for Diversity & Inclusion.)

Currently, the map of gender-neutral bathrooms included here (and downloadable from the college website) showcases what seems, at first glance, to be an impressive array of facilities. Upon closer inspection, however, one can see that the majority of these were unisex bathrooms to begin with, built to meet ADA requirements or to save space in smaller buildings. Some are available only during business hours, many are in dormitories (which may not be accessible to students who do not live there), and still others are private—meaning they are attached to a student's room and are not usable by anyone else. Nonetheless, the college publicizes their existence as a powerful, dramatic statement of the school's priorities. In essence, existing facilities are simply being remarketed for strategic purposes, and many students, staff, alumni, and other community members (seeking signs of Davidson's progressive culture) are falling for it—hook, line, and sinker. While the physical safety and emotional well-being of trans students are crucial aspects of the bathroom debate, we must be willing to discuss the limitations of gender-neutral bathrooms within an institutional context, particularly when colleges present them as a "win" for diversity.[22]

Responsible Reckoning: Implications and Future Directions

The trends toward assimilation that are discussed here do not in any way to diminish the antiracist student work that has been and remains a central part of campus life. Since Davidson altered its racist admissions policy and began admitting first African and then African American applicants, beginning in the 1960s and 1970s, Black students have fought against the institution's exclusionary ideologies and paved the way for the contemporary culture of activism on campus.[23] Similarly, it is important to recognize that the administrators who listen to and assist queer students are overwhelmingly Black deans. This essay should not be taken as a critique of them or of any individual actors; rather, it is a critique of the white supremacist structures that we all inhabit and the degree to which the institution as a whole has collapsed any efforts to dismantle those structures into a form more palatable to its predominantly white neoliberal board members, donors, and stakeholders. As previously mentioned, Davidson College has never directly and collectively addressed or reckoned with the pervasive nature of white supremacy on its campus, yet the impacts of that white supremacy on contemporary campus culture remain inescapable.

This conscious silence is precisely why it is critical to address the responsibility of white queer students in these spaces. In these contexts of ever-shifting power dynamics, institutions can appropriate white queer bodies and narratives for their own reputation and prestige. Although we as white queers may not consciously prioritize the interests of our whiteness and queerness over those of other stakeholders, the social instinct to cling to the institution is an inherited legacy of white supremacy and settler colonialism that all white queers, by nature of our whiteness, have felt drawn to or still feel drawn to. As demonstrated here, there are many ways institutions can capitalize on queer identities to build their own reputation without delivering meaningful change, and they will continue to do so until we make it clear that such efforts never have been and never will be enough.

After all, what does it mean for white queers to feel safe, secure, or comfortable on stolen land? What does it mean for us to celebrate inclusion in an institution that relied on enslaved labor and proudly embodied the Confederate cause well into the twentieth century? What does it mean for us to secure our right to gender-neutral spaces when the people who build, clean, and maintain those facilities are perpetually disenfranchised and underserved by the school they serve? For white queers, the danger of searching for happiness in an institution is that we will seek it at the expense of the collective good.[24]

So, what do these patterns and our potential complicity in them mean for our presence within institutions? First, white queers must rid ourselves of the assumption that all queer identities and spaces are inherently freeing for everyone. Instead, we must actively develop liberatory positions by educating ourselves and following the lead of antiracist, anticolonial organizers. This means finding our appropriate place in movements that challenge racist hierarchies and lasting inequality and prioritize the return of Indigenous land.[25]

Second, white queers must reject the institution's attempts to confer on us social capital and must move from seeking institutional acceptance to mobilizing with our nonwhite peers for our collective interests. Particularly for white queers who hold class-, citizenship-, and ability-based privileges, queerness as an identity can feel so all-encompassing that it appears to be the most powerful (and, sometimes, the singular) determinant in our experiences in the world. While that *feeling* may be legitimate, treating queerness as our defining characteristic invisibilizes the whiteness that shapes every aspect of our lives and has the potential to invalidate the struggles of our queer peers of color. Instead, we must shift from developing communities simply based on LGBTQ+ *identity* categories to forming coalitions around a shared queer *politic* that guides us in how to think and act against queer hegemony and assimilation.[26]

There can be no queer liberation without the eradication of all that upholds and relies upon cisheteropatriarchy, including colonialism and white supremacy; the construction of these systems has been and remains inextricably linked, and the same must be true of their destruction. Institutions like Davidson College are mired in racist and settler-colonial histories, and their violent rhetoric of inclusion (as opposed to self-reflection or responsibility) is a logical extension of that past. While all white people within institutions should work to make them less violent for those who already inhabit them, white queers cannot settle for breadcrumbs bestowed at others' expense. Repeated reforms to an institution that is fundamentally rooted in structures of inequity and harm will only temporarily ease the troubles of some and will free no one. After all, who is *us*, if not *all* of us?

As a queer person (and especially as a trans queer), I am often forced to exist in certain margins, but I know that not all margins are created equal.

Even as my queerness pulls me from the center of some spaces, my whiteness reaffirms my place and power in institutions like Davidson College. If, as Ahmed warns, pursuing normative notions of happiness strengthens the hold of whiteness and white privilege, I do not want to feel happy *in* my gendered body or at Davidson—I would rather feel freed *from* both.[27]

Institutions like Davidson College already surveil, mistreat, and remove our queer bodies from our control every day that we exist in a cishet world, and white queers must do everything in our power to prevent the whiteness of our bodies from being weaponized within a white supremacist world. I believe that queer liberation is not only a project of building and holding onto but also of letting go: sometimes, we must be willing to "kill some forms of joy" to open ourselves up to our own potential.[28] In essence, we must be ready and willing to trade the promise of happiness for the possibility of freedom, which means always holding our institutions to a higher standard until we are able to render them obsolete. I believe that in a queer future in which we have actively divested from systems of control, surveillance, and oppression, liberation will be sweeter and more thrilling than happiness ever could have been.

Notes

1   Craig Steven Wilder, *Ebony and Ivy: Race, Slavery, and the Troubled History of America's Universities* (New York: Bloomsbury Press, 2013); Leslie M. Harris, James T. Campbell, and Alfred L. Brophy, *Slavery and the University: Histories and Legacies* (Athens: University of Georgia Press, 2019).

2   Leslie Feinberg, *Transgender Warriors: Making History from Joan of Arc to Dennis Rodman* (Boston: Beacon Press, 1996), 21–30; E. Patrick Johnson, *Appropriating Blackness: Performance and the Politics of Authenticity* (Durham, NC: Duke University Press, 2003).

3   Sara Ahmed, *On Being Included: Racism and Diversity in Institutional Life* (Durham, NC: Duke University Press, 2012), 51–52.

4   Himani Bannerji, *The Dark Side of the Nation: Essays on Multiculturalism, Nationalism and Gender* (Toronto: Canadian Scholars Press, 2000), 37; Rosemary Deem and Jenny Ozga, "Women Managing for Diversity in a Postmodern World," in *Feminist Critical Policy Analysis: A Perspective from Post-Secondary Education*, ed. Catherine Marshall (London: Falmer Press, 1997), 25–40; Ahmed, *On Being Included*, 53.

5   Following conventions of gender and sexuality studies and queer theory, I use queer as an umbrella term to include all individuals who claim LGBTQ+ identities and to refer to the processes of people, places, and things being marked queer by extension. For more on this, see Heather Love, "Queer," *TSQ: Transgender Studies Quarterly* 1, nos. 1–2, (May 2014), 172–76, accessed May 31, 2022, https://read.dukeupress.edu/tsq/article/1/1-2/172/91750/Queer.

6   C. Riley Snorton, *Black on Both Sides: A Racial History of Trans Identity* (Minneapolis: University of Minnesota Press, 2017); Raquel Willis, "Trans Visionaries: How Miss

Major Helped Spark the Modern Trans Movement," them, March 8, 2018, accessed May 31, 2022, https://www.them.us/story/transvisionaries-miss-major.

7   Jasbir Puar, *Terrorist Assemblages: Homonationalism in Queer Times* (Durham, NC: Duke University Press, 2007), 4–11. There is significant scholarship on the relationship between race and queer identity; for further reading on the danger and detriment of white queerness and the power and resilience of nonwhite queer identities and sexual culture, see James Baldwin and Quincy Troupe, *James Baldwin: The Last Interview and Other Conversations* (Brooklyn, NY: Melville House Publishing, 2014); Allan Bérubé, "How Gay Stays White and What Kind of White It Stays," in *The Making and Unmaking of Whiteness*, ed. Birgit Brander Rasmussen, Eric Klinenberg, Irene J. Nexica, and Matt Wray (Durham, NC: Duke University Press, 2001); Gloria Wekker, *The Politics of Passion: Women's Sexual Culture in the Afro-Surinamese Diaspora* (New York: Columbia University Press, 2006).

8   Ahmed, *On Being Included*, 147.

9   Sara Ahmed, "A Phenomenology of Whiteness," *Feminist Theory* 8, no. 2 (August 2007): 149–68, accessed May 31, 2022, https://tinyurl.com/2p8p7nux; Sara Ahmed, "Multiculturalism and the Promise of Happiness," *New Formations* no. 63 (Winter 2007): 121–37, accessed May 31, 2022, https://tinyurl.com/4799kmb4; Ahmed, *On Being Included*.

10   Ahmed, "A Phenomenology of Whiteness."

11   Ibid., 149.

12   Cornelia Rebekah Shaw, *Davidson College: Intimate Facts* (New York: Fleming H. Revell Press, 1923), 11–20; Stone Bynum and Janet Stovall, "BSC Proposes Project '87," *Davidsonian*, 1983; F.A. Sondley and Theodore Davidson, *Alexander-Davidson Reunion, Swannanoa, N.C., August 26, 1911* (Raleigh: North Carolina State Library, 1911), accessed May 31, 2022, https://archive.org/details/alexanderdavidsooosond/mode/2up.

13   Shaw, *Davidson College*; *Always Part of the Fabric* (Davidson, NC: Davidson College Archives and Special Collections, 2015), accessed May 31, 2022, https://davidsona rchivesandspecialcollections.org/archives/always-part-of-the-fabric.

14   The first members of the Davidson family to arrive in the United States (in the late seventeenth and early eighteenth centuries) have long been celebrated as foundational colonists who facilitated the westward expansion of white settlers. There are multiple accounts of blackface, Confederate reenactments, and cross burnings on campus during the nineteenth and twentieth centuries. The school allowed a student club to conduct an imitation lynching of a Black employee in 1920, put on and publicized a blackface minstrel group during the 1920s, and held a popular show in the mid-twentieth century, known as the "Playful Pickaninnies." Unfortunately, many of the sources that describe these events are held only by the Davidson College Archives and Special Collections, and, as such, are rarely accessible to the general public; much of the information about the college's past has been unearthed and highlighted through student projects, such as Jonathan Shepherd-Smith's thesis work and Tian Yi and Sarah Melin's "Davidson Disorientation" initiative, as well as the work of the Davidson College Archives and Special Collections team, including the film *Always Part of the Fabric* and various interviews, oral history transcripts, and collected student papers. More about the history of the college can be found in the department's physical collections or through digitized sources available at their website, accessed July 13, 2022, https://davidsonarchivesandspecialcollections.org/archives.

15   Ahmed, "Multiculturalism and the Promise of Happiness."

16   Ibid., 12–3, 130–31.

17   *Slavery and Justice: Report of the Steering Committee on Slavery and Justice: Brown University Steering Committee on Slavery and Justice* (Providence, RI: Brown University, 2005); Wilder, *Ebony and Ivy.*

18   Dean Spade, *Normal Life: Administrative Violence, Critical Trans Politics, and the Limits of the Law* (Durham, NC: Duke University Press, 2015).

19   This event, hosted by a student organization called Queers & Allies, was well received by many, but it is important to note that multiple queer students I talked to during and after this event believed that Davidson's framing of the event misrepresented and even directly contradicted the reality of the queer experience at the college. Afterward, one of my friends admitted that she was disheartened by the general response to the event; echoing concerns shared by myself and others, she noted that while white cishet students and staff were willing to promote and attend events like this one for food, drinks, and entertainment, those same people are "not ever there to support us when it comes down to it."

20   *Model District Policy on Transgender and Gender Nonconforming Students: Model Language, Commentary and Resources* (Washington, DC: Gay, Lesbian, and Straight Education Network/National Center for Transgender Equality, 2018), accessed May 31, 2022, https://www.glsen.org/blog/gender-neutral-bathrooms-are-radical-not-how-you-think.

21   Jeremy Bauer-Wolf, "More than Just Bathrooms," Inside Higher Ed, July 25, 2018, accessed May 31, 2022, https://tinyurl.com/nhaz482d.

22   This is particularly important in states where access to bathrooms (based on perceived sex or gender) has been legislated and has stirred significant debate, as was the case in North Carolina with the passage of House Bill 2 in 2016.

23   Bynum and Stovall, "BSC Proposes Project '87"; *Always Part of the Fabric.*

24   Ahmed, "Multiculturalism and the Promise of Happiness," 123.

25   Ta-Nehisi Coates, "The Case for Reparations," *Atlantic*, June 2014, accessed May 31, 2022, https://www.theatlantic.com/magazine/archive/2014/06/the-case-for-reparations/361631; Ronald Gamblin, "Land Back! What Do We Mean?," 4Rs Youth Movement, accessed May 31, 2022, http://4rsyouth.ca/land-back-what-do-we-mean.

26   Cathy J. Cohen, "Punks, Bulldaggers, and Welfare Queens: The Radical Potential of Queer Politics?" *GLQ* 3, no. 4 (May 1997), accessed May 31, 2022, https://tinyurl.com/2p9bmp8b; Spade, *Normal Life.*

27   Ahmed, "Multiculturalism and the Promise of Happiness."

28   Ibid., 135.

Refusing Queer Settler Colonialism in Canada

History and Trajectories of a Movement

Kai Rajala

Despite a few moments of convergence, there has never been a sustained relationship of solidarity between Indigenous sovereignty movements and a queer liberation/rights struggle in Canada. For reasons that are perhaps self-evident, Indigenous nations have threatened the legitimacy of the Canadian state by asserting their own inherent rights and title to land occupied by settlers, while queer settlers have reaped the benefits of collaborating with the country as heritors. Though there has certainly existed a history of queers criticizing both the United States and Canada as so-called democratic nations, little urgency has been placed on the status of queer settlers. If a radical queer movement in Canada or elsewhere is ever to succeed at liberating itself from the heterosexist, patriarchal, and carceral structures of the modern nation-state, it must move beyond focusing simply on the way the queer is treated by the state and, instead, interrogate its own complicity within the structure of settler colonialism.

Developing from this introspection, queers must not only challenge the unequal governmental distribution of wealth among settlers under capitalism or any other colonially imposed economy, as well as looking at how the origins of wealth and the rights of Canadians (aka "The Canadian Dream"), including for queer settlers, came at the expense of Indigenous displacement and violent dispossession. To build toward and prefigure a future of collaborative struggle between queer settlers and Indigenous sovereignty movements, the errors of the past—in which a gulf of ignorance and disinformation separated settlers from Indigenous political organizing and knowledge—must be corrected. Exploring this past may help elucidate why we haven't been able to build this relationship and the importance of reattempting to.

In 1969, just as the omnibus Criminal Law Amendment Act was being ushered in by Pierre Elliott Trudeau's cabinet, in an effort to partially decriminalize certain homosexual acts between consenting adults in Canada, the same government was attempting to further dispossess Indigenous peoples of their lands and resources and assimilate them into the nation-state with the white paper proposal.[1] This concurrence helped form the hypothesis of much my research on the matter: i.e., that the rise of the gay rights movement in Canada was inextricably tied to the suppression of Indigenous title and sovereignty due to the actions of the Liberal government at the time. While Indigenous groups pushed back against the white paper, what followed the criminal law code reforms was an identity-based gay liberation movement that emerged as both a reaction and a response to the government's shifting attitudes and geared itself toward state recognition and rights acquisition. Even though several chapters of the gay liberation movement had employed antistatist/communist lenses in their activism, this essay asks whether gay liberation in Canada ever had any concept of anticolonialism as a theory and movement. I am invested in locating historical points of contact between gay liberation and Indigenous resurgence movements—as well as points where the two movements remain incompatible and where they are able to imagine collaborative prefiguration. The act of looking back allows us to forge forward.

The 1969 White Paper and the Criminal Law Amendment Act

At the end of the 1960s, a decade in Canada that was characterized by the radicalism of social movements and the statecraft of liberal policy reform, there were, concurrently, two distinct attempts at assimilation taking place: that of Indigenous peoples and that of homosexual men. To forge a future of middle-class prosperity and expand its project of occupation, the socially liberal politics of the Canadian state sought to deal with subalterns, people who challenged both the social reproduction of Canadian society and posed a threat to Canadian state sovereignty.[2] While, as citizens, gay men had never been completely outside of its legal structure, the criminalization of white homosexual men by the Canadian state meant that they occupied a grey area in terms of social acceptability and mobility. The incorporation of white homosexual men into the fold of nationhood was a decision that ensured the Canadian state could expand the viability of its capitalist economy and maintain its assumed authority and legitimacy in the minds of its subjects. It was also a political move that worked rather seamlessly; homosexual men were, in fact, so eager to penetrate into the body politic of the Canadian nation that they named a periodical after it.[3]

Settler colonialism is not only a social and psychological project, however; it operates primarily in a material way, relying on access to land and resources to continue the process of capitalist accumulation by colonial dispossession. Indigenous nations stood in the way of Canada's access to that land. During the transformative era of the 1960s, Canadian government actors were retiring the overtly genocidal tactics of segregation, starvation, and eradication that their predecessors had employed against Indigenous peoples, opting instead for more covert ways of dealing with sovereignty claims, by way of legislation that would effectively attempt to trade title to land for Canadian citizenship. When Pierre Trudeau was elected prime minister of Canada in 1968, he promised to enact his vision of a "Just Society," a plan that would incorporate those previously left out of the project of Canadian nation-building.[4] Aspects of this strategy were to be achieved through the Criminal Law Amendment Act (Bill C-150), as well as the proposed 1969 white paper. The white paper, introduced by Pierre Trudeau's government and then minister of Indian affairs Jean Chrétien, sought to eliminate Aboriginal treaty and title rights by abolishing the Indian Act as it stood and assimilating Indigenous people into Canadian society. The trade was essentially land for citizenship. Indigenous radicals involved in the burgeoning Red Power movement in Canada understood the Indian Act to be a mechanism of colonial control and, thus, sought to abolish it. But they understood the white paper to be just as disenfranchising and so their overarching purpose was to regain control of their lands and communities through self-governance and repatriation.[5]

The growing Red Power movement was in part a result of Indigenous people's refusal of the insulting tactics of Trudeau's government and the Canadian state. At the same time, the Canadian gay liberation movement emerged as a response to the Criminal Law Amendment Act, as queers demanded increased rights and accommodation from the state, encouraged by the Stonewall riots in the United States and by the olive branch Canada had extended with its progressive reforms. At this historical moment, there was certainly room for the radical potential of settlers and Indigenous people uniting against the assimilatory actions that Pierre Trudeau's government attempted to enact toward each group, but no coalition materialized. Canadian gay activists claimed their mission was to fight for the "liberation of gays from their personal and collective ghettos."[6]

Thus, the struggle for gay liberation, like many other siloed identity-based movements at the time, was framed as a single issue that was complementary to but separate from the liberation struggles of other groups. At this time, gay liberation movements were firmly rejecting assimilation into heterosexual society. Yet this notion of gay liberation as a separate struggle failed to take into account the existence of queer Indigenous, Black, and people of color who were also fighting for rights and self-determination from different positions. The gay rights movement also demonstrated the inability of the queer settler imaginary at the time to understand its own role as a beneficiary and agent in the colonial project. The settler political climate of the late 1960s and early 1970s in Canada manifested in the isolation of radical movements into separate struggles.

Searching for Solidarities between Gay Liberation and Red Power in Canada

In the mid to late 1960s, Vancouver, BC, was a hotbed for emerging counterculture movements and sectarian leftist struggles. Even before the American Indian Movement emerged in the United States, the Native Alliance for Red Power formed in Vancouver, drawing inspiration and a theoretical framework of anti-imperialism from the Black Panther Party in the United States.[7] The influence of the Black Panther Party helped shift the understanding that some Indigenous political organizers in Canada had of themselves as victims of racism at the hands of white Canadian society toward what they described as "an internal colony of the Canadian imperialist settler-state."[8] Heavily influenced by settler Marxist movements, some Indigenous activists began to articulate an argument that the system of reservations imposed by Canada produced the same imperial oppression and occupation that the Canadian state inflicted on its external colonies. While Indigenous people within Canada had always carried a long tradition of political opposition against their oppressors, who regulated every aspect of their existence, other disenfranchised groups, including gays, were only beginning to organize as a result of a newfound political awakening and unification around what they perceived to be the shared oppression of a heterosexist society.

Records and testimonies indicate that, much like the Red Power movement, Canadian gay movements were in conversation with and evolving alongside other liberatory groups. In 1971, after significant assessment, the League for Socialist Action in Canada issued a statement announcing its solidarity with gay liberation.[9] The statement indicated the belief that homosexuality was a natural occurrence, and that along with the women's movement and the antiwar movement, socialists could agree that gays were subjugated under the capitalist economic system. Meanwhile, in the United States, from the Bay Area to Philadelphia, there were clear traces of comradery and solidarity between gay liberation and Black Power in the late 1960s.[10] In 1970, an invitation from the Black Panther Party was extended to members of the Gay Liberation Front to attend the Revolutionary People's Constitutional Convention in Philadelphia in September of that year.[11] The attendees were queers of color who identified as part of the Third World diaspora, and they represented Third World gay liberation from Chicago at the convention.[12] Members of the American Indian Movement were also present at the convention. Regardless of whether groups within the broader gay liberation were communicating with Indigenous liberation struggles, they were sharing space and revolutionary community in convergences that sought to raise collective consciousness and inform the independent struggles involved.

While the criminal law code reforms of 1969 under Prime Minister Pierre Trudeau (which decriminalized aspects of homosexual sex) did little to shift societal attitudes toward the gay lifestyle or to curb police violence and crackdowns on bathhouses and bars, in the eyes of many it was the beginning of the state's acceptance and incorporation of gays into its narrative of multiculturalism. The Canadian state showing the slightest interest in gay issues had the effect of reducing the militancy of the movement since, for some, their goals were already on their way to being achieved. When more radical factions of the gay movement appeared in Canada, they were short-lived and fizzled out, as more conservative and assimilationist groups, such as the Canadian Gay Activist Alliance, which was primarily fighting for rights and recognition instead of liberation, drew many of those interested away from the far left of the movement.[13]

Self-Determination, Settler Colonialism, and Gay Liberation

The gay movement in Canada was seemingly unaware of Indigenous struggles for sovereignty, but it had encountered the principles of autonomy and self-determination elsewhere. By being forced to reckon with issues like abortion, due in part to its decriminalization in the 1969 criminal law code reforms, as well as the community proximity and associations between gay men and lesbian women, the gay liberation movement understood itself to be struggling alongside women's liberation. In fact, gay liberation often spoke out against the attempts by men to determine women's health and control their bodies and acknowledged the specific oppression experienced by lesbian women to be a "double oppression."[14] Perhaps the most promising introduction to the concept of self-determination came from the Front de Libération Homosexuel in Montréal, which drew many of its political positions, as gay sovereigntists, from the Front de Libération du Québec (FLQ). After a reciprocal FLQ and Gay Alliance Toward Equality (GATE) teach-in, a GATE member declared in a full-page spread in Vancouver's *Gay Tide* newspaper that supporting Quebec's "democratic right to self-determination ... in no way negates or violates [gay liberation's] single issue focus."

Self-determination as a concept was new to those organizing within the struggle for gay liberation in Canada; however, militant queers saw that those fighting for the separation of Quebec from the rest of Canada favored self-governance as a people and subsequently applied the concept to those who sought bodily autonomy from state repression—that is to say, "self-determination for women and gays." The position paper even acknowledged the state's "assimilation" and declared that "as for gays, blacks, and native people, a whole anti-Quebec ideology to justify ... and to make acceptable the historically imposed inequality of the Quebecois, has been created."[15] Unfortunately, while it seemed to go as far as mentioning the conquest of Quebec by the British in 1759, the paper drew no further comparisons of the assimilation of gays and the Quebec people to the attempts of colonization and assimilation of Indigenous people by the Canadian state. These positions are also part of a problematic trend that fails to challenge the Quebec people's own understanding of themselves as colonized by English Canada, when, in fact, they too are agents of settler colonialism.

Evidence of any encounters between the Canadian gay liberation movements and Red Power in the archives are scarce. The manifesto published during the North American Conference of Homophile Associations on August 28, 1969, mentions a "general attempt to oppress all minorities and keep them powerless" and names "the struggles of black, feminist, Spanish-American, the Indian, the hippie, the young, the student, the worker, and other victims of oppression and prejudice."[16] In fall 1974, a Canadian gay magazine drew attention to a militant action undertaken by several hundred Indigenous people and supporters in Ottawa, the nation's capital. Ron Daymon wrote a piece republished in the *Body Politic* that underlined the importance of the direct-action tactics of a Native People's

Caravan, which offered an alternative to requesting rights from the state. Daymon argued that the gay movement could learn from these protests.[17]

Former GATE Vancouver organizer Don Hann does not remember any Indigenous leftist comrades or Indigenous gay men in and around GATE's organizing and social circles, nor was there a broader understanding of their unique struggles. "Settler colonialism wasn't a concept back in the 1960s," he recalls.[18] While the observation that the term "settler colonialism" had not yet permeated the gay movement was probably true across the landscape of settler politics, it is still possible that the relationships of solidarity between white gay settlers and Indigenous peoples could have and did, in fact, develop. But this anecdotal piece of obliviousness allows us to interpret the extent to which the social fabric of white settler society was saturated by a colonial mindset that rendered it difficult for even the most well-meaning settler liberation struggle to empathize with those who existed outside of or in complete resistance to the imposed Canadian state.

When exploring why Canadian radical queers were not organizing alongside or discussing the articulations of the burgeoning Red Power movement of the late 1960s, it is perhaps helpful to understand the sociopolitical context in which these struggles were emerging. Besides the phenomenon of the "gay ghetto," which kept the gay community insular and atomized from the rest of society, settler colonialism as a political theory and a framework for understanding the process of colonialism, occupation, and the dispossession of land was still developing. Settler colonialism was not widely accepted as a framework of analysis by the left in Canada until much later. Leftists in North America largely identified as being antiwar and anti-imperialist, and when they did draw from anticolonialism, it was usually in reference to Frantz Fanon and often misapplied or misappropriated.[19] The usage of the critical term "settler colonialism," particularly in Canada, came about, most importantly, as a result of the material struggles of land defense and self-determination against the state led by Indigenous peoples.[20] As a theory, it has been expanded upon by historians, sociologists, and Indigenous theorists.

Twenty-First Century Pink Statecraft and the Erasure of Genocide

The twenty-first century saw a new marriage of sorts between queers and the Canadian colonial project. For queer settlers, the promise of recognition in the eyes of the progressive state did not end with the passing of the Civil Marriage Act in 2005. In the years that followed Justin Trudeau's election, assimilationist gays, lesbians, and transgender settlers who already desired upward mobility within the capitalist order were offered even more fruits from the state.[21] In his role as prime minister, Trudeau marched with his family at the head of a slew of Pride celebrations from 2016 to 2019, emphasizing the importance of family values. In response to the violent repression that queers had endured at the hands of the Canadian policing, Trudeau performed a very public and very emotional apology.[22] In March 2019, when President Donald Trump moved to ban transgender troops from the US military, the Canadian Armed Forces (CAF) overhauled its existing policy to extend a hand and "welcome [Canadians] of all sexual orientations and gender identities."[23] Like the US military under the Barack Obama presidency, the revised policy incentivized transgender Canadians to enlist in the army, offering support services for those who wished to medically transition, as well as insisting that the CAF would create an environment where transgender members were free from harassment and discrimination.

In the months leading up to Canada 150 in 2017, the sesquicentennial celebration of the Canadian state's confederation, I began to observe, record, and think through the ways that Canada was marketing itself as progressive, tolerant, and (perhaps unsurprisingly) gay-friendly. On the now-defunct official website of Canada 150, the narrative boasted about how the Canadian state—at least when under the control of what is often referred to as its "natural governing party," the federal Liberals—had been advanced in its efforts to decriminalize and legalize aspects of homosexuality throughout the twentieth century and beyond. Plotted along the interactive and all too self-congratulatory timeline of selective (if not outright revisionist) historical events was the aforementioned 1969 Criminal Law Amendment Act, as well as the legalization of gay marriage in Canada (the Civil Marriage Act), which passed nearly a decade before similar legislation in the UK and the US. This specific focus on Canada's progress in lesbian, gay, and transgender rights, particularly as a way to obfuscate state violence, is sometimes referred to as pinkwashing.

The response to Canada 150 from certain Indigenous organizers and allied settlers was one of anticolonial resistance and of pushing back against the rhetoric of progress and celebration, rebranding the celebration as "150 years of genocide." While normative gays and lesbians continued to collude with the Canadian state, radical queer groups had spent the better half of the previous decade loosening the soil of the settler imaginary by troubling the narrative of Canada as a welcoming, neutral safe haven for sexual and gender minorities.[24] Instead, they had insisted, through demos and publications, that Canada has been no less capitalist than any other nation-state and no less violent to those it criminalized and saw as being in the way of its expansive and extractive project.

If 2017 was a celebration of a false narrative, then 2019 was another chance for Canada to proudly reconstruct history and lay claim to the idea that it was an early adopter of rights for the queer settler. In anticipation of the fiftieth anniversary of the 1969 criminal law code reforms, Canada announced it would issue a commemorative dollar coin, quite literally a token of gay capitalism.[25] Beyond mere pinkwashing, Trudeau was, in more ways than one, continuing the project of assimilation, the fabled construction of the "Just Society" that his father had begun in the late sixties. Among several disruptions, queer activists and academics, including myself, gathered in Ottawa in March 2019 for the "Anti-69" conference, to trouble the mythology of omnibus Criminal Code reform bill and to shed light on the Canadian state's ongoing crimes on Indigenous people within Canada and abroad.[26]

Queers against Canada: Refusing State Recognition

Though we can only speculate on the radical potential of the combined forces of the gay liberation and Red Power movements as they emerged simultaneously in 1960s and 1970s Canada, a queer anticolonialism exists today among the queer, trans, and Two Spirit Indigenous youth on the frontlines of resistance against the Canadian state. The current generation is leading the #ShutDownCanada and Land Back movements, as well as efforts to abolish the Canadian colonial police force, the Royal Canadian Mounted Police (RCMP), and defund municipal police bodies in major Canadian cities. A radical political analysis rooted in a necessity for Indigenous sovereignty has been gaining momentum, as radical queer and anarchist organizers continue to learn alongside and build relationships of solidarity with Indigenous peoples and nations. As Canada moves to secure land for resource extraction amid a global pandemic and pacify conversations around repatriation and abolishing the police, all settlers, but especially queers, must commit to push back against their own governance structures, which will continue to erase voices of resistance and mount their own narrative of benevolence.[27]

In his book *Red Skin, White Masks*, Glen Coulthard applies the theoretical concept of the "politics of recognition" to post-1969 Canadian society, expanding upon Frantz Fanon's ideas about the shift from the overt violence of colonial control over colonized subjects to recognition and accommodation as a form of state management.[28] Coulthard concludes that because rights and permission are distributed by the state, the cycle of colonization continues, and the rights must be rejected. He extends this strategy of rejecting state management to other "subaltern groups, not just the colonized," which would include the working class, people of color, and gender and sexual minorities.[29] Because the Canadian state privileges the treatment of respectable and middle-class gay, lesbian, and transgender settlers at the expense of Indigenous people, it makes sense for queers to turn this recognition and accommodation provided by Canada on its head.

The practice of queer refusal of the settler colonial project is not an ideological attainment or position but, instead, an ongoing commitment to the disruption of settlement and the economies that sustain it. Radical queer settlers who choose to align ourselves with Indigenous nations and peoples whose lands we continue to occupy and whose stolen wealth we continue to benefit from must start by refusing the recognition and the gifts that nation-states offer us, as well as actively disrupting the ways in which our identities are used to advance Canada's myth of progress. Armed with the lessons of the past, we must help to enact decolonization in its fullest, most literal sense, moving beyond the perfunctory gestures of acknowledgment and toward outcomes that are material. This project is one that destabilizes queer utopian ideals and settler agency in imagining alternatives to capitalism and colonial governance and, instead, centers the repatriation of lands and the reclamation of laws, Indigenous governance structures, and Indigenous economies that have been suppressed. It is a commitment to action and relationship building, to solidarity and learning. Beyond the body politic, a disembodied politic of sorts that rejects the narratives of queer progress and challenges the very nature of queer identity formation exists. The greatest threat to the Canadian settler state, then, should not be seen as the radical queer's lifestyle or rejection of heterosexist society and social and sexual reproductive norms but the rejection of state power and capitalist accumulation.

Notes

1   An earlier version of this essay, "Retracing Queer Settler Complicity within Canadian Nation-State Formation," was presented in April 2018 at the "Toward a Queer Abolitionist Movement" conference at University of North Carolina, Asheville, and was later reworked into "Searching for Solidarities between Gay

Liberation and Indigenous Struggles for Self-Determination in 1970s 'Canada'"
for the "Anti-69: Against the Mythologies of the 1969 Criminal Law Code Reform"
conference in Ottawa in March 2019.

2   Lorenzo Veracini, "'Settler Colonialism': Career of a Concept," *Journal of Imperial
and Commonwealth History* 41, no. 2 (June 2013): 315, accessed May 31, 2022, https://
tinyurl.com/yck632z5. Veracini describes how settler colonialism requires its
subjects to conform and to help generate its core traits: "mononuclear familial
relations and reproduction, and the production of assets transferable across
generations."

3   *The Body Politic*, which was published from 1971 to 1987, was one of Canada's first
gay magazines.

4   "The Just Society will be one in which the rights of minorities will be safe from the
whims of intolerant majorities. . . . The Just Society will be one in which our Indian
and Inuit populations will be encouraged to assume the full rights of citizenship
through policies which will give them both greater responsibility for their own
future and more meaningful equality of opportunity"; Pierre Elliott Trudeau, "The
Just Society", June 10, 1968, accessed May 31, 2021, https://www.edu.gov.mb.ca/
k12/cur/socstud/foundation_gr6/blms/6-4-4a.pdf.

5   For more information on the white paper and Indigenous political organizing
in 1960s Canada, see Arthur Manuel, *Unsettling Canada: A National Wake Up
Call* (Toronto: Between the Lines, 2015), 29–39; Paul Tennant, *Aboriginal Peoples
and Politics: The Indian Land Question in British Columbia 1849–1989* (Vancouver:
University of British Columbia Press, 1990).

6   "Gay Rights Now!" *Body Politic*, July–August 1975, 16.

7   Ray Bobb, "Red Power and Socialist Study: 1967–1975" (2012), accessed March 22,
2021, unavailable May 31, 2022, https://revolutionary-initiative.com/2012/04/26/
overview-of-red-power-movement-in-vancouver-1967-1975.

8   Bobb, "Red Power and Socialist Study"; Bryan Palmer, *Canada's 1960s: The Ironies of
Identities in a Rebellious Era* (Toronto: University of Toronto Press, 2009), 378–79.

9   "The Gay Movement 1971: A Tentative Assessment," in *Gay Liberation in Canada:
A Socialist Perspective*, Socialist History Project, accessed May 31, 2022, http://www.
socialisthistory.ca/Docs/1961-/Gay/Gay-Lib-3.htm.

10   Jared Leighton, "'All of Us Are Unapprehended Felons': Gay Liberation, the Black
Panther Party, and Intercommunal Efforts against Police Brutality in the Bay Area,"
Journal of Social History 52, no. 3, (Spring 2019): 860–85.

11   Leslie Feinberg, "Early Left-Wing Liberation: 'Unity with All the Oppressed,'"
Lavender and Red, Part 75, Workers World, October 5, 2006, accessed May 31, 2022,
https://www.workers.org/2006/us/lavender-red-75.

12   "Oral History: Watch Joel Hall Talk About Third World Gay Liberation," Out History,
accessed May 31, 2022, http://outhistory.org/exhibits/show/queer-bronzeville/
part-4/gay-liberation.

13   Robert Rothon, "Vancouver's Gay Liberation Front," *Xtra Magazine*,
October 22, 2008, accessed May 31, 2022, https://xtramagazine.com/power/
vancouvers-gay-liberation-front-14389.

14   "Sister Struggles: Gay Liberation and Women's Liberation," *Gay Tide*, accessed
December 2018, The ArQuives.

15   Gay Alliance Toward Equality, "Gay Liberation and Quebec Self-Determination,"
Gay Tide, September 1977, accessed December 2018, The ArQuives.

16   Archival material, accessed in December 2018, The ArQuives.

17   Ron Dayman, "A More Militant Movement," *Body Politic*, November–December 1974, accessed December 2018, The ArQuives; for more information on the 1974 Native People's Caravan, see "Native People's Caravan" Canadian Encyclopedia, accessed May 31, 2022, https://www.thecanadianencyclopedia.ca/en/article/native-people-s-caravan.

18   Don Hann, personal communication with author, March 5, 2019.

19   Bryan Palmer, *Canada's 1960s: The Ironies of Identities in a Rebellious Era* (Toronto: University of Toronto Press, 2009), 248.

20   Notable Indigenous struggles that doubtless informed this theoretical articulation were the rejection of the 1969 white paper, the 1969 protest by the Kanien'kéhaka (Mohawk) of Akwesasne, the 1990 Mohawk community defense of Kanesatake (the so-called Oka Crisis), as well as the 1995 Gustafsen Lake standoff between the Ts'peten Defenders and the RCMP.

21   Justin Trudeau, who was elected as prime minister in November 2015, overturning nearly a decade of Conservative leadership in Canada, ran his first campaign on a socially liberal platform that emphasized the need for diversity throughout government and society. The Liberal government's agenda was also purportedly focused on renewing and repairing the fraught relationship between Canada and the Indigenous people, a gargantuan task his father Pierre Trudeau had spent most of his political career attempting to address.

22   Kathleen Harris, "'Our Collective Shame': Trudeau Delivers Historic Apology to LGBT Canadians," CBC News, November 28, 2017, accessed May 31, 2022, https://www.cbc.ca/news/politics/homosexual-offences-exunge-records-1.4422546.

23   Kathleen Harris, "Canada's Military Issues New Policies to Welcome Transgender Troops as Trump Insists on Ban," CBC News, March 19, 2019, accessed May 31, 2022, https://www.cbc.ca/news/politics/military-transgender-caf-policy-1.4978669.

24   Radical queer organizing in Canada in the past decade included the Pink Bloc out of Vancouver; see "Pink Bloc Intervention in Rally for Civil Liberties in Vancouver, July 17 2010," Vancouver Media Co-op, July 29, 2010, accessed May 31, 2022, https://vancouver.mediacoop.ca/blog/pink-bloc/4321; Queers against Israeli Apartheid, accessed May 31, 2022, https://quaiavancouver.wordpress.com/2014/08/07/quaia-vancouver-statement-on-vqff-pinkwashing; as well as Black Lives Matter Toronto, accessed May 31, 2022, https://www.blacklivesmatter.ca.

25   Dean Beeby, "New Loonie to Commemorate End of Laws against Homosexuality," CBC News, December 20, 2018, accessed May 31, 2022, https://www.cbc.ca/news/politics/coin-loonie-royal-canadian-mint-cabinet-trudeau-homosexuality-1.4954537.

26   For more information on the "Anti-69" conference, see Anti-69 Network, accessed May 31, 2022, https://anti-69.ca.

27   The process of settler-colonial expansion is considered "essential work."

28   Glen Sean Coulthard, *Red Skin, White Masks* (Minneapolis: University of Minnesota Press, 2014) 31–49.

29   Karl Gardner and Devin Clancy, "From Recognition to Decolonization: An Interview with Glen Coulthard," *Upping the Anti* 19, August 2, 2017, accessed May 31, 2022, https://uppingtheanti.org/journal/article/19-from-recognition-to-decolonization.

Reportbacks from Militant Queers

"Gay Shame Hates Everything"

Anarcho-Trans/Queer Politics against Neocolonial Conquest

Stasha Lampert and Toshio Meronek

San Francisco has long held a reputation for being a socially and politically liberal-progressive place. In the imagination of outsiders, it's a city broadly accepting of counterculture, home to prominent figures in the arts and impactful social movements, all topped with rainbow flags. Corporate media, politicians, and religious leaders outside and inside the city still embrace the optics of progress, and those in power use San Francisco's left utopian image to discipline or disappear the left, radical minority in the city to embed their own center-right or right-wing politics. Liberal Democratic rulers have long held power in San Francisco, and in many cases, because of this, social inequalities exist or are widening, particularly along lines of race and class. The establishment has worsened oppressive dynamics through a craven insistence on satisfying the appetites of capitalist vultures and property owners, while innovating institutional violence by lending it a facade in the form of liberal diversity and tolerance theater. As socioeconomic pressures and contradictions mount, the demands of radical trans/queer politics remain essential—dissent is kept alive by organizers in the city who have been refusing for years to be placated with hollow compromises or to be silenced.

In 2001, Gay Shame San Francisco started out as a resistance to the increasing corporatization of queer politics. (One of the most obvious symbols of this was the turn in the 1990s toward apolitical Pride parades and away from commemorating the 1969 antipolice riots at the Stonewall Inn in New York City.)[1] From its inception, the group has planned and engaged in direct action as one of its primary tactics for confronting oppressive forces. The group makes decisions using a consensus model—a strategic, political choice in contrast to defaulting to majority rule, winner-takes-all

Image 1: Walk of Shame to the second annual Gay Shame Awards, 2003.

regimes of decision-making. As much as the group's enemies and detractors in neoliberal San Francisco try to characterize its members as wholly white, moneyed twenty-somethings fresh from academia, in the recent meetings we've attended, the most consistent membership is nonwhite, with an age range of people in their twenties to people in their seventies. There's a vibrant dynamic between newer members and members who have been active for years. As new members begin to take on more of the group's essential functions, older members cede space for newcomers to take on all aspects of the work, including proposing new political projects, making propaganda, and running social media—responsibilities that often end up stodgily stratified in organized groups.

Gay Shame's organizing work over the years has been a bold example of a radical queer political practice that tackles the most pressing contemporary problems faced by queers in San Francisco, which some nonprofits have criticized as too broad to be considered "queer issues." Gay Shame sees this wide focus as integral: trans/queer people won't survive unless our resistance includes assessing the ravages of capital everywhere, starting with how that violence manifests in gentrified and hyperpoliced neighborhoods and cities.

In many ways, the San Francisco Bay Area has been a proving ground for a menacing representation-industrial complex, as administered by corporatized, 501(c)(3)-centric gay politics. In 2022, the realpolitik ruling the region promotes vacuous, fungible versions of marginalized people and identities for profit and institutional cache. The representation politics and its obsession with optics above all else has also facilitated and provided cover for some of the most violent policies of neoliberal austerity regimes, often in the form of brand activists with deliberately curated and cultivated cults of personality who may have some marginal connection to left movements. These are the people who cozy up to more traditional figures in power. Today's nightmarish new normal involves elites using trans/queer identities to bestow pride upon the act of working for—or collaborating with—the military, weapons manufacturers, police, and dystopian tech and financial companies. Meanwhile, whole blocks, neighborhoods, and cities are being emptied of any person of a nonwhite complexion whose salary falls below six figures. Incidentally, this displacement, particularly in San Francisco, has impacted a disproportionate number of trans/queer people of color who live and work in marginalized conditions and professions, including the work and legacies of historically significant movement figures and moments (in the Bay Area, for example: ACT UP San Francisco, Compton's Cafeteria Riot, June Jordan), which are celebrated and, frankly, *used* by the elite and its supporters, while queer people of color's continued existence in the city is rendered untenable.

These are the neoliberal consequences Gay Shame warned about and resisted when corporate nonprofit careerists hatched their "Gay Marriage or Bust" campaigns of the early 2000s. When establishment politicos chose gay marriage as the community's most pressing issue, it sucked up resources and sidelined radical organizing power that came out of fights around, for example, HIV/AIDS and queer anti-imperialist solidarity across borders. To liberal onlookers who had long understood the "LGBT community" as a monolith, Gay Shame's critique may have seemed like a benign point of conflict among the gays, at the time.[2] Politically, however, the co-optation strategically maligned the more radical demands of queers organizing against police harassment or the malicious neglect experienced during the AIDS crisis—both of which signaled the critical need for steep institutional and societal change. Put another way, energy directed toward an assimilationist issue like gay marriage followed the usual trajectory of settler state political theater: the optics of representation and acceptance were used to further consolidate state power and the state's authority to confer legitimacy on those it had brutalized.

As an anarchist-leaning group, the centrality and necessity of anticapitalism and decolonization are at the heart of what informs Gay Shame's antiassimilationist analysis of the variety of issues the group organizes around, including the emerging dominance of the tech sector, gentrification, the policing of unhoused people, and the perpetual betrayal at the hands of politicians and bureaucrats, among others. In many ways, Gay Shame is just repeating and reapplying what Black, Indigenous, trans/queer radicals have been saying for centuries. In spectacular fashion, the group continues to collaboratively strategize ways of resisting the elimination of trans/queer Black and brown people in San Francisco and beyond.

The Gentrifiers Have Names and Addresses

Many of Gay Shame's actions over the past several years have involved demystifying the goings-on that makes gentrification possible, profitable, and continuous. There are a variety of political actors in the city—including well-meaning advocates at nonprofits—who rely on corporate models that maintain the state and the state of things or hide behind unintelligible, invisible "market processes" that *regrettably no one can ever do anything about because our hands are tied, or maybe we should wait a few more decades—oh, well.* The force of this vacuum is overwhelming and totalizing enough that it has become an essential part of Gay Shame's work and that of other antigentrification organizations, however arduous and Sisyphean, to continually recontextualize and reiterate that gentrifiers are people making avoidable decisions that wreak havoc on our collective livelihoods. This effort to historicize might involve putting someone's face on a flyer—with sarcastic but politically thoughtful commentary about their role in accelerating the widespread housing crisis that is a profitable endeavor for a wealthy few—or it might even involve planning pickets at their events.

Actions have recently targeted an emerging, astroturfed advocacy front for real estate industrialists posturing as progressive housing activists. These groups and actors self-describe as "pro-housing advocates," and, in 2014, started popularizing the "Yes in My Back Yard" (YIMBY) movement. The acronym YIMBY is meant to highlight their alleged opposition to the "Not in My Back Yard" (NIMBY) antidevelopment tendencies of some residents, usually homeowners who work against changes to their neighborhoods. NIMBYs, at the time of this writing, are probably best exemplified by the self-appointed neighborhood watchmen of Nextdoor.com, who are quick to call police on nonwhite neighbors and publicly rage about "quality of life" issues. This makes NIMBYs a convenient bogeyman against which YIMBYs can position themselves as nonregressive, coolly policy-driven, and favorable to popular needs like shelter. NIMBYs are a force the YIMBYs blame for lack of affordable housing due to frequent

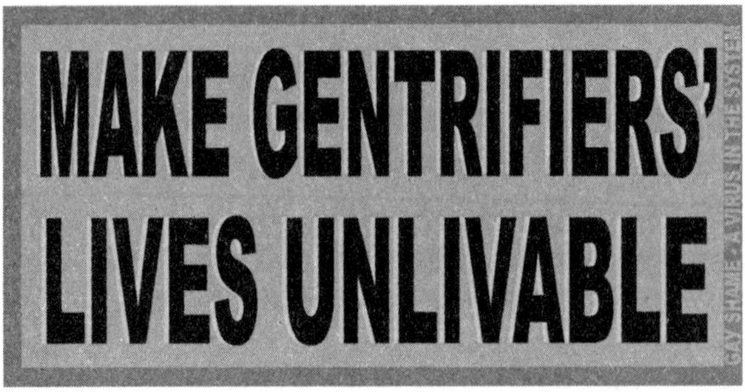

Image 2: An antigentrification sticker produced and distributed by Gay Shame, 2017.

homeowner opposition to new developments, usually for aesthetic or property value–related reasons. YIMBYs perform this faux opposition despite their own propensity to support primarily luxury housing developments in neighborhoods already vulnerable to displacement, justified through trickle-down economics, which belies their self-designation.[3] Their campaigns are funded by a wealthy real estate donor mill made up of those who stand to benefit from market rate developments that are unaffordable for nonelites. Among the YIMBY and gentrifier ranks are the tech entrepreneurs who like to dismantle existing meager services or infrastructure, force people onto a publicly funded app to access whatever social programs remain, up charge them for the inconvenience, then finally starve the people who staff the services so that they can continue to be unprofitable to all but their most esteemed investors. Then, there are the politicians who are *really, truly for the people but just can't stop voting for more cops and more luxury condos, because it's essential that they win the next election,* after which point they can't help but get back in there and vote for even more cops and luxury condos. Finally, there are the landlords and developers, who are usually salivating behind the curtains over the millions of dollars of market speculation windfall that could be theirs, if only they could get rid of pesky tenants and the poors, with their evil rent control and their contemptible need for shelter. This is just a short list and is hardly comprehensive, but it roughly demonstrates the landscape in which Gay Shame formulates their actions and targets.

Dress to Express Die-versity
Pride's first incarnation in June 1970 was a day of protest to mark the one-year anniversary of the Stonewall riots. Today, June's Pride Month is described by many corporations, tourism boards, and nonprofits soliciting donations as Pride *season*, stretching roughly from early spring to

Image 3: A banner for the 2017 Gay Shame Awards, which took place in the Castro.

fall. The 2017 Gay Shame Awards updated the group's early tradition of celebrating Pride Month by awarding the city's most noxious political and business establishment homos and their allies a mock trophy via a street pageant ceremony and presentation. Taking place in the streets of the Castro, highlighted by a large banner reading, "No Pride in Cops, Condos, Capital," the action provided a space for costumes, performance, music, and light-hearted mayhem with the intention of highlighting businesses, events, people, and venues that foreclose the possibility of a vibrant life in the city. One such award was "Most Likely to Host a Klan Rally," presented to Beaux, a nightclub in the Castro. The LGBTQ film festival Frameline, longtime proud beneficiary of Zionist money, got the "Pinkwashing Drone Joystick Circle Jerk" award. Bold, colorful, but mostly plainly worded shit talk of this variety is part of demystifying the violence these actors commit in their various lines of work. It's no surprise, for instance, that the award for "Throwing Black People in the Big House" went to neoliberal California state legislator Scott Weiner, who had just that year gone out of his way to get a Black woman jailed for allegedly stealing his cell phone: a small personal amenity that he could have quite easily replaced and then moved on with his life with relative ease.

In general, Gay Shame's actions attempt alternatives to the "march and chant" style of protest. The format provides an opportunity to use play and levity—drawing from the general affect of *camp*—to confront otherwise grave and devastating issues. The group also often engages its targets by simply clowning them, which makes fun of the facade of serious respectability many establishment figures try to put on, if not outright mandate, in the exclusive spaces of public comment, appearances, or presentations. With these vital, playful displays, Gay Shame tries to compose and perform visions of the world in opposition to the dead world that landlords, development barons, politicians, and their media backers create.

Give Back the House Keys and Get the Fuck Out

In 2018, Gay Shame and organizers from a Los Angeles–based antigentrification group held a joint panel in which the two groups shared their perspectives on fighting back against gentrification in a manner that holds a hard line against the aesthetic and cultural symbols of gentrification. Symbols such as cafés, art galleries, sleek murals, and other smaller institutions and emblems that many have come to recognize as omens of incoming displacement and expropriation. The event, which began with a presentation and discussion, was organized to immediately become an action after the talk concluded, manifesting the idea that spectators are also participants, and that political discourse is immediately actionable. The march went to a development at 55 Dolores, which had previously been rent-controlled apartments but saw all of its prior tenants evicted and replaced with million-dollar condos occupied by Google, Apple, and Tesla employees. A flyer for the event encouraged attendees to "come dressed as your favorite condo or techie." Several dozens of people, flanked by a friendly motorcycle rider, marched blocks from the event venue to the condos while chanting, acting out the parodic characters of their costumes, and handing out informational flyers to onlookers. When the group arrived at the building, they projected a few messages onto the facade of 55 Dolores in rotation, including: "Give Back the House Keys and Get the Fuck Out" and "Don't Buy the YIMBY Lie; More Condos = More Evictions."

Gay Shame has also taken on some figures who help to make flipped tragedies like 55 Dolores possible: the developers, landowners, and property managers who make up a great deal of the less public-facing or visible apparatuses that administer the finer details of gentrification. Take, for instance, the real estate firm Starcity. In San Francisco, single-occupancy rooms (SROs) are a form of dwelling that has provided a low-income, affordable option in the city for decades. Most are located around the city's Chinatown, Mission, and Tenderloin neighborhoods—neighborhoods that have long been home to Chinese, Latinx, and Black residents. The city's

Image 4: Gay Shame and Defend Boyle Heights action at 55 Dolores Street, the site of a recent eviction and high-end house flip (following a joint Gay Shame– Defend Boyle Heights panel), 2018.

poorest residents, as well as its highest percentages of people of color, often live in these SRO units. As the city becomes more affluent, SROs are being either administratively starved of support or outright targeted. Starcity took the particularly diabolical route of monetizing these displacements to bring trendy "tech dorms" to the market for lonely, maladjusted tech bros seeking an overpriced, congregate-living setting with others of their ilk. Ultimately, sixteen units at 2072 Mission Street were culled from an increasingly dwindling supply of space affordable to low- to no-income residents, as unit rents went from $450 to $2,000 a month. Gay Shame created flyers highlighting Starcity's scandalous history, also calling out city officials and departments that allowed for such cynical maneuvers. In 2019, the group picketed outside of a Starcity event being held at the Roxie, a historic community arthouse movie theater, flyering and holding a banner reading: "Fuck Starcity."

Lawyers and Lawfare

Gay Shame led several actions against the locally infamous eviction lawyers Daniel and Jonathan Bornstein—siblings who had devoted their careers to helping so-called mom-and-pop landlords find loopholes in San Francisco's tenant laws, thereby allowing those landlords to get rid of low-income tenants covered by any number of protections, such as rent control. With the Bornsteins as their emissaries, landlords could capitalize on the increasingly large bags of money they could make catering to young tech professionals who decided they wanted the color and conveniences of

Image 5: Gay Shame serves an eviction notice to Bornstein & Bornstein, eviction lawyers who pioneered "Eviction Boot Camps" for landlords, during an action dubbed "Project Lawyer Connect," 2014.

the city over the bland, office park–saturated suburbs where tech giants like Apple, Facebook, and Google had built their headquarters. Of the brothers' many antics, the more salacious included their series of "Eviction Boot Camps": free-of-charge consulting events for inquiring landlords curious about how to utilize their capital more greedily.

Within the lofty auspices of a conference center atop Fort Mason—a historic pier with a fabulous view of the Golden Gate Bridge—green and eager property-owners were treated to PowerPoint presentations filled with slides detailing just how much money their current tenants were "costing" them in potential and future profits. At one of these conference meetings, a dozen or so Gay Shame members arrived dressed as quirky San Francisco land barons, having previously RSVPed online under Waspy names. Twenty minutes into the Bornsteins' cloaked classist and racist rhetoric, Gay Shame members stood up in tandem, with several people chanting "Evict the Evictors" while holding a banner bearing the same slogan, a confrontation that caused some audience members to leave, and someone with the Bornsteins to call the police. Upon the group's exit from the conference center, the cops nabbed the first Black person they saw—a member of Gay Shame—handcuffed them, pushed them to the ground, and brusquely ordered other people, including passersby walking along the piers, to move a few yards away. . . *or else.*

Another Gay Shame member leveraged a mixture of white privilege and experience in talking cops down from their adrenaline pulpit, and the detained member was eventually released.[4]

The Profitability of Burning Your Tenants to Death

Documented landlord arson is much rarer than the projected number of actual incidents. As the former fire chief of Fairfield, a town near San Francisco, told one of us in an interview: it's a "perfect crime."[5] Much of the direct evidence literally goes up in flames. In one tragic example in the Mission, the local, mostly Latinx, community grieved the death and homelessness resulting from a January 2015 burning down of a building that contained a large Latinx market and more than sixty tenants. In spite of their numbers, they lacked the resources and powerful allies necessary to negotiate strong terms of return or retribution. Ultimately, the San Francisco Fire Department declared the fire "likely accidental." Hawk Ling Lou, the slumlord whose fire alarms failed the night of the enormous fire in a building with windows that were painted continues to own and rent hundreds of apartments in the city. If anything, a freshly vacated 0.49 acres of land speculated to be worth tens of millions of dollars appears to be a boon for him. In some cases, the mostly low-income, undocumented Latinx people who lived there left the city altogether. The largest number relocated to Treasure Island, a waterlocked former naval base accessible only by car, a single San Francisco Municipal Transportation Agency bus line, or private boat for those so fortunate.

Next door, condos were superficially harmed by smoke from the fire. The luxury development, Vida (some marketing executive's name for the complex, referencing the area's Latinx culture), opened about a year before the fire at 2588 Mission Street to almost exclusively white tenants who paid upwards of $8,000 per month for two-bedroom apartments—an obscene amount even by the standard of an upper-middle-class sub-administrator techie in the nation's most expensive city. The area surrounding the now burned-down apartment building and Vida has been a hot spot for luxury developments. The attempt to push residents and small businesses out so that the properties can be sold and developed has been multifaceted. Community groups have also been succumbing to the pressure. Previously, a few shady nonprofits based in the Mission sold out to Vida's developer by signing a letter supporting the project to the San Francisco Planning Commission. In exchange, the nonprofits received one-time payments that, pooled together, wouldn't pay for a single two-bedroom unit at Vida.

Gay Shame collected a small amount of money for some of the survivors. In May 2016, the group rolled out a red-carpet for a "Lights, Camera, Arson!" direct action adjacent to the empty, fenced-in plot, and in front

Image 6: Flyer for the Lights, Camera, Arson action outside an Alamo Drafthouse theater and Vida luxury condo complex adjacent to the Latinx lives, homes, and market incinerated by the slumlord owners of twenty large properties in San Francisco. (Hawk Ling and Ketty Lou, 2016.)

of the new gentrified buildings: the mammoth Vida, a franchised adjacent boutique beer and movie theater called Alamo Drafthouse, and a $20,000-per-year charter elementary school called Alta Vista, formed by execs from locally headquartered Twitter and Zynga (whose cash cows were the cellphone games FarmVille and Words with Friends) and funded by tech overlords and charter school fans Peter Thiel and Mark Zuckerberg.[6] Gay Shame members dressed as archetypal Bay Area gentrifiers: Burning Man Festival fans, landlords, and techies. Notably featured as a figure of mockery was a locally loathed techie Sarah Slocum, who briefly made national news when she claimed to be the subject of an "anti-tech hate crime" after she was offended by bar staff who asked her to remove her since-discontinued Google brand augmented eyeglasses (a failed enterprise by Google to sell wearable surveillance gear for your face).[7] One of San Francisco's remaining local news outlets, Mission Local, deleted a reporter's coverage of the action, a decision by its editor.[8] A dynamic Gay Shame frequently faces is the lack of willingness on the part of establishment press outlets or figures in power to engage with radical critiques or actions, effectively keeping these politics marginal and hiding the negative implications of their own policies.

The Castro Was Never Home

Tourism industrialists have worked for decades to solidify San Francisco's Castro district as the "gay mecca" of the West Coast. Starting in the 1960s, it has been the place where gay assimilationists went to escape homophobia, bringing their own phobias with them. Despite the promises of an accepting, liberated society that halo San Francisco, there are strict limits to this in practice. Classist, racist, and transphobic loathing persists, resulting in the ejection of Black queers from the dwindling gay bars on 18th Street, the evictions of low-income queers with HIV, and a special cop unit formed to harass houseless queer youth out of the gayborhood. In the 2000s, groups such as the business-centric Castro Merchants Association and the property owner–led Noe Valley Community Workgroup acted as a civilian police unit. They spread through media and mailers upper-class nightmare scenarios of poor, queer kids preying on their children, focusing on threats to "safety" and "sanitation." Businesses spoke to the potential effects on the microeconomy of the gayborhood. As summed up by homeless queer twenty-two-year-old Darien (no last name given) in the *Noe Valley Times:* "Some parents are very uncomfortable with a lot of the kids who are hanging out there because they wear makeup, have weird hair, and might have lice."

The homeowners and business associations had their way and convinced city officials that the threat of queer homeless youth was so serious that they had to overturn plans for a large queer youth shelter. "People should not be scared of what they see. We, the homeless gay kids, are also very vulnerable, and people have to understand that it is very hard to live on the street," Darien said.[9]

The Castro was never home to the trans and gender nonconforming people who live(d) in the nearby Tenderloin district and created the closest thing to a safe haven that exists/ed. Attempts by actors like the real estate industry to make the Tenderloin ("the TL" for short) into another Castro, with its allure for high-end prospective renters, tourists, and property seekers, have largely failed, despite an inordinate number of officers hired to police the area and corporate media's attempt to rally City Hall to transform what the *San Francisco Chronicle* commonly casts as little more than a dangerous vice land and "open-air drug market," populated by residents who are less than human.

Repurposing methods of groups like the Castro Merchants and Noe Valley Community Workgroup, whose members connect over a hatred of poor people, try to remake the TL time and again. Among the most eager and energetic try-hards is a married duo named Carolynn Abst and Ronald Case, who in 1999 descended on the neighborhood's Polk Street armed with a lot of self-confidence and a relatively big bank account. In the area of the city with the highest concentration of homeless people, where the number of renters far outweighs owners, Abst and Case purchased a couple of large buildings for cheap, flipping them into condos meant for newcomers with money. They formed Lower Polk Neighbors (LPN) to combat what Abst told the *Wall Street Journal* was a "filthy" area that the city had abandoned to the filthy people who survived there in spite of countless earlier versions of Absts and Cases. The near-extinction event that was the beginning of the HIV/AIDS crisis had failed to disappear communities of trans/queer people or people who use drugs from the Tenderloin, but Lower Polk Neighbors emerged for a moment as a new force that could finish them off.

Polk Street's gentrification, combined with Abst and Case's cruel, self-serving intentions, made the couple an obvious target for Gay Shame, whose members religiously attended LPN meetings, where Abst and Case served as cochairs for years. Gay Shame called out the subtle and not so subtle racism during the meetings, which, like so many neighborhood association meetings, are scenes of administrative violence, where noise complaints act as weapons and kitschy beautification projects, such as commissioning of bland, deliberately apolitical murals, are used by businesses and luxury developments to paper over the loss of communities, cultures, artists, and others affected by displacement—a tendency that Gay Shame has referred to as "artwashing." Gay Shame created and circulated a map of all the queer spaces lost to the efforts of people like Abst and Case. They also created a "wanted" poster with an image of Abst, who tag-teamed with city overseers to import and install forty palm trees, costing upwards of eight million dollars, and founded a program offering local low-income youth—the literal targets of LPN's gentrification—less than minimum wages to paint over street art.[10]

The law came for Gay Shame years later, in 2013, when Abst hired a lawyer to serve a cease and desist notice to the host of the collective's website, freespeech.net. Freespeech.net's operators ultimately sided with Abst's allegation that Gay Shame's wanted poster amounted to libel.

A decade after LPN planted them, the palm trees began drooping. The city hired additional police, who now harass homeless people from luxury RVs dubbed San Francisco Police Department "Mobile Command Centers." Meanwhile, the Department of Public Works hoses down people living on the street in the early hours of the morning, when the department isn't throwing away or requisitioning their medication, tents, and walkers.[11] There are also the "ghost condos"—a nickname for the expanding phenomenon of residences never lived in, because they are investment properties, with owners who can afford to keep them vacant while they wait for the market to reach higher peaks or use them as a temporary asset to launder money or rarely used pieds-à-terre. They'll likely stay empty as tech industry consultants advise Silicon Valley's largest companies to further virtualize their offices and outsource their labor forces. Still, for now, the Tenderloin remains un-Castrofied.

Over the past ten years, Gay Shame actions have served as examples of what a small, anticapitalist, antifundraising collective can do to thwart many of the most destructive forces for communities in San Francisco: developers and landlords, accompanied by the web of gentrifiers, neighborhood groups, nonprofits, politicians, and unions at their service. While the effect of actions like these can't be quantified (quantifying acts is better left to nonprofit administrators and campaign strategists who labor over their organizational year-end donor reports), Gay Shame continues to exist in part because the actions *do* have some effect. These impacts can take the form of making life annoying for profit-driven landlords or reminding wealthy techies that their unimaginative, redundant apps and boutique cafés are just another way to drive displacement in low-income neighborhoods.

Most importantly, perhaps, the group spreads alternative visions of the world through self-published media and, in the tradition of queer radical groups before it, fosters camaraderie through years of efforts refining complicated political stances and personal relationships within a group that operates by consensus. As fleeting as a two-hour action or meeting can seem, it provides a crucial opportunity to interface with others in the city who may be disillusioned by presenting an alternative to the brutally anti-poor politics typical of the city's more conventional avenues for political engagement (such as nonprofits) and pushed by San Francisco's most

Image 7: A flyer advertising Gay Shame's Cops Out of Dyke March action is defaced with the words: "GAY SHAME HATES EVERYTHING IDIOTS."

Image 8: Participants in costume at the 2017 Gay Shame Awards as a techie-landlord arsonist and a pro-condo development politician.

prominent political figures and news outlets. The US tech industry's most dystopian corporations and their libertarian leaders compete to hatch a more terrifying algorithm than the last, with the aim of caging us all within the narrowest physical and psychological boxes possible. As the likes of Mark Zuckerberg and Jeff Bezos menace California and the rest of the world with vicious drives to deregulate labor markets, further monopolize supply chains, and index every affective and biometric aspect of our existence—we cheap units of human labor that fill their databases must face down these attacks and find ways to create a world rich with meaning and connection with one another. Gay Shame continues to counterorganize and dream up a world without technologies of policing and exploitation.

The Gay Shame group has no singular leader and resists any form of vanguardism or cult of personality. All its ideas and propaganda are replicable; it encourages others to take and remake its posters, its actions, and its decision-making structure, in contrast to Silicon Valley's model of innovation, where ideas are only good if they can be trademarked and sold. Some of the group's messaging may come off as hypercritical and curmudgeonly, but underneath the apparent cynicism there is an earnest idealism, a vigorous refusal of nihilism, and a shared belief that an anticapitalist world is worth twenty years of organizing, and probably twenty more.

Notes

1   "Five-O Out of Pride 50," *Gay Shame*, accessed June 10, 2022, https://gayshame.net/index.php/five-o-out-of-pride-50.

2   For a decent representation of the confusion of liberals outside of "the community," see the reaction of Amy Goodman, host of the progressive news show *Democracy Now!* to a gay marriage "debate" between then member of Gay Shame Mattilda Bernstein Sycamore and Dan Choi, a gay military veteran discharged from the Army for publicly coming out while enlisted, October 22, 2022, accessed June 1, 2022, https://www.democracynow.org/2010/10/22/does_opposing_dont_ask_dont_tell.

3   For a lengthier explanation on how YIMBYs and NIMBYs are not opposing forces, as the YIMBY's false narrative suggests, see Erin McElroy and Andrew Szeto, "The Racial Contours of YIMBY/NIMBY Bay Area Gentrification," *Berkeley Planning Journal* 29, no. 1 (January 2017), accessed June 1, 2022, https://escholarship.org/uc/item/4sw2g485.

4   As of 2020, Daniel Bornstein continues to practice eviction law despite the brothers' professional, and perhaps personal, relationship dissolving in 2016, when they sued each other over money and their brand name, eventually leading to Jonathan's ousting from the firm they jointly ran.

5   Prisca Carpenter, Toshio Meronek, and Clio Sady, "Hot Rental Market Sparks Suspicions of Landlord Arson in San Francisco," Al Jazeera, April 2, 2015, accessed June 1, 2022, https://tinyurl.com/2p9xkuxb.

6   See Issie Lapowsky, "Inside the School Silicon Valley Thinks Will Save Education," *Wired*, May 4, 2015, accessed June 1, 2022, https://www.wired.com/2015/05/altschool; Russ Klettke, "We Built a School," *Modern Counsel*, June 15, 2016, accessed June 1, 2022, https://modern-counsel.com/2016/renee-lawson.

7   Kurtis Alexander, "Sarah Slocum: The Infamous Face of Google Glass," SF Gate, March 25, 2014, accessed June 1, 2022, https://www.sfgate.com/news/article/Sarah-Slocum-the-infamous-face-of-Google-Glass-5348911.php.

8   Laura Wenus, "Radical Group Takes Aim at Landlords and Others," Mission Local, May 28, 2016, accessed June 1, 2022, https://gayshame.net/wp-content/uploads/2021/05/missionlocal-vida-protest.pdf.

9   Anne Sengès, "Some Residents Wary of Homeless Youth Shelter Set to Open in Castro," *Noe Valley Voice*, March 1999, accessed June 1, 2022, http://www.noevalleyvoice.com/1999/March/shelter.html.

10 In 2006, the *San Francisco Bay Guardian* reported that a defender of the upper class, then local district attorney Kamala Harris, attended a Lower Polk Neighbors meeting to show her support for the association's work. Harris's office "responded to [LPN] agitation by having representatives of the District Attorney's Office walk the neighborhood with police and installing high-tech surveillance equipment to gain more criminal convictions"; Joseph Plaster, "The Death of Polk Street," *San Francisco Bay Guardian*, August 29, 2007, accessed June 1, 2022, https://sfbgarchive.48hills.org/sfbgarchive/2007/08/29/death-polk-street.

11 "Stolen Belonging Project Interview with Former DPW Worker: Disclosing Human Rights Violations, Theft and City Workers Profiting Off of Items They Take in the Sweeps," Stolen Belonging, 2019, accessed June 1, 2022, https://www.stolenbelonging.org/dpw-disclosure.

How to Survive without Assimilating

Resisting Pinkwashing and Antisemitism

Beth Bruch and Sandra Y.L. Korn

In April 2018, Durham, North Carolina, made international headlines by becoming the first city in the United States to end police exchanges with foreign militaries, including Israel's.[1] The two of us are proud to have been part of the organizing work that led to this victory. Demilitarize! Durham2Palestine, the coalition-driven campaign from 2016 to 2019 that made this victory possible, challenged the collaboration between Durham law enforcement and Israeli security forces as part of a larger project to dismantle state violence and racial discrimination in both countries.

Palestinian land has been stolen and occupied over hundreds of years of colonialism, genocide, nationalism, and capitalism—and, today, that occupation is being carried out in the name of Jewish people worldwide, whether Jewish people personally support it or not.[2] We hope that our work with the Demilitarize! Durham2Palestine campaign can provide a model for internationalist organizers hoping to address the structures of violence and oppression that endanger so many people at home and overseas—and for Jewish people and queers looking for political work that affirms collective liberation rather than assimilation.

The two of us came to our organizing work from different trajectories: Beth grew up in Durham and has been organizing here for much of her adult life. Sandra grew up in a suburban/rural town in New Jersey and moved to North Carolina just six years ago. Both of us are white Jews living in diaspora and in contradiction: we are the descendants of European Jews who suffered pogroms and whose relatives were murdered in the Holocaust. Our people were ethnically cleansed from much of Europe. Yet our families became settlers on land that was stolen through genocide (we are writing this on the stolen land of the Occaneechi Band of the Saponi Nation). As Jews, we face antisemitism and white nationalism, but as white people, we benefit from structures of white supremacy. Many of our dearest ones are service workers, artists, and creators who lack regular income or work on the front lines as the US economy crumbles under the crisis of the COVID-19 pandemic, but we both enjoy class privilege and are still employed by large and resilient institutions (a public school system, a private university). These contradictions, along with our queer identities and queer politics, have led us to a vision of mutual solidarity.

This account of the campaign highlights a possible response to two assimilationist bargains that have pervaded our Jewish communities. First, we confront the narrative that the state of Israel, a nuclear power built on occupied Palestinian land, keeps lesbian and gay people safe—this is known as "pinkwashing." Second, we challenge the idea that, in a time of rising antisemitic violence, Jewish communities in the US should hire police to guard the doors of our synagogue. Instead, we want to offer collective action as a model for liberation that challenges these assimilationist narratives of safety.

Pinkwashing Occupation

As queers in the Palestine solidarity movement, we cannot be involved in advocating for Palestinian human rights and liberation without running up against pinkwashing. The term *pinkwashing* was first coined by breast cancer activists concerned that corporations that manufactured products containing carcinogenic substances were then branding them in pink and pledging to donate money to breast cancer research, thereby cleansing their reputations.[3]

When used in reference to militarization, the term *pinkwashing* refers to the practice of presenting a military occupation as progressive, feminist, and LGBTQ-friendly—such as highlighting the progressive sexual freedoms of an occupying country to distract from the profoundly unprogressive nature of military occupation itself. Scholars like Lila Abu-Lughod and Jasbir Puar have shown how the United States government justifies its War on Terror and military occupation of Iraq with chatter about making the Middle East a safer place for women and gay people. This assertion presumes that Muslim women want to be liberated from their own families and hijabs by US soldiers.[4] Similarly, the Israeli government and its supporters around the world tout Israel as a gay tourist destination, lifting up Tel Aviv Pride and openly gay Israeli soldiers as evidence that Israel is a lesbian- and gay-friendly nation, despite same-sex marriage remaining illegal in Israel.[5]

Worse, when contrasted with the presumed homophobia of Palestinian society, this ideal of Israel as a lesbian- and gay-friendly nation creates a narrative that not only erases queer Palestinian identity but also provides a supposedly "progressive" justification for Israel's occupation. The organization alQaws for Sexual and Gender Diversity in Palestinian Society notes, "Israel is interested in portraying itself as positive, progressive, liberal, and democratic by, on the one hand, expressing its support for LGBT rights/people and, on the other, by presenting itself as queer Palestinians' savior." In actuality, Palestinian LGBTQ organizations are working to take care of their own people: alQaws runs community centers throughout Palestine, operates a national hotline, and builds partnerships with established institutions, all while challenging divisive political forces and working against Israeli colonialism and occupation.[6]

Activists in Palestine and the US have been fighting back against pinkwashing agendas pushed by US and Israeli-based Zionist advocacy organizations. In "Israel/Palestine and the Queer International," Jewish American lesbian writer Sarah Schulman is interviewed about being invited to present the keynote address at the Tel Aviv Lesbian and Gay Studies Conference. Jewish colleagues made her aware of the academic and cultural boycott of Israel, leading to her public decision to respect the boycott. She made the trip, but instead spoke in anti-occupation venues, met with Palestinian BDS leaders, and learned from Palestinian queer organizers like Haneen Malkey of alQaws. When confronted by the sight of Israeli soldiers attacking a largely queer group of protestors for Palestinian rights, she realized, "They [the soldiers] were just not my 'we.'"[7] In another instance, chronicled in the video *Pinkwashing Exposed: Seattle Fights Back!* created by Dean Spade, queer Palestine solidarity activists successfully lobbied to cancel a 2012 tour stop of Israeli government-sponsored lesbian and gay activists that had been scheduled by the City of Seattle. The local activists educated Seattle's LGBT Commission on pinkwashing and its propaganda agenda.[8] A few years later, in 2016, the pan-LGBTQ conference Creating Change scheduled an "LGBT Israel" reception. The reception was hosted by "A Wider Bridge," an organization funded by right-wing Zionist organization Stand With Us, along with the Israeli Consulate, with the performative goal of showing how queer-friendly Israel and Zionism can be. After organized protests by a diverse group of queer organizers, however, Creating Change canceled the reception.[9]

We too have encountered pinkwashing efforts. We are both members of the North Carolina Triangle chapter of Jewish Voice for Peace (JVP), a group of people rooted in Jewish community and committed to justice for Palestine that supports BDS. Recently, an article in our local newspaper accused JVP Triangle of being antisemitic and anti-LGBTQ.[10] Incidentally, when we read the article, we happened to be in a room full of queer JVP leaders painting a banner. We put down our glitter paint and drafted a response:

> Conflating anti-Zionism with antisemitism is an old political tactic that insults our identities and our Jewish values. [The article's author] frames JVP as an anti-queer and anti-Semitic organization—a strange accusation, since we've never seen him at an LGBTQ event and rarely at any of our Jewish community institutions. There have always been Jews with differing opinions about Israel/Palestine. Our bodies and our sexualities cannot be used as a wedge to divide the Jewish community.

Pinkwashing erases the identities of queer, anti-Zionist Jews. More importantly, pinkwashing enables US and Israeli military occupations by providing a progressive veneer for apartheid. Queer Palestinians have documented blackmailing by the Israeli army, which threatens to expose their sexuality unless they inform on families and friends.[11] Pinkwashing, and even its critiques, tend to erase cultural differences and impose a Western lens on Palestinians. Haneen Malkey brilliantly teaches on behalf of alQaws: "We have taken many terms out of our discourse, such as 'acceptance' (we are not working so 'you' can accept us), and 'equality' (we don't want 'your' privileges), replacing them with other words that better communicate our vision as people working to create society." Malkey goes on to point out that pinkwashing makes it appear that queer Palestinian liberation can "be separated from political action against occupation and colonization, which do not distinguish between gay and straight."[12] As Palestinian poet and activist Zaina Alsous points out, Palestinians are not passive victims. Palestinians are rising up and fighting the occupation.[13] Organizations based in Palestine and the Palestinian diaspora—including Palestinian Queers for BDS and alQaws—are actively organizing for the liberation of Palestinian queers.

How Do We Keep Our Own People Safe?

We turn our queer analysis of community safety from occupied Palestine to our own Jewish communities here in the US. In October 2018, white supremacist Robert Gregory Bowers shot and killed eleven Jewish elders during Shabbat morning services at the Tree of Life Synagogue in Pittsburgh, Pennsylvania. Jewish communities across the US and the world were confronted with the question: How do we keep our people safe?[14]

Donald Trump suggested publicly that if the Tree of Life synagogue had had armed guards inside, the "results would have been far better."[15] To our horror, many in the mainstream Jewish community, including at our own Reform synagogue, seem to agree with Trump's claim. For example, the Union for Reform Judaism suggested that synagogues should consider applying for Federal Security Grants from the Department of Homeland Security.[16] We saw many congregations, ours included, increase security or off-duty police details at services, Sunday school, and other events. It is noteworthy that the president's suggestion was, in many ways, not a new idea: many synagogues have employed armed guards during services and on High Holidays for years.

Not all Jewish communities moved toward more policing, however: the New York–based Jews for Racial and Economic Justice launched a "Community Safety Pledge," asking congregations to commit to "interfaith collaboration and crisis de-escalation" instead of expanded policing.[17] Yet most congregations ignored this call. We witnessed synagogues around the country becoming increasingly policed and militarized.

Who is made safer when there are police at the door of a place of worship? For many in our community—largely those who are white, cis, straight, and able-bodied—the sight of an armed guard can foster comfort. Yet many of our life experiences, and even the history of European Jews, belie this sense of comfort. Our ancestors grew up in cultures where official government policies and propaganda often discriminated against Jews: denying Jewish people citizenship, casting us as scapegoats for everything from economic precarity to disease, and displacing Jewish people from their homes and homelands. The Nazis and their sympathizers killed more than half of the global Jewish population in the 1940s, ethnically cleansing Jewish people from Europe and attempting to do so in North Africa.[18] For example, Poland was 10 percent Jewish before Nazi occupation. Three million Polish Jews were killed primarily by the Nazis, but also by Poles.

Today, fewer than ten thousand Jewish people live in Poland, out of a total population of over 37.8 million.[19]

During this time, the US government was hesitant to accept Jewish asylum-seekers. This country turned away a ship of 937 Jewish refugees from Europe, many of whom ended up dying at the hands of the Nazis.[20] Later, though, post–World War II multiculturalism meant that European Jews, along with Irish, Italian, and other European ethnic groups, were suddenly welcomed into the US "melting pot."[21] Our white ancestors took the bargain: assimilate into whiteness and gain the protection of the US state. They attended school with funding from the GI bill (which wasn't available to Black veterans), purchased properties in redlined neighborhoods, and moved their families and their synagogues out to the suburbs.

Some Jewish people are unable to participate in this bargain, however. At least 12 to 15 percent of US Jews are people of color—many suggest that 20 percent of Jewish families include people of color—and many more of us are queer, trans, disabled, chronically ill, or from poor and working-class backgrounds.[22] Many of us who face structural violence from the government and the police are less likely to find the Department of Homeland Security to be a source of comfort and trust. US law enforcement has a long and troubled history of violence against Black and brown people, and the Department of Homeland Security, founded after September 11, 2001, is deeply steeped in anti-Muslim and anti-Arab surveillance and fearmongering.[23] Black Jews in particular have led our community in conversations about why we cannot rely on the police to protect us from antisemitic violence.[24]

Fundamentally, the Department of Homeland Security and the police not only make our synagogues less safe for people of color and queers—they make synagogues less safe for us all.

Our work for community safety is troubled by a lack of consensus about whom, exactly, Jews need to be kept safe from. We are familiar with the long history of Klan violence against white Jews, as well as Black folks and people perceived as queer.[25] Since 2016, the world has seen a rising number of violent anti-Jewish incidents, from synagogue shootings through cemetery vandalism to swastikas drawn on windows or the sides of buildings. These actions are generally perpetrated by white nationalists, for whom antisemitism is an integral part of their ideology.[26]

Unfortunately, a lack of accurate information muddles our work against antisemitism. The Anti-Defamation League (ADL), which has established itself as the premier authority on antisemitism, counts acts of Palestine solidarity activism and anti-Zionist protests as "antisemitic."[27] A new report by the ADL defines the seven tropes of antisemitism as "power, loyalty, greed, deicide, the blood libel, Holocaust denialism and anti-Zionism."[28] Prominent Jewish intellectual Bari Weiss, in her book *How to Fight Antisemitism*, pretends that this so-called "left-wing antisemitism" is a greater threat to American Jews than the violent attacks carried out by those on the right.[29] These pundits, along with Jewish and non-Jewish people on the right, find it convenient to mobilize Islamophobia and racism to scapegoat Muslim women like Linda Sarsour and US Representative Rashida Tlaib as emblems of antisemitism, simply because of their unabashed support for Palestine. Yet these women have acted in solidarity with Jewish communities targeted by antisemitic violence over and over again.[30] The media are eager to amplify stories of Black thinkers and public figures accused of antisemitic comments—without mentioning that these tropes are perpetuated in US discourse by white nationalists on the internet and in government positions.

When the right leverages false or exaggerated accusations of antisemitism to silence the voices of progressive activists, this also confuses and distracts Jewish people and our allies from the fight against dangerous white nationalism. We've witnessed this in our own community: after the success of the Demilitarize! Durham2Palestine campaign, we faced backlash from some organized Jewish community institutions, which fruitlessly enlisted countless hours of staff and volunteer time to oppose the statement on militarized police training. They claimed that because he had singled out Israel in his statement, our Jewish mayor had done something antisemitic. At the same time, the same organizations failed to even issue any comment when a known local white supremacist charged into a group of Jewish students, screaming that they were plotting a Goldman Sachs takeover of the US, during a vigil on UNC's campus mourning the victims of the Pittsburgh shooting.[31] Who, here, is more of a threat to Jewish people's safety?

We know that the same people plotting to harm Jews are also plotting anti-Muslim, anti-Latinx, and anti-Black violence. What we need in response is solidarity, not Islamophobia.[32] A few visionary rabbis have taken the lead in imagining what collective safety might look like for Jewish communities. Rabbi Ariana Katz of Hinenu congregation of Baltimore has noted that this work must start by reckoning with the generational trauma that leads Jewish people to fear that no one will show up for us. In her Yom Kippur drash (or sermon) in October 2019, entitled "We Will Not Abandon the Waters," Rabbi Katz says: "It is exactly in these times of increased fear that we must stay committed to our values. . . . We will not sacrifice the safety of some of us for others of us. . . . The answer is to look outside ourselves. Building radical kinship between our communities."[33]

In practice, this means envisioning safety plans for our congregations that do not involve law enforcement. In the Jewish newspaper the *Forward*, rabbinic student Lara Haft calls on us to "focus on building interfaith defense networks to support the places of worship that are most vulnerable to attacks by neo-Nazis and white supremacists, including synagogues, Mosques, Black churches, and LGBT congregations."[34] Of course, not all Jewish people attend congregational services, and our communal visions for how to fight rising antisemitism must include secular Jews as well.

We have witnessed parallel discussions about safety within our queer communities. Increasingly assimilated LGBT people—especially white cispeople—invite the police to protect our gayborhoods, Pride parades, and nightclubs. Multinational banks, which put Black, Indigenous, and people of color at risk through investments in prisons and extractive projects like the Dakota Access Pipeline, are frequently invited to sponsor queer conferences and bankroll LGBTQ nonprofits.[35] Black queers have taken the lead in calling out queer assimilation and how it puts all of us in danger. In fall 2015, Black Lives Matter activists staged disruptions of North Carolina Pride in Durham and Greensboro. We were marching in the Durham parade with our Jewish Voice for Peace chapter. The Black Lives Matter leaders invited white people like us who wanted to support the disruption to hand out leaflets with information about why the parade was halted: "We interrupt your regularly scheduled state-sanctioned celebration to remind you that we are not ready to celebrate the countless murders of our Transgender Black Women. We are not ready to give into silence and privilege and respectability politics that only continue to increase the pockets of some while depleting the pockets of many."[36] We are inspired by the leaders who are generating and carrying out community solutions to violence that do not rely on the police.[37] Transformative justice and community-based methods of safety are vital work, and we hope to accompany that work with strategic, coalition-based campaigns to dismantle the oppressive structures impeding community safety.

Counternarratives through Coalition: Demilitarize from Durham2Palestine

To challenge the politics of assimilation, we must build coalitions representing different communities to work for a shared goal of collective liberation. The Demilitarize! Durham2Palestine campaign began with a series of listening sessions: conversations with diverse local activists committed both to a more just and equitable Durham and a Palestine free from occupation. We strove to build a local campaign in solidarity with national and international justice movements, taking inspiration from the Movement for Black Lives Platform, as well as the Palestinian civil society call for Boycott, Divestment, and Sanctions, or BDS.[38] Our first step would be challenging police exchanges that brought Durham Police Department into conversation with Israeli military and law enforcement.

During trips to Israel, US law enforcement agents—including police, Border Patrol, and Immigration and Customs Enforcement (ICE)—receive training and instruction from Israeli military, police, intelligence agencies, and private defense companies. Officials visit checkpoints and prisons while learning about Israeli practices of surveillance and racial profiling. These programs facilitate an exchange of what the US-based organization Jewish Voice for Peace has termed "worst practices."[39] The group Researching the American-Israeli Alliance, in partnership with JVP, has demonstrated how counterterrorism trainings "instill militarized logics of security into the civilian sphere, normalizing practices of mass surveillance, criminalization, and the violent repression of communities and movements the government defines as threatening."[40] Counterterrorism trainings purport to teach civilian police forces how to protect a civilian populace by using racial profiling and other techniques that cause harm to targeted groups, as honed by Israel through the military occupation of Palestine and the genocide and containment of Palestinian people.

Of course, Israel isn't the first country with which the US has engaged in a deadly exchange; for example, we have a long history of exporting horrifying military tactics to Central America, in part through the notorious School of the Americas/Western Hemisphere Institute for Security Cooperation.[41] Currently, though, Israel seems to be the only country intent on training US law enforcement in "counterterrorism" tactics. Durham's former police chief Jose Lopez went on a trip to Israel called a "National Counterterrorism Seminar," funded by the ADL,[42] and two commanders in the Durham Police Department traveled to Washington,

DC, to receive training from the Israeli police.[43] In her previous position, Durham's current police chief C.J. Davis established the Atlanta Police Leadership Institute International Exchange Program, which coordinated exchanges with Israel.[44] Groups like the ADL, the Jewish Institute for National Security of America, and Georgia International Law Enforcement Exchange have sponsored and arranged trips for dozens of US police departments, university police, ICE officials, and Department of Homeland Security officers, as well as bringing Israeli law enforcement here to the US. The NYPD has even maintained a branch office in Tel Aviv since at least 2012.[45]

Challenging this interconnected and transnational web of state violence requires a broad coalition. JVP–Triangle was one of ten organizations in the initial Demilitarize! Durham2Palestine coalition—along with Students for Justice in Palestine (SJP) Duke, SJP UNC Chapel Hill, SpiritHouse, Inside-Outside Alliance, Muslims for Social Justice, Muslim American Public Affairs Committee, Abrahamic Initiative on the Middle East, Durham for All, and BYP100. More recently, the Coalition for Peace with Justice, Migrant Roots Media, and the Piedmont Chapter of Democratic Socialists of America joined the coalition.[46]

Every group in our coalition had an essential role. It was and remains important to the coalition to recognize the integral leadership of Palestinians, Black people, and Latinx people in working toward prison abolition, maintaining an internationalist perspective, and advocating for their own human rights. We also recognize the important role that Jewish people can play in advocating for Palestinian liberation. Zionism is often conflated with Judaism by both people on the left and people on the right. Therefore, Jewish people stepping up into leadership of BDS work becomes necessary, both because we are well positioned to explain how critiquing Israel is not antisemitic, and because we demonstrate that not all Jewish people are in favor of a colonial occupation. JVP also provided significant support to the Demilitarize! Durham2Palestine campaign at a national level and launched an aligned campaign that named these US-Israel law enforcement programs a "deadly exchange."

The Durham2Palestine coalition organized for three years. Finally, in spring 2018, Durham's Mayor Steve Schewel circulated a policy statement he had drafted on the topic, which was unanimously approved by our city council two weeks later: "The council opposes international exchanges with any country in which Durham officers receive military-style training since such exchanges do not support the kind of policing we want here in the City of Durham."[47]

The statement didn't adopt the abolitionist framework that our campaign had hoped for, yet it did include an explicit mention of Israel, the focus of our internationalist campaign and the only country currently attempting to train US police officers in militarized "counterterrorism" measures.

Multiracial Coalitions Create Safety through Solidarity

As white, queer Jews in the South, we are aware of our strengths and limitations—when we work with other people, our power increases dramatically. Our analysis deepens as we fill in the lacunae in each other's understandings, and our understanding of community deepens as we plumb each other's relationship networks. In coalition, our capacity to do strong work multiplies. It is dangerous when white people organize without taking direction from and setting the table with people of color. So, as Jews positioned in a predominantly white, predominantly Jewish organization, it is not only strategic for us to build movements alongside more people of color, it is necessary if we want to win. Furthermore, it is a moral and ethical imperative. Not all of us have the same stakes in this fight, but all of us are essential. bell hooks tells us: "All too often our political desire for change is seen as separate from longings and passions that consume lots of time and energy in daily life.... The shared space and feeling of 'yearning' opens up the possibility of common ground where all these differences might meet and engage one another."[48]

How do we choose where to focus our organizing energy within the vast common ground that emerges in a time of multiplying crises? We fear that the multinational corporations profiting from borders, incarceration, and militarization also see an opportunity in economic and political crisis. It's not a coincidence that companies like Elbit Systems, G4S Secure Solutions, Motorola Solutions, Geo Group, and Palantir are engaged with the Israeli occupation, with US border detention and ICE deportations, with US "defense" contracts in the Middle East, and with militarized policing in our cities. These companies—based in Israel, the US, and the UK—have business growth models that are premised on increasing militarization, surveillance, and incarceration. They are already huge, and we can only imagine that they will leverage the instability of the economic crisis triggered by the COVID-19 pandemic to fill their coffers with more and more government contracts.

198 Surviving the Future

All around the US, Jewish communities, Muslim communities, and Black, migrant, Latinx, Arab, disabled, working-class and poor, and queer communities are forming relationships of mutual accountability and mutual aid to protect and support each other. Right now, we are inspired by Mijente's No Tech for ICE campaign, by the success of the Stop Urban Shield coalition in the San Francisco Bay Area, by the Dream Defenders, and by collectives of Muslims and Jews enacting community safety.[49]

It is clear that the combined forces of militarism, Zionism, and antisemitism distinctly harm Black and brown communities in the US, Palestinians living under occupation, and Jewish people. We see the pull that assimilation has had on LGBT communities seeking equality and on our own families who migrated to the US after generations of antisemitic trauma in Europe. Yet we know that antisemitism and homophobia are only pieces of larger systems of racial and economic oppression at play. We know from history that queers, people of color, and political dissidents are all targeted by the right (from the GOP to the Nazis). So, it makes sense from both an intuitive and a strategic perspective—and from both altruism and self-interest—that we work together to fight them. Again and again we learn: ultimately assimilation will not protect us. Whiteness will not protect us, and, for those of us with light complexions, our complacent assimilation into whiteness actively harms others.

We see the way that pinkwashing efforts attempt to create enmity between US queers and Arab people, never mind the overlap. Zionist ploys to co-opt our experiences and claim our loyalty are all the more reason that Jewish queers must resist and participate in multiracial coalitions fighting white supremacy and militarism. Such participation yields our own safety, our people's future, and the safety and well-being of our neighbors and all oppressed people. These supportive relationships and powerful collaborations are what we all need to survive the disasters of today and to thrive in our collective future.

We are so grateful for the following friends, comrades, and family for reading and providing comments on this chapter: Ajamu Dillahunt, Alana Krivo-Kaufman, Aman Aberra, Beth Korn, Kathy Bruch, Leila Nashashibi, Noa Nessim, Noah Rubin-Blose, Sam Wohns, and Trude Bennett—as well as for the thoughtful feedback and editorial vision of Scott Branson and Raven Hudson.

Notes

1   For some of the news coverage of our campaign, see "In the News," Demilitarize! Durham2Palestine, accessed June 1, 2022, https://www.durham2palestine.org/in-the-news.

2   Edward Said, *The Question of Palestine* (New York: Penguin, 1979); Ilan Pappe, *The Ethnic Cleansing of Palestine* (New York: One World, 2006); Ali Abunimah, *The Battle for Justice in Palestine* (Chicago: Haymarket Books, 2014).

3   Sarah Schulman, "A Documentary Guide to Pinkwashing," HuffPost, updated February 2, 2016, accessed June 1, 2022, https://www.huffpost.com/entry/israel-pinkwashing_b_1132369; Joy Ellison, "Recycled Rhetoric: Brand Israel 'Pinkwashing' in Historical Context," June 2013, DePaul College of Liberal Arts and Social Sciences Theses and Dissertations, 149, accessed June 1, 2022, https://via.library.depaul.edu/cgi/viewcontent.cgi?article=1151&context=etd.

4   Jasbir Puar, *Terrorist Assemblages* (Durham, NC: Duke University Press, 2007); Lila Abu-Lughod, *Do Muslim Women Need Saving?* (Cambridge, MA: Harvard University Press, 2013).

5   Sarah Schulman, "Israel and 'Pinkwashing,'" *New York Times*, November 22, 2011, accessed June 1, 2022, https://www.nytimes.com/2011/11/23/opinion/pinkwashing-and-israels-use-of-gays-as-a-messaging-tool.html?_r=0.

6   "alQaws Statement Re: Media Response to Israel's Blackmailing of Gay Palestinians," alQaws, September 19, 2014, accessed June 1, 2022, https://tinyurl.com/5n8pfceb.

7   Sarah Schulman and Karma R. Chávez, "Israel/Palestine and the Queer International," *Journal of Civil and Human Rights* 5, no. 5 (2019): 139–57; also see Sarah Schulman, *Israel/Palestine and the Queer International* (Durham, NC: Duke University Press, 2012).

8   Dean Spade, dir., *Pinkwashing Exposed: Seattle Fights Back*, Vimeo, 2015, accessed June 1, 2022, https://vimeo.com/126391030.

9   Bashar, "#CancelPinkwashing: No Room for Pinkwashing at Creating Change," Tarab NYC, accessed June 1, 2022, https://tarabnyc.org/cancelpinkwashingoriginal.

10   Peter Reitzes, "Letter to the Editor," *Herald Sun*, March 11, https://www.heraldsun.com/opinion/letters-to-the-editor/article204001669.html.

11   Ashley Bohrer, "Against the Pinkwashing of Israel: Why Supporting Palestinians Is a Queer and Feminist Issue," Al Jazeera, August 9, 2014, accessed June 1, 2022, https://www.aljazeera.com/indepth/opinion/2014/08/against-pinkwashing-israel-20148910454343031.html.

12   Haneen Malkey, "Signposts from alQaws: A Decade of Building a Queer Palestinian Discourse," alQaws.org, April 3, 2013, accessed June 1, 2022, https://tinyurl.com/4rb9tppp.

13   Conversation during an organizing meeting that Bruch and Alsous attended years prior to the D2P campaign; confirmed by text message exchange between Alsous and Bruch on April 8, 2020.

14   We choose to name the murderer as part of a framework of holding perpetrators of violence responsible for their actions.

15   Michael Zennie, "President Trump Says 'Results Would Have Been Far Better' if Pittsburgh Synagogue Had Armed Guard," *Time*, October 27, 2018, accessed June 1, 2022, https://time.com/5436877/trump-synagogue-armed-guard.

16   The Union for Reform Judaism is the body that issues advice and guidance for the Reform Movement, the denomination of the synagogue we belong to; see Union for Reform Judaism, accessed June 1, 2022, https://urj.org.

17   "Commit to the Community Safety Pledge," Jews For Economic Justice, November 1, 2018, accessed June 1, 2022, https://www.jfrej.org/news/2018/11/commit-to-the-community-safety-pledge.

18   Robert Satloff, "Jews in Nazi-Occupied Countries: North Africa," Jewish Virtual Library, July 4, 2004, accessed June 1, 2022, https://www.jewishvirtuallibrary.org/jews-in-nazi-occupied-north-africa. Not all displaced Jewish people are the result of the Nazi occupation of Europe. Cultural studies scholar Ella Shohat writes about the displacement of Arab Jews from their homelands in the Middle East after the end of the Second World War; see Ella Shohat, *On the Arab-Jew, Palestine, and Other Displacements: Selected Writings of Ella Shohat* (London: Pluto, 2017).

19   "Jewish Life in Poland Before the Holocaust," Facing History and Ourselves, accessed June 1, 2022, https://www.facinghistory.org/resource-library/resistance-during-holocaust/jewish-life-poland-holocaust; Poland Population (Live), accessed June 1, 2022, https://www.worldometers.info/world-population/poland-population; for more on Polish violence against Jewish people in Poland after the Nazi occupation ended, see David Engel, "Patterns of Anti-Jewish Violence in Poland, 1944–1946," Yad Vashem, accessed June 1, 2022, https://www.yadvashem.org/articles/academic/patterns-of-anti-jewish-violence.html.

20   On the USS *St. Louis*, see Daniel A. Gross, "The U.S. Government Turned Away Thousands of Jewish Refugees, Fearing That They Were Nazi Spies," *Smithsonian Magazine*, November 18, 2015, accessed June 1, 2022, https://tinyurl.com/2p822dvr; also see Yael Schacher, "Coronavirus Can't Be an Excuse to Continue President Trump's Assault on Asylum Seekers," *Washington Post*, March 21, 2020, accessed June 1, 2022, https://tinyurl.com/mr44kjer.

21   Karen Brodkin, *How Jews Became White Folks and What That Says About Race in America* (New Brunswick, NJ: Rutgers University Press, 1998).

22   Ari Y. Kelman, Aaron Hahn Tapper, Izabel Fonseca, and Aliya Saperstein, *Counting Inconsistencies: An Analysis of American Jewish Population Studies, with a Focus on Jews of Color*, Jews of Color Field Building Initiative, May 2018, unavailable June 1, 2022, https://jewsofcolorfieldbuilding.org/wp-content/uploads/2019/05/Counting-Inconsistencies-052119.pdf.

23   Khaled A. Beydoun, *American Islamophobia: Understanding the Roots and Rise of Fear* (Berkeley: University of California Press, 2018); Moustafa Bayoumi, *This Muslim American Life: Dispatches from the War on Terror* (New York: New York University Press, 2018).

24   For example, articles by Bentley Addison, "Arming Synagogues Will Make Them Less Safe—For Black Jews. Stop Erasing Us," *Forward*, November 5, 2018, accessed June 1, 2022, https://forward.com/opinion/413590/arming-synagogues-will-make-them-less-safe-for-black-jews-stop-erasing-us; and Nylah Burton, "As a Black Jew, I'm Begging You: Don't Arm Your Synagogue," *Heyalma*, November 6, 2018, accessed June 1, 2022, https://www.heyalma.com/as-a-black-jew-im-begging-you-dont-arm-your-synagogue.

25   We learn from Southern queer elder Mab Segrest about her work fighting the Klan in North Carolina in the 1970s. Mab entered this work feeling compelled to fight white supremacist organizations that her own family members helped prop

up—but she soon came to realize that she personally was a target of the Klan due to her queerness; see Mab Segrest, *Memoir of a Race Traitor* (New York: New Press, 2019).

26   Eric Ward, "Skin in the Game: How Antisemitism Animates White Nationalism," *Political Research Associates*, June 29, 2017, accessed June 1, 2022, https://www. politicalresearch.org/2017/06/29/skin-in-the-game-how-antisemitism-animates-white-nationalism.

27   "Antisemitism in the US," Anti-Defamation League, unavailable June 1, 2022 https://www.adl.org/what-we-do/anti-semitism/anti-semitism-in-the-us. Even Jewish human rights activists are not free from these allegations (for example, Sandra lost her job teaching in our Jewish community when major donors threatened to withdraw funding, and Beth's principal received a letter calling her antisemitic and racially divisive), but the consequences of criticizing Israel are often harsher for non-Jews.

28   "Antisemitism Uncovered: A Guide to Old Myths in a New Era," Anti-Defamation League, accessed June 1, 2022, https://antisemitism.adl.org.

29   See Judith Butler's review of Bari Weiss, *How to Fight Antisemitism*; Judith Butler, "Bari Weiss's Unasked Questions," *Jewish Currents*, September 23, 2019, accessed June 1, 2022, https://jewishcurrents.org/bari-weisss-unasked-questions.

30   See JTA, "Colorado Jewish Cemetery Receives Money from Linda Sarsour's Fundraising Campaign," December 7, 2017, accessed June 1, 2022, https://tinyurl. com/mnu7ukyk; Marcy Oster, "Rashida Tlaib Attended Jewish Voice for Peace Shabbat Service after Cancellation of Israel Trip," *Forward*, August 18, 2019, accessed June 1, 2022, https://forward.com/fast-forward/429759/rashida-tlaib-israel-trip-jewish-voice-for-peace-shabbat; "Jews and Allies Celebrate Passover with Rep Rashida Tlaib," JVP Action, April 13, 2020, https://www.jvpaction.org/ passover-rashida-tlaib.

31   Lyell McMerty, "Vigil Honoring Victims of White Supremacy Disrupted by Provocateur," November 12, 2018, accessed June 1, 2022, https://www.dailytarheel. com/article/2018/11/vigil-disrupted-1112. A tweet from the group Take Action Chapel Hill reads, "Tonight, Jews at a prayer vigil in Chapel Hill were charged at by a man in a Trump 2020 hat who was non-stop screaming anti-Semitic abuse. Chapel Hill Police seized one of the Jewish folks the man charged into and then charged the *Jewish* person with assault." Accessed June 1, 2022, https://web.archive.org/web/20200523195827/https://twitter.com/takeactionch/ status/1061466269927567361.

32   Jewish Voice for Peace, *On Antisemitism: Solidarity and the Struggle for Justice* (Chicago: Haymarket Books, 2017).

33   Rabbi Ariana Katz, "We Will Not Abandon the Waters: Yom Kippur Drash," October 10, 2019, accessed June 1, 2022, https://www.hinenubaltimore.org/blog/ yomkippurdrash5780.

34   Lara Haft, "It's Time for Jewish Communities to Stop Investing in the Police," *Forward*, March 23, 2018, accessed June 1, 2022, https://forward.com/opinion/397377/ its-time-for-jewish-communities-to-stop-investing-in-the-police.

35   Christina B. Hanhardt, *Safe Space: Gay Neighborhood History and the Politics of Violence* (Durham, NC: Duke University Press, 2013).

36   Brian Howe, "Did an NC Pride Official Assault a Black Lives Matter Marcher in the Pride Parade?" *Indy Week*, October 28, 2015, accessed June 1, 2022, https://indyweek.com/

news/northcarolina/nc-pride-official-assault-black-lives-matter-marcher-pride-parade.

37 Some of those we are learning with include Ejeris Dixon and Leah Lakshmi Piepzna-Samarasinha, eds., *Beyond Survival: Strategies and Stories from the Transformative Justice Movement* (Oakland: AK Press, 2020); Dean Spade, *Normal Life: Administrative Violence, Critical Trans Politics, and the Limits of Law* (Durham, NC: Duke University Press, 2015); Mariame Kaba, @prisonculture on twitter.

38 Vann R. Newkirk II, "The Permanence of Black Lives Matter," *Atlantic*, August 3, 2016, accessed June 1, 2022, https://www.theatlantic.com/politics/archive/2016/08/movement-black-lives-platform/494309, "Palestinian Civil Society Call for BDS," BDS: Freedom, Justice, Equality, July 9, 2005, accessed June 1, 2022, https://bdsmovement.net/call. The BDS movement calls on all of us to end support and collaboration with the Israeli government in its occupation of indigenous Palestinian lands by boycotting goods produced in occupied territories and boycotting cultural institutions funded by the Israeli government for the purpose of bolstering its image internationally. BDS arose out of a 2005 statement by Palestinian civil society organizations, as part of a strategy inspired by South Africa's anti-apartheid movement and the US Civil Rights Movement. The statement invites the world to engage in and maintain "non-violent punitive measures . . . until Israel meets its obligation to recognize the Palestinian people's inalienable right to self-determination and fully complies with the precepts of international law."

39 Deadly Exchange, accessed June 1, 2022, https://deadlyexchange.org.

40 Researching the American-Israeli Alliance and Jewish Voice for Peace, *Deadly Exchange: The Dangerous Consequences of American Law Enforcement Trainings in Israel*, September 2018, accessed June 1, 2022, https://deadlyexchange.org/wp-content/uploads/2019/07/Deadly-Exchange-Report.pdf; also see Angela Y. Davis, *Freedom Is a Constant Struggle: Ferguson, Palestine, and the Foundations of a Movement* (Chicago: Haymarket Books, 2016). For more on the Movement for Black Lives, see "Statement: Demilitarize! Durham2Palestine Coalition on the Movement for Black Lives and an End to Imperialism," Demilitarize! Durham2Palestine Coalition, August 21, 2010, accessed June 1, 2022, https://twitter.com/ztsamudzi/status/1278843418698027009 and https://www.durham2palestine.org/our-work/statements#h.p_CkpvO5D43rwj.

41 Dévora González and Azadeh Shahshahani," Shut Down the School of the Americas/WHINSEC," *Jacobin*, November 15, 2019, accessed June 1, 2022, https://www.jacobinmag.com/2019/11/shut-down-school-of-the-americas-whinsec-ice-border-patrol.

42 Anti-Defamation League National Counterterrorism Seminars, September 9–17, 2017, "Agencies with Executives Trained in NCTS."

43 "City Panel OKs Policy Banning Exchanges with Israeli Police," AP News, April 17, 2018, accessed June 1, 2022, https://apnews.com/9bf366cca607484b8dfd926 97c211823.

44 Lincoln Anthony Blades, "How Policing in the US and Security in Israel Are Connected," Teen Vogue, July 25, 2018, accessed June 1, 2022, https://www.teenvogue.com/story/how-policing-in-the-us-and-security-in-israel-are-connected; Alice Speri, "Israel Security Forces Are Training American Cops Despite History of Rights Abuses," Intercept, September 15, 2017, accessed June 1, 2022,

https://theintercept.com/2017/09/15/police-israel-cops-training-adl-human-rights-abuses-dc-washington; Deputy Chief Cerelyn "C.J." Davis (résumé), accessed June 1, 2022, https://durhamnc.gov/DocumentCenter/View/9799/Davis-Resume-Final-2016.

45 Aviva Stahl, "Report Criticizes NYPD Collaboration with Israel," Documented, September 12, 2018, accessed June 1, 2022, https://documentedny.com/2018/09/12/report-criticizes-nypd-collaboration-with-israel.

46 Although they were involved in the initial victorious campaign, SpiritHouse and Inside-Outside Alliance are no longer coalition members, and the Coalition for Peace with Justice and Abrahamic Initiative on the Middle East have merged.

47 Dawn Baumgartner Vaughan, "Durham City Council Rejects 'Militarization of Our Police Force.' Chief Says No to Israeli Training," *Herald Sun*, April 5, 2018, accessed June 1, 2022, https://www.heraldsun.com/news/local/counties/durham-county/article207967584.html.

48 bell hooks, *YEARNING: Race, Gender, and Cultural Politics* (Boston: South End Press, 1990), 12–13.

49 Critical Resistance, "Letter of Support to AC Supervisors for Backing Communities," Stop Urban Shield, May 10, 2019, accessed June 1, 2022, http://stopurbanshield.org; Ari Feldman, "Jews from Manhattan Synagogue Created Welcome Path in Front of Mosque," *Forward*, March 18, 2019, accessed June 1, 2022, https://forward.com/fast-forward/421052/new-zealand-mosque-jews-manhattan-synagogue; Avery Anapol, "Hundreds of Muslim Canadians Form 'Rings of Peace' to Protect Synagogues after Pittsburgh Shooting," Hill, November 6, 2018, accessed June 1, 2022, https://tinyurl.com/7yxnujfz.

Forgotten on the Front Lines

Past and Present Black Queer Invisibility in Black Liberation Movements

Yold Yolande Delius

In the wake of George Floyd's murder, a Zoom call begins. The nonprofit I am working for has organized a town hall meeting for the participants in their youth services program. As part of the youth programs, I lead a queer-inclusive sex education initiative, the only queer program in the otherwise very straight, very traditional nonprofit. Moderating the town hall was a straight Black male activist and actor based in New York City. His message of encouragement and political activism energized the young people listening to him. Yet when he was asked which Black activists the young people should be following on social media, the first person he mentioned was Dr. Umar Johnson.

Surprised and upset, I noted in the chat of the video call that Dr. Johnson is homophobic toward Black queer folks, suggesting that he probably isn't someone to endorse to impressionable young people. When he read my comment in the thread his smile disappeared and was replaced by an awkward look to his keyboard. "Okay, we're not all going to agree," he pleaded, and the topic was dismissed. He started talking about the importance of the Black vote, and my concerns were swept into and beyond the flow of conversation.

Dr. Umar Johnson is a doctor of clinical psychology and a self-proclaimed expert on "the education and mental health of Afrikan and Afrikan-American children." Claiming to be a "paternal kinsman" to Frederick Douglass, he is known for his messages on Black collectivity and homophobic exclusionary politics. More specifically, in a YouTube video with DJ Vlad, he mentioned that he would not hire "sexually confused" people in his school for Black children. Later, in that same video, he claimed that queerness does not come from Africans, as it is a European export.

These claims are violent at the very least. These views are oppressive and encourage the institutional erasure of Black queer folks; it is dangerous to pass these ideas off as valuable to young people.

More than that, I am concerned about the origins of Black queer invisibility within Black liberation movements. Being confronted with violently homophobic rhetoric during the attempted genocide of Black transwomen in the United States, I am personally horrified by the dismissal of such an honest and evident concern. This is evidence of a glaring oversight in today's antiracist discourse—the interlocking oppressions of race and gender. As Adolph Reed Jr. writes in "The Limits of Anti-Racism," "The contemporary discourse of 'antiracism' is focused much more on taxonomy than politics. It emphasizes the name by which we should call some strains of inequality ... over specifying the mechanisms that produce them or even the steps that can be taken to combat them."[1] I argue that because my challenge to the moderator went beyond the confines of the strictly racial analysis he employed, it was dismissed as irrelevant. A race and gender analysis of the oppression of Black folks would, as the Combahee River Collective puts it, call "into question some of the most basic assumptions about our existence, i.e., that sex should be a determinant of power relationships."[2] As the moderator was an ardent follower of Dr. Johnson's rhetoric, this goes without question.

I argue that while ineffective, antiracist logic also limits Black liberation, because it homogenizes Black folks, rendering Black queer folks invisible. This logic also whitens queerness, disappearing Black queer folks twice over. As an alternative, I suggest a Black queer feminist lens in Black liberatory politics. This lens offers a framework where Blackness itself is queered, providing it the oppositional positionality to critique the state and to see clearly the range of oppressions not including their own. In this, I hope to reimagine what we call "Black liberation" to truly heed Charlene A. Carruthers's call in the opening chapter of *Unapologetic*: "All of us or none of us."[3]

Competing Histories

As Adolph Reed Jr. writes in "The Limits of Anti-Racism," "contemporary anti-racist activists understand themselves to be employing the same tactics and pursuing the same ends as their predecessors in the period of high insurgency in the struggle against racial segregation. This view, however, is mistaken."[4] In this section, I will argue that the mainstream contemporary recollection of the Stonewall riots of 1969 reveal a deliberate separation of queerness and Blackness as a result of the emergence of a neoliberal logic. In this way, I hope to uncover a queer Black radical tradition underneath the invented, parallel histories of gay liberation and Black liberation.

Lisa Corrigan, along with other contemporary queer thinkers, argues that the Stonewall riots "had opened up the opportunity for an alliance between gays, blacks, and antiwar activists that could work to restructure American society."[5] Unfortunately, this argument is evidence of an invented history that excludes queer Black activists from pre-Stonewall events. Perhaps most famously, Marsha P. Johnson was a queer Black activist on the frontlines of many gay rights demonstrations before, during, and after Stonewall. As Elena Kiesling writes, queer Black artists such as Countee Cullen, Claude McKay, and Langston Hughes significantly shaped the Harlem Renaissance, arguably one of the most influential literary periods. In addition, Bayard Rustin, an openly Black gay civil rights activist, "was at the forefront of the civil rights movement, while other queer civil rights activists, such as Pauli Murray, have worked rather unnoticed."[6]

Clearly, there is an incongruence between the history Corrigan is proposing and the history Kiesling writes. Perhaps most dangerous is the popular assertion that gay liberation activism started during and after Stonewall, when in actuality Stonewall was merely "one moment in a series of events confronting the most marginalized—queers and of color—staged by those most affected by state-sanctioned violence."[7] More than that, Kiesling writes about "the eradication of queer people of color from the neighborhood in which the Stonewall Inn is located... hav[ing] been forced out of the area through massive gentrification measures," including but not limited to "increased police presence," signaling safety for the white neighbors and tourists who frequent the area.[8] As such, Christina Hanhardt argues in *Safe Space* that the advancement of queer activism and the "economic policies of the neoliberal city" have led to a conceptualization of queerness that must be removed from other markers of identity to function, leaving queerness as solely whiteness.[9] The omission of these historic events leads me to agree with Kiesling that "black queerness has not become part of the collective memory of the nation."[10]

Neoliberalism should not be taken lightly in our reevaluation of American social movement history. At the same time as queerness was being whitened by neoliberal policies, Blackness was becoming criminalized, as similar policies destabilized its movements and the goals of those movements. In *From #BlackLivesMatter to Black Liberation*, Keeanga-Yamahtta Taylor refers to this phenomenon: "By the end of the 1970s, there was little talk about institutional racism or the systemic roots of Black oppression."[11] Michelle Alexander speaks of this plainly in *The New Jim Crow*: "The conflation of blackness with crime did not happen organically; rather, it was constructed by political and media elites as part of the broad project known as the War on Drugs. In the era of colorblindness, it is no longer permissible to hate blacks, but we can hate criminals."[12] As Kiesling writes: "Dean Spade and Morgan Bassichis claim: 'Because "blackness" and "criminality" are wedded in the US lexicon . . . any claims to not being a criminal—or on the flipside, to being a citizen—must literally be made on the backs of black people.'"[13]

Both the actions of whitening queerness and of criminalizing Blackness led to "the historical specificities of those struggles [becoming] smoothed out of sight in a romantic idealism that homogenizes them into timeless abstractions."[14] As such, a heteronormative emphasis on Blackness and a white emphasis on queerness emerge, leaving no room for the narratives and contributions of Black queer folks. Within the context of a distorted past and a silenced present, it makes sense that the keynote speaker at my workshop would dismiss the concerns of Black queer folks in a town hall. If our identities and accurate histories are of no concern, then our issues are not either. Analyzing the histories of Black queerness not only requires the incorporation of gender and sexuality in our oppression analysis, it also calls us to move from an individual to a systemic critique of oppression.

Reimagining the Black Radical Tradition

In *Unapologetic*, Carruthers defines the Black radical tradition as such: "The Black radical tradition comprises cultural and intellectual work aimed at disruptive oppressive political, economic, and social norms, and its roots are in anticolonial and antislavery efforts of centuries past."[15]

Carruthers uses Haiti as a central example of the possibilities of Black radical imagination, as France's colony, Saint-Domingue was the site of the first successful slave revolution in the Western Hemisphere. While the revolution happened in what is now Haiti, a key feature of the Black radical tradition is its insistence on transcending borders. Carruthers writes that "the struggle for Black liberation has always been global. Full of contradictions, enslaved Africans forged movements that were hyper-local but that also transcended enforced borders. In part, they were responding … to the collective punishment of Black people."[16] Similarly, the Black American left in the 1960s saw the same struggle against collective punishment. Taylor mentions a quote from Martin Luther King Jr. in the months before he was killed, emphasizing the importance of collectivity in movement building: "In these trying circumstances, the Black revolution is much more than a struggle for the rights of Negroes. It is forcing America to face all its interrelated flaws—racism, poverty, militarism and materialism. It is exposing the evils that are rooted deeply in the whole structure of our society."[17] The Black radical tradition is interested in freeing Black people from the chains of racism but also in destroying the machine that produces those chains that encircle others as well. In the Black radical tradition, "the struggle for racial justice and the general struggle for social and industrial democracy" are "inseparable … the victory of the former depend[s] largely on the success of the latter."[18] Indeed, this call catalyzes us to think more broadly about racial oppression including a gendered analysis, bringing forth what the Combahee River Collective sees as "the fact that the major systems of oppression are interlocking. The *synthesis* of these oppressions creates the conditions of our lives."[19] As such, to get a broader view of the Black radical tradition, we also must have an in-depth look at the ways race and gender interlock in the resistance of oppressions.

Just as the moderator demonstrated by saying, "We're not all going to agree" to my honest concerns over Dr. Johnson's violent rhetoric toward Black queer folks, Carruthers points out that "feminism and queer politics (and the people who engage in them) are often slandered and called divisive."[20] But, as we have seen, the Black radical tradition *depends* on the collaboration of *all* oppressed peoples to make Black folks and oppressed people everywhere free. Black queer and trans activists understand this deeply. Despite the violence Black queer and trans people face, Carruthers correctly prophesied Black queer and trans folks' heavy activism and support in the wake of George Floyd's murder: "We have been there after Black men and boys have been slain by police officers and vigilantes."[21] Decades before Carruthers, Amy Jacques Garvey, Pan-Africanist feminist and editor of the women's page in the *Negro World*, the United Negro Improvement Association's (UNIA) newspaper, "wrote extensively about the need to be anticapitalist and anti-imperialist and about the interlocking oppressions due to race, class, and gender."[22] Within Marcus Garvey's gargantuan movement of the early twentieth century, calls for a synthesis of oppressions were already being made, illustrating the centrality of feminist and queer perspectives in Black movement building.

Blackness as Queerness: The Black Queer Feminist Lens

As I have suggested, a gendered analysis of racial oppression is imperative to understanding the breadth of injustice in the United States. I, along with other scholars, go further to assert that thinking about Blackness as queerness is useful for positioning Blackness in opposition to the state to critique it, instead of positioning Blackness in opposition to queerness. I place Philip Brian Harper's understanding of "[q]ueer theory [as] an articulating principle functioning in, across, between, and among various social domains and political experiences . . . [that] is therefore consciously provisional and dynamic, strategic and mobilizing, rather than prescriptive or doctrinal"[23] alongside Carruthers's understanding of the Black Queer Feminist (BQF) lens as "a political praxis . . . based in Black feminist and LGBTQ traditions and knowledge [in] which people . . . bring their full selves into the process of dismantling all systems of oppression."[24] In other words, as Kiesling writes: "Ultimately, the discourse surrounding black queerness, re-queers the nation by, paradoxically, bringing queerness back into a marginal position from which it can be critical of the state."[25] To be in the optimal position to build liberation movements—and, therefore, critique the state—we must queer our politics to fully see the range of oppressions from the margins.

While the moderator of the town hall endorsed the Black Lives Matter movement and repeated the phrase, I am not sure if their politics align with his. Thankfully, the Black Lives Matter movement is specific precisely where his antiracist discourse was not. Thus, an exploration of the Black Lives Matter movement's principles is warranted. Indeed, it provides an important model for a BQF framework to thrive.

As a powerful response to the moderator's dismissal of my concerns, Kiesling writes that "#Blacklivesmatter . . . does not eschew the messy terrain of politics at the intersection of queerness and blackness."[26] Indeed it would be silly to suggest that an actual conversation about Dr. Johnson's politics would be simple and lovely, but seeing as how Black Lives Matter "centers blackness while employing a queer framework to recognize and acknowledge the multiple intersections of both blackness and queerness," the topic would be a *central* question instead of a marginal one.[27] A BQF framework is one that is "full of contradictions" as Carruthers writes.[28] Thus, BQF asks us to lean into the discomfort at the intersection of race and gender, as it is there that radical possibilities abound.

The film *The Same Difference* by Nneka Onourah provides insight into the ability of Black queerness to destabilize and reimagine both queerness and Blackness.[29] In the documentary, Onourah highlights Black queer women and discusses discrimination against nontraditional gender performances in the Black lesbian community. By doing so, Onourah reflects a politic that "challenges the supposed homogeneity of the black community as well as the whiteness of queerness."[30] Four nontraditional stud women are interviewed for the film to highlight their deviance from the typical masculine stud script, revealing their marginalization within an already marginalized community. One stud in particular, Jordan, is pregnant and struggles with discrimination by an online community that is repulsed by Jordan's pregnancy. At the same time, Onourah includes other studs who offer rigid rules for stud representation, including "you have to be stud or femme, no in between" and "no stud on stud," while also presenting Black lesbians who break those rules, suggesting radical possibilities of being. Kiesling adds: "The black queer women in *The Same Difference* disrupt the normative gender expressions and sexualities of a dominant heterosexual majority at the same time as they challenge normative ideas about queerness. Countless couples and individuals that do not stick to the relationship rules, or somehow invalidate authentic masculinity, challenge blackness and queerness simultaneously."[31] I read this as a queerness within queerness that can go on ad infinitum. Applying a BQF lens to the possibilities of queer politics, knowing that there is always a smaller margin, another difference to consider, also means there are more complex ways of being Black and queer beyond our current grasp.

The nontraditional studs in the film reflect this sentiment of specificity, while also emphasizing the importance of collective action, stating that "none of us are like each other" and "we all need to come together for the greater good and work together to advance our movement." Indeed, this is a primary concern of the Black radical tradition: collective action as opposed to specific struggles. As Carruthers writes, "radical Black cultural workers . . . have had to . . . tell more complete stories about Black history that don't simply add women and LGBTQ folks but that center us."[32] Blackness as queerness gives us an intellectual vantage point that helps us both see further and imagine greater.

Conclusion

Although his words annoyed me, I am grateful for the moderator's dismissal at the virtual town hall, as it was a powerfully illustrative example of the kind of Black liberation movement I do not want to be a part of. The politics of Black Lives Matter and of the women in *The Same Difference* reflect a radical queerness that embraces the messy social struggles of those most marginalized. In doing so, they enable a powerful critique of mainstream queerness and Blackness, while encouraging collective action from a BQF lens. In other words, by centering the margins, we center all of us. By using a BQF lens to transcend the fictive borders that encircle us, we are better able to leave the confines of the mainstream, individualistic discourse in favor of a dynamic, complex, challenging framework that includes every being touched by the sting of oppression.

While the moderator said, "We're not all going to agree" to avoid a tough conversation, he unwittingly reflected the variety, rigor, and radical possibility of a Black queer feminist lens. Humorously, he could consciously use this framework as well, by engaging with the discomfort instead of dismissing it. The Black radical tradition has liberated countless folks using this paradigm—it is one worth resurrecting today.

Notes

1   Adolph Reed Jr., "The Limits of Anti-Racism," *Left Business Observer*, 121, September 2009, accessed June 1, 2022, https://www.leftbusinessobserver.com/Antiracism.html.

2   Combahee River Collective, *The Combahee River Collective Statement: Black Feminist Organizing in the Seventies and Eighties* (Latham, NY: Kitchen Table/Women of Color Press, 1986).

3   Charlene Carruthers, *Unapologetic: A Black, Queer, and Feminist Mandate for Radical Movements* (Boston: Beacon Press, 2018).

4   Reed, "The Limits of Anti-Racism."

5   Linda Corrigan, "Queering the Panthers: Rhetorical Adjacency and Black/Queer Liberation Politics," *QED: A Journal in GLBTQ Worldmaking* 6, no. 2 (2019): 3, accessed June 1, 2022, https://files.libcom.org/files/CorriganQueeringthePanthers2019.pdf.

6   Elena Kiesling, "The Missing Colors of the Rainbow: Black Queer Resistance," *European Journal of American Studies* 11, no. 3 (January 2017): 3–4, accessed June 1, 2022, https://tinyurl.com/48dspfcm.

7   Ibid., 5.

8   Ibid.

9   Christina B. Hanhardt, *Safe Space: Gay Neighborhood History and the Politics of Violence* (Durham, NC: Duke University Press, 2013).

10 Kiesling, "The Missing Colors of the Rainbow," 4.

11   Keeanga-Yamahtta Taylor, *From #BlackLivesMatter to Black Liberation* (Chicago: Haymarket Books, 2016), 51.

12   Michelle Alexander, *The New Jim Crow: Mass Incarceration in the Age of Colorblindness* (New York: New Press, 2012), 199.

13   Kiesling, "The Missing Colors of the Rainbow," 6.

14   Reed, "The Limits of Anti-Racism."

15   Carruthers, *Unapologetic*, 19.

16   Ibid., 29.

17   Taylor, *From #BlackLivesMatter to Black Liberation*, 56.

18   Reed, "The Limits of Anti-Racism."

19   Combahee River Collective, *The Combahee River Collective Statement*; emphasis added.

20   Carruthers, *Unapologetic*, 5.

21   Ibid.

22   Ibid.

23   Phillip B. Harper, *Are We Not Men? Masculine Anxiety and the Problem of African-American Identity* (Oxford: Oxford University Press, 1998), 1.

24   Carruthers, *Unapologetic*, 43.

25   Kiesling, "The Missing Colors of the Rainbow," 10.

26   Ibid.

27   Ibid., 7.

28   Carruthers, *Unapologetic*, 10.

29   Nneka Onourah, dir., *The Same Difference* (New York: Women Make Movies, 2015).

30   Kiesling, "The Missing Colors of the Rainbow," 12.

31   Ibid., 14.

32   Carruthers, *Unapologetic*, 61.

Queer Archives

Exceeding Survival

Militant Memory as a Praxis of Black Feminist, Anarchist World-Making

aems dinunzio

"We reject attempts to document this moment that fails to center the Black experience or that fails to document the facts about the State's role in inflicting Black pain. We commit to modeling care in our memory work because Black people deserve care. We commit to doing ethical memory work that protects Black people because racist state-sanctioned violence also resists documentation. We commit to archival practices that support accountability and historical accuracy because when the dust settles attempts will be made to rewrite the history."

—Zakiya Collier

"These institutions were not created for us ... but we can find ways to burrow in and to get what we need out of these institutions, even though those institutions may be fighting us all the way. . . . How do we dream community-based archives as well? How do we deal with what already exists [and] also say 'What do we want?' What would be the vision for a truly liberated archive created by the people who are directly impacted, held by the people that are directly impacted, and used for the liberation and freedom of people who are directly impacted (and therefore for all of us)? What would that look like?"
—Walidah Imarisha

"We in the fight for freedom must use memory work as a bullet for liberation."
—Doria Johnson

Collier, Imarisha, and Johnson articulate a vision of memory work that responds to the compounded crises of racial capitalism, climate devastation, white supremacy, settler colonialism, and patriarchal cisheteronormativity.[1] Black archivists, librarians, and other memory workers often bear the brunt of this labor, calling for radical interrogation of violent dynamics while being delegitimized in favor of superficial reform that fails to disrupt hegemonic power.[2] For example, Yusef Omowale of the Southern California Library (SCL) describes how dominant institutions have offered "affirmation, recognition, and legitimacy of minoritized life" in response to "social movements demanding acknowledgement that we too deserve breath and the joy of life."[3] Accepting this institutional legitimacy, he warns, means "to be incorporated into the existing order of capitalism, American exceptionalism, patriarchy and violence" at the expense of "others who do not meet the requirements of empire."[4] In response, Omowale proposes "refusing offers of inclusion and recognition, and instead demanding redistribution" of life-giving care, resources, and community sovereignty.[5] He concludes that "if we are to restore and document our humanity . . . we must first seek to archive lives lived in spaces of impossibility," referring to those "suffering slow deaths of incarceration, poverty, and environmental toxicity."[6]

Drake, Hathcock, and Omowale identify how institutions founded upon and buttressed by white supremacy, racial capitalism, and settler colonialism will ultimately work to diffuse the potentials of radical memory work, while continuing to profit materially and symbolically from it. These profits represent neoliberalism's "stripped-down, non-redistributive form of 'equality' . . . compatible with continued upward redistribution of resources."[7] Instead, activist memory workers call for a disruption of institutional enticements that seek to neutralize the subversive potentials of alternative praxes. As Omowale says, "The values we must practice are ones of refusal. Refusal not as an act of negation, but as a condition of possibility."[8]

Since my formal entry into the archives field via enrollment at the University of Texas's School of Information in 2017, preceded by years of organizing with the Inside Books Project (IBP), Texas After Violence Project, Austin Anarchist Black Cross, and other groups informed by prison abolitionist praxis, I have worked to articulate how this organizing fundamentally informs my archival work.[9] Documenting prison practices, responding to book and information requests, conducting oral histories with survivors of state violence, and visiting people in juvenile and death row facilities expanded my role beyond that of an information worker to relations of affinity, solidarity, and mutual aid. These relationships were often curtailed by state-sanctioned execution and other forms of hegemonic violence, embedding my growth as an archivist with a sense of critical urgency.

These intersections of memory work, intimate affinities, and carceral violence cultivated what I describe as a *militant memory praxis* (MMP). This praxis contextualizes archival and documentation efforts in the state of perpetual crisis engendered by racial capitalism, settler colonialism, imperialism, and all appendages of the carceral state.[10] I draw on *militancy* rather than the closely aligned concept of *liberatory* memory work to reflect my specific identification as a queer, nonbinary anarchist committed to abolition, not only of prisons but all forms of statist and hierarchical power; this commitment is not driven by a hope of reconciliation, but by an embrace of insurrection.[11]

Archivists, activists, scholars, and academics have developed diverse understandings of *liberatory memory work* (LMW) that is "premised on the need to work with the past, to insist on accountability, to acknowledge and address pain and trauma, and to reveal hidden dimensions of human rights violations."[12] One dialogue series on LMW expressed a set of "necessary processes" in "reckoning with the past," which include "storytelling, research, memorialization, redress and reparation, and punishment for those responsible for violation."[13] In this final process, they add that "the state must ensure a process of punishment for those responsible for past violations" (in the context of this series, discussion centered on "crimes against humanity" and "human rights violations").[14] All of these "necessary processes," they argue, "require 'liberatory memory work,'" as "justice is unimaginable without it"; consequently, at times it is warned that their work "may be seen to be in opposition to the state."[15]

Given the diversity of backgrounds and participant perspectives in this dialogue series, there were points of divergence and contention. In a reflection coauthored by Doria Johnson, Jarrett Drake, and Michelle Caswell, they discuss the importance of holding "action, critique, and vision in tandem," and acknowledging "reformational inputs cannot birth transformational outputs."[16] They continue: "[We] must imagine new methods of memory work that extend beyond standard modes of memorialization that receive state funding, university support, or capitalist endorsement. These new methods might involve approaches that are guerilla in nature yet grand in purpose. . . . To engage in memory work within ongoing conflicts is to step in the line of fire with a vest and a vision to advocate for justice over peace and for truth over reconciliation. . . . In order to generate these futures, memory work should be dangerous."[17]

My conception of militant memory praxis is aligned with their vision and builds on it through Black feminist, queer, and decolonial anarchism. Militant memory is intentionally and unrepentantly in opposition to the state and its appendages, with whom there is no point of restoration or reconciliation. Militant memory is a *praxis,* in that it centers putting theory into practice via sabotage, piracy, insurrection, expropriation, and redistribution. Drawing on these tactics, MMP seeks to disrupt the ongoing sequestering of resources by statist institutions, actively sabotaging the capacity of minoritized communities to survive and mobilize in the here and now. Militant memory identifies statist hegemony for what it is, because the more we skirt around naming violence in fear of offending its agents, the more we delegitimize those who are dying to dismantle it. It is a praxis that responds to the call to action from those shouldering the brunt of this labor by asking: How can we as queers, criminals, deviants, dykes, anarchists, and other coconspirators against the state, radically dismantle its appendages of power, and what does it actually look like to draw on an archival praxis informed by Black feminist, decolonial anarchist, and critical trans imaginaries?

Before exploring these questions, I want to clarify the concept of *archive(s)*, the *archival field, profession,* and *memory work.* First, the Society of American Archivists (SAA) defines *archives* as "the permanently valuable records—such as letters, reports, accounts, minute books, draft and final manuscripts, and photographs—of people, businesses, and government. These records are kept because they have continuing value to the creating agency and to other potential users. They are the documentary evidence of past events. They are the facts we use to interpret and understand history." In other words, archival objects are sources of evidence through which we can formulate understandings of the past. These understandings are informed by Western, white, settler-colonialist, and racial-capitalist notions of linear time, value, truth, and objectivity. *To archive* is to identify, acquire, and preserve these materials of historic value, as understood (or assigned) by the individual or organization assessing said materials. A capital "A" *Archive(s)* is "an organization dedicated to preserving the documentary heritage of a particular group: a city, a province or state, a business, a university, or a community."[18] The *archives profession* generally refers to archivists with formal education (i.e., graduate-level degrees) and certification that dubs them qualified to "assert control and order over bodies of records."[19] They work in business administration, state and local government, higher education, museums, and libraries, doing work that is purportedly "too important, complex, and demanding to be handled satisfactorily by people who lack professional training and experience."[20] Professional organizations create the standards, certifications, and policies meant to structure practices across the field. It is this concept of professionalization that Omowale refuses, asserting that communities have long possessed the knowledge and skill sets to document their histories, even when deprived of institutional sanctioning and resources.[21]

Alternatively, the language of the *archives field* and *memory work* encompasses noninstitutionalized labor often excluded from (or intentionally distanced from) professionalization. These types of archives are often described as community-based, grassroots, or independent, referencing their autonomy from dominant organizations.[22] They often serve as spaces of activism, education, and camaraderie.[23] *Memory work* comprises forms of cultural preservation and transmission beyond strict notions of "archives," like oral histories in Indigenous communities, a shelf of zines in an anarchist bookshop, or binders of incarcerated people's poetry collected by pen pal groups. I conceive of memory work as any activity taken to intentionally collect and preserve information (such as documents, art, stories, and other forms of cultural expression) due to its perceived value in representing, constructing, or challenging understandings of the past. Memory work plays a crucial role in *world-building*, by which I mean engaging in acts to construct the type of society we would like to live in.

So-Called Impossible Worldviews

Anarchism can be described as a philosophy, praxis, and/or a worldview that is exceedingly diverse in its range of tactics and theoretical frameworks. Some commonly shared tenets include the abolition of statist, hegemonic political power in favor of nonhierarchical modes of organization, the redistribution of resources from dominant minorities to dispossessed majorities, direct-action methods for achieving change and combating oppression (methods ranging from pacifism to insurrection, depending on the school of thought), and social relations based on mutual aid, solidarity, and autonomy.[24] Some anarchist intellectual traditions include collectivism, mutualism, primitivism, green or eco-anarchism, anarcho-communism, feminist and queer anarchisms, and anarcho-syndicalism, to name a few.[25] There is also "anarchism without adjectives," embracing all these forms, so long as they fall under the broad umbrella of anarchy, which "admits of any kind of organization, so long as membership is not compulsory."[26]

The anarchism I draw upon is informed by an array of these traditions, but specifically draws on Black feminist, decolonial, queer, and trans epistemologies. I center these epistemologies, despite leftist condemnation of "identity politics," because canonical anarchism is steeped in Eurocentric, settler-colonial, cisheteronormative, and patriarchal domination that necessitates critical recognition and disruption. On the tendency of predominantly white cisgender anarchists who debase "[so-called] 'identity politics' for dividing the ranks of workers," Zoé Samudzi aptly responds, "as though employing 'proletariat' is not an identity politic or as if 'working class' is not an identity."[27] In other words, an analysis of hegemonic class oppression cannot be detached from analyses of racial capitalism, settler colonialism, ableism, patriarchy, and cisheteronormativity. A Black feminist anarchism does not construe Black women as a monolithic or essentialist abstraction; rather, it draws on "black feminism [as] a modality for understanding how the anti-black settler state is a fundamentally illegitimate construction."[28] Black liberation is antithetical to the existence of the settler state, because the state will always position Blackness as "exploitable, commodifiable, and enslaveable."[29] These analyses are not new; as Saidiya Hartman says, "Black people have been abandoned by the law, positioned outside the nation, and excluded from the terms of the social contract—and this recognition is in fact hundreds of years old."[30] Rather than arguing for neoliberal reform and inclusion, Samudzi and Anderson warn that corporate capitalism and the nonprofit-industrial complex are "inextricably linked to the anti-Black carceral system [that works to] compromise and neutralize political movements."[31]

Similarly, Dean Spade's framework of a "critical trans politics" is informed by feminist, queer, antiracist, and disability studies analyses that challenge neoliberal imperatives.[32] He specifically critiques liberal capitalist discourses of human rights and hate crimes legislation that work to perpetuate carceral statist hegemony, while failing to actually prevent violence in the day-to-day lives of trans people.[33] As an alternative, Spade offers: "[a]

transformative approach . . . that accurately conceptualizes the conditions trans people face and more directly strategizes change that impacts the well-being of trans people . . . It is rooted in a shared imagination of a world without imprisonment, colonialism, immigration enforcement, sexual violence, or wealth disparity. It is sustained by social movement infra-structure that is democratic, nonhierarchical, and centered in healing."[34]

This "shared imagination" Spade points to is particularly resonant with my conception of the role of memory work in grassroots social move-ments. Public memory is largely informed by hegemonic "official" histories promoted by the state in the mass media, by heritage institutions, and in academia. Speaking about transformative justice, Alexis Pauline Gumbs says that "the moments in which prisons became a dominant feature of the US, our imaginations . . . also became imprisoned. The way we imagine work, our relationships, the future, family, everything, is locked down."[35] Spade's critical trans politics seeks to intervene in this collective lockdown through direct action to support the lives of trans people and nonhierar-chical mobilization based on collective visions of justice. These visions are built from "the so-called impossible worldview of trans political existence," referring to the ways that dominant discourses construe trans people as "impossible people who cannot exist, cannot be seen, cannot be classified, and cannot fit anywhere . . . that we are not politically viable; our lives are not a political possibility that can be conceived. Inside this impossibil-ity, I argue, lies our specific political potential—a potential to formulate demands and strategies to meet those demands that exceed the contain-ment of neoliberal politics."[36]

Here, again, "impossibility" serves as a site of world-making, anti-hegemonic memory work and coalition building against neoliberal racial capitalism. There are many archives and documentation projects draw-ing on these Black feminist, queer, and trans epistemologies; for example, the BYP100 "She Safe, We Safe Story Collection Project" works to create "visions for what our communities need in order to build a world without state and gender violence," representing the revolutionary potentials of an archival praxis that is "abolitionist . . . unapologetically Black . . . gener-ative and empowering."[37] This pairing of storytelling and documentation with the capacity to act, mobilize, and construct liberatory imaginaries is central to my concept of militant memory praxis. In the following section, I will reflect on how these "impossible worldviews" have informed my own archival work and praxis of militant memory.

The Inside Books Project Archive

The Inside Books Project (IBP) was founded in 1998 by a handful of anarchists and antiauthoritarians, to send free books to incarcerated people in Texas.[38] Collective members show volunteers how to read and respond to incarcerated patrons' information requests by compiling a package of books and writing a letter of care and solidarity. In return, many incarcerated patrons send IBP creative works as a "thank you" for the free resources, as an outlet for expression, and as testimony to their everyday experiences within the prison system. Creative works include crafts, poetry, prose, essays, and photographs. The intimate process of responding to patrons' letters and engaging with their creative works is often a transformative, even radicalizing, encounter for volunteers, who are pushed to examine assumptions they may hold about imprisoned people. Materials produced by the prison, such as censorship documents, also challenge volunteers' assumptions. Seeing white supremacist, patriarchal logics at work in the rhetoric of these documents challenges popular conceptions of the prison-industrial complex that are disconnected from its roots in slavery, colonization, and racial capitalism; it provokes a historical remembering that we are meant to forget.

Over the years, I observed how these narrative exchanges between incarcerated patrons, prison mailrooms, and IBP volunteers challenged the memory construction of carceral regimes. I felt an online space that preserved and shared both incarcerated people's narratives and the prison system's censorship records would expand the terrain of these disruptions. I founded the IBP Archive (IBPA) in 2015, which I reflect on as an ongoing experiment in cultivating militant memory, transformative justice, and abolition. These concepts are often ridiculed as unrealistic, in large part because so often we fail to articulate how we have put our theories into action (i.e., we fail to articulate our praxis), avoiding the seemingly banal everyday practices that are the substrate of mobilization work. To avoid this trap, I will describe some everyday practices and policies of the IBPA informed by militant memory, not as a blueprint but as an open reflection on the ways that grassroots archival work can create spaces of prefigurative experimentation and world-making.

Appraisal and Acquisition

The archives profession identifies a set of "core archival principles" that include appraisal, acquisition, description, access, preservation, and

Image 1: Pen drawing by Inker Nora, "Thank you IBP."

"controlling and promoting use" of archives.[39] All of these principles are embedded in legacies of white supremacist, settler-colonialist looting, dispossession, and genocide. *Appraisal*, the process determining what has historical value and warrants long-term preservation, and *acquisition*, the process of procuring and taking these items into custody, particularly demonstrate capitalist and colonialist logics. Rather than taking possession of materials and treating them like commodities, militant memory centers tenets of autonomy, consent, and sovereignty. The IBPA affirms the agency of incarcerated creators in processes of preserving and sharing their narratives. The appraisal policy does not conceal the power and subjectivity at play but transparently states that those disproportionately targeted by state violence are prioritized for publishing. Archival items do not belong to IBPA; the creator can remove or change the way their content is shared at any time.

Preservation and Use

Another traditional archival function is "controlling and promoting the use" of materials.[40] These guidelines include "considering possible theft," and only allowing those who "abide by the archives' rules and regulations" to access materials.[41] Guidelines for accessing archives usually include

Image 2: Color pencil drawing by Edee E. Davis, "Pride."

supervision, requiring a government issued ID to document the name and the records a person will be accessing. Surveillance in reading rooms targets identities that have been historically construed as criminal or disruptive, such as Black, gender "nonnormative," and disabled people. Furthermore, strict policies on access and use constrain the intentions of creators, who imagine their creative works as sites of intimacy, communication, and engagement.

Militant memory seeks to disrupt barriers to access and participation in our own histories. Rather than performing respectable normativity, it is a guerilla praxis embracing transgression, expropriation, and redistribution. MMP facilitates radical access to our cultural legacies, not strictly for academic research but for radical mobilization, joyful affinity, and intimate identification. It aligns with "preservation through use," or "using the materials . . . as a means of helping others (re)discover marginalized social histories and continue to build new social movement culture" and "activating materials via their accessibility."[42] For example, many submissions to the IBPA are writing or crafts meant to be directly engaged with by volunteers. Storing these away in folders removes the intimacy and intention of multimodal, tactile engagement, so these are redistributed after digitization. Furthermore, in contrast to traditional archives, the IBPA encourages communication between incarcerated creators and people accessing the archive to view their works. The subject/object relations upheld in traditional institutions curtail these potentials. Militant memory recognizes that abolitionist social movements must engage in dialogue and collaboration with incarcerated communities and facilitate transgressive narrative exchanges across physical and digital space.

Description, Access, and Provenance

The Society of American Archivists states that the purpose of description is "to facilitate the work's identification, management, and understanding."[43] Description—through the use of tags, metadata, and tools like finding aids—enables people to locate items and understand their provenance, which is particularly bound up in racial-capitalist and colonialist logics of ownership, hierarchy, and bureaucratic power.[44] While these processes are meant to be standardized and objective, Samudzi reminds us that "'objectivity' is the subjectivity of power and hegemony," and "authoritative claims to knowing and describing the world, rather, are part of a social-structural apparatus that act in service of empire."[45] This is particularly relevant for the IBPA, which is engaging with data produced, structured, and leveraged by the carceral state, such as socially constructed categories of gender, race, ethnicity, and even intelligence.[46] Unaccountable use of this data can reify state surveillance and administrative violence. For example, content published online could result in legal or extralegal repercussions for creators. Trans creators may want to publish under a name different from the one they use in prison or to remain anonymous. MMP asks, how can we disrupt hegemonic normalization and compulsory integration into the nation-state's notion of citizenship and subjecthood? Militant memory draws on critical trans politics, which challenges the constructed norms of administrative bureaucracy that regulate capacities to survive.[47] It deploys strategic descriptive practices that subvert surveillance while affirming individual identities and survival. For the IBPA, incarcerated creators define their own terms of legibility. Rather than census-style documents that reflect settler state logics, description forms for creators to fill out and return with submissions utilize both standardized tags and free-text fields. There are no compulsory categories or replication of carceral language, such as "offender" and "perpetrator." Creators provide their own language and range of anonymity. Alternatively, descriptive practices for prison records disrupt the desired anonymity of carceral administrative violence, providing public access to data on administrative practices that can be accessed for both legal and extralegal mobilization and for *sousveillance*.

Militant Memory as *Sousveillance*

The last application of MMP I will discuss is in relation to "racializing surveillance" and *sousveillance*. Simone Browne's concept of "racializing surveillance" describes "a technology of social control where surveillance practices, policies, and performances concern the production of norms pertaining to race and exercise a power to define what is in or out of place."[48] The archive of prison censorship records digitized in the IBPA exemplifies these practices, laying out how carceral logics criminalize and destroy particular narratives deemed "out of place." For example, works like *Narrative of the Life of Frederick Douglass, an American Slave, The Autobiography of Malcolm X*, and Stephen Duncombe's *Cultural Resistance Reader* are banned,[49] because, according to the prison, they "contain material that a reasonable person would construe as written solely for the purpose of communicating information to achieve the breakdown of prisons through offender disruption such as strikes, riot, or security threat group activity."[50]

Other texts are deemed "detrimental to offenders' rehabilitation" because they would "encourage deviant criminal sexual behavior."[51] This is applied to Alice Walker's *The Color Purple*, Toni Morrison's *The Bluest Eye*, and Ann Moody's *Coming of Age in Mississippi*,[52] all books by Black women that discuss issues around race, gender, and sexuality. In the document under "remarks," where employees explain their censorship reasoning, they often write "racial," indicating the ways that intersections of gender and sexuality inform "racializing surveillance."[53] By producing these portraits of criminality, the state construes, regulates, and reifies those lives that are possible, or impossible. This ideological power seeps into broader understandings of criminality and deviancy sustained through cultural, political, and social institutions (including archives, museums, and libraries). In sum, the "Texas Department of Criminal Justice (TDCJ) Censorship Collection" attests to the ways that nation-states produce discourse, propaganda, and public knowledge in an act of "aggressive memory construction" that holds "immense mobilizing potential" and works to "legitimize current political regimes."[54]

Alternatively, a militant memory praxis deploys technologies of sousveillance. *Sousveillance*, literally *to watch from below*, is *both a technology and social practice* reflecting situations where top-down surveillance is inverted (e.g., "cop watches" that follow and record police).[55] Collecting, preserving, and providing access to prison administrative records subverts the unquestioned power of racializing surveillance and builds up sites of information that can be drawn on to challenge state practices. For the IBPA, geolocation on Omeka allows us to map out which prison units have created the corresponding censorship record, unveiling the architectural and ideological panopticism of carceral logics.[56]

By removing the identifying data of incarcerated patrons whose books are banned and instead highlighting information about the prison and its practices, the IBPA subtly subverts carceral administrative power. For example, we find the unit codes in the censorship records, matching these with a key on the TDCJ website and inputting the address in the geolocation field on Omeka.[57] This process directly connects censorship records to prison unit data, such as the type and size of facilities as well as agricultural, manufacturing, and logistics operations (i.e., unpaid prison labor).[58] Other documentation tools, like the Internet Archive's "Wayback Machine," also act as technologies of sousveillance, by preserving web page changes over time, Wayback allows one to access prison data across decades, even after it's altered or removed from the prison website.

These small, day-to-day practices of sousveillance disrupt the layers of opacity the prison system depends on to assure that its arbitrary and violent logics go unquestioned and unchallenged.[59] In this way, militant memory praxis intervenes in the ideological, sociocultural, and political logics of racial capitalist settler colonialism, contributing to a collective imaginary built on abolition.

Militant Memory and "Archives of Survival"

Since the outbreak of the COVID-19 pandemic, the IBPA has collaborated with the Texas After Violence Project (TAVP) to document the intersections of COVID-19 and mass incarceration through the Sheltering Justice Project.[60] This project is what TAVP's executive director Gabriel Solis describes as an "archive of survival," i.e., an archive that has "emerged as a direct response to state violence happening in our communities in real time [to] reflect life, energy, and resistance in the face of this violence, annihilation, and erasure."[61] In this way, "archives of survival" are direct-action methods to combat ongoing violence and carceral logics permeating public memory. These logics seek to normalize, individualize, or invisibilize the onslaught of violence waged against criminalized identities. By digitizing the narratives of incarcerated people in the context of the pandemic and of mass protests against police violence and contextualizing these narratives within legacies of racial capitalist settler violence, the IBPA collaborates with TAVP to subvert hegemonic history and knowledge; as Solis says, "the insurrection of subjugated knowledges *is* the archive."[62]

Herein lies the essence of *militant memory praxis*: insurrection. Hegemonic institutions have enjoyed profiting from the voices, labor, and theorization of insurrectionists. They enjoy giving selected discounts on exorbitant registration fees while retaining broad-based inaccessibility, publishing on the unacknowledged labor of others, and selectively allocating funds to projects deemed legitimate. They invite insurrectionists to conduct workshops and give keynotes, applauding from a comfortable distance and maintaining the accumulation of resources kept behind ivory gates. Well, now we're at the gates, and we demand more than the right to survive.

Conclusion

> "There are mechanisms in our stories that can be re-imagined as a living practice of Abolition. How do we begin to not just rehearse revolution in this way, but realize it too?"[63]
> —Afrofuturist Abolitionists of the Americas

As I critically interrogate the role of archives in a project of neoliberal upward distribution, I situate myself within these embedded power relations that are integral to the functioning of the profession and of academia. My intention is not to reinforce binary or simplistic notions of institutional versus community-based, oppressor and oppressed, but to be in dialogue with those who share commitments to disrupting power as it operates across these spaces and through our day-to-day lives. I hope more memory workers leverage their power to redirect funds, refuse reformist compromise, and tear out the roots of statist hegemony rather than pruning its leaves. People who benefit from white supremacy, myself included, should be particularly cognizant of the ways that the capacity to engage in undermining practices within institutional spaces is not evenly distributed. We should embrace the role of race traitors, and "traitors to our institutions," as Scott writes in the introduction to this volume, by collectively engaging in antihegemonic action and resisting neoliberal solutions of visibility and inclusion. Even minor resistances to hierarchical power can destabilize job stability and access to resources necessary for survival. Therefore, militant memory should be practiced in such a way that we collectively dismantle power while critically reflecting on the ways our identities, bodies, and affinities are disparately targeted by racial capitalist settler state power. In "Accomplices Not Allies," Indigenous Action describes how the "ally-industrial complex" leverages the language of "grassroots" and "community-based," while gatekeeping, co-opting, or philosophizing on structural violence.[64] Instead of allies, they call for "accomplices," "a person who helps another person commit a crime," those who will "become complicit in a struggle toward liberation [and] seek ways to leverage resources and material support and/or betray their institution to further liberation struggles . . . they must strategize with, not for, and not be afraid to pick up a hammer."[65] It is my hope that more memory workers in positions of power choose to take up this hammer, unapologetically dismantling neoliberal and reformist discourses meant to tamper with our radical imaginaries. I also hope that more anarcho-queer comrades and coconspirators against the state consider archives, documentation, and memory work as tools for mobilization; acknowledging too Omowale's reminder that many already are. At the intersection of my desires lies a coalitional insurrection that deploys militant memory as praxis of liberation exceeding survival.

Notes

1   Zakiya Collier, "Call to Action: Archiving State-Sanctioned Violence against Black People," Medium, June 6, 2020, accessed June 2, 2022, https://tinyurl.com/44kz2xxu; originally published in *Sustainable Futures*. "Transcript of Walidah's Liberated Archives Keynote," Walidah Imarisha" (blog), August 22, 2017, accessed June 2, 2022, http://www.walidah.com/blog/2017/8/22/transcript-of-walidahs-liberated-archives-keynote. Doria Johnson, cited in Jarrett M. Drake, "In the Direction of Freedom," Medium, March 9, 2021, accessed June 2, 2022, https://medium.com/texas-after-violence-project/in-the-direction-of-freedom-8a75094988f7; originally published by Texas After Violence Project. Robin D.G. Kelley, "What Did Cedric Robinson Mean by Racial Capitalism?" *Boston Review*, January 12, 2017, accessed June 2, 2022, http://bostonreview.net/race/robin-d-g-kelley-what-did-cedric-robinson-mean-racial-capitalism.

2   April Hathcock, "White Librarianship in Blackface: Diversity Initiatives in LIS," In the Library with the Lead Pipe, October 7, 2015, accessed June 2, 2022, http://inthelibrarywiththeleadpipe.org/2015/lis-diversity; Jarrett M. Drake, "Diversity's Discontents: In Search of an Archive of the Oppressed," *Archives and Manuscripts* 47, no. 2 (March 2019): 270–79; Joseph V. Femia, "The Concept of Hegemony," in *Gramsci's Political Thought: Hegemony, Consciousness, and the Revolutionary Process* (Oxford: Clarendon Press, 1981).

3   Yusef Omowale, "We Already Are," Medium, September 3, 2018, accessed June 2, 2022, https://medium.com/community-archives/we-already-are-52438b863e31;

originally published in *Sustainable Futures*; I.E. Smith, "Minority vs. Minoritized," Odyssey Online, September 2, 2016, accessed June 2, 2022, https://www. theodysseyonline.com/minority-vs-minoritize.

4   Omowale, "We Already Are."

5   Ibid.

6   Ibid.

7   Lisa Duggan, *The Twilight of Equality? Neoliberalism, Cultural Politics, and the Attack on Democracy* (Boston: Beacon Press, 2003), xi.

8   Omowale, "We Already Are."

9   aems dinunzio, "Abolition in the Archive: Impossible Futurities Imagined through a Critical Trans Politics," course paper for "Archival Enterprise II," taught by Ciaran Trace, University of Texas, Austin, May 1, 2019. Many other archivists have written on the intersections of carcerality and memory work, including Tonia Sutherland, "The Carceral Archive: Documentary Records, Narrative Construction, and Predictive Risk Assessment" *Journal of Cultural Analytics* 4, no. 1 (2019), accessed June 2, 2022, https://tinyurl.com/397nket8; Jarrett M. Drake, "'Graveyards of Exclusion:' Archives, Prisons, and the Bounds of Belonging," Medium, March 27, 2019, accessed June 2, 2022, https://tinyurl.com/vd833n4u; originally published in *Sustainable Futures*; Gabriel Solis, "Reflections on Archives of Violence and Transformative Justice," Medium, September 10, 2018, accessed June 2, 2022, https://tinyurl.com/25b4vrfb; originally published in *Sustainable Futures*; Randall C. Jimerson, "Embracing the Power of Archives," *American Archivist* 69, no. 1 (Spring–Summer 2006): 19–32, accessed June 2, 2022, https://www2.archivists. org/history/leaders/randall-c-jimerson/embracing-the-power-of-archives.

10   Dean Spade, *Normal Life: Administrative Violence, Critical Trans Politics, and the Limits of Law* (Durham, NC: Duke University Press, 2015).

11   I am indebted to Jane Field, archivist and associate director of the Texas After Violence Project (TAVP) for talking out these ideas with me.

12   Chandre Gould and Verne Harris, "Memory for Justice," Nelson Mandela Foundation 1, 4, accessed November 11, 2022, https://www.nelsonmandela.org/uploads/ files/MEMORY_FOR_JUSTICE_2014v2.pdf.

13   Ibid., 3–4.

14   Ibid., 4.

15   Ibid.

16   Doria D. Johnson, Jarrett M. Drake, and Michelle Caswell, "From Cape Town to Chicago to Colombo and Back Again: Toward a Liberation Theology for Memory Work," Reflections from the 2016 Mandela Dialogues, February 27, 2017, accessed June 2, 2022, https://www.nelsonmandela.org/news/entry/reflections-from-the-2016-mandela-dialogues.

17   Johnson, Drake, and Caswell, "From Cape Town to Chicago to Colombo and Back Again."

18   Society of American Archivists, "What Are Archives," accessed June 2, 2022, https://tinyurl.com/ysyjveyd.

19   Bruce Dearstyne, "The Archival Profession: Meeting Critical Institutional and Social Needs," Academy of Certified Archivists, accessed March 1, 2021https:// www.certifiedarchivists.org/archival-profession.

20   Ibid.

21   Omowale, "We Already Are."

22 For more on the rhetoric of "community-based" archives, see Jarrett M. Drake, "Seismic Shifts: On Archival Fact and Fictions," *Medium*, August 20, 2018, accessed June 2, 2022; originally published in *Sustainable Futures*.

23 Alycia Sellie, Jessie Goldstein, Molly Fair, and Jennifer Hoyer, "Interference Archive: A Free Space for Social Movement Culture," *Archival Science* 15, no. 4 (December 2015): 453–72; The Long Haul, "About Us," accessed June 17, 2022, https://thelonghaul.org/about-us; MayDay Rooms, accessed June 2, 2022, https://maydayrooms.org.

24 Black Rose/Rosa Negra Anarchist Federation, "Who Are the Anarchists and What Is Anarchism?" June 7, 2017, accessed June 2, 2022, https://blackrosefed.org/who-are-the-anarchists-and-what-is-anarchism; Voltairine de Cleyre, "Anarchism," in *Selected Works of Voltairine de Cleyre* (New York: Mother Earth Publishing Association, 1914); Lucy Parsons and Albert Parsons, *Anarchism: Its Philosophy and Scientific Basis as Defined by Some of Its Apostles*, ed. Lucy Parsons (Chicago: MrsARParsons Publisher, 1889); Sam Dolgoff, ed., *Bakunin on Anarchy: Selected Works by the Activist-Founder of World Anarchism* (New York: Alfred A Knopf, 1972).

25 C.B. Daring, *Queering Anarchism: Addressing and Undressing Power and Desire* (Oakland: AK Press, 2012); Lorenzo Kom'boa Ervin, "Anarchist Theory and Practice," in *Anarchism and the Black Revolution* (London: Pluto Press, 1979), accessed June 2, 2022, https://theanarchistlibrary.org/library/lorenzo-kom-boa-ervin-anarchism-and-the-black-revolution; Peter H. Marshall, *Demanding the Impossible: A History of Anarchism* (Oakland: PM Press, 2010); Rudolf Rocker, *Anarcho-Syndicalism: Theory and Practice* (London: Pluto Press, 1989 [1938]).

26 Kevin Carson, "Joseph Labadie—Anarchists without Adjectives," Center for a Stateless Society, March 29, 2016, accessed June 2, 2022, https://c4ss.org/content/44250.

27 Zoé Samudzi, "Race, Class, and Reparations, Zoé Samudzi in Conversation with James Wilt," *Geez*, January 31, 2019, https://geezmagazine.org/magazine/article/race-class-and-reparations.

28 Zoé Samudzi, "On a Black Feminist Anarchism (OC Anarchist Bookfair 2017)," YouTube, March 28, 2017, accessed June 2, 2022, https://www.youtube.com/watch?v=Fo9BowIVEQo&ab_channel=FoxAlive.

29 Willian C. Anderson and Zoé Samudzi, *As Black as Resistance: Finding the Conditions for Liberation* (Oakland: AK Press, 2018), 33–34.

30 Saidiya Hartman, "On Insurgent Histories and the Abolitionist Imaginary" (interview by Catherine Damman), *Art Forum*, July 14, 2020, accessed June 2, 2022, https://www.artforum.com/interviews/saidiya-hartman-83579.

31 Anderson and Samudzi, *As Black as Resistance*, 41.

32 Spade, *Normal Life*, 14.

33 Dean Spade, "What's Wrong with Rights?" in ibid.

34 Spade, *Normal Life*, 15–16.

35 Walidah Imarisha, Alexis Gumbs, Leah Lakshmi Piepzna-Samarasinha, Adrienne Maree Brown, and Mia Mingus, "The Fictions and Futures of Transformative Justice," New Inquiry, April 20, 2017, accessed June 3, 2022, https://thenewinquiry.com/the-fictions-and-futures-of-transformative-justice.

36 Spade, *Normal Life*, 19.

37 "She Safe, We Safe Black Queer Feminist Curriculum Toolkit," BYP100, accessed June 17, 2022, https://communityresourcehub.org/resources/she-safe-we-safe-black-queer-feminist-curriculum-toolkit.

38   Skot Oh and Dani King, personal correspondence, March 2, 2021.

39   "Core Archival Functions," Society of American Archivists, accessed June 3, 2022, https://www2.archivists.org/node/14804.

40   Ibid.

41   Ibid.

42   Sellie, Goldstein, Fair, and Hoyer, "Interference Archive."

43   "SAA Dictionary: Description," Society of American Archivists, accessed June 3, 2022, https://dictionary.archivists.org/entry/description.html.

44   Jarrett M. Drake, "RadTech Meets RadArch: Toward a New Principle for Archives and Archival Description," Medium, April 7, 2016, accessed June 3, 2022, https://tinyurl.com/94jy5y4z; originally published in On Archivy.

45   Zoé Samudzi, "Shifting Objectives: On Methodology and Identity Politics," Versobooks.com, July 6, 2017, https://www.versobooks.com/blogs/3310-shifting-objectives-on-methodology-and-identity-politics; also see Wendy M. Duff and Verne Harris, "Stories and Names: Archival Description as Narrating Records and Constructing Meanings," *Archival Science* 2, no. 3 (September 1, 2002): 263–85, accessed June 17, 2022, https://yalearchivalreadinggroup.pbworks.com/f/Duff&Harris.pdf.

46   "Offender Search," Texas Department of Criminal Justice, accessed June 18, 2020.

47   Spade, *Normal Life*, 57.

48   Simone Browne, *Race and Surveillance* (Milton Park, UK: Routledge, 2012), 16.

49   Frederick Douglass, *Narrative of the Life of Frederick Douglass, an American Slave* (Boston: Anti-Slavery Office no. 25, 1847); Malcom X with Alex Hayley, *The Autobiography of Malcom X* (New York: Grove Press, 1965); Stephen Duncombe, *Cultural Resistance Reader* (London: Verso, 2002).

50   Texas Department of Criminal Justice, "Denial Form for *Narrative of the Life of Frederick Douglass, an American Slave*, by Frederick Douglass," Inside Books Project Archive, August 29, 2012, accessed June 3, 2022, http://ibparchive.texasafterviolence.org/items/show/342; Texas Department of Criminal Justice, "Denial Form for *Cultural Resistance Reader* by Stephen Duncombe," Inside Books Project Archive, April 12, 2017, accessed June 3, 2022, http://ibparchive.texasafterviolence.org/items/show/314.

51   Texas Department of Criminal Justice, "Uniform Offender Correspondence Rules," February 11, 2010, accessed June 3, 2022, https://www.prisoncensorship.info/docs/r152.pdf.

52   Alice Walker, *The Color Purple* (San Diego: Harcourt Brace Jovanovich, 1982); Toni Morrison, *The Bluest Eye* (New York: Holt, Rinehart and Winston, 1970); Ann Moody, *Coming of Age in Mississippi: The Classic Autobiography of Growing Up Poor and Black in the Rural South* (New York: Bantam Dell, 1968).

53   Browne, 17; Texas Department of Criminal Justice, "Denial Form for *Coming of Age in Mississippi* by Anne Moody," Inside Books Project Archive, March 28, 2013, accessed June 3, 2022, http://ibparchive.texasafterviolence.org/items/show/262; Texas Department of Criminal Justice, "Denial Form for *Meridian* by Alice Walker," Inside Books Project Archive, July 2, 2013, accessed June 3, 2022, http://ibparchive.texasafterviolence.org/items/show/260.

54   "Texas Department of Criminal Justice (TDCJ) Censorship Documentation," Inside Books Project Archive, accessed June 3, 2022, https://ibparchive.texasafterviolence.org/collections/show/20; Lizaveta Kasmach, "Victory Day:

Between Remembrance and Militant Memory," BelarusDigest, May 10, 2016, accessed June 3, 2022, https://belarusdigest.com/story/victory-day-between-remembrance-and-militant-memory.

55 Vian Bakir, "Sousveillance," in *The SAGE Encyclopedia of Surveillance, Security, and Privacy*, edited by Bruce A. Arrigo (Thousand Oaks, CA: SAGE Publications, 2016), 943–46; A People's Archive of Police Violence in Cleveland, accessed June 3, 2022, https://www.archivingpolniceviolence.org.

56 "Browse Items on Map (42 Total)," Inside Books Project Archive, accessed June 3, 2022, http://ibparchive.texasafterviolence.org/geolocation/map/browse.

57 "Unit Codes: Key to Operator and Type of Facility," Texas Department of Criminal Justice, accessed June 3, 2022, https://www.tdcj.texas.gov/unit_directory/index.html.

58 "Clemens (CN)," Texas Department of Criminal Justice, July 31, 2009, accessed June 3, 2022, https://web.archive.org/web/20100725200949/http://www.tdcj.state.tx.us/stat/unitdirectory/cn.htm.

59 For example, I was born in the same county as the above-cited Clemens unit, but only learned of its history and simultaneous present years later, while archiving censorship records. The prison was established in 1893 by sugar plantation owner and Texas Prison Board chairperson William Clemens and almost only housed African American men. These men were exploited through the convict leasing and "state account" systems that allowed the state of Texas to continue profiting from coerced labor and agricultural production post -emancipation. Even today, the unit continues to serve as a source of unpaid agricultural labor; the only real change is that it now houses juveniles along with adults. Near the present-day dog kennels lie the bodies of imprisoned people who died during virus epidemics in the early twentieth century or of heat stroke in the fields. Heat stroke continues to kill incarcerated people in Texas, where over 75 percent of units do not have air conditioning. These archival excavations vividly connect carceral pasts to the present, laying out the lineage of racial-capitalist slavery, colonization, and genocide; see "Memorials in Clemens Unit Prison Farm Cemetery," Find A Grave, accessed March 26, 2021, accessed June 3, 2022, https://www.findagrave.com/cemetery/2508032/memorial-search#srp-top; Texas Department of Criminal Justice, *History of the Texas Department of Criminal Justice* (Nashville, TN: Turner Publishing Company, 2004), 62; "Fear, Force, and Leather—The Texas Prison System's First Hundred Years, 1848–1948: Convict Leasing and State Account Farming (1883–1909)," Texas State Libraries and Archives Commission, updated August 22, 2019, accessed June 3, 2022, https://www.tsl.texas.gov/exhibits/prisons/convictlease/page3.html; Jolie McCullough, "A Judge Told Texas to Put Some Inmates in Air Conditioning. Lawyers Say Prison Officials Are Violating That Order," *Texas Tribune*, September 5, 2019, accessed June 3, 2022, https://www.texastribune.org/2019/09/05/texas-prison-air-conditioning-heat-contempt-motion.

60 "Sheltering Justice: Stories from the Intersection of COVID-19 and Mass Incarceration," Inside Books Project Archive, accessed June 3, 2022, http://ibparchive.texasafterviolence.org/collections/show/15; Sheltering Justice (Texas After Violence Project), accessed June 3, 2022, https://shelteringjustice.texasafterviolence.org.

61 Gabriel Solis, "Sheltering Justice," Medium, May 29, 2020, accessed June 3, 2022, https://medium.com/texas-after-violence-project/sheltering-justice-

737f9209e1c1; originally published in Texas After Violence Project; Gabriel Solis, "What Are Archives of Survival?" Medium, June 17, 2019, accessed June 3, 2022, https://medium.com/texas-after-violence-project/what-are-archives-of-survival-9868af5400cc; originally published in Texas After Violence Project.

62   Ibid.

63   "What Is an Abolition Futurist?" Afrofuturist Abolitionists of the Americas, October 15, 2018, accessed June 3, 2022, https://afanarchists.wordpress.com/what-is-an-abolition-futurist.

64   "Accomplices Not Allies: Abolishing the Ally Industrial Complex, An Indigenous Perspective," Indigenous Action, May 2, 2014, accessed June 3, 2022, https://tinyurl.com/3k6at8b7.

65   Ibid.

The Figa

Jonesy and Jaime Knight

In 2015, we formed the artist collective die Kränken. The name is the translation of the German term "the sick" and references both the historic
pathologization of homosexuality and the AIDS pandemic that decimated a
generation of gay men. It's also a nod to the Blue Max, a Southern California
motorcycle club founded in 1968, which fetishized Prussian military
uniforms and culture. It was actually in response to an archive of the Blue
Max MC that we created the exhibition "Die Kränken: Sprayed with Tears,"
with curator David Evans Frantz at the ONE Gallery, at ONE National Gay
and Lesbian Archives, at the University of Southern California Libraries,
in Los Angeles. The Blue Max archive, the primary inspiration for the
exhibition, consists of nineteen boxes of material, including photographs,
meeting minutes, videotapes, and other ephemera. Along with the material
work for the show, we planned to do a series of videos made with artists,
activists, and scholars about the history, ideas, and important moments
in the development of leather subculture. Each of these videos involved
an interview with an important figure in the LGBTQ/leather community,
intertwined with a conceptual reenactment of a historical moment. Our
first, called Black Pipe Intervention, included an interview with activist
Reverend Troy Perry and was a requiem to a police raid at an LA leather bar.

The work of die Kränken is centered in leather and gay motorcycle club
culture, but there is a wider interest in what we consider the fight against
gay assimilation and homonationalist culture in the gay community.[1] In
highlighting these, in certain aspects, "unco-optable" communities and
sexual practices through aesthetic interventions, we hope to make a
statement about the radicality of these communities and practices and
the importance for a continued specifically queer relationality that exists

outside of the mainstream normative culture. For our part, we are tired of the neoliberal capitalist project of our contemporary moment and yearn for the days when gays and lesbians were saying, "Let us show you something different," rather than "Look how we can be just like you."

When in conversation with Joseph Hawkins, director of ONE, after having completed "Sprayed with Tears," it came up that certain aesthetic decisions made in relation to the archival material were inspired by essays in Gayle Rubin's *Deviations*.[2] Gayle is an important figure in the leather community and in the academic world of sexuality and women's and gender studies. A cultural anthropologist, she is most widely known for her writing on sex and its political economy. For us, it was her ethnographic work on the legendary San Francisco sex (fisting) club the Catacombs that was of interest.

After an initial email introduction by Joseph, we met Gayle in the fall of 2016 to discuss the possibility of interviewing her. Leather is often called "a second coming out," and Gayle's writing provides a portal to understanding myriad pleasures and the permission to act upon them. In fact, Jonesy considers Gayle's writing to be his own "Leatherman's Handbook,"[3] in reference to Larry Townsend's classic study. The anthology *Deviations* remains an essential reference to consult when considering empowerment, as well as conflict and struggle, in the realm of sexual practices, where power and submission play an important role in the realization of fantasy and pleasure.

Every once in a while, we're lucky enough to meet our idols in person. We have felt utterly inspired and honored to get to know someone whose work has had such a profound effect on us, both personally and in terms of our academic and artistic interests. We weren't expecting the vast resources of Gayle's archive and, after successfully blowing us away with a show of books, art, ephemera, and cultural artifacts, Gayle invited us into a long discussion. Over the course of five or so hours, Gayle enlightened us on topics as varied as the pornography wars, police harassment, the history of leather, and her involvement with BDSM communities. Eventually Gayle provided us with a personal account of the Catacombs that paralleled her infamous *Drummer* magazine article, "The Catacombs: A Temple of the Butthole."[4] Gayle's descriptions of the club became the inspiration for our next collaboration.

In *The Figa*, we take the description of Gayle's anthropological fieldwork at the Catacombs and turn it into a video that Gayle herself best describes

Image 1: Still from *The Figa* (showing Gayle Rubin with overlay with Fist Fuckers of America patch), Jonesy and Jaime C. Knight, Single Channel Video, 28 min., 2018.

as "the perfect combination of history, art, and poetics." The work interweaves portions of the interview with documentation of a performance created with artists, dancers, and choreographers. This performance is an interpretive reenactment of Gayle's descriptive narration loosely broken into three parts. The first part is a "bar" or "club" scene in which "patrons" file in, some beginning with a quotidian or menial task (setting up the bar, painting a mural) and others moving into the space to begin a series of repetitive motions. Eventually every actor/performer is engaged in some such motion. The second "chapter" is a simulated fisting scene, beginning with the setting up of a sling and the greasing of the top's fist.

Throughout *The Figa*, aside from the initial claim, the viewer doesn't hear any questions posed to Gayle, and her dialogue seems to flow naturally. This was an editorial/aesthetic choice that allows the video and interview to proceed seamlessly with Gayle's description of the Catacombs. The interstitial spaces between the topics Gayle covers are used as places to focus on the visual and sound aspects of the work. The interview took on a traditional format as it took shape, with questions posed and answered.

The generosity of Gayle and the knowledge she has shared with us while working on and screening *The Figa* is immeasurable. This has been one of the best experiences of our artistic lives and has helped to inspire our collaboration on a large body of work and several events. Gayle has truly expanded our knowledge beyond the topics of *The Figa* and has given

Image 2: Still from *The Figa* (depicting day-glo fist being painted on the wall by Jaime), Jonesy and Jaime C. Knight, Single Channel Video, 28 min., 2018.

us a glimpse into a life that is fully lived with passion, deep curiosity, absolute academic rigor, and a love of community that makes collecting and preserving the history of that community of the utmost importance. The world at large owes a debt to Gayle for her commitment to her craft on behalf of the leather community and queers in general, and we feel lucky to call her a friend.

The video opens with a black screen bearing the following statement: "It has been said that fisting is the only contemporary sexual practice that is new to the last century." The images fades to a shot of Gayle addressing the statement. (Following are from Gayle's dialogue in *The Figa*):

Now that's an interesting comment, because one can't know whether a fist was ever in a rectum before the twentieth century. I wouldn't say, yes, I wouldn't say, no. Who knows? But there's a difference between something people do and something that becomes a marked category with a social world built around it. So in terms of a social world around fisting, that is definitely late twentieth century. But I've been very curious about this, because I do have some dateable artifacts, and one of the things I wanted to figure out is when did fisting really start? I can't tell you that, but I can tell you when there are dateable artifacts of fisting.

The first dateable artifact I have of fisting is a poem about it written by the poet Paul Mariah. Paul Mariah was not only a poet, he was

Image 3: Still from *The Figa*, Jonesy and Jaime C. Knight, Single Channel Video, 28 min., 2018.

also a printer, he was an activist, he was a publisher, he had a little magazine called *Manroot*, which was full of gay poetry; and he wrote a poem called "The Figa." The *figa* is a word for this Mediterranean charm that's basically a fist. The *figa* literally means the fig, but it also means the fist. And he wrote this poem, and he actually printed it as a poster, and I have his own copy framed on the wall over there . . . still has Crisco stains on it (laughs). What's interesting is I can date this poem at least as early as 1969, because in 1969 Paul Mariah was a student at San Francisco State, and he submitted a book of poems called *Poems: Metaphysical Caverns*—a creative work submitted in part for the fulfillment for the requirements for the degree of master in arts, August 1969, and "The Figa" is in here. So I know that fisting [was] prevalent enough by 1969 that Paul Mariah wrote a poem about it.

I'm also told by a number of people that fisting happens as part of the impact of the counterculture on the leather community, and one of them was Chuck Arnett, the artist who did the iconic mural of the toolbox. Well, by 1967 or so, he's doing dayglow paintings over at the Stud with black light on them that have sixties colorations, with a whole different look. My suspicion is that it's the drugs of the counterculture that powered the emergence of fisting as a mass phenomenon, as opposed to something a few people are doing.

In the following excerpt Jonesy asks about the "absence of the phallus" in fisting. Gayle speaks to the influence drug culture had on the development of fisting as a sexual practice. The final scene of the video emulates the ecstatic climax and loving denouement from Gayle's description:

> After a while, I kind of looked around, and one of the things that was pointed out to me was that because most of the people were mostly doing drugs, you know, acid, MDA, those kind of drugs, they didn't really get hard-ons early in the evening. So it wasn't until about 4:00 a.m., when the drugs started to wear off, that you started to see hard-ons. So I wouldn't say that the phallus—well, first of all, I wouldn't say the penis was removed, it's not like people weren't turned on or never got turned on, but, at least early in the evening, there wasn't a lot of penis action. There were a lot of penises, but they were mostly kind of, you know, just there, and, really, it was just hands and holes, which was something, as a lesbian, I could relate to (laughing). It was like, I looked around, and I thought, "This is almost like lesbian sex." There was a sense of commonality that came out of that, because it wasn't as genitally focused; and, really, the main eroticism was around the anus and the hand. That was really interesting, it was a hole and a hand. You know, when Foucault talked about fisting, he talked about the de-genitalization . . . and the taking the focus away from the genitals as a way of making the whole body something that is sensate and part of a broader notion of sexuality or erotic experience. There really was a displacement so that the penis wasn't the central object of attention. The hand and the anus were the central objects of attention, and how to extract the most pleasure out of these things, not just pleasure but experience. That's why, I think, people describe fisting as spiritual, in that the experience could be extremely intense, not quite sexual, and certainly not distressing, but like something else. It was like going to another plane of experience.

Gayle goes on to speak about the closing of the Catacombs. For us, this final exposition by Gayle became the most profound, because she details what many normative or traditionally conservative people would never consider when thinking about fisting, a sex club, or BDSM culture. Gayle's words are paired with of a group of performers participating in a kind of "come down" dance that ends in what Jonesy lovingly dubbed the "cuddle puddle."

Image 4: Still from *The Figa*, Jonesy and Jaime C. Knight, Single Channel Video, 28 min., 2018.

As the institutional collapses happened, not just because of the [HIV/AIDS] epidemic, but because of the political response to the epidemic, you know, there was a lot of institutional damage that happened . . . and the institutions changed, and I never had the same access, as a female, to these intimate gay male sexual spaces that I had had. I should say, I didn't start out being particularly interested in or focused on fisting. I was much more interested in more formal S/M; but what I found when I got here was that, for reasons that had preceded me, other people had carved little trails into this world. I had access to the fisting world in a way that I didn't have to much else, so I ended up being very engaged with it and doing a lot of my best ethnography at the Catacombs, and that was unexpected. It's one of the ways that fieldwork is always surprising. You never know where you're going to go and where you're not going to go. As that particular environment was no longer accessible to me, a lot of other things never were as accessible. So I learned a lot there. I think I said this in the article I wrote, but, as a female, I was always an alien there, but there was so much comfort with just the body. And these were not all leather icons, Tom of Finland or Drummer models with lots of muscles. These were normal people with ordinary bodies who just were having a wonderful—I won't just say fun—they had a lot of fun, but they also had just really wonderful intense and intimate

Image 5: Still from *The Figa*, Jonesy and Jaime C. Knight, Single Channel Video, 28 min., 2018.

experiences of their bodies. They were unashamed and really just completely casual and relaxed about it. It was something I had never run into anywhere else in this culture, and I think it just changed me profoundly. I just got much easier in my own body. You know, I was raised as a female in this culture, where you're always uptight, you're never skinny enough, never pretty enough, you're never this, you're never that. Just to relax and enjoy the body you have, that was the lesson I learned there, and it was really a gift. The body you have is the body you have, so get into it, and enjoy it while you can.

In this, Gayle encapsulates so many of the ideas we find important in our work as cultural producers interested in the archives of communities that exist outside of what we see as an increasingly banal and ineffective normative culture. A sexual practice that can become beyond sexual and (to quote Gayle, paraphrasing Foucault) create a "body sensate" removes the gender-obsessed, future-thinking, appropriative compulsion of contemporary capitalist culture from the equation of intimate sensual relationality. That it can produce a shattering of the conception of a body diametrically opposed to the popular image of what a body is and should be is radical even in our time of body positivity and acceptance. As artists our initial compulsion is to make something beautiful. Beyond that is to create something that, to quote Claire Bishop, "implies a questioning of how the world is organized, and therefore the possibility of changing or redistributing that same world."⁵ We situate *The Figa* and its folklore in a tradition that seeks to highlight the communities, practices, aesthetics, codes, and radicality of queer cultures that don't adhere to normative society and that resist co-optation, so as to offer something different, a way toward a new, hopefully better, world.

Image 6: Still from *The Figa* (showing imagined recreation of the Catacombs with choreography), Jonesy and Jaime C. Knight, Single Channel Video, 28 min., 2018.

Image 7: Still from *The Figa* (showing imagined recreation of the Catacombs with choreography), Jonesy and Jaime C. Knight, Single Channel Video, 28 min., 2018.

Notes

1   Jasbir Puar, *Terrorist Assemblages: Homonationalism in Queer Times* (Durham, NC: Duke University Press, 2017).

2   Gayle Rubin, *Deviations: A Gayle Rubin Reader* (Durham, NC: Duke University Press, 2011).

3   Larry Townsend, *The Leatherman's Handbook* (Los Angeles: L.T. Publications, 1972).

4   Gayle Rubin, "The Catacombs: A Temple of the Butthole," *Drummer* 139 (May 1990): 28–34; reprinted in *Deviations*.

5   Claire Bishop, *Artificial Hells: Participatory Art and the Politics of Spectatorship* (London: Verso, 2012).

Into History and Out of *Quarantine*

A Reparative Poet's Survival Kit

Scott Chalupa

Since the onset of the COVID-19 pandemic, I have been asked about reso-nances between the current pandemic and the HIV/AIDS pandemic at the core of my book. It is important to resist the temptation to draw too many connections between the two pandemics. HIV/AIDS is transmitted through sexual and other specific behaviors; COVID-19 is spread through casual contact, like the flu, a disease to which it has unfortunately been compared. It is also important to recognize the disparate impact of COVID-19 on queer communities, particularly queer youth. Queers suffer from higher rates of mental illness, suicide, homelessness, and substance abuse because of our abject positions in US society, and COVID-19 is a vector for exacerbating preexisting social, economic, and political conditions that endanger queer persons. We cannot understand the depth and nature of all this until clearer lines can be drawn between the lives and deaths of queer individuals during the COVID-19 pandemic.

I came into the community in the mid-1990s among queers surviving quotidian decimation from HIV/AIDS. From 1992 to 1995, roughly thirty thousand to forty thousand Americans died annually. The survivors I met then gave me a queer history education against the backdrop of a nation content to look past the escalating death rate. My peers and I learned about pre-Stonewall resistance groups like the Daughters of Bilitis, formed in 1955 by Del Martin and Phyllis Lyon, and the Mattachine Society, founded in 1950 by Harry Hay and others. We learned about gender outlaws like Sylvia Rivera and Marsha P. Johnson, founders of Street Transvestite Action Revolutionaries, and the always-coiffed and painted author Quentin Crisp. They and many other revolutionaries dropped from consciousness long ago as new legal protections—with widely disparate impacts—were/

are reluctantly granted to the most performatively "normal" persons. US culture thrives on an amnesia that blots out the tragic realities of its most abject persons with ahistorical narratives that privilege progress over acknowledgment and reckoning.

My book *Quarantine* is an attempt to fight that amnesia, to render the queerness of the early HIV/AIDS pandemic visible, to reify the pervasive grief and horror of the period, while queering it with the joy and love necessary for survival. Many of the poems in *Quarantine* are expressions of José Esteban Muñoz's concept of ecstatic time: "the moment one feels ecstasy, announced perhaps in a scream or grunt of pleasure, and more importantly during moments of contemplation when one looks back at a scene from one's past, present, or future."[1] For me, reading and writing queer stories into the past has been a necessary step to engage ecstatic time, to release our stories from the "stranglehold" of linear "straight time."[2] *Quarantine* consistently engages ecstatic moments of the past to reexamine contemporary realities. Knowing how our *then* intersects with our *now* allows us to imagine future horizons for queerness.

Given the present manageability of HIV/AIDS for those with access to care and meds, it is easy to forget that tens of thousands of people continue to die from AIDS-related diseases each year in the US. It is easy to forget that AIDS used to be an unequivocal death sentence. In the 1980s and early 1990s, diagnosis often meant six to eighteen months to live, perhaps more if one was lucky. A person suddenly symptomatic and admitted to the hospital one day was often dead days later. Family therapist David Nord, writing in 1994, observes that for persons with AIDS (PWAs) and their families of choice "concurrent grief processes overlap" because of "insufficient time to work through the process of grieving one person before another death occurs."[3] Further compounding concurrent grief was the reality that families of choice who caretook dying and grieving PWAs were often vectors of HIV/AIDS transmission. Nord notes that queer persons have "been forced by necessity to create families of choice because their family of origin is nonsupportive, rejecting, or hostile,"[4] defining a family of origin as "relatives connected by blood, marriage, or adoption."[5] Families of choice filled the roles left vacant when queer persons fled their families of origin for larger cities, where they might find love and support among more sizeable queer populations.

After death, parents and siblings often publicly enacted social shaming by banning PWAs' former lovers and adopted family from funerals or forcing them to sit in silence. Douglas Crimp writes of that "social oppro-brium" that families of origin—indeed all arbiters of the dominant US culture—placed upon families of choice.[6] To participate in these important rituals, queer families of choice had to "conceal their grief . . . their fond memories," and such "ruthless interference with our bereavement," Crimp adds, was "as ordinary an occurrence as reading the *New York Times*."[7] One of the personal obituaries excerpted from *Quarantine* reenacts and under-mines the erasures committed by long-estranged families who appeared from nowhere to claim authority over bodies, property, and funeral rites. Another obit mimics some of the obits I found in archives that read like deeply intimate love letters to the deceased. Grief is an encounter with nonlinear time: living down the trauma of sudden or protracted death, memories looping back into our past, musings about what the deceased might think or say about some current or future life event. For most people, the intensity of grief ebbs over time. For survivors of the early HIV/AIDS pandemic, however, grief could be indefinitely delayed, extending and multiplying the initially intense pains of past and present grief far into the future.

The unprecedented experience of grief shouldered by communities of PWAs and their loved ones is part of a larger history of queer abjec-tion stretching back more than a century. In *Feeling Backward: Loss and the Politics of Queer History*, Heather Love is wary of becoming entranced by that "long history of association with failure, impossibility, and loss" that often accompanies queer people and communities.[8] In her exploration of early twentieth-century queer literature, Love eschews interpretive/critical lenses in favor of descriptive readings to show how queer histories of "disconnection, loss, and the refusal of community" allow a more profound embrace of "the dark, retrograde aspects of queer experience."[9] Prior to HIV/AIDS and Stonewall, many cities and states enacted and enforced laws banning public congregations of homosexuals, making queer spaces and patrons into targets of law enforcement. Laws prohibiting people from dressing in clothing different from their birth-assigned gender were also common. These prohibitions pushed queers and queer identities into the shadows, criminalizing the means by which queers could live authentic lives.

In *Lonely Hunters: An Oral History of Lesbian and Gay Southern Life, 1948–1968*, interviewee Merrill Mushroom remembers a friend "coming in late to the bar," because "officer so-and-so [had] caught [her] again" and demanded sexual favors in exchange not arresting her.[10] More striking is her observation, "No one got incensed. There was *nothing* we could do, and this was *not* that unusual."[11] Another interviewee in *Lonely Hunters* remembers that "you didn't think of yourself as a victim unless you were careless, [but] we were all victims. There was such an utter sadness about it all."[12] My poem "Sacrifice of Isaac" recounts a bar raid but undermines this historical tragedy by giving readers a queer wink through the gay male victim's ability to turn violence into fantasy. Though a problematic gesture on multiple levels, it demonstrates the way that gay male encounters with various powers were/are transposed into sexual fantasy—a fact made obvious by Tom of Finland's artwork and his artistic inheritors.

I would like to return briefly to the COVID-19 pandemic and the demands for self-quarantine in its early months to honor the vast differences between quarantine discussions during HIV/AIDS and those of today. As COVID-19 was (and still is) a rapidly spreading respiratory disease, and because it has not been equated with abject groups in the ways that HIV/AIDS was equated with homosexuals, the current pandemic's quarantine and contact tracing demands/efforts have served different sociopolitical urges and functions than similar demands/efforts did during the early HIV/AIDS pandemic. Because HIV/AIDS was so deeply associated with homosexuals well into the late 1990s and early 2000s, admission of one's HIV/AIDS status was tantamount to an admission of queerness. Thus, HIV/AIDS was often a vector for intense discrimination and hate crimes.

California's 1986 state ballot Proposition 64, had it passed, would have granted the state government power to bar PWAs and those suspected to be carriers from public and private schools and from commercial food handling facilities and would potentially have established state-wide isolation and quarantine for PWAs and suspected carriers.[13] Quarantine discourse in the early decades of HIV/AIDS was, on its face, about fear of AIDS; however, that discourse was grounded in an older fear of the metaphoric contagion/disease of homosexuality. The American Psychiatric Association (APA) categorized homosexuality as a sexual deviation until 1973, when it was removed from that category in the APA *Diagnostic and Statistical Manual*. Supreme Court Justice William Rehnquist wrote in 1978 that protecting a gay group's First Amendment right to assemble was "akin" to recognizing the rights of "those suffering from measles ... to associate together and with others who presently do not have measles," and thereby spreading the disease of homosexuality.[14] I see this history of abjection and separation as a form of quarantine—keep queers hushed and in the shadows to minimize their effects on the general population. We continue to observe fear of queer contagion in today's demands of hetero and homonormativity: the impulse to "protect" children from transgender and gender nonconforming persons, the reticence to allow children to express gender in the way that best suits them, and the continued conceptualization of sexuality and gender identity in discrete categories instead of fluid and coexistent spectra.

In *Covering: The Hidden Assault on Our Civil Rights*, Kenji Yoshino analyzes the social phenomenon of covering: toning one's queerness down or up to present more normatively. Yoshino observes that our current society discriminates "not against the entire group, but against the subset of the group that fails to *assimilate* to mainstream norms."[15] When writing *Quarantine*, I was particularly interested in how the demand/desire to cover one's queerness—as well as the more extreme demands to convert or to closet—creates the self-destructive need for one to quarantine a piece of oneself within oneself to achieve an existence mistaken for survival. In *Quarantine*, the poems that deal most explicitly with these ideas are the poems formatted as dictionary definitions of quarantine. One definition poem included here explores a religious individual who volunteers for a reparative therapy, or a conversion program. The other included definition poem explores an educator covering his queerness to better assimilate into his work environment.

The AIDS Coalition to Unleash Power (ACT UP) emerged in New York City in 1987 as one of the first organizations to publicly challenge and call attention to the governmental neglect and the societal shaming at the heart of the mushrooming HIV/AIDS death rates. In his 1989 essay, "Postcards from America: X Rays from Hell," artist activist David Wojnarowicz wonders "what it would be like if, each time a lover or a friend or a stranger died of [AIDS], their friends, lovers or neighbors would take the dead body and drive with it in a car a hundred miles an hour to washington d.c. and blast through the gates of the white house and come to a screeching halt before the entrance and dump their lifeless form on the front steps."[16]

In 1992, ACT UP answered that call when several members dumped the ashes of their loved ones on the White House lawn. Though hundreds of ACT UP protesters participated, the event garnered only a small blurb on a back page of the *New York Times*. In a sense, *Quarantine*, also attempts to fulfill Wojnarowicz's call. All the obituaries in *Quarantine* anonymize the dead with missing names and photos, replacing titles with birth and death dates. The poems formatted as dictionary definitions of quarantine and other poems mimic the columnar format of obituaries to queer their poetic rubrics, adding to the exploding mass of nameless bodies. However, I knew *Quarantine* must do more than pile nameless bodies at the feet of my readers.

I could not engage with that history and still break through the anger of Wojnarowicz, until I embraced another emotional process. In *Reclaiming Queer: Activist and Academic Rhetorics of Resistance*, Erin Rand discusses "the unification of ACT UP's members ... through communal anger" and the mobilization of that anger alongside other coexistent emotional intensities into direct action.[17] Eve K. Sedgwick, borrowing from Melanie Klein, argues that by working from a position that is "anxiety-mitigating," we can marshal our resources to "repair" the oppressive and/or "murderous" parts of the world.[18] For ACT UP and many PWAs, collective acceptance of grief, anger, and shame mobilized the activists from paralytic stasis into productive action.

ACT UP's famed Monday night meetings were not just "a place to fight AIDS," they were also "cruising grounds, a chance to channel one's grief and frustration ... an opportunity to enact newly emerging queer identities, and a place to reimagine the world."[19] While the poem "[first] meeting/s" is a direct homage to those Monday night meetings, all the poems in *Quarantine* are the result of working through my grief and frustration over our past and our present, as well as my occasional cynicism about our future. Like ACT UPers, I had to be trained in how not to be destroyed.

To make *Quarantine* a reparative project, I reappropriated "reparative" from life-destroying therapies and redeployed it creatively. This required that I engage a process of real survival, that I reckon with the ways that communities decimated by benign neglect (the Reagan administration's official AIDS policy) survived and transformed the world. Through that reckoning, I could begin to imagine new possibilities for queerness in history and in the future. This reparative process lies at the heart of living in ecstatic, nonlinear time. One of my chief guides for reckoning and reimagining has been Michelangelo Merisi da Caravaggio, a queer sixteenth-century Italian painter who hired petty thieves and courtesans of late Renaissance Rome as models for his religious artworks. Many poems in *Quarantine* are ekphrastic responses to Caravaggio's works, commandeering his biblical images to retell queer history: Quentin Crisp as Christ,

Isaac as a sissyboy relishing his arrest in a bar raid. Placing queer stories and persons at the center of religious iconography breathes pedestrian life into these mythic figures, in much the same way as Caravaggio's choice to detail the saints' dirty feet.

Queerness is a thing that we must make visible, especially in historical contexts, as it can be and has been erased by millennia of heteronormative excuses and rationalizations. Muñoz argues that we must "map our repression, our fragmentation, and our alienation," and that this confrontation with our past allows us "to imagine and potentially make a queer world."[20] In this confrontation, we "call on the past, [we] *animate it*, understanding that the past has a performative nature," and we then discover that "the past does things."[21] To see the world differently requires that we see ourselves differently by actively seeing ourselves in history. My hope is that *Quarantine* and the histories it presents encourage continual reimagination to reshape our past through fresh methodologies for critique and action—and, thus, to propel ourselves into spaces and realities we have yet to conceive.

3/6/63–2/8/82

Is it wrong of me
to miss your
motorcycle more
than you? Classic
black bike thirty
years your senior:
an   Indian   Four
that,   like   you,
wore its works out in the open,
air-cooled. I loved your small seat—
ample and accommodating enough
for one, but too sensible for two.

All those CCs rumbling my lithe
legs, hands clamped hard on low-
slung custom handles, chest pressed
against the gold flame detailed
gas tank... Oh God, how I wanted
to ride your ghost into the future.

04/21/1961 – 11/30/1988

Last Thursday, our best gay
gal-pal crashed the pearly gates at
home after a last
long   bout
with over-fabulous
youth—once again
proving he always
knew   the   best
moment   to   exit.   Let
us   not   forget   that
chillier-   than   -usual
spring   when   he
breezed like a clumsy zephyr
into our icy gay-borhood with all
the grace and charm of a farm boy
from Bumpkin-land. A quick study
in all things tragi-camp, he soon
endeared himself as one of our
happy hamlet's beloved bearded
ladies.

We ask that you join us
in celebrating his several favorite
forms of debauchery at The Eagle
this weekend during a revelry
lesser folk might mistake for a
memorial. Please be sure to come
wearing your best leather harness,
angel wings, and a codpiece to
make your mother blush. Though
his blood relations have whisked
his remains back to who-cares-where,
an open casket will be provided at
the back bar where you can toss in
your offerings for the after-party
to follow.

In lieu of sad Sally spirits,
please bring satin flowers, brass
clamps, fairy glitter, and poppers.

Sacrifice of Isaac

he says the night he got arrested was
his side-door entrée into S&M
when a gray-beard plainclothes vice
pinned his faggot face against the bar
even pulled a knife some queens
love a grizzled daddy any way
they can get one lost in the thrall of not
knowing if it all ends one night
in the hot hands of fag-killer pigs
how familiar how cliché and he
would not be the first trotted off to cop
cruiser instead of paddy wagon fresh
with threat driven to a narrow alleyway
dragged out fucked and knifed lifeless
who would report such a man missing
who would dare risk speaking his name
connecting their own with a known homosexual
but that night in LA's Black Cat
another cop as if an angel of the Lord
appeared and whispered a few terse words
to the snarling silver fox pinning the fairy's
face to the bar and that cop so ready to
sacrifice another nameless limp-wristed
lamb to the coming year yanks him up
jackboots him into the waiting wagon
and in the next day's paper that silly
sissy smiling wide having made
his covenant with power his routine rush
to the rush of reenactment how close each of us
every night to our needful little deaths

Suppers at Emmaus

Your London life was full of crucifixion.
A sassy sissy who failed every time
you *pretended to be a real person*.

In Manhattan you discovered
you only understood happiness,
and spent your last decades spinning parables

at suppers supplied by friends and strangers:
A man who hardly worked a day, lived *like
Blanche DuBois* from gifted meal to miracle

rent check, a pauper philosopher swallowed up
in swirling sleeves, outstretched hand
dividing the table in two, making more emphatic

the lesson: One ought not keep up
*with the Joneses; drag them down to your level.
It's cheaper*. Resurrected in America,

you take tea with the grace a wide-brimmed derby
demands, lavender nails aglow
in the soft light of the restaurant, apostles

enrapt and incensed at a wrinkled fruit's
prophesies that *AIDS is just a fad*
and *homosexuality is a horrible disease*.

Messengers are oft misunderstood,
and it's likely you were only thinking aloud,
at least that's how East Village queens

tell the story now. They have forgiven you
such eccentricities, swooning at your naked
civil service. *I am always the same*, you quipped.

Only the way people see me has changed.
And each time they see your prancing
phantasm, how they bow.

Quar • an • tine

VERB

3. cover; live openly but butch it up; refuse to
    perform faggotry

    a. You stand afront the class / buttoned down
        & sleeves ¾ cuffed // pre-noon slacks
        barely rumple a subtle break over insensible
        shoes / this [you think] is how it must be
        // for every gay nearly here / a classroom
        persona / a front just legible enough // no
        need for you to be a prancing affront //

    b. Yoshino [you think] wagged an e-ink finger
        at you / this morning from the Kindle
        crisp coffee & fresh fruit rush // his words
        afront your furrowed forehead / admonish
        you: // *to tone down* [your] *disfavored*
        identity / is to the cool prof who happens
        to be gay // as to hybrid seedy tangerine /
        is to the clementine // & this bargain enacted
        each morning not because / you've been
        asked to not because // you're an affront
        to the university not because // you're still
        some self-hating gay //

    c. but because it *feels* good & right to have
        stable work / *feels* more natural than
        leather codpieces & glittered jackboots
        buried two decades back // the marching
        [the screaming] & the ashing of White House
        lawns with bone chips / all that advocation
        to come to this place of rest // where you
        no longer feel // how you've always felt:
        a front / afront // affront

Quar • an • tine

NOUN

2. conversion; psychiatric or religious erasure of
   self; electric soul-cleanse

   a. of course I give it all up and hand over
      even my collected middle school journals
      then stand with the others stripping
      to our skivvies post-pat-down the doctor
      says no trace of our outside lives can live
      here but were there room enough and time
      to hide I'd tackle that beautiful blond
      who took those journals and incinerated
      my hand-written interiors God I desire
      to fold him beneath the bare collapsible
      tables dear Jesus this is why I'm here
      to pray away my fear of living
      right pray that He redirect my desire
      on bended knee please Lord push deep
      in me and cut out what offends thee

   b. .   .   .

   c. not remembering is the most merciful part
      of Thursday mornings as they gurney
      me to a room I can't place dreaming
      of an ocean pier waves shouting against
      tall struts and sand to meet my secret
      much older lover when I resurface with
      the bends the whole ocean is a fog
      I have to swim my way out of the ceiling
      tiles sharpen and I am made to rise
      and swivel stand and shuffle to the sofa
      a paper-gown man helps me cloud back
      into my skin this is how we emerge
      flash-fried mercifully forgetful our ears

awaken to electric wails down the hall
our waiting room a sea of free-will
forgetters in dys-unison each new scream
adjoins as the last removes as the next
penitent in paper raiment gets silently
gurneyed in

[first] meeting/s

you wonder: how to keep grief.   Private when
every.   Faggot.   You ever met is.   Veiled
remember: sitting shiva.   As a child
know: no Manhattan man would   [stand again]
if that were queer custom.   And this is why—
this: Monday night.   You wander   settle in
a metal folding chair.   Sit somewhere near
the rear.   A panel of gay lays: debates
up front: an anger.   You did not know
you didn't need permission to.   Feel this
[you think   ] could be our real liberation
[   ] wonder why we don't blare: Britten's *Dies
Ire* for every[   ]body in New York
wish: you could be   brave like that [queer quartet]
up front   ...intend to stay...   handshake your hellos
but all that grief.   And all those guys: it was
so heady.   [   ] aphrodisiac: anger
and ass: supplied.   To slake sorrow.   [and now
incomprehensible: how some small few
all.   Who's left.   Alive.   —inconsolable
sadness assuaged.   [how   ] comfort the comrade
who?   Next week   you may: bury or infect
those were they   [and you among them]   who lay/ed
dead.   In the streets: a marching scream—   made up
of the coming.   Decade's dead.   Pool.   Célèbre

Notes

1   José Esteban Muñoz, *Cruising Utopia: The Then and There of Queer Futurity* (New York: New York University Press, 2009), 32.

2   Ibid.

3   David Nord, "The Impact of Multiple AIDS-Related Loss on Families of Origin and Families of Choice," *American Journal of Family Therapy* 24, no. 2, (1996): 133.

4   Ibid., 131.

5   Ibid., 130.

6   Douglas Crimp, "Mourning and Militancy," *October* 51 (Winter 1989): 3–18, accessed June 3, 2022, https://www.academia.edu/5756612/Mourning_and_Militancy.

7   Ibid., 8.

8   Heather Love, *Feeling Backward: Loss and the Politics of Queer History* (Cambridge, MA: Harvard University Press, 2007), 29.

9   Ibid., 146.

10   James T. Sears, *Lonely Hunters: An Oral History of Lesbian and Gay Southern Life, 1948–1968* (Boulder, CO: Westview Press, 1997), 43.

11   Ibid., 43; emphasis in the original.

12   Ibid., 33.

13   HIV was not part of public discourse at this time, and "carriers" was the term commonly used for people who had the virus but not the syndrome that defines AIDS; "HIV/AIDS Compilation," NBC Universal Archives, June 16, 1982, 27:26, unavailable June 3, 2022, https://www.nbcuniarchives.com/asset/1209242.

14   Quoted in Kenji Yoshino, *Covering: The Hidden Assault on Our Civil Rights* (New York: Random House Trade Paperbacks, 2006), 45.

15   Ibid., 22; emphasis added.

16   David Wojnarowicz, *Close to the Knives: A Memoir of Disintegration* (New York: Vintage Books, 1991), 122.

17   Erin J. Rand, *Reclaiming Queer: Activist and Academic Rhetorics of Resistance* (Tuscaloosa: University of Alabama Press, 2014), 131.

18   Eve K. Sedgwick, *Touching Feeling* (Durham, NC: Duke University Press, 2003), 146.

19   Deborah B. Gould, *Moving Politics: Emotion and ACT UP's Fight against AIDS* (Chicago: University of Chicago Press, 2009), 202.

20   Muñoz, *Cruising Utopia*, 55.

21   Muñoz, *Cruising Utopia*, 27–28, emphasis mine.

Making
Queerness

How to Queer the Grammar of the Body by Eating Bread

Cassius Kelly and emet ezell

"I write theory to make my feelings seem legitimate."
"Cis-opinions call themselves science."
—alok v menon

"Corporate processes privilege and imagine only one kind of body on
either side of the desk: on one side, the docile body of the contingent,
replaceable instructor; on the other, the docile body of the student
dutifully mastering marketable skills and producing clear, orderly,
efficient prose."
—Robert McRuer

This chapter was born from an assignment in an undergraduate feminist
studies class. At the time, we were students at Southwestern University—
roommates in a tiny apartment. From our couch (likely manufactured in
a private prison) and our kitchen (likely designed by an architect who
also built prisons), we agonized over our participation in a system that
wanted to crush us. How could we learn radical feminist theory in conditions like these? Academic, structural demands were in constant tension
with our basic needs. We were forced to choose between sleeping, writing,
and eating. Why did we never have enough time to write papers *and* cook
dinner? What were we to do with this illusion of choice between productivity and survival? No matter what we compromised, we were repeatedly
left physically and emotionally depleted, consumed by a sense of guilt over
our apparent failure to "manage time" effectively.

In actuality, no amount of time management could give us the time we
needed: the problem was structural. As students recovering from eating

disorders (EDs), we felt this tension between our formal academic writing and our eating habits become more pronounced during the school year. We struggled to choose between cooking dinner and finishing an essay or between grocery shopping and going to class. From both the corporate university and the medical model of ED treatment, we received the same message of individualism: this is *your* problem to overcome. The more we researched and the more we talked with each other, the more we felt the impossibility of eating and academic writing as contingent acts. How, then, were we to forge a viable future as students in recovery?

The university structure is built upon a colonial model of self-making: to produce a properly academic written product is, at the same time, to produce a rational self. From this sense, we began to understand our activities of eating and writing as intertwined within a corporate university structure. We recognized that the university system is built on a history of racism undergirded by Enlightenment philosophy. This structure compels the reproduction of white, "rational" bodies and white, "rational" writing. According to queer and crip theorist Robert McRuer: "We inherit an Enlightenment legacy where the production of writing and production of the self converge, but the corporate university also extends that legacy in its eagerness to intervene in, and thereby vouchsafe, the kinds of selves produced. The call to produce orderly and efficient writing/docile subjects thus takes on a heightened urgency in our particular moment."[1] The call to create/produce orderly subjects is not only made by the corporate university, but is also made by—and converges with—diet culture. Take, for example, the requirement to take two semesters of physical education to graduate from our private undergraduate institution. What message does this requirement send about the kinds of bodies that are worthy of graduating, not to mention what kinds of bodies fit into the tiny desks the university provides?

Looking at the histories of the corporate university and the medical model of eating highlights the ways in which fatphobia and racism are intertwined with the demand for self-control and productive, orderly bodies. Fatphobia and racism also extend to writing, as does homophobia. Any deviant body becomes a threat to the dominant social order.

The enforcement of rational writing within academic institutions mirrors the enforcement of heterosexuality: both are "impossible to embody fully, permanently, or without incoherence."[2] Composure and composition are embodied experiences. We understand composure to be based upon this same colonial legacy of contorting one's body and one's writing to become legible to a white, wealthy, orderly audience. Instead, we followed McRuer's *decomposure*, which suggests that attention be placed elsewhere: in one's incoherence. Decomposure is an embodied refusal to solidify a compliant "self." Furthermore, the goal is not just to survive our own illegibility, but to desire it. Desiring a self that is decomposed—that disrupts and refuses to comply with colonized demands—is aligned with antiracist and anticolonial projects.

McRuer notes that one's failure to comply with the standardized order does not automatically translate into critical decomposition. Rather, critical decomposition "actively [involves] resisting the corporate university and disordering straight composition;" at the same time, "critical decomposition is impossible on an individual level."[3] Critical decomposition needs collective, active disordering. It needs us to write and think in collaboration. It needs us to find new ways of writing, eating, and cooking together. We understand both writing and eating to be self-making processes. By writing and eating outside the inherited colonial order, in a decomposed manner, we create queer and resistant selves.

If, as McRuer writes, "composition in the corporate university remains a practice that is focused on a fetishized final product," then a disordered composition demands a shift in both practice and focus.[4] This essay attempts to follow such a shift—moving away from the solidified final product and toward an unpredictable future. Desiring decomposition opens the possibility for constructing alternative selves through alternative processes. As students, we were disenchanted by academia's incessant demands for rigidity. Inspired by the queer and crip theory we were learning in class and seeing on the streets, we took our academic participation and used it as an opportunity for intervention. We deviated from writing separate, single-authored essays and decomposed into something different. Rather than divorcing the self-making processes of eating and writing, we prioritized doing these activities simultaneously and collaboratively. Rather than disciplining our queer bodies into straight performance, we centered a composition that undermines heteronormativity rather than reaffirming it.

To decompose our writing, we had to bring our attention to the ways in which the isolated individualism of academia manifests in our own bodies. Corporate university models and their precedents depend upon an imposed order, composure, and docility. The ordering that universities consciously and unconsciously demand of faculty, students, and other campus workers stratifies power and authority in a visible, palpable way. Writing and legibility are deeply implicated in this process: one's conformity (or lack thereof) translates into evaluations that directly impact material realities. In our particular case, conformity translated into grades, which in turn affected scholarship eligibility, graduation dates, career possibilities, and the level of cortisol in our bodies.

The academic research methods we were taught as students prioritized transcending the body to arrive at some objective, emotionless, and "reasonable" truth. This way of writing presupposes that the body is not a source of knowledge but, rather, something to overcome. Take, for example, the phenomenon commonly called writer's block. When we can't focus or think anymore, when we have run out of words to say, it is an inconvenient experience. Overcoming writer's block is a trope in the hypermasculine, ascetic, heroic narrative of writing. It involves physically isolating yourself—ideally in a single room, or maybe a cabin in the woods, with only orange peels and dry gin for sustenance—where you redirect your body and harness a manly "superhuman" willpower. Starve yourself, deprive yourself, destroy any semblance of regulated sleep—just finish the goddamn essay. In the process, you will prove yourself to be a good student, a successful moral agent. The process of academic writing involves resisting the body, shedding any vestige of it from the final product: a document that is simultaneously individualized (penned by a single author) and homogenized (in accordance with a standardized structure). Put another way, discipline and abstinence constitute a moral self.

Our academic institutions demanded composure from our writing and from our bodies. *Have you chosen the right word? Can you be clearer? How about trimming down the flowery language? Did you turn the essay in on time? Why can't you focus?* A grammatically correct essay depends upon these questions. McRuer points out that "the demand for certain kinds of finished projects in the writing classroom is congruent with the demand for certain kinds of bodies."[5] A grammatically correct body depends upon discipline and individualization; it is white, straight, able-bodied, thin, smart, and, of course, arrives on time. In other words, composed writing demands composed bodies. The illusion of bodily stability and the illusion of singular authorship are mutually constitutive myths. Any deviation from academic composure can be read as a personal grammatical error—a moral failure.

In a similar way, diet and exercise are moralized tools for producing an orderly, gendered body. Prescribed methods of dieting and discipline surrounding food often require a direct resistance to—or rejection of—bodily needs, such as food and rest. When we internalize self-ordering, it can take a pathological turn. We have observed this phenomenon in both the corporate university and the medical-industrial complex: it is called "disorder."

EDs provide a useful example here. A strict food regimen and commitment to hegemonically determined healthy aesthetics is almost universally understood as good. Distancing oneself from fatness and its associated moral degradation becomes a way to practice a continual overcoming of the body. Yet we know firsthand that EDs are a complicated matter: our own compulsions to order became disorders that required a medical reordering. In this process, the initial practice of ordering is rarely put into question; on the contrary, its necessity is reinforced in conventional ED treatment.

A composed self is a moral self in this paradigm. Anthropologist Sigal Gooldin's research demonstrates how eating becomes associated with moralistic meaning through the narratives that patients create for themselves in treatment. For many of the participants in Gooldin's research, patients translated the cutting sensation of hunger into an experience of power and productivity. Her findings show how anorexic women use the sensation of hunger to actively write their own drama; overcoming one's hunger through resistance and restriction is a means of enacting self-composure.[6] Hypercontrol and manipulation function as "selfing device[s]," forms of asserting agency over one's body that are then "experienced as a heroic way of being in the world."[7] The stories Gooldin recorded demonstrate how ED practices forge a body centered around individualized self-improvement, productivity, and achieving morality through the manipulation of hunger.

Gooldin's writing responds to that of Susan Bordo, a renowned theorist who links modern consumer culture to the formation of the female body. Contrary to Bordo's focus on visual images, Gooldin is interested in how particular eating behaviors—such as restriction, vomiting, or late-night bingeing—form a moralistic self.[8] She suggests that anorexia needs to be questioned beyond its culturally symbolic meanings. While media images certainly affect our bodily perceptions, EDs are not reducible to a mere internalization. By focusing on experience, Gooldin is able to research how the phenomenological struggle with hunger translates into a sense of superiority and heroism. Consequently, failure to control the hunger of one's body translates to an overwhelming sense of guilt and shame. These feelings fuel the impulse to correct ourselves by rigidly moralizing eating behaviors that are buttressed by narratives of "self-composure."

The phenomenological struggle with hunger translates across practices of eating and writing. Both academic writing and the manipulation of diet and hunger involve overriding the body again and again to produce a disciplined self. Historian Nina Mackert observes how keeping detailed records of food can also be a forceful tool in composing a moral, "rational" self. For Mackert, diaries are objects of self-documentation, often used concurrently with restrictive dieting. If eating and writing can be mutually reinforcing "technologies of the self," then hypercontrolled eating and detailed record keeping help build the individualized, calculable self.[9]

Mackert's research uses Maxwell Roscoe Rhoads as a case study. Rhoads was a white middle-class man at the turn of the nineteenth century who sought treatment for his health concerns at John Harvey Kellogg's Battle Creek Sanitarium. There, he was prescribed a highly restrictive diet and advised to keep copious notes on his eating habits—a practice he continued long after he was discharged. Through measuring and documenting his food consumption, Rhoads tried to make himself and his improvement calculable. By tracking his progress and failures, Rhoads's diary archives the intrinsic connection between these understandings of both health and morality: two interdependent ideologies that are upheld by practices of scientific eating and methodical record keeping.

Rhoads's diary also chronicles an important historical turn toward a medical and white supremacist model of "'hygienic' or 'scientific' eating." In this model, "dietary knowledge" became a central tenet in the attainment and maintenance of health and whiteness.[10] While this quantitative view of health presents itself as neutral, dieting has clear Christian and eugenic roots. Battle Creek Sanitarium was "founded as a convalescent home by Seventh Day Adventists in 1866."[11] Ten years after its founding, Dr. John Harvey Kellogg, a "recently graduated medical doctor from a well-known Adventist family" became the director. From this position, Kellogg rebranded the sanitarium, substituting its Christian framework for a secularized model.[12] This turn came "at a time when fear of racial decline was widespread" across white America. As Mackert makes clear, Kellogg's "later project, the Race Betterment Foundation, vividly demonstrated the eugenic ethos of food reform in the Progressive Era."[13] Historicizing the rise of what we now call the diet industry exposes the racist and Christian roots of "healthy eating," a subject that might otherwise be seen as benign. The deeper we went into our research concerning the historical practices and meanings of eating, the more we found its systemic racism, which is invested in composing white, docile, and nutritious selves/bodies.

Historic links between the science of nutrition and religious morality continue to play out in today's culture of dieting and contemporary medical practice. Moral imperatives to control the body transform into moral imperatives to maintain recovery during treatment. As our own experiences, the medical-industrial complex, and the educational system all demonstrate, the push for bodily composure is fraught with contradiction. Sociologist Helen Gremillion describes treatment for EDs as a "core contradiction," problematizing the way in which the body is perceived as "raw material that patients shape and develop."[14] Seeing one's body as entirely malleable dissociates the body from the impact of everything it encounters. In this way, individuals come to perceive their bodies as the problem rather than as historically situated within multiple systems (where the medical-industrial complex and the corporate university are just two examples). Mainstream, institutionalized forms of writing and ED treatment both depend on notions of moral agency and individual selfhood.

As Gremillion's account demonstrates, ED treatments often reinforce the very structures that perpetuate the problem. While doctors might issue new mandates around intake and dietary habits, these new diets are enforced just as strictly as when an individual applies their own restrictive behaviors, thereby still composing a moral self, albeit using a different method. In treatment, eating is used to fashion an autonomous, healthy self—as defined by doctors and treatment staff—yet treatment specialists send mixed signals to their patients suffering from EDs. If the health of the body is still dependent on quantitative external measures, then patients are only internalizing a new authoritative measure of the same general form of objectification. For Gremillion, this paradoxical phenomenon raises important questions originally posed by Bordo: "Whose body is this? And whose will it become?" Given the inherent contradictions of medicalized ED treatment, how do we understand ourselves in a way that allows for resistant writing, resistant eating, and resistant subjectivity?

These are important questions to ask in the process of forging a resistant subjectivity. Claiming ownership and direct agency over our bodies only reaffirms hegemonic systems of power. While thinking of ourselves as individual actors may be empowering at the surface level, this self-conception can never abolish the oppressive forces of medical and academic institutions.

These systems can never be evaded or undone entirely; we are always forced into or performing some type of composure (i.e., racialization, incarceration, wage labor, gender assigned at birth); however, deviance is possible within our habits of writing and eating. We can contaminate an otherwise orderly social fabric.

We forge composed bodies through practices of eating and writing, as we have found across treatment records, personal diaries, anthropological research, and our own narratives. Systems of education and medicine share a certain grammar in their compulsive commitments to ordering. These grammatical forms have been enforced in our bodies, internalized, and then reproduced with our cooperation. We internalize the authoritative order so deeply that it becomes habit. Reflex. Knee-jerk. Ritual. How can we actively take up a subjectivity of decomposition, of queer deviation from the dominant order? Part of this imaginative work involves disrupting notions of agency that fetishize individual self-control and hypercomposition.

Through collaborative writing, we expose the multiplicity that is always already festering around the edges of composure. Singular authorship is a joke. When we erase our inherent multiplicity, we fail to notice that we are "only part of an agentic network" that includes other people, objects, our own organs, histories, institutions, microorganisms—all of which animate and condition (and are animated and conditioned *by*) the actions we take.[15] As a way to participate more fully in undermining notions of individual selfhood, we write from our prison labor–made university couch and recognize ourselves as interdependent. This is not to say that we are passive "victims of bodily or 'outside' forces"; in fact, just by acknowledging what's already here, we become more present to the world than we ever could be when we imagined ourselves as separate.[16]

Gloria Anzaldúa's approach to writing and to selfhood engages with history, object, myth, ritual, subject, and her own ghosts. She theorizes the body as our source and container for these knowledges. If "the body is the ground of thought," as Anzaldúa teaches, and if the body is only subjected to conscious control and vigilance, then our access to selfhood becomes warped.[17] After all, "you can never live up to the white dominant ideal you've been forced to internalize"; the body will always find a way to deviate.[18] Controlling the body is not the path to producing knowledge, writing theory, or constructing a self. The task at hand, then, is not to *think* differently about something but to *do* and *be* differently about it. This essay is our attempt at writing not by controlling the conscious mind but by surrendering to a decidedly collaborative, queer, and resistant process.[19] This allows us to refuse the moralizing compulsion toward a predetermined formal logic, instead taking up the draft and the recipe as valid modes of writing. We embrace this writing project as a draft, one with a future that can't be anticipated. It is a queer, feminist starting point for a process. It is always collaborative, corporeal, and has a specific known history, like a recipe.

In our kitchen, we found that deviating from the cultural conditioning to value some foods as good and others as bad opened up a new way of self-making that was no longer dependent upon internalized food standards. Eating bread made us neither good nor bad; the act could simply be joyful. As Mackert notes, "writing and eating emerge as different assemblages of human and nonhuman actors: desk, pen, diary, hand, writer; and food, fork, mouth, eating."[20] Writing and eating happen both in the body and outside the body, "taking into account diverse enactments of agency."[21] Deviance includes multiple objects and actors; it is always already a communal affair.

In our tiny university dorm room, while writing this paper, emet set about learning how to bake challah to connect with their newfound Jewish lineage. I remember the weeks in a row that emet baked flat challah, and the one Shabbat we realized that the yeast was not activating (it had died somehow). Their willingness to bring the flat loaves to dinner was actually amazing—a moment of sharing "failure," a revelation that making bread is an ongoing process—a weekly ritual that is not driven by final outcomes and does not end with the perfect loaves. It is built on ancestral knowledge; the recipes and techniques emet learned have been passed down from friends and adapted through generations. Being part of emet's failure gave me permission to start baking my own bread according to my mother's recipe. Both of our bread recipes yield two loaves—reminding us that food is always intended to be shared, not to mention that making and eating bread resists diet culture's obsession with food restriction and the fatphobic notion that carbs and bread will corrupt your body. Isn't bread one of the few things we have had to nourish ourselves across time

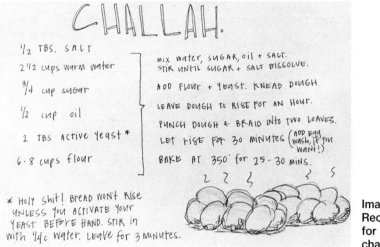

Image 1: Recipe for challah.

and place, through diaspora and famine and poverty? Isn't it a symbol of revolution and vitality, the staff of life?

Following the wisdom of Gloria Anzaldúa, who teaches us to refuse "to write from any single disciplinary position," we turn to our beloved self-making technology of the recipe. Above is emet's challah recipe, which has been and continues to be necessary to our writing process.[22] We know that the bread will not always rise, nor will the writing always follow a rational formula. Either way, we are committed to nourishing and making resistant selves.

If we come to recognize the cracks in the system, encouraging one another to find diverse, interdependent enactments of agency, then perhaps we can more easily tap into our own decomposition, engaging deviance as a legitimate ontology. It encourages us to speak and write and eat in a new language, with uncontrolled tongues and leaking pens, refusing to translate our self into the predetermined, precoded "right" form.

Notes

1   Robert McRuer, "Composing Bodies; or, De-Composition: Queer Theory, Disability Studies, and Alternative Corporealities," *JAC* 24, no. 1 (2004): 55.

2   Ibid., 50.

3   Ibid., 56.

4   Ibid., 53.

5   Ibid., 60.

6   Sigal Gooldin, "Being Anorexic: Hunger, Subjectivity, and Embodied Morality," *Medical Anthropology Quarterly* 22, no. 3 (September 2008): 290.

7   Ibid.

8   Ibid., 278–79.

9   Nina Mackert, "Making Food Matter: 'Scientific Eating' and the Struggle for Healthy Selves," in *Food, Power, and Agency* (London: Bloomsbury Academic, 2016), 105.

10   Ibid.

11   Ibid.

12   Ibid., 108.

13   Ibid., 109.

14   Helen Gremillion, "Epilogue: A Narrative Approach to Anorexia," in *Feeding Anorexia: Gender and Power at a Treatment Center* (Durham, NC: Duke University Press, 2003), 4, 47.

15   Mackert, "Making Food Matter," 120.

16   Ibid.

17   Gloria Anzaldúa. *Light in the Dark/Luz en lo Oscuro: Rewriting Identity, Spirituality, Reality* (Durham, NC: Duke University Press 2015), 6.

18   Ibid., 87.

19   Ibid., 25.

20   Mackert, "Making Food Matter," 120.

21   Ibid.

22   Anzaldúa, *Light in the Dark*,156.

Ways of Seeing

Radical Queerness

Jamie Theophilos

A corporation's ability to profit from the representation of marginalized communities is more prominent and evident now than it has ever been. Individuals, organizations, and communities using media platforms to present themselves have become so prolific that the social media of corporations have become a quintessential part of how identities form and social movements function. While technology rapidly grows and new social movements emerge, we must ask what is at stake in the possibilities of representation for identity-based social movements like radical queer subculture.

Throughout the past half-century, the use of media has been a continuously contentious topic among queer communities. In a 2008 newsletter, the now-defunct queer insurrectionary group Bash Back! made a statement regarding queer activism and media: "The reality is that the hip queers who seek to make their careers as … filmmakers are in fact servants of abstraction. They seek to socially and monetarily capitalize on the image of queer revolt while contributing nothing to its possibility."[1] This perspective broadly shows the conflict surrounding the prioritization of media production and representation among LGBT movements. Groups like Bash Back! argue that the act of creating representation just for the sake of representation functions purely as a spectacle (an abstraction) without honestly confronting the systematic disenfranchisement of LGBT people and their intersecting identities.

At the same time, there is a complex interplay between our labor systems, technology, and communication methods that makes it impossible to reject outright the usefulness of representation in media. As with all other institutions, the media industry has an intrinsic relation to capitalism. The inevitability of media usage and the long-standing, tumultuous relationship radical queer movements have with media representation leaves me with a long list of looming questions: What value does representation hold for radical queer politics? Can producing, consuming, and examining media advance queer anticapitalist movements even though this engagement feeds into capitalist profits? How do different media forms provide different political possibilities for the image? How is radical queerness represented on different mediums when they contain vastly different intentions and story lines?

My list of questions could continue endlessly. As a filmmaker, graphic designer, and media educator, I am confronted with these questions both in my pedagogy, my artistic productions, and my commitment to anarchist-inflected politics. This essay attempts to address these questions, as well as pose the ultimate question: What does it mean to see radical queerness in mass media? With such a broad topic at hand, I focus on several aspects of media representations: the aesthetics, the story line, and characters who present militantly queer in media. I choose these three because they have been significant components in my attempt to imagine what militant queer representation looks like and in my interpretation of how many other media makers imagine it. I intentionally cover a wide variety of media to see how different forms, historical moments, locations, and styles address queer representation in media production. I hope to continue the discordant dialogue of queer representation with other radical media creators who are also as enthusiastic, driven, and eager to create queer media as they are skeptical, bored, and disillusioned with what is out there.

In a 2017 research study, Brand Innovators analyzed the most prominent companies that focused their themes, advertisements, and creative strategies on LGBT consumers. At the top of their list was Apple.[2] When Apple released their first personal computer, they decided to stray away from the famous Sony computer hardware styles and create a new personal computer style. It was a style influenced by minimalism, Bauhaus architecture, and a Zen-like simplicity. Through choices like these, Apple made a name for itself with its creative design. That appeal became more important to liberal consumers over the decades due to ongoing developments, such as founder Steve Jobs's relationship with Pixar and the public announcement of current CEO Tim Hook's homosexuality. However, the idea that Apple Inc. is the more creatively suited and politically progressive choice is a myth. There is no technical superiority with Apple computers that makes them more suitable for creative production or more adept for LGBT populations but, rather, the marketing and computer design catered to a liberal audience.[3] By combining their design approach with specific marketing campaigns, Apple has meticulously built an image of LGBT inclusion and made itself the token computer of the arts and humanities.[4]

Apple's long-term marketing plans show how aesthetic choices can both target audiences explicitly (such as their rainbow-colored advertisements on the gay hookup social media application Grindr), as well as implicitly (founder Steve Jobs's documented choice to emulate esteemed artistic movements like Bauhaus in his early computer case designs). Examining the subsequent correlation of the use of the Apple computer by the LGBT community and the humanities shows how design choice is political: major corporations set the terms for how designs become interpreted as social approbation and support and, thus, become popular or ubiquitous with the approved or welcomed group. Seeing that even something like the design of a computer impacts the cultural tastes of our time points to how commercial practices generate cultural value.[5] A product's design is not merely a decorative feature, it is at the center of a business's attempt to target consumers.

Joanne Entwistle's theory of aesthetic economy analyzes the way aesthetics affect the functioning of the free-market labor system. Entwistle argues that most commodities are no longer intended for consumption but, rather, for the staging of our lives. Thus, design forms sell "atmospheres" rather than filling a "need." The aesthetics of design create cultural climates and their political relations. There are political consequences to this: the illusion of personalized customization becomes more desirable than supplying the actual need itself.[6] It also becomes an insidious way that dominant regimes impose various aspects of their ways of living onto other nondominant cultures, also known as cultural imperialism.

The idea of a style being profitable is central to one of the main issues regarding militant queer abolitionist politics: the consequences of LGBT assimilation into mainstream heteronormative culture. Queer politics originated in a steadfast belief in resisting and ultimately abolishing dominant forms of oppression and coercive power, which includes a general abhorrence of the capitalist economy. Many queer activists see acceptance into capitalist institutions and mainstream culture as countering the defining nature of queerness. To confront LGBT inclusion into systems of coercive power, radical queers subscribe to an antiassimilationist politic. This politic involves the belief that queer culture should not prioritize inclusion and that societal assimilation is not a marker of real equity and liberation. Instead, radical queer culture enthusiastically seeks out participatory practices of rebellion against the state, as well as against gender and sexual social norms. Radical queers abhor the idea of LGBT culture and identity conforming to hegemonic culture; thus, radical queer communities involve themselves in a wide array of political tactics to attack capitalist institutions and offend mainstream cultures. These provocative acts of agitation and offensiveness often take the form of radical queers choosing ways to present themselves and the general sense that queerness should not aim to be made appropriate for a mass audience.

Yet what is considered culturally appropriate undoubtedly changes across location and time. Mass media promotes LGBT assimilation through representation that enables people, communities, and ideologies to be absorbed into hegemony. We can evaluate the assimilation of a particular idea by the frequency and tendency of its representation in the media. For queerness especially, the largest indicator of assimilation is how widely queer culture gets broadcast or, in other words, how signs of queerness become commodified. An example is how "skinny" jeans have ebbed and flowed in the way they have symbolized effeminacy: changing from something seen as distinctly demasculinizing and off-beat if worn by a man to one that became more noticeably acceptable as higher-end fashion lines remarketed the garment as "slim-fitting, urban-style" pants. When something is seen as socially acceptable on a national scale, it no longer retains its subcultural codes. Thus, the aesthetic design of products helps us gauge what the status quo is—in other words, what the threshold of assimilation is.[7] Since aesthetic tastes frequently change, their economic value and political charge do as well. Understanding this can give us insight into how cultural industries, such as film, advertising, and television, use aesthetics as a central point to producing a commodity, as well as for communicating political rhetoric.

For decades, queer cultures of all kinds have used style as a central point of communication and connection: LGBT film directors signified homoeroticism surreptitiously during the William B. Hays Code era, Black butch women of New York City built camaraderie through "stud" style, and gay male bars invented "handkerchief flagging" for cruising purposes. The signifying markers of a counterculture community rely on style to communicate. Yet we now know that these specific symbols are not as relevant today. There is no more Hays Code in Hollywood, and LGBT-specific dating apps have essentially removed the need for things like dress codes. Therefore, queer aesthetics and their ability to communicate sexual and gender rebellion are specific to the sociopolitical context and the technological advancements of that time in history. There is no particular marker (like a color, geometric figure, hairstyle, camera movement, or sound) inherent to seeing militant queer media outside of that historical context. If we are to begin to parse what militant queer imagery looks like today, we must understand that the power of subversive or reactionary aesthetics depends on the politics of our time.[8]

Militant queer media must look for styles and imagery that are antithetical to what is popular and lucrative to confront the social constructs of gender and sexuality. While antiassimilationist aesthetics cannot exist independently, the distinctions between mainstream and subcultural LGBT imagery show us that we must inspect the political landscape and understand the economy of design to confront mainstream media's current depictions of queerness. For example, the depiction of queerness has changed throughout the history of the moving image. Before the Hays Code, many gay figures were portrayed as the "sissy," exuding no sexual preference and serving as a comedic relief. Then the Hays Code and the Cold War era transformed the homosexual and transgender characters into antagonistic predators, preying on innocent men and women.[9] The AIDS crisis shifted things further, with queer figures, specifically gay men and transgender people of color, being seen as sickly, victimized, and in need of saving. However, with the advent of the VHS camcorder in the late 1980s and the increased ability to make one's own media, artists and filmmakers created a rebuttal against AIDS-related tropes. The queer activism that resulted from the AIDS crisis showed the public what it meant to create rebellious aesthetic signifiers of queerness and how to rewrite the story lines of queer livelihoods. Filmmakers such as Marlon Riggs, Bruce LaBruce, Vaginal Davis, and Gregg Bordowitz addressed how identity is shaped by mass media, rejecting stereotypical story lines as well as centrist nonprofit organizations and political parties that promote queer assimilation. Marlon Riggs's film *Tongues Untied* (1989) and Gregg Bordowitz's documentary *Fast Drip, Long Drop* (1993) found ways to address harmful narratives relating to gender, race, and sexuality during the late 1980s and early 1990s, all while being incredibly distinct in aesthetic. Media like these two films portrayed class conflict and difference particular to their directors' life experiences. Riggs and Bordowitz replicated, remixed, and mocked the use of popular media production strategies (such as traditional documentary film formats), which marked their difference from mainstream LGBT images of that time.

There is a stark contrast between filmmakers who set provocative terms to represent their LGBT characters, imagery, and story lines and filmmakers who only sought representation for its monetary value. In "Gay Activists and the Networks" (1981), Kathryn Montgomery talks about the history of depictions of LGBT characters deemed acceptable in mass media.[10] She states that an image must be palatable and relatable enough to a mass audience to be lucrative and, thus, worth producing. The popular 1990s television show *Will and Grace* featured representations of supposed queerness that domesticated markers of sexuality, making them relatable and innocuous enough for a broad audience. The mainstream audience can then gaze at a unique, othered figure that had previously been relatively hidden within mass media without having their ultimate ideologies of sex and gender disrupted. This kind of placated representation of queer identity still occurs today. For example, Cameron Tucker's lubberly role on the ABC network sitcom *Modern Family* as an effeminate caretaker who employs hyperbolic and even comical heterosexual gender norms. Shows like this are profitable for stations like ABC Family because they mollify the politics of deviant sexuality and gender performances and remove all implications of gay sexual acts. An effeminate gay male character can serve as comic relief, while also removing the possibility of imagining him having anal sex by focusing on his parental role in an upper-middle-class suburb. While LGBT characters have more possibilities for gender and sexual expressions than in past decades, the incentives behind LGBT imagery—why an image or story line is being shown— should always be highlighted. The drive for mass appeal and profit will always conflict with genuine radical queer media representation.

At the same time, we do not have to fully accept that radical queer representation cannot exist in mass media. Before writing this essay, I intended to argue that sexual perversion and explicit gender rebellion must be present when displaying radical queerness, mostly to offend mass populations and, hence, disallow any economic value for major production studios and cable television channels. However, spending an afternoon babysitting my two-year-old nephew made me begin to question this rigid opinion.

While aesthetics will always play a role in the direct combat of institutionalized power systems that impact marginalized people's oppression, it is tangential to the story line. Narrative and design both serve as vital organs of the body of queer anticapitalist social movements. In many instances, an opaque story line with radically political themes of state abolition, societal rebellion, and queerness is more accessible, perhaps, than a burning cop car with two trans women having sex next to it. While accessibility can apply to many instances (whether it be about literal access to a form of media or the ability of an individual to comprehend it), my experience with my nephew made me realize how political mobilizations leave out a crucial location of struggle if we do not focus on the effect gender and sexual representation has on children. I bring up accessibility not only to acknowledge that many more explicit means of depicting nonnormative sexuality may be censored for various populations across the country, but also to note that alternative underground media is not something younger children are readily capable of accessing themselves without adult guidance. There must be ways to represent queerness that offend identity hierarchies and coercive power systems, while reaching audiences who may never have access to independent underground media or simply have no interest in the content.

While watching my baby nephew, I looked for the animations, story lines, and music he found most enticing. I was curious about what drew him to a show like *Thomas the Tank Engine*, but not to a sitcom that would be appealing to an adult. This topic of children's entertainment has been something psychologists and media researchers have analyzed for decades: how and why specific aesthetic and narrative properties are digestible and entertaining to specific age groups, depending on where they are in their brain development. I began to think about what queer media would look like beyond things we may explicitly associate with anticapitalism and queerness. Not only would my nephew's parents not allow me to show content like that to my two-year-old nephew (regardless of a character's sexual preference), but he would most likely have little interest in it visually. So if we know that our conceptions of ourselves, our identities, personalities, and sense of community get formulated most powerfully during childhood, what story lines and images can attract these audiences and expose them to radical queerness?

Looking at children's media is an example of the necessity of representation to a political strategy. The intentionality of the story line, imagery, and delivery is foundational to its production. The impact of children's media not only points out that in demeaning the importance of LGBT representation (especially in mass media) we fall short of our radical aims, it also showcases how we can build depictions of queerness that can expand beyond sexual explicitness and overt state violence. This assertion means that the struggle to shift how queer representation functions should recognize the psychological impact of visual representation on youth. Furthermore, that representation should not be exclusively concerned with sexual and gender identity or with a story line about societal acceptance. Instead, it should explore how individuals of any age can creatively and boundlessly define themselves. Queer representation in media can mean imagining identities and ways of life that break with gender and sexual norms, including LGBT norms, and starting to develop in children countering identities that exceed the state's grasp. Ultimately, queer representation should be provocative in how it imagines gender and sexualities. The show should depict gender and sexuality beyond just a label and expand them into something that exceeds the state's use of them.

In *The Queer Art of Failure* (2011), Jack Halberstam suggests that the way to captivate the child audience parallels queer theory. A children's film cannot deal only with success and perfection but must also grapple with the domain of failure, because "childhood is a long lesson in humility, awkwardness, limitation, and [growth]."[11] Expressions of failure and vulnerability are primary ways radical queer children's media can flourish. Halberstam focuses on animation, because the limitlessness of animation and motion graphics can help us, especially kids, envision alternatives to the ways nature, the body, and the world function around us. With animation, there are ample opportunities to produce other worlds and show bodies, shapes, figures, and societies in unfamiliar forms that are imaginative and ever-shifting. While I could point to many examples of this, two have specifically struck me.

In Cartoon Network's animated show *Adventure Time* (whose intended target audience is children ages two to eleven), the character BMO (abbreviated from Be More) is an ideal onscreen character to analyze given their amalgamated personhood. BMO is a personified video game console, music player, camera, alarm clock, toaster, flashlight, and oven who also self-identifies as nonbinary. There is something fun, exciting, and striking about the idea of an animated character like BMO, who is not only multidimensional as an object but in their gender personification as well. The creation of BMO invites curiosity and humor, while also presenting a muscular tenderness between BMO and the main characters, Jake the dog and Finn the human. BMO is loved, and the gender exploration of BMO is never questioned as inappropriate nor does it ever take precedence in the show's plotline.

My second example is the wildly popular e-sports game *League of Legends*, with its design choice of three specific queer-influenced characters: Neeko, a colorful Latinx chameleon whose ability to shapeshift into other characters takes explicit preference for other females; Taliyah, an ostensibly transgender teenage girl whose primary battle ability involves transforming rock formations in the game's battleground layout; and Varus, a ravenous bow and arrow hunter made from the souls of gay male lovers. Without much background on their lore, you would not know that these characters are LGBT. While these characters and their story lines representing nonheteronormative gender and sexuality are subtle, they are by no means conventional in performance. As an example, Neeko illuminates her sexual preference in her in-game voice lines. Her primary power is shapeshifting into her teammates to confuse the enemy team. When she takes shape, Neeko comments on feeling beautiful when formed into a feminine character and then, conversely, shows disdain and discomfort when the user chooses to shapeshift her into a hypermasculine teammate. Neeko's sexuality plays no influential role in her lore; she is purely a chameleon exploring the depths of the tropical rainforest of *League of Legends*'s fantasy realm, who just so happens to love women. Varus, on the other hand, gives no in-game hint of his relationship to homosexuality; it only shows up in his biographical lore when Riot Games goes into lengthy detail—through blog posts, cinematic trailers, and comic strips—about his relationship history with another male warrior. Finally, Taliyah's experience as a teenage trans woman is mentioned (elusively) only once in the lore. Yet her ability to transform the landscape around her indicates how she has transformed herself and the power that this ability holds. This variety in how *League of Legends* presents unconventional gender and sexuality is noteworthy. It leads its audience members, who are almost all in their teens and early twenties, to explore the characters' multidimensional story lines through different interaction functions.

Of course, the two companies that produce these media pieces are themselves large corporations that should be held to the same standards of critique as all other major corporations, regardless of any praise. Nevertheless, while I am a thorough believer in consuming independent media outside of large-scale marketing schemes, these two media outlets are more attractive and accessible for children and teenagers for the reasons stated above. These characters deserve attention for how they cleverly shed light on the artificiality of gender and sexuality through supernatural and otherworldly forms. This kind of representation psychologically impacts children in perceiving and conjuring their gender sexuality. Moreover, these creations focus on obscurity and imagination when presenting an identity that can be interpreted as positively utopian. This kind of representation gives children and teenagers a way to envision rule bending and breaking within rigid societal norms.

Performances like these help youth imagine new, uncategorical, imaginatively boundless, and culturally dynamic ways of living. Showing children more abstract and exploratory ways of identifying oneself is more developmentally influential and in alignment with radical queer ideology than mere representation of diversity and inclusivity. Queer-related children's media (such as *Steven Universe*, *She-Ra and the Princesses of Power*, and *The Owl House*) is a place that deserves the attention of radical media makers who can use style and narrative to create visions of new gender and sexual worlds for developing queers. Media like this can serve as a gateway that ignites inspiration for our future generation to fight for liberatory practices—meaning that the ability to abundantly explore gender and sexuality outside the scope of our traditional presentations of queerness is set on our terms rather than those of the dominant regime. Rather than believing the answer is to entirely reject mass media imagery, we should find imagery that aligns with our queer politics. Moreover, while doing so, we must reject, in the ways we can, mass corporate producers who dictate what our lives can and should look like.

Analyzing how queer-related story lines and aesthetics are customized for children's media points to the need for intentionality behind the act of representation. In other words, it is essential to understand why and how something is being represented. As digital media progresses into a stage wherein choosing to be "offline" is nearly impossible, making choices in how and when we create digital media is essential.[12] Thus, the location where queer media is to be represented, be it on social media, in a magazine, or in a film, impacts the content's power. For example, less popular media, such as zines or film photography, inform queer social movements differently than a social media platform. Zines provide hands-on experiences, growing and delivering untold histories that have been previously censored.

In another vein, social media platforms interact with queer representation in a particular way compared to other media platforms. Mass social media companies invite the creation of multiple accounts, suggesting that different components of ourselves can be portrayed in unique ways depending on the mechanism, filter, hashtag, icon, background photo, or avatar used.[13] In addition, contemporary society consumes and produces digital media at such a rapid rate that the corporate profit incentive gets obscured behind the idea of "being your own producer, content creator, or entrepreneur."

Despite the many slogans social media applications use to market personal customization and the perceived and strictly bounded freedom to create a personal social media account for free, we are not our own producers but, rather, profit makers for these digital media corporations. The options for presenting a video for queer people on sites like TikTok are regulated by the filters, stickers, and emojis available, as well as the algorithms themselves. This regulation points to how digital technologies tend to force users to make choices that are all too neatly situated within our roles as consumers.[14] Instagram and Facebook algorithms reinforce the idea that these choices are truly customizable and, therefore, liberatory, while simultaneously turning our interactive lives into fodder for consumer research entrenched in biases that stem from the tech marketing interest conglomerates we rely on to communicate. Therefore, in an age of user-generated content, radical queer abolitionist strategies must surpass simply attacking the point of production and instead also extend into the multifarious realms of distribution, exhibition, and consumption, and the nebulous ranges in between.[15]

To reiterate, the choice of where and how you deliver a form of imagery should be as intentional as the construction of the story line and choice of aesthetic. Queer media must not only invoke our ability to use design and narrative as a means to nonconformity; it must also invoke our ability to decide when, how, and why to use specific platforms. It must also be understood that the platforms we, as artists, use have political implications and shape the story line, aesthetics, and audience's reach. This idea brings the audience's attention to the makers' subjectivity as a fundamental factor in informing how reality is documented—questioning our truths about what can even be considered reality. Further, to stay aligned with anticapitalist political practices, militant queer media should focus less on the individual producer and more on the collective movement, all while still critiquing the commonly held notions of truth and authorship.

The scholar and activist Gregg Bordowitz speaks eloquently on this topic. Bordowitz plays out his relationship to authorship, particularly television broadcasting, in his essay "Operative Assumptions," in which he speaks to the importance of subordinating the identity of an artist to the identity of a radical activist.[16] Bordowitz states: "I made a commitment against any mystifying practices assigning privilege to an author, a figure, a signature, a gesture. I resisted the notion of the artist as a lonely alienated soul who is the bearer of a unique mark, the product of his individuality, a testament to the universal and transcendent nature of the human spirit."[17] "Operative Assumptions"—as well as his films—reckons with the tumultuous, often confusing dynamic of making media concerned with representing the self and making media that focuses on the external: be it a social movement, public issue, or marginalized audience or, in his case, representing people with AIDS. This discussion around authorship, intention, and political ideology is a requisite to discussing queer media. The very idea of rejecting or abolishing identity has to be at the core of queerness and must extend into our roles as media producers and consumers. By exploring the radical queer politics of aesthetics, narrative, and productions in media, we can continue a legacy of inciting action both among our media creations and our social movements, all while understanding that media is thoroughly bound to how we mobilize. The ultimate standard we have is seeing how the representation of queerness (be it in a character, style, medium, or story line) incites action to connect, empower, and expand class consciousness through impactful subversive visuals and rituals. These forms of media can support the ideologies that queerness so historically and profoundly strives for. Media becomes essential for connecting with ourselves and signaling our political affinities. Analyzing past and present media shows that radical queer imagery is most effective when it invites rebellion, imagination, community, and a rejection of normalcy.

The looks, form, function, and design of contemporary queer anticapitalist movements will continuously change as our political landscapes and mass media technology grow. If media creators want to stay aligned with the militancy of queerness, they need to focus on making, distributing, and consuming media that strikes at the existing world order. This attack can involve inspiring direct action, but it can also include influencing children to envision different and diverse ways of expressing gender and sexuality in direct opposition to patriarchal and heterosexual norms, as well as societal conformity in its entirety. Despite our inescapable relationship to mass media representation, the moving image, sound, graphics, and general technology have scaled up in ways that allow for more opportunities to celebrate and interrogate the complexities of sexuality, gender, and their intersecting means of tyranny. Media's ability to build connections is also useful to militant queerness for how it can galvanize collective action and sustain solidarity during political lulls and retrenchment. When formed with the burning desire to abolish the systems of domination, radical queer media provides vital energy that is critical to helping queer people build a sense of identity and community purpose and create ways of achieving liberation.

Notes

1   Teagan Eanelli and Fray Baroque, *Queer Ultraviolence* (Oakland: AK Press, 2013), 20.
2   Walter Isaacson, "How Steve Jobs' Love of Simplicity Fueled A Design Revolution," *Smithsonian Magazine*, August 31, 2012, accessed June 3, 2022, https://tinyurl.com/2p87re2r.
3   Tim Carmody, "Without Jobs as CEO, Who Speaks for the Arts at Apple?" *Wired*, August 29, 2011, accessed June 3, 2022, https://www.wired.com/2011/08/apple-liberal-arts.
4   Erica Sweeney, "Absolut, Apple and Calvin Klein among Most LGBTQ-Friendly Brands, Study Finds," Marketing Dive, March 14, 2018, accessed June 3, 2022, https://tinyurl.com/3ntj8vur.
5   Joanne Entwistle, "The Aesthetic Economy: The Production of Value in the Field of Fashion Modelling," *Journal of Consumer Culture* 2, no. 3 (November 2002): 317–39.
6   Gernot Böhme, *Critique of Aesthetic Capitalism* (Italy: Mimesis International, 2017), 14.
7   Dick Hebdige, *Subculture: The Meaning of Style* (London: Routledge, 1979), 2.
8   Ibid., 101.
9   Rob Epstein and Jeffrey Friedman, dirs., *The Celluloid Closet* (Hollywood: Sony Pictures Classics, 1996).
10   Kathryn Montgomery, "Gay Activists and the Networks," *Journal of Communication* 31, no. 3 (September 1981): 49–57.
11   Jack Halberstam, *The Queer Art of Failure* (Durham, NC: Duke University Press, 2011), 29.
12   Ryan Conrad, *Against Equality: Queer Revolution Not Mere Inclusion* (Oakland: AK Press, 2015), 9.
13   Douglas Rushkoff, *Program or Be Programmed: Ten Commands for A Digital Age* (New York: Soft Skull Press, 2011), 40.
14   Robert W. McChesney, *Digital Disconnect* (New York: New Press, 2013), 203.
15   Chris Robé, *Breaking the Spell: A History of Anarchist Filmmakers, Videotape Guerrillas, and Digital Ninjas*, (Oakland: PM Press, 2017), 10.
16   Gregg Bordowitz, "Operative Assumptions," in *The AIDS Crisis Is Ridiculous and Other Writings*, ed. James Meyer (Boston: MIT Press, 2005), 180.
17   Ibid., 183.

Genderless Siberia

Wriply Marie Bennet

Image 1: Genderless Siberia by Wriply Marie Bennet.

You ever done something. Something... big. Something that could shift the conversation! And then afterward, you're, like, wow that was a gigantic waste of time?

There are certain *ah-ha* moments that you run into in life,
I am going to tell you about a few of mine.
The *ah-ha* moments that lead to me believing that divestment is the only true liberation that people like me and other people who are marginalized will ever receive.

My presence in this country wasn't of my choosing.
Yet my skin and the body that lies within are under attack from all sides.

Do you know what it's like to grow up with no doors open to you? Left in a gender Siberia.
Not allowed to have boyhood because of your high voice and your femininity. You're excluded by the young boys!
Not allowed to have a girlhood, by your parents and society. Not allowed to have manhood by the men in your community—even the gay boys excluded your brand of queer from their particular path of manhood. They've even got a catchy phrase for it.
Who knows the gay exclusionary catch phrase??

No fats!
No femmes!
No Asians!
No Blacks!

And once you finally find the language for who you are as a Black trans women/femme... even women continue to close the door in your face because of what's on your birth certificate and what might be between your legs!
Left in a gender Siberia.
You can't imagine how stifling that is, to not be allowed to have an identity because of what your body looks like, and to not even be allowed to have an identity that "you should've had" because of the way your "body looks".........
So what the fuck????

But... there is a but.
But what if your body doesn't look that way?
What then?
And when it doesn't look the other way either... ???

Let me tell you a story,
I've been calling it.

The tale of two titties.
The intersex intersection, Destruction of the little God.

Once upon a time there was a little god in the making... her name isn't important at this junction!

This little god always knew who she was.
But her mortal mother always told her... never speak out loud the truth of her Divinity, for fear that other mortals would see she's different.

"There's only one woman in this house." Her mother's favorite phrase that sliced through her like the thinnest of blades!
Her life... was a never-ending series of verbal, physical, and sexual abuse.
Every night the little god would pray to the "God her family gave her."
"Please jehovah god..." (yes they were jehovah's witnesses!!!
Which was a wild upbringing, trust me!)

Anyway, "Please jehovah god, make me a girl, or end my suffering... I can't bear much more of this!!"

This went on for years... every night, she'd pray for freedom from her earthly torment, and for understanding of her Being.

Until the 4th grade when the little god sprouted some mole hills that swiftly became mountains.

The kids all teased her, especially the little girls... "Look he's got tits"... her response: "jealous???"

Oh, the little god developed a swift tongue and hands even quicker for the little boys, and few grown men didn't appreciate how she and her body made them feel!

But her mortal mother had enough of the fighting. . . over something she and the rest of the world felt "shouldn't" be on her body.

They were a clear sign of her Divinity. They made others think, "well, if her body can do that. . . what can mine do?"
So like wings sheared off of an angels back. . . they were taken from her.
And for a little while she lost herself.
She lost her way, and forgot who she was.
And fell into a box that couldn't hold her, one built for someone without so much fullness!!

For years, before and after. . . I went to bed terrified that one day I would wake up a man.
And I woke up here. . . Not a Man, not yet a Woman.
Genderless Siberia.

About the Authors

zuri arman is a writer and poet based in Providence, Rhode Island. His work can be found in *Collision Literary Magazine* and *Alluvia Magazine*. Their current research and creative writing interests are grappling with the residues of religious frameworks and grammars in contemporary culture and politics, radical Black political thought, and the relationship between Blackness, nature, and the human. His work is informed by his experience working in the environmental and environmental justice movements while an undergraduate at the University of Pittsburgh. Outside of work, he dabbles in various artistic mediums, including lo-fi music and visual productions, trying to find new ways to express the same thoughts but in forms accessible and appealing to wider audiences. He is the descendent of Southern sharecroppers whose survival in an anti-Black world made his existence possible. They are currently pursuing their PhD in the Department of Africana Studies at Brown University.

Ryan Becker was born in a small town in Central Illinois. Ryan is a machine operator/supervisor and also an artist, drawing portraits and animals.

Wriply Marie Bennet is a proud self-taught illustrator and activist/organizer born and raised in Ohio. Her art and organizing work started with the Trans Women of Color Collective and expanded in Ferguson, when she and a few others were freedom riders traveling to stand with the family and community of Mike Brown. Wriply is also well known for an action held in Columbus, Ohio, during which she and three other Black, queer, and trans folk (known as the Black Pride 4) were arrested while holding the community accountable for divisive actions against folks of color in the queer community. Her art has been used in numerous social justice flyers, fundraisers, online gallery shows, and citywide campaigns and made its first film debut in *MAJOR!*, a documentary at the 2015 San Francisco transgender film festival.

Raxtus Bracken is a white, queer, and transgender student organizer who graduated from Davidson College, in Davidson, North Carolina. They are committed to transformative abolitionist community work that centers the experiences of marginalized peoples and promotes collective liberation from structural, institutional, and interpersonal injustice.

Scott Branson is a queer/trans anarchist writer, translator, community organizer, and teacher. They were one of the organizers of the two UNC Asheville/Davidson College queer conferences that inspired this book. They have translated Jacques Lesage de la Haye's *The Abolition of Prison* (AK Press, 2021) and Guy Hocquenghem's second book of essays addressing the May 1968 uprising in France, *Gay Liberation after May '68* (Duke University Press, 2022), for which they also wrote a critical introduction. Scott is the author of *Practical Anarchism: A Daily Guide* (Pluto Press, 2022) and is also working on a book about the institutionalization of queerness for Duke University Press as well as a book on trans-anarcha-feminism. They often contribute to *The Final Straw Radio*, a weekly anarchist radio show and podcast.

Beth Bruch works as a high school librarian in rural North Carolina and is a member of the Jewish Voice for Peace–Triangle North Carolina chapter, the Sacred Monsters havurah, and the Movement to End Racism and Islamophobia (MERI).

Scott Chalupa is the author of *Quarantine* (PANK Books, 2019), described by Pulitzer Prize–winning poet Jericho Brown as "melancholy and meditative ... a beautiful book." Chalupa lives and writes in South Carolina, where he earned an MFA in poetry at the University of South Carolina and currently teaches at Central Carolina Technical College. His work is primarily concerned with queering stories and experiences not usually seen as queer, often through ekphrastic response to art, music, and other media. His current creative obsessions are the intersection of queerness and quantum/astrophysics and queering biblical text/history to comment on the world now. One poem from that obsession is forthcoming in an Orison Books anthology on the biblical figure Eve. His work has appeared in *HIV Here & Now*, *PANK*, *pacificREVIEW*, *Nimrod*, *Beloit Poetry Journal*, *South Atlantic Review*, *Tupelo Quarterly*, and other venues.

Yold Yolande Delius is a Haitian American interdisciplinary artist based in Brooklyn, New York. Her work focuses on the artistic expression of Haitian diasporic narratives. Their mediums include academic writing, cultural critique, short stories, acrylic and watercolor painting, and dance. As a first-generation immigrant, she is passionate about complicating what it means to be within the Haitian diaspora by engaging the community. Along with creating the blog *Raja's World*, their work has been featured in *Plantin Magazine*, *Sounds and Colours*, and the *Diasporic African Dream Anthology*.

aems dinunzio is an archivist, anarchist, and organizer from rural Texas. Since 2012, they have worked with Inside Books Project (IBP), in Austin, Texas, sending books and information resources to people in Texas prisons. In 2015, they founded the IBP Archive to preserve, digitize, and amplify the narratives of imprisoned people and to expose censorship occurring in the Texas Department of Criminal Justice. They are working on their PhD at the University of Arizona School of Information, exploring how archives can act as sites of prison abolitionist and transformative justice activism, education, and mobilization. They spend their free time exploring desert cactus with their dog glitch.

Zaria El-Fil is an African and African diaspora studies and humanities honors double major at the University of Texas at Austin. In general, her research places the experiences of enslaved women at the forefront in order to acknowledge the symbolic violence, social injury, and forms of cultural domination and oppression that have reduced enslaved women to asterisks in the telling of history. However, since the recent uprisings, she has been consulting with the work of Caribbean theorists to engage in imaginative practices of worlding from the standpoint of the histories of Black people. Consistent with her commitment to becoming a public historian, she also lends her talents to dramaturgical work, historical exhibitions, and curriculum building throughout Austin, Texas.

Amalia Golomb-Leavitt is a healer/social worker/friend/organizer living in Chicago on Potawatomie, Kickapoo, and Peoria land. She is invested in politicizing and decolonizing health care, as well as bringing racialized and intergenerational trauma into conceptions of trauma-informed work. She works with conflict resolution and accountability and survivorship. She fights for the abolition of prisons and police. She is interested in movements working to build systems for accountability and safety that encourage change, equity, and harm reduction, rather than responding to violence by causing more violence.

Che Gossett is a Black nonbinary femme writer and PhD in women's and gender studies. They were a 2019–20 Helena Rubinstein fellow in critical studies, in the Whitney Independent Study Program, as well as a 2020–21 graduate fellow at the Center for Cultural Analysis at Rutgers University. Their work has been published in anthologies including *Trap Door: Trans Cultural Production and the Politics of Visibility* (MIT Press, 2017), *Death and Other Penalties: Continental Philosophers on Prisons and Capital Punishment* (Fordham University Press, 2014), *The Transgender Studies Reader* (Routledge, 2014). They also coedited a special issue of *Transgender Studies Quarterly* (Duke University Press), with Professor Eva Hayward, on trans in a time of HIV/AIDS.

Raven Hudson is an activist, writer, and researcher with a BA in English and gender and sexuality studies from Davidson College, where they cofounded the Asian American Initiative (AAI), coedited the student literary magazine *Libertas*, and helped create and host AAI's *Coalasian: A Southern Podcast*. Their recent work centers on wounds and the melancholic subject within contemporary queer Asian American poetry.

Jonesy and Jaime Knight met in January 2015 at the Los Angeles home of Sini Anderson, director of the Kathleen Hanna documentary, *The Punk Singer*. It was a birthday party for their mutual friend Tammy Rae Carland, and they shared the "fraternal recognition" moment (a term Jonesy invented about a shared brotherhood), as often happens in the queer community with its miniscule degrees of separation. While passing a joint with photographer Catherine Opie, Jonesy told Jaime about a project he was working on at the ONE Archives at USC about the history of Southern California gay motorcycle clubs. They started meeting up to hang out and go drinking, cruising at the Eagle Bar and sharing their queer histories. Finding more than just social connections in common, they realized they had similar goals in their creative practice and started on a journey, making a large body of work. Having now shown in institutions, bars, clubs, and galleries, at festivals, and in the streets of Los Angeles, it's overwhelming to each of them how much they've made in such a short span of time. While Jaime relocated to the Bay Area in 2017 to teach at California College of Art, Jonesy remains in Los Angeles, and they continue their collaboration through correspondence, late night phone calls, and working trips to each other's homes and studios

Cassius Kelly and **emet ezell** have been baking bread and making home together since their undergraduate days at Southwestern University. Emet is a community organizer, public song leader, and poet, and the author of *Between Every Bird, Our Bones* (Newfound, 2022), which was selected by Chen as winner of the Gloria Anzaldúa Poetry Prize. They live in Berlin and research gaps in lineage and spiritual ghosts: what's passed down when there is no down? Cassius is a graduate student at the University of Texas at Austin, pursuing degrees in women and gender studies and information studies. Their research is at the intersection of decolonial feminism and disability studies, with a particular focus on madness and resistance. Despite the fact that emet lives in Germany and Cassius lives in Texas, they still read each other's tarot and discuss fat studies late into the night.

Sandra Y.L. Korn is assistant editor at Duke University Press, focusing on books on religion, and a member of the Jewish Voice for Peace–Triangle North Carolina chapter.

Stasha Lampert is an organizer and artist living in San Francisco. Their work, which focuses on housing justice and gentrification, labor rights, racial justice, and queer/trans liberation, has appeared in a number of activist periodicals, short documentaries, and zines.

Toshio Meronek's writing on the Bay Area, housing, prisons, and queers appears in publications such as *In These Times* and Truthout, and anthologies like *Captive Genders: Trans Embodiment and the Prison Industrial Complex* (AK Press, 2011) and *Trap Door: Trans Cultural Production and the Politics of Visibility* (MIT Press, 2022). Their most recent project is *Miss*

Major Speaks (Verso, 2023), a collaborative book with the trans activist Miss Major Griffin-Gracy.

Yasmin Nair is a writer, academic, and activist based in Chicago, and the cofounder, with Ryan Conrad, of the queer radical collective Against Equality. Her work can be found at www.yasminnair.com.

Mimi Thi Nguyen is associate professor of gender and women's studies at the University of Illinois, Urbana-Champaign. Her first book is *The Gift of Freedom: War, Debt, and Other Refugee Passages* (Duke University Press, 2012). Her following project is called The Promise of Beauty. She has also published in *Signs, Camera Obscura, Women & Performance, positions: asia critique, Radical History Review*, and *ArtForum*. Nguyen has made zines since 1991, including *Slander* and the compilation zine *Race Riot*. She is a former *Punk Planet* columnist and *Maximumrocknroll* volunteer. In June 2013, Sarah McCarry's Guillotine (a series of erratically published chapbooks focused on revolutionary nonfiction) released *PUNK*, a conversation between Nguyen and Golnar Nikpour.

E Ornelas is a PhD candidate at the University of Minnesota. As the descendant of a survivor of the Sherman Institute, a Native boarding school in Riverside, California—and, therefore, robbed of cultural, linguistic, and tribal identity—E's research interests focus on the continued survivance and futurity of Indigenous peoples, particularly through the use of literature. E studies community-based, abolitionist-informed responses to gendered, racialized, and colonial violence that Black and Indigenous fiction authors write about. When not on campus, E can be found reading feminist sci-fi, making music, and walking their dog.

Kai Rajala is a queer, nonbinary, white settler of Finnish and other European descent. They are a writer, radio host, and an anarchist anti-academic working and living on the unceded territories of the Kanien'kehá:ka peoples on the island colonially referred to as "Montréal," and known otherwise as Tiohtià:ke. They are currently pursuing studies as an independent researcher and are interested in sites outside of the university where knowledge production occurs. When not attempting to undermine the Canadian state through their writing, Kai enjoys reading, making memes, and cycling. You can find Kai on twitter at @anarcho_thembo.

Darian Razdar is an organizer, researcher, and artist currently based in Toronto. His writing explores tensions within and across movements and spaces to build (r)evolutionary consciousness and incite change. He holds a dual BA in social theory and practice and French and francophone studies from University of Michigan, Ann Arbor (2018) and a masters of planning from University of Toronto (2020).

Bry Reed is a queer Black feminist from Baltimore, Maryland, currently pursuing a doctorate in American studies at Purdue University. She is committed to prison abolition, pleasure, and care work as tools for Black liberation. Beyond her doctoral studies, she is a writer, educator, and radical troublemaker.

Adrian Shanker (he/him) is editor of the critically acclaimed anthology *Bodies and Barriers: Queer Activists on Health* (PM Press, 2020) and the executive director of the Spahr Center, serving Marin County, California's LGBTQ+ and HIV communities. He previously founded and led Bradbury-Sullivan LGBT Community Center in Allentown, Pennsylvania. A specialist in LGBTQ+ health policy, he has developed leading-edge health promotion campaigns to advance health equity through behavioral, clinical, and policy changes. Adrian is also a member of the Presidential Advisory Council on HIV/AIDS.

Kitty Stryker is a queer juggalo anthropologist and an anarchist cat mom prepping a doomsday bunker in the East Bay. She started the website consentculture.com after calling out abuse within the BDSM and altsex communities in 2011. Her first book, *Ask: Building Consent Culture*, addressing consent culture in and out of the bedroom, was published by Thorntree Press in 2017.

Mattilda Bernstein Sycamore (mattildabernsteinsycamore.com) is the author of two memoirs and three novels and the editor of five nonfiction anthologies. Her most recent title, *The Freezer Door* (MIT Press, 2020), was a New York Times Editors' Choice, one of *Oprah Magazine*'s Best LGBTQ Books of 2020, and a finalist for a 2021 PEN/Jean Stein Book Award. Her previous title, *Sketchtasy* (Arsenal Pulp Press, 2018), was one of NPR's Best Books of 2018, and her first memoir, *The End of San Francisco*, won a Lambda Literary Award. Her new anthology is *Between Certain Death and* *a Possible Future: Queer Writing on Growing Up with the AIDS Crisis* (Arsenal Pulp Press, 2021). Sycamore lives in Seattle, and she still goes outside every day at 8:00 p.m. to scream Black Lives Matter, Abolish the Police. Join her.

Jamie Theophilos enjoys making videos, designing stuff, writing things, and playing music. They are a PhD candidate at Indiana University School for Media Arts and Sciences, where they also teach. Additionally, Jamie edits and produces films with Submedia Collective. They spend most of their time hanging with their Australian shepherd named Cassie, who is indeed a very good girl.

Rebecca Valeriano-Flores is a PhD candidate, activist, and musician residing in Chicago, Illinois. Her dissertation in philosophy is an antiracist and anticolonial project that focuses on the work of Frantz Fanon. She is a researcher and archivist for Black and Pink Chicago, a prison abolition organization that advocates for LGBTQ+ people who are incarcerated or formerly incarcerated. With Black and Pink Chicago, she is working on a community-based, participatory action research project on Rushville Treatment and Detention Facility in Illinois. As a musician, she has released three full-length albums and has toured across the US and Europe.

Index

Page numbers in *italic* refer to illustrations. "Passim" (literally "scattered") indicates intermittent discussion of a topic over a cluster of pages.

ABOUT PM PRESS

PM Press is an independent, radical publisher of books and media to educate, entertain, and inspire. Founded in 2007 by a small group of people with decades of publishing, media, and organizing experience, PM Press amplifies the voices of radical authors, artists, and activists. Our aim is to deliver bold political ideas and vital stories to people from all walks of life and arm the dreamers to demand the impossible. We have sold millions of copies of our books, most often one at a time, face to face. We're old enough to know what we're doing and young enough to know what's at stake. Join us to create a better world.

PM Press
PO Box 23912
Oakland, CA 94623
www.pmpress.org

PM Press in Europe
europe@pmpress.org
www.pmpress.org.uk

FRIENDS OF PM PRESS

These are indisputably momentous times—the financial system is melting down globally and the Empire is stumbling. Now more than ever there is a vital need for radical ideas.

In the many years since its founding—and on a mere shoestring—PM Press has risen to the formidable challenge of publishing and distributing knowledge and entertainment for the struggles ahead. With hundreds of releases to date, we have published an impressive and stimulating array of literature, art, music, politics, and culture. Using every available medium, we've succeeded in connecting those hungry for ideas and information to those putting them into practice.

Friends of PM allows you to directly help impact, amplify, and revitalize the discourse and actions of radical writers, filmmakers, and artists. It provides us with a stable foundation from which we can build upon our early successes and provides a much-needed subsidy for the materials that can't necessarily pay their own way. You can help make that happen—and receive every new title automatically delivered to your door once a month—by joining as a Friend of PM Press. And, we'll throw in a free T-shirt when you sign up.

Here are your options:

- **$30 a month** Get all books and pamphlets plus a 50% discount on all webstore purchases

- **$40 a month** Get all PM Press releases (including CDs and DVDs) plus a 50% discount on all webstore purchases

- **$100 a month** Superstar—Everything plus PM merchandise, free downloads, and a 50% discount on all webstore purchases

For those who can't afford $30 or more a month, we have **Sustainer Rates** at $15, $10, and $5. Sustainers get a free PM Press T-shirt and a 50% discount on all purchases from our website.

Your Visa or Mastercard will be billed once a month, until you tell us to stop. Or until our efforts succeed in bringing the revolution around. Or the financial meltdown of Capital makes plastic redundant. Whichever comes first.

Queercore: How to Punk a Revolution: An Oral History

Edited by Liam Warfield, Walter Crasshole, and Yony Leyser with an Introduction by Anna Joy Springer and Lynn Breedlove

ISBN: 978-1-62963-796-9
$18.00   208 pages

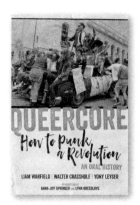

Queercore: How to Punk a Revolution: An Oral History is the very first comprehensive overview of a movement that defied both the music underground and the LGBT mainstream community.

Through exclusive interviews with protagonists like Bruce LaBruce, G.B. Jones, Jayne County, Kathleen Hanna of Bikini Kill and Le Tigre, film director and author John Waters, Lynn Breedlove of Tribe 8, Jon Ginoli of Pansy Division, and many more, alongside a treasure trove of never-before-seen photographs and reprinted zines from the time, *Queercore* traces the history of a scene originally "fabricated" in the bedrooms and coffee shops of Toronto and San Francisco by a few young, queer punks to its emergence as a relevant and real revolution. *Queercore* is a down-to-details firsthand account of the movement explored by the people that lived it—from punk's early queer elements, to the moment that Toronto kids decided they needed to create a scene that didn't exist, to Pansy Division's infiltration of the mainstream, and the emergence of riot grrrl—as well as the clothes, zines, art, film, and music that made this movement an exciting middle finger to complacent gay and straight society. *Queercore* will stand as both a testament to radically gay politics and culture and an important reference for those who wish to better understand this explosive movement.

"Finally, a book that centers on the wild, innovative, and fearless contributions queers made to punk rock, creating a punker-than-punk subculture beneath the subculture, queercore. Gossipy and inspiring, a historical document and a call to arms during a time when the entire planet could use a dose of queer, creative rage."
—Michelle Tea, author of *Valencia*

"I knew at an early age I didn't want to be part of a church, I wanted to be part of a circus. It's documents such as this book that give hope for our future. Anarchists, the queer community, the roots of punk, the Situationists, and all the other influential artistic guts eventually had to intersect. Queercore is completely logical, relevant, and badass."
—Justin Pearson, The Locust, Three One G

Y'all Means All: The Emerging Voices Queering Appalachia

Edited by Z. Zane McNeill

ISBN: 978-1-62963-914-7
$20.00   200 pages

Y'all Means All is a celebration of the weird and wonderful aspects of a troubled region in all of their manifest glory! This collection is a thought-provoking hoot and a holler of "we're queer and we're here to stay, cause we're every bit a piece of the landscape as the rocks and the trees" echoing through the hills of Appalachia and into the boardrooms of every media outlet and opportunistic author seeking to define Appalachia from the outside for their own political agendas. Multidisciplinary and multi-genre, *Y'all* necessarily incorporates elements of critical theory, such as critical race theory and queer theory, while dealing with a multitude of methodologies, from quantitative analysis, to oral history and autoethnography.

This collection eschews the contemporary trend of "reactive" or "responsive" writing in the genre of Appalachian studies, and alternatively, provides examples of how modern Appalachians are defining themselves on their own terms. As such, it also serves as a toolkit for other Appalachian readers to follow suit, and similarly challenge the labels, stereotypes and definitions often thrust upon them. While providing blunt commentary on the region's past and present, the book's soul is sustained by the resilience, ingenuity, and spirit exhibited by the authors; values which have historically characterized the Appalachian region and are continuing to define its culture to the present.

This book demonstrates above all else that Appalachia and its people are filled with a vitality and passion for their region which will slowly but surely effect long-lasting and positive changes in the region. If historically Appalachia has been treated as a "mirror" of the country, this book breaks that trend by allowing modern Appalachians to examine their own reflections and to share their insights in an honest, unfiltered manner with the world.

"These deeply personal and theoretically informed essays explore the fight for social justice and inclusivity in Appalachia through the intersections of environmental action, LGBTQA+ representational politics, anti-racism, and movements for disability justice. This Appalachia is inhabited by a queer temporality and geography, where gardening lore teaches us that seeds dance into plants in their own time, not according to a straight-edged neoliberal discipline."
—Rebecca Scott, author of *Removing Mountains: Extracting Nature and Identity in the Appalachian Coalfields*

Crisis and Care: Queer Activist Responses to a Global Pandemic

Adrian Shanker
with a Foreword by Rea Carey

ISBN: 978-1-62963-935-2
$15.95   128 pages

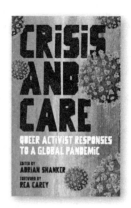

Crisis and Care reveals what is possible when activists mobilize for the radical changes our society needs. In a time of great uncertainty, fear, and isolation, Queer activists organized for health equity, prison abolition, racial justice, and more. Nobody who lived through the COVID-19 pandemic will soon forget the challenges, sacrifices, and incredible loss felt during such an uncertain time in history. *Crisis and Care* anthologizes not what happened during COVID-19, or why it happened, but rather how Queer activists responded in real time. It considers the necessity to memorialize resiliency as well as loss, hope as well as pain, to remember the strides forward as well as the steps back. Activist contributors Zephyr Williams, Mark Travis Rivera, Jamie Gliksburg, Denise Spivak, Emmett Patterson, Omar Gonzales-Pagan, Kenyon Farrow, and more provide a radical lens through which future activists can consider effective strategies to make change, even or perhaps especially, during periods of crisis.

"Adrian Shanker has emerged in recent years as an urgent and prescient voice on matters concerning queer health. Crisis and Care: Queer Activist Responses to a Global Pandemic *is timely, important and shares a message we ignore at our own peril. The response to COVID-19 from LGBTQ communities is informed by our own experience with a deadly pandemic made vastly worse by poor presidential leadership. Our lived experience over the past 40 years has valuable lessons for how we should be addressing today's viral threats."*
—Sean Strub, author of *Body Counts: A Memoir of Politics, Sex, AIDS, and Survival*

"How did we respond? That is the central question in Crisis and Care. *Lots of books will look at COVID-19, but this book looks at how LGBTQ activists responded to one of the most challenging moments of our lives."*
—Igor Volsky, author of *Guns Down: How to Defeat the NRA and Build a Safer Future with Fewer Guns*

"In Crisis and Care, *Adrian Shanker and the contributing authors make the bold case that we are defined not by the bad things that happen in our society, but by how our community responds."*
—Robyn Ochs, editor of *Bi Women's Quarterly*

The George Floyd Uprising

Edited by Vortex Group

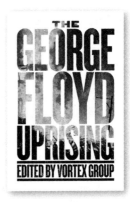

ISBN: 978-1-62963-966-6
$22.95   288 pages

In the summer of 2020, America experienced one of the biggest uprisings in half a century. Waves of enraged citizens took to the streets to streets in Minneapolis to decry the murder of George Floyd at the hands of the police. Battles broke out night after night, with a pandemic weary populace fighting the police and eventually burning down the Third Precinct. The revolt soon spread to cities large and small across the country where protesters set police cars on fire, looted luxury shopping districts and forced the president into hiding in a bunker beneath the White House. As the initial crest receded, localized rebellions continued to erupt throughout the summer and into the fall in Atlanta, Chicago, Kenosha, Louisville, Philadelphia, and elsewhere.

Written during the riots, *The George Floyd Uprising* is a compendium of the most radical writing to come out of that long, hot summer. These incendiary dispatches—from those on the frontlines of the struggle—examines the revolt and the obstacles it confronted. It paints a picture of abolition in practice, discusses how the presence of weapons in the uprising and the threat of armed struggle play out in an American context, and shows how the state responds to and pacifies rebellions. *The George Floyd Uprising* poses new social, tactical, and strategic plans for those actively seeking to expand and intensify revolts of the future. This practical, inspiring collection is essential reading for all those hard at work toppling the state and creating a new revolutionary tradition.

"*Exemplary reflections from today's frontline warriors that will disconcert liberals but inspire young people who want to live the struggle in the revolutionary tradition of Robert F. Williams, the Watts 65 rebels, and Deacons for Defense and Justice.*"
—Mike Davis, author of *Planet of Slums* and *Old Gods, New Enigmas*

"*This anthology resists police and vigilante murders. It is not an easy read. We will not all agree on its analyses or advocacy. Yet, its integrity, clarity, vulnerability, love and rage are clear. As a librarian who archives liberators and liberation movements, I recognize essential reading as a reflection of ourselves and our fears. With resolution, this text resonates with narratives of mini-Atticas. The 1971 prison rebellion and murderous repression by government and officialdom reveal the crises that spark radical movements and increasing calls for self-defense. This volume offers our cracked mirrors as an opportunity to scrutinize missteps and possibilities, and hopefully choose wisely even in our sacrifices.*"
—Joy James, author of *Resisting State Violence: Radicalism, Gender, and Race in U.S. Culture*

Your Place or Mine? A 21st Century Essay on (Same) Sex

Gilles Dauvé

ISBN: 978-1-62963-945-1
$17.95   224 pages

In a fascinating and radical critique of identity and class, *Your Place or Mine?* examines the modern invention of homosexuality as a social construct that emerged in the nineteenth century. Examining "fairies" in Victorian England, transmen in early twentieth-century Manhattan, sexual politics in Soviet Russia, and Stonewall's attempt to combine gay self-defense with revolutionary critique, Dauvé turns his keen eye on contemporary political correctness in the United States and the rise of reactionary discourse.

The utopian vision of *Your Place or Mine?* is vital to a just society: the invention of a world where one can be *human* without having to be classified by sexual practices or gender expressions. Where one need not find shelter in definition or assimilation. A refreshing reminder that we are not all the same, nor do we need to be.

"*Do you ever ask yourself why there is so little class analysis applied to the assimilation of the 'gay movement,' or even of the previously glamorous and revolutionary 'subcultures' denoted by the word 'queer,' why today's 'activists' are so keen on reformist political strategies, why the current LGBTQQIP2SAA configuration used to describe the 'gay' or 'queer' community indicates a factionalization of sexual identity that has become so inclusive as to become almost meaningless ? I have, and if you have too, Gilles Dauvé's* Your Place or Mine? A 21st Century Essay on (Same) Sex *is the right book to be holding in your hands.*"
—Bruce LaBruce